An Introduction to Africana Philosophy

In this book Lewis R. Gordon offers the first comprehensive treatment
of Africana philosophy, beginning with the emergence of an Africana
(i.e. African diasporic) consciousness in the Afro-Arabic world of the Middle
Ages. He argues that much of modern Africana thought emerged out of
early conflicts between Islam and Christianity that culminated in the
expulsion of the Moors from the Iberian Peninsula, and out of the
subsequent expansion of racism, enslavement, and colonialism which in
their turn stimulated reflections on reason, liberation, and the meaning of
being human. His book takes the reader on a journey from Africa through
Europe, North and South America, the Caribbean, and back to Africa, as
he explores the challenges posed to our understanding of knowledge and
freedom today, and the response to them which can be found within
Africana philosophy.

LEWIS R. GORDON is the Laura H. Carnell Professor of Philosophy,
Religion, and Judaic Studies at Temple University, Philadelphia.

An Introduction to Africana Philosophy

LEWIS R. GORDON

Temple University

CAMBRIDGE UNIVERSITY PRESS
Cambridge, New York, Melbourne, Madrid, Cape Town, Singapore, São Paulo, Delhi

Cambridge University Press
The Edinburgh Building, Cambridge CB2 8RU, UK

Published in the United States of America by Cambridge University Press, New York

www.cambridge.org
Information on this title: www.cambridge.org/9780521675468

First published 2008

Printed in the United Kingdom at the University Press, Cambridge

A catalogue record for this publication is available from the British Library

Library of Congress Cataloguing in Publication data

Gordon, Lewis R. (Lewis Ricardo), 1962–
An introduction to Africana philosophy / Lewis R. Gordon.
    p.   cm.
Includes bibliographical references and index.
ISBN 978-0-521-85885-4 (hardback) – ISBN 978-0-521-67546-8 (pbk.)
1. Philosophy, African.   I. Title.
B5305.G67 2008
199′.6–dc22   2007053044

ISBN 978-0-521-85885-4 hardback
ISBN 978-0-521-67546-8 paperback

In Memory of Yvonne Patricia Solomon
(1943–2004)
and
Lewis Calwood Gordon
(1943–2004)

Contents

Preface   *page* ix

Introduction: Africana philosophy in context   1

Part I Groundings

1 Africana philosophy as a modern philosophy   21

2 Classic eighteenth- and nineteenth-century foundations   33
    Anton Wilhelm Amo   35
    Quobna Ottobah Cugoano   40
    From David Walker's *Appeal* to the founding of the
        American Negro Academy   46
    Two Caribbean men of letters: Anténor Firmin and
        George Wilmot Blyden   56
    Conclusion   65

Part II From New World to new worlds

3 Three pillars of African-American philosophy   69
    Anna Julia Cooper and the problem of value   69
    W. E. B. Du Bois and the problem of double consciousness 73
    Fanon's critique of failed dialectics of recognition   80

4 Africana philosophical movements in the United States
  and Britain   91
    Prophetic and other recent forms of African-American
        pragmatism   93
    Black feminist and womanist thought   100
    Afrocentrism and Afrocentricity   106
    African-American analytical philosophy   110

African-American and Afro-British European continental philosophy   120
Cedric Robinson's anthropology of Marxism   128
African-American existential philosophy, phenomenology,
    and their influence   132

5 Afro-Caribbean philosophy   157

6 African philosophy   185
African humanism   186
The theme of invention in recent African philosophy   195
African critiques of invention   200
Recent African political thought   220

Conclusion   249

Guide to further reading   251
Index   260

Preface

This book came about through an odd series of circumstances. I was asked to write up a proposal for it while tending to the last rites for the man whose first and last name I share. Those were harrowing times. It was at the end of a year in which, through losing both my parents, I became an orphan. Proposing a text that invokes ancestors as witnesses was something I thought I would not have been able to bear. I found strength and inspiration articulating their contributions and representing this field for Cambridge University Press.

Africana philosophy has experienced growth among professional philosophers in the past two decades. Although this book explores a constellation of thought over the course of a millennium, pioneering work in the academy belongs to William R. Jones, Leonard Harris, and Lucius T. Outlaw for offering a way of writing about this field that has had enormous impact on its participants. The difference between them and their predecessors was that they brought the metaphilosophical question of African diasporic philosophy – its conditions of possibility – to the forefront of professional philosophical debates in the 1970s and 1980s. It was a privilege to enter the academy in the 1990s on the shoulders of their pioneering work. An even greater privilege is this opportunity to advance my position on the problematics they have outlined. My own work argues for the expansion of philosophical categories. Thus, when the question of introducing the field of Africana philosophy became concrete in my agreement to write this book, it became clear to me that the text itself required philosophical inquiry. How, in other words, does one introduce an area of philosophy whose basis has been a challenge to philosophy and related fields such as political theory and intellectual history?

The task at hand transcended the history of philosophy by demanding an interrogation of the distinction between historical work in philosophy and philosophical work in the history of ideas. This is not my first encounter with such issues. I raised such questions in 1995 in the introduction to my book *Fanon and the Crisis of European Man*, when I argued against the tendency to reduce black thinkers to their biographies and to treat them as writers without ideas. I saw my efforts as engagements with Fanon's thought rather than writing on him. A study of Karl Jaspers who, like Fanon, was a psychiatrist who wrote philosophical work in the middle of violent events, would be remiss if it offered only a biographical account. And even if such an endeavor were announced, the author would be expected to explain and evaluate Jaspers's *thought*. A similar concern would be raised in a biographical study of John Locke, another philosopher who was also a physician.

As a study of Western philosophy would seem odd if it focused on the philosophers but not their ideas, one on Africana philosophy requires also engaging the thought raised by such a constellation of thinkers. An additional difficulty is that this project involves the examination of thought by professional philosophers and contributions by other thinkers whose identity is not necessarily that of philosophers. For some professional philosophers such a path stimulates much suspicion. I recall an emeritus colleague's recount of his experience at an august American institution in the 1950s, when he consulted the director of graduate studies (DGS) about asking Paul Tillich to be his main advisor. The DGS responded, "Why do you want to work with him? He is a thinker, not a philosopher."

Africana philosophers could not afford to abandon thought for professional recognition. The road to inclusion continues to be a rocky one, with obstacles that include the inability of professional philosophy to affect the vision of many professional philosophers. In spite of philosophical demands on the category, it continues to be a stretch for many white philosophers to see Africana philosophers as human beings, and even more so as philosophers. This form of polite racism, in which Africana philosophers are often more tolerated than engaged, has occasioned an almost neurotic situation for Africana philosophers. Is there any way of responding to such behavior by custodians of reason other than by advancing reason? Would not such a response ultimately rely more on faith or devotion than anything else? This question of human minimum affects dynamics of appearance. Who are Africana philosophers? Who counts as an Africana philosopher? Is there Africana philosophy? If so, what is it? These kinds of question presuppose an initial absence. Introducing Africana philosophy is, to use a phrase wrought with significance in the African diasporic context, an act of unveiling. Since the thought unveiled is one that has been around for some time, the tale to be told is one of disappearance as well as reappearance. But what returns is not exactly as it has been before. There was not, after all, a panoramic discussion of African diasporic philosophy as offered here. In effect, this organization of what has been is the advancement of something new.

Africana philosophy offers the appearance of a people with the articulation of ideas. Most of them are now in the pantheon of witnesses known in this tradition of thought as the ancestors. I hope I have done justice to them.

There are those among the living to whom I owe much gratitude. The first is Hilary Gaskin for her commitment to bringing this area of research to the oldest continuous publishing house. Her faith and patience are immeasurably appreciated. I presented some of the ideas in this book at the 2006 meeting of the Philosophy Born of Struggle Society conference at the New School University and then as a public lecture hosted by the Africana Studies Department, the Philosophy Department, and the Humanities Center at Stony Brook University. Thanks to J. Everet Green and Leonard Harris for organizing the former and David Clinton Wills and the welcoming community of colleagues at Stony Brook for the latter. I also presented some of these ideas through a series of lectures as the Metcalfe Chair in Philosophy at Marquette University that year and the Political Theory Workshop at the University of Pennsylvania. I would like to thank the members of the philosophy department at Marquette, especially Michael Monahan, for their generosity and the theorists in the department of political science at the University of Pennsylvania, especially Anne Norton and Rogers Smith, for their valuable feedback. I also benefited from comments from the following scholars who read the manuscript closely: Molefi Asante, Myron Beasley, Doug Ficek, David Fryer, Leonard Harris, Paget Henry, Joan Jasak, Kenneth Knies, Anthony Monteiro, Marilyn Nissim-Sabat, Neil Roberts, Jean-Paul Rocchi, Susan Searls-Giroux, Kwasi Wiredu, and the anonymous referees at Cambridge University Press. The text also benefited from Shabbat discussions with Walter Isaac, Gregory Graham, Frank Castro, Qrescent Mason, Devon Johnson, Denene Wambach, and José Muniz.

No one, however, has read this text more closely and has offered more suggestions at every stage of the project than Tom Meyer and Jane Anna Gordon. Their eye for precision and abilities as the proverbial devil's advocates have made them my most trusted colleagues at Temple. With Jane I am also fortunate that she has continued to be so much more, as the face I am lucky enough to see when I open my eyes each morning.

Thanks also to Mathieu, Jennifer, Sula, and Elijah Gordon for their love and patience as I devoted so much time to the completion of this book.

The two people to whom this book is dedicated are my mother and father. They have become ancestors. Through my brothers, children, and me, they continue to speak and remain loved.

Introduction: Africana philosophy in context

Africana philosophy is a species of Africana thought, which involves theoretical questions raised by critical engagements with ideas in Africana cultures and their hybrid, mixed, or creolized forms worldwide. Since there was no reason for the people of the African continent to have considered themselves African until that identity was imposed upon them through conquest and colonization in the modern era (the sixteenth century onward), this area of thought also refers to the unique set of questions raised by the emergence of "Africans" and their diaspora here designated by the term "Africana."[1] Such concerns include the convergence of most Africans with the racial term "black" and its many connotations.[2] Africana philosophy refers to the philosophical dimensions of this area of thought.

There is, however, perhaps no greater controversy in philosophy than its definition. As we will see even the claim to its etymological origins in the Greek language is up for debate.[3] This may seem rather odd since the word "philosophy" is a conjunction of the ancient Greek words *philia*, which means a form of respectful devotion, often defined as "brotherly love," and *sophia*, which means "wisdom." The source of controversy is that it could easily be shown, as scholars such as the Argentinean philosopher, historian, and theologian Enrique Dussel, the Irish political scientist and archaeolinguist

---

[1] For discussion see V. Y. Mudimbe, *The Invention of Africa: Gnosis, Philosophy and the Order of Knowledge* (Bloomington, IN: Indiana University Press, 1988); Lucius T. Outlaw, *On Race and Philosophy* (New York: Routledge, 1996), ch. 4; and Lewis R. Gordon, *Existentia Africana: Understanding Africana Existential Thought* (New York: Routledge, 2000), ch. 1.

[2] *Ibid.*

[3] See Théophile Obenga's discussion of the etymology of "philosophy," which he argues is not of Greek but African origin, in his book, *Ancient Egypt and Black Africa* (Chicago, IL: Karnak House, 1992), pp. 49–53. See also his *African Philosophy: The Pharaonic Period, 2780–330 BC* (Popenguine, Senegal: Ankh, 2004).

Martin Bernal, and the Congolese philosopher, historian, and archaeologist Théophile Obenga have demonstrated, that these words are transformed versions of ancient Phoenician and Hittite words, which in turn are varied and adopted words from the Old Kingdom of ancient Egypt.[4] The work of these scholars alerts us to a tendency to limit the historical reach in etymological and archaeological work. To end one's search for the origin of Western words in the Graeco-Latin classical past is to treat that world as civilizations that emerged, literally, *ex nihilo*, out of nothing or nowhere. They too had to have been built on earlier civilizations, and with that came even more archaic linguistic resources. Put differently, all languages, at least in the basic stock of organizing grammar and terms, are built on the linguistic foundations of the most primordial human languages and thus, logically, on early human beings and the geographical terrain from which they came. A prime example is the word "Egypt," which is based on the ancient Greek *Aigyptos*, which was in turn based on the Amarnan word *Hikuptah* (or *Ha[t]kaptah*), which was one of the names of what is today known as Memphis. The ancient indigenous peoples referred to the civilization that encompassed a vast region of northeast Africa as Km.t, today often written as Kam, Kamit, or Kemet, which means "black lands" or "dark lands." As we will see, this is not the only instance of the imposition of representing an entire network of kingdoms, or even an entire continent, under the name of one of its parts. Crucial here is the story that is revealed by pushing etymology a little bit further. The upshot of this call for a more radical linguistic archaeology is that it challenges an organizing myth in the study of Western intellectual history and the history of philosophy – the notion of ancient Greece as the torch from which the light of reason was brought into history and then on to the rest of humanity. The most famous example, in recent times, was Martin Heidegger's (1889–1976) famous encomium and effort to draw upon the reflections of the pre-Socratics for a more direct engagement with beings themselves.[5]

---

[4] See Enrique D. Dussel, "Europe, Modernity, and Eurocentrism," *Nepantla: Views from South* 1, no. 3 (2000): 465–78; Martin Bernal, *Black Athena: The Afroasiatic Roots of Classical Civilization (The Fabrication of Ancient Greece 1785–1985*, vol. I) (New Brunswick: Rutgers University Press, 1987) and *Black Athena Writes Back: Martin Bernal Responds to His Critics*, ed. Martin Bernal and David Chioni Moore (Durham, NC: Duke University Press, 2001), and Obenga, *African Philosophy*.

[5] See Martin Heidegger, *Being and Time*, trans. John Macquarrie and Edward Robinson (New York: Harper Collins, 1962). My subsequent etymological references should, thus,

Although it does not follow that the elements of a concept in the present entail the presence of the concept in the past, for concepts could exist independently and in terms of very different life challenges in their differing times, and the organization of those elements could be what was uniquely brought together by subsequent civilizations, it is also the case that some concepts echo older ones as part of an ongoing problematic governed by the precepts of mythic life. Thus, the question of how one engages reason is crucial for the understanding of the development of philosophy, in addition to understanding that its etymology suggests that such intellectual activity was not conducted in isolation.

The critics of the claim that the Greeks invented philosophy have shown that this notion was a creation of European Renaissance intellectuals, many of whom wanted a connection to a classical past that brought coherence to the rapidly changing world that was eventually created by the age of modern exploration (which began in the fifteenth century and ended by the late eighteenth century) or the scramble to reach India, which was in medieval times regarded by Mediterranean peoples as the center of the world. Being west of center, it was their hope to find a short cut around a believed-smaller globe. The commerce stimulated by the shift to the Atlantic Ocean decimated the status of the Mediterranean as a site of sea trade, and the realization of continents to the west that were not Asian led to a literally new "orientation" of those people's perspective. Once west of the center, the new alignment created a geological and political shift in which a new "center" was born.[6]

Additionally, as Walter Mignolo, Enrique Dussel, and Cedric Robinson have shown, there is an important missing element in this narrative of expansion.[7] That element is the fact that the Mediterranean world as far north as most of the Iberian Peninsula was ruled under the name of

be distinguished from the kinds Heidegger had in mind, and although I may not always go further for the sake of brevity, the reader should at all times take these exercises as encouragement for further inquiry.

[6] See for example Enrique Dussel, *Beyond Philosophy: Ethics, History, Marxism, and Liberation Theology*, ed. Eduardo Mendieta (Lanham, MD: Rowman & Littlefield, 2003), especially ch. 3, "The 'World-System': Europe as 'Center' and Its 'Periphery' beyond Eurocentrism," pp. 53–84.

[7] *Ibid.*; Walter Mignolo, *The Darker Side of the Renaissance: Literacy, Territoriality, and Colonization*, 2nd edn (Ann Arbor, MI: University of Michigan Press, 2003); Cedric Robinson, *An Anthropology of Marxism* (Aldershot: Ashgate, 2001).

al-Andalus by the Moors (black, brown, and "red" Muslims from Africa) for nearly eight hundred years. A crucial, and often overlooked, dimension of the fifteenth-century expansion of Christendom was that 2 January 1492 was marked by the victory of Queen Infanta Isabella I of Castile (1451–1504) and King Fernando de Aragón or King Ferdinand V of Castile (1452–1516) in *Reconquista* (reconquest), which was achieved by pushing the Moors southward back into Africa. Reconquest is an appropriate term since Iberia went from Vandals to Visigoths, who exemplified Germanic Catholic conquest until falling to the Muslim Moors. The Christian reconquest continued through an edict on 31 March expelling nearly 200,000 Jews and forcing the conversion of other non-Christians, and spread with a tide onto the African continent and into the seas, where investments paid off in the form of Columbus's landing on the shores of the Bahamas on 12 October of the same year. Some of these events are recounted by Niccolò Machiavelli (1469–1527) in his discussion of Ferdinand:

> In our own times we have Ferdinand of Aragon, the present king of Spain.
> This man can be called almost a new prince, since from being a weak ruler,
> through fame and glory he became the first king of Christendom. If you
> consider his deeds you will find them all very grand, and some even
> extraordinary. In the beginning of his reign he attacked Granada, and that
> enterprise was the basis of his state . . . Besides this, in order to be able to
> undertake great enterprises, he had recourse to a pious cruelty, always
> employing religion for his own purposes, chasing the Marranos out of his
> kingdom and seizing their property. No example of his actions could be
> more pathetic or more extraordinary than this. He attacked Africa under
> the same cloak of religion.[8]

The making of this new "center" was not, then, solely a commercial affair but also a military one and, subsequently, a racial-religious one, for the darker populations of people were pushed more southward in a war that continued back and forth throughout the modern world as Christianity sometimes dominated but Islam fought back well into the present. Another outcome was the mixed population of north Africa becoming dominated by lighter peoples than in its ancient and medieval past, with the consequence today of that region being considered more a part of the Middle

---

[8] Niccolò Machiavelli, *The Prince*, trans. Peter Bondanella (Oxford: Oxford University Press, 2005), ch. 21, p. 76.

East than the African continental world on which it rests and in which it resides.[9]

This new center sought explanations for its emergence, and it did so through an increasingly eroded sense of inferiority as it looked farther westward. Now being neither East nor West, the many kingdoms and small states that comprised today's Portugal, Spain, and Italy began to develop a new consciousness, one in which "Europe," as we now understand it as a geopolitical place, was born; with that new consciousness, the notion of this new being ever having suffered a disconnection from the mechanisms of its emergence began to erode. Europeans began to forget that there was not always a Europe. As Cedric Robinson relates:

> Reviewing a map of the Old World, one inevitably discovers that Europe is not a continent but a peninsular projection from a continent. It might as easily have come to be known as the Asian continent. In point of fact the continent became the locus of several civilizations, most if not all of them prior to the invention of Europe. Indeed, Europe as the marker of a distinct civilization came into being as a colonial backwater of the ancient civilizations which had appeared and flourished in Asia, the Indus Valley, the Near East, and Africa. As such it would be anachronistic, at least, to state that the development of Europe – which is normally assigned at the close of the Dark Ages (6th to 11th centuries) – required access to the non-European world. The more significant error, however, is the presumptive one: since there was no Europe, the notion of the non-European conceals the truer positivity; that is, Europe emerged from the negation of the real. In order to fabricate Europe, institutional, cultural and ideological materials were consciously smuggled into this hinterland from afar by kings and popes, episcopals, clerics, and monastic scholars. No reality, then, substantiates the imagined, autonomous European continent.[10]

The European began to develop a sense of the self in which there was sup- posedly a primal, mythical exemplification of wisdom itself, and the place

---

[9] See Mignolo, *The Darker Side*, and Dussel, "Europe, Modernity, and Eurocentrism" and *Beyond Philosophy*. An often overlooked element of this conflict is that the African pop- ulations also enslaved white Christians whose descendants became part of the north African Muslim populations; for discussion see e.g. Robert Davis, *Christian Slaves, Mus- lim Masters: White Slavery in the Mediterranean, the Barbary Coast and Italy, 1500–1800* (New York: Palgrave Macmillan, 2003) and *Golden Age of the Moor*, ed. Ivan Van Sertima (New Brunswick: Transaction Publishers, 1992).

[10] Robinson, *An Anthropology*, p. 33.

that became the epitome of this sense of self became Hellenic civilization, a place whose foundational role took racialized form in nineteenth-century scholarship on the history of philosophy.[11]

We encounter at the outset a unique problem in Africana philosophy. The love of wisdom seems to have a history fraught with racial and ethnic allegiance. The notion that philosophy was a peculiarly European affair logically led to the conclusion that there was (and continues to be) something about European cultures that makes them more conducive to philosophical reflection than others. But the problem that immediately emerges is one of accounting for and supporting such a claim when the people we call Europeans were (and continue to be) constantly changing. Just as the global concept of the African emerged in the modern world, so too did the notion of the European. In many ways, as we will see, the two concepts are symbiotically related.[12]

The notion of Europeans' intrinsic connection to philosophy is, in other words, circular: it defines them as philosophical in the effort to determine whether they were philosophical. The effect is that the many Germanic groups who were considered barbarians to the ancient Greeks, Romans, Phoenicians, and Egyptians become realigned genealogically into the very groups who denied them membership. Thus, it really becomes the identification with ancient classical civilizations that determines the European identity instead of the link in itself from the ancient to the modern worlds.

To conclude that the kinds of intellectual activity that were called philosophical in the past and have joined the fold in the present were thus limited to one group of people, most of whom were artificially lumped together to create false notions of unity and singular identity, requires a model of humanity that does not fit the facts. The first, and most obvious one, is that philosophical activity existed in ancient China at least a few thousand

---

[11] Bernal, in *Black Athena*, outlines the scholarship that framed this interpretation of the past; but for the best-known example in philosophy, see G. W. F. Hegel's *The Philosophy of History*, with prefaces by Charles Hegel and the translator, J. Sibree, and a new introduction by C. J. Friedrich (New York: Dover Publications, 1956).

[12] Sylvia Wynter, one of the scholars whom we will later discuss, has written quite a bit on the shared dynamics that created Europe and Africa and the modern world. See discussions of this theme in *After Man, Towards the Human: Critical Essays on the Thought of Sylvia Wynter*, ed. B. Anthony Bogues (Kingston, Jamaica: Ian Randle, 2006) and *The Sylvia Wynter Reader*, ed. B. Anthony Bogues (Kingston, Jamaica: Ian Randle, forthcoming).

years before Thales of Miletos (624–526 BCE), the first known Greek philosopher, attempted to figure out the constitution of the universe. The *I Ching*,
for instance, is generally believed to have been written in about 2852 BCE.[13]
Although an objection could be made, as did Karl Jaspers (1883–1969), that
ancient Chinese philosophy is more mystical and lacks a sophisticated treatment of nature, and that a similar claim holds for ancient and traditional
African philosophy, I would encourage, in response, the following pedagogical experiment.[14] After introducing students to such works, present any
collection of pre-Socratic philosophy for their perusal. I do just that when I
teach courses on African philosophy, and the students immediately see the
point: philosophers of color engaging with the same questions are treated
as naive, simple, or mystical but ancient Greek philosophers are revered for
their supposed genius, or, in Heideggerian language, their attunement with
beings instead of Being. We need not, however, pick on Heidegger. Bertrand
Russell (1872–1970) goes to great lengths to spell out the sophistication of
nearly every effort of the pre-Socratics, and that nearly every work that
comes out under the title "ancient philosophy" pretty much ignores the
rest of the ancient world continues to exemplify this prejudice.[15]

The second fact is that the unique upheavals associated with the development of philosophy – cross-fertilization of cultures; abstract and logical
reasoning; collapse in concrete manifestations of authority, which stimulates critical reflection – are all found in earlier civilizations such as
Egypt/Kamit and Kush. Think, as well, of mathematics. Wherever human
communities are large enough to stimulate anonymous relationships

---

[13] See *The Classic of Changes: A New Translation of the I Ching as Interpreted by Wang Bi*, new
edn, trans. Richard John Lynn (New York: Columbia University Press, 2004).

[14] Karl Jaspers, *Way to Wisdom: An Introduction to Philosophy*, trans. Ralph Manheim (New
Haven: Yale University Press, 1951). I focus on Chinese thought because Jaspers criticized it. The argument could apply to Egypt/Kamit as well, where thought often
focused on problems of value and the fragments that remain are often those from
ritualistic contexts. The most famous are perhaps the funeral rites prepared by Ani
and now known as *The Egyptian Book of the Dead: The Book of Going Forth by Day*, 2nd
rev. edn, trans. Raymond O. Faulkner, introduction by Ogden Goelet, preface by Carol
Andrews, and produced by James Wasserman (San Francisco, CA: Chronicle Books, 2000);
but see as well the twelfth-dynasty (*c.* 1991–1786 BCE) text *Debate between a Man Tired
of Life and His Soul* [ba], trans. R. O. Faulkner. Available online at the following URL:
http://nefertiti.iwebland.com/locmntl/hotfreebies.html.

[15] See Bertrand Russell, *A History of Western Philosophy* (New York: Simon and Schuster,
1972).

between people and the organization of social life, mathematics is necessary.[16] Whether it is among the ancient cities of Africa, Asia, or those of the Americas, the reality is that some degree of mathematics is needed for the ongoing operations of civil society. It is difficult to imagine such development without some of the abstract problems raised even by basic mathematics, such as infinity (counting in sequence from whole numbers onward) and infinitesimality (fractions).

We have then come to a basic aspect of philosophical thought. All such thought is reflective and abstract. Philosophy emerges where problems that stimulate critical reflection come to the fore. By critical reflection I mean subjecting each assumption to conditions of evidence, rational assessment, or reason. But simply thinking about one's assumptions and prejudices, while a necessary aspect of philosophical work, is insufficient to make such thought itself philosophical. Thought transcends mere critical reflection when it begins to raise certain questions. These include, but are not limited to, "What is there? How should we conduct our lives? What can we know? How is knowledge possible? How do we know what we know? What matters most? Why is there something instead of nothing? What must be the case?" or "What is reality? What kinds of things can be otherwise? How should we organize living together?" In academic philosophy these questions are associated with specialized areas of inquiry: ontology, ethics, epistemology, metaphysics, and political philosophy. Understanding that all areas of philosophical inquiry have correlated fundamental questions should make it clear that this is not an exhaustive list. To it could be added, for example, aesthetics ("What is beautiful and what is ugly? What are the conditions for something to be transformed into the interesting – for example, a work of art?"), the philosophy of logic ("What are valid and cogent arguments, and what are their ontological, metaphysical, or epistemological implications?"), and, more familiar, the philosophy of existence ("How is life meaningful? What does it mean to emerge, to live, to exist?"). And then there is metaphilosophy

---

[16] See one of the many texts on ancient mathematics, such as Gay Robins and Charles Shute, *The Rhind Mathematical Papyrus: An Ancient Egyptian Text* (New York: Dover, 1990); Corinna Rossi, *Architecture and Mathematics in Ancient Egypt* (Cambridge: Cambridge University Press, 2004); Christopher Cullen, *Astronomy and Mathematics in Ancient China: The "Zhou Bi Suan Jing"* (London: Cambridge University Press, 1996); Frank Swetz and T. I. Kao, *Was Pythagoras Chinese? An Examination of Right Triangle Theory in Ancient China* (State College, PA: Pennsylvania State University Press, 1977); and Richard Mankiewicz, *The Story of Mathematics* (Princeton, NJ: Princeton University Press, 2000).

or the philosophy of philosophy. This includes all the reflections on philosophy from antiquity to the present, such as "What is the significance of thinking? What is *this kind of thinking* which devotes itself to thinking?"

Plato, for example, in his *Symposium*, took the question of *eros* (erotic love) and transformed it into a discussion of what it means to love Socrates (the lover of wisdom or the *philosophon*). Writing through the voice of Socrates' lover, Alcibiades, Plato, rather poignantly, argued that loving the philosopher (and by implication loving the wise or wisdom) entailed encountering that which at first appeared very ugly yet revealed an inner core so beautiful that it was "intoxicating."[17] This is paradoxical because, as the term suggests, to be intoxicated is to be poisoned. And as is well known, as Jacques Derrida (1930–2004) later reminds us in his essay "Plato's Pharmacy," most medicines are also poisonous.[18] Philosophy is, in other words, something that is good for us but it is achieved through a process that is not at first appealing and often even dangerous, as revealed by the four texts that chronicle the last days of Socrates, one of which is marked by the memorable dictum, "I tell you that . . . examining both myself and others is really the very best thing that a man can do, and that life without this sort of examination is not worth living."[19]

This sense of philosophy as not immediately beautiful is a function of its difficulty. Philosophy requires hard work; it requires thinking in ways to which most of us are not used, and it often requires appealing to things that are not immediately evident.

Philosophers have also argued about which of the above questions is most important. We could call this the search for a *philosophia prima* or first philosophy. Depending on which one dominated which period and in which region, unique forms of philosophies have emerged. In China, for instance, the question of conduct was paramount in the thought of Confucius (*K'ung-fu-tzu*, 551–479 BCE), whereas among the Hindus and Buddhists of India concerns with reality affected questions of conduct as relevant only

---

[17] See Plato's *Symposium* in *The Works of Plato*, trans. B. Jowett (New York: McGraw-Hill Humanities/Social Sciences/Languages, 1965).

[18] Jacques Derrida, *Dissemination*, trans. with introduction and notes by Barbara Johnson (Chicago, IL: University of Chicago Press, 1981).

[19] I am of course referring to Plato's *Euthyphro*, *Apology*, *Crito*, and *Phaedo*, brought together, in addition to *The Works*, in *The Last Days of Socrates*, reprint edn, trans. Hugh Tredennick and ed. Harold Tarrant (London: Penguin Classics, 1993). The quotation is from the *Apology*, which appears on p. 63 of this compilation.

for achieving higher consciousness. In many African communities one would see much emphasis on conduct as well, but this would be misleading in cases where the basis of thinking about conduct flowed from an ontology in which reality itself had an originary moment of creation of all beings and ultimate value. The ontological and the axiological, or value, would be one.[20] And in different periods of Western civilizations the shift has gone from the good as paramount to the modern philosophical advancement of epistemology as first philosophy.[21] Some philosophers have mistakenly focused on only one of these questions as the only real philosophical question. This has led to views in which only ontological, epistemological, or ethical inquiries prevailed. Yet such conclusions are often contradicted by the fact that some of the best-known philosophers made no contribution to the areas chosen as the unique province of philosophy. Many political philosophers, for example, made no contributions to metaphysics or ontology; and many famous epistemologists made no contribution to ethics. And then there are the grand philosophers, such as G. W. F. Hegel (1770–1831) and Arthur Schopenhauer (1788–1860), who seem to have touched on nearly every area of philosophical thought.

It could easily be shown, however, that thinking through one philosophical category or question eventually leads to another. Exploring what there is leads to the methodological question of how to go about such an inquiry, which leads to the epistemological question of the knowledge wrought from such thinking, which raises the ethical question of whether such thought ought to be pursued. We could even reflect on the beauty of such thought or on its political implications, as many critics of philosophy have charged and for which many philosophers had to provide a defense over the ages.[22] In addition to being lovers of wisdom and reason, then, philosophers

[20] See e.g. Kwame Gyekye's discussion of Akan philosophy in *An Essay on African Philosophical Thought: The Akan Conceptual Scheme*, rev. edn (Philadelphia, PA: Temple University Press, 1995).

[21] Cf. e.g. the distinction between Plato's *Republic* and René Descartes's *Meditations on First Philosophy*. See *The Works of Plato* and René Descartes, *Descartes' Philosophical Writings*, trans. and ed. Norman Kemp Smith (London: Macmillan, 1952).

[22] Cf. Iris Murdoch, *The Sovereignty of the Good* (London: Ark Paperbacks, 1985) and Antonio Gramsci's *Selections from the Prison Notebooks*, trans. and ed. Quintin Hoare and Geoffrey Nowell Smith (New York: International Publishers, 1972) as well as the many reflections of John Dewey, such as those in his *The Reconstruction in Philosophy*, enlarged edn (Boston, MA: Beacon Press, 1957), and again Gyekye, *An Essay*.

are also paradoxically the greatest critics and defenders of philosophical thinking.

Philosophical thought is guided by reason. The meaning of reason is, however, a philosophical question. Most modern philosophers have attempted to fix reason through transforming it into a species of rationality. Others, such as David Hume (1711–1776), took this route and denied in *A Treatise of Human Nature* that reason could be anything else than what could be called instrumental rationality, which focuses simply on the means by which actions are achieved.[23] And then there are those who reject such approaches and argue that reason is the language in which things emerge as making sense. For some, such as René Descartes (1596–1650), Elisabeth von der Pfalz or Elisabeth of Bohemia or Princess Palatine (*c.* 1618–1680), or Quobna Ottobah Cugoano (*c.* 1757–*c.* 1803) this language is literally the thought or words of God.[24]

Many definitions of science are available in philosophical and scientific literature. Peter Caws, for instance, defines science as imagination constrained by evidence. To this definition we should add that scientists do not think imaginatively about everything but do so about one thing – namely, nature.[25] The famed contemporary physicist Sylvester James Gates agrees but adds that the concern of science is primarily descriptions of how things work. In his view the scientist is like someone who enters a house and is concerned with how it functions. The scientist does not question why the house exists, whether the house should exist, or even how to make it more beautiful. He or she simply asks how the lights are turned on, how

---

[23] David Hume, *A Treatise of Human Nature* (London: Penguin Classics, 1969).

[24] Descartes, *Philosophical Writings*; see also *Cartesian Women: Versions and Subversions of Rational Discourse in the Old Regime*, ed. Erica Harth (Ithaca, NY: Cornell University Press, 1992); Jacqueline Broad, *Women Philosophers of the Seventeenth Century* (Cambridge: Cambridge University Press, 2003); Ottobah Cugoano, *"Thoughts and Sentiments on the Evil of Slavery" and Other Writings*, introd. and notes by Vincent Carretta (New York: Penguin Classics, 1999).

[25] Peter Caws, *Ethics from Experience* (Boston, MA: Jones and Bartlett Publishers, 1996). Some earlier efforts include *The Philosophy of Science: A Systematic Account* (Princeton, NJ: D. Van Nostrand, 1965) and *Science and the Theory of Value* (New York: Random House, 1967). See also his recent *Yorick's World: Science and the Knowing Subject* (Berkeley, CA: University of California Press, 1993). For discussion of Caws's thought on science, see Lewis R. Gordon, "Making Science Reasonable: Peter Caws on Science Both Human and 'Natural,'" *Janus Head: An Interdisciplinary Journal of Literature, Continental Philosophy, Phenomenological Psychology, and the Arts* 5, no. 1 (2002): 14–38.

the water flows, how the ceiling remains aloft, how the house stands up, and so forth, and in the physicist's case that house is physical reality.[26]

Religion, however, is concerned with questions such as who built the house (provided that the house has to have been built in the first place), for what purpose the house exists, and how we should live in the house. More, religion is concerned about what we should believe about the house and other sets of belief that follow from such beliefs. Although religion is not antipathetic to reason, it is not as reliant on reason as philosophy is. Religion, in other words, places faith in faith itself, in, by the end, what should be believed.

The poet, as one might guess, is not as constrained by evidence as the scientist or the philosopher or even the theologian. This is because, whereas the philosopher looks at reason, the scientist at nature, and the theologian at faith, the poet is guided by imagination itself without constraints beyond those internal to imaginative play.

All this leads to the following set of limits. Philosophy is guided by reason and questions that stop short of religion. It is not that philosophy cannot examine religious questions, but that it does so in philosophical terms, which means within the realm of reason. Religion, on the other hand, is willing to go where philosophy cannot, namely, within the realm of faith itself. And poetry has fewer limits. Science, on the other hand, is compelled to stop where philosophy begins. Science talks about the world (the house), but it is philosophy, ironically, that talks about science, religion, poetry, and philosophy itself. Although there is religious thought on philosophy and on poetry, it is bound by the dictates of faith, whether it is in a deity or a set of customs over the ages. Because of this, religion can speak to the part of us that wishes not to be alone in the universe. Whether it is from a voice without a speaker is a question that converges in philosophy and theology.[27]

Philosophical questions also pertain to conditions of possibility. These are what must be understood for there to be the emergence of a certain idea or concept. Immanuel Kant (1724–1804) famously advanced such arguments

---

[26] Sylvester James Gates, Jr., "How Diversity Likely Matters in Science and Mathematics," Keynote Address, Caribbean Philosophical Association Conference (San Juan, Puerto Rico, 2005).

[27] These ideas can be consulted in Jaspers, *Way to Wisdom*; Søren Kierkegaard, *Stages on Life's Way*, trans. Walter Lowrie (Princeton, NJ: Princeton University Press, 1940); Keiji Nishitani, *Religion and Nothingness*, trans. Jan Van Bragt (Berkeley, CA: University of California Press, 1982).

in his *Critique of Pure Reason* (1781) as transcendental ones, which he later, in *Prolegomena to Any Future Metaphysics* (1783), called "critical philosophy."[28] They ask, "How is an idea possible?" "What ideas are necessary for the emergence of other ideas?" This famous turn in philosophy has influenced much of what most philosophers of all backgrounds have been doing since at least the nineteenth century. In part this is due to the world dominance of European civilization by that period. The influence of Kant's thought on European thinkers meant that it would spread through places dominated by Europeans. Transcendentalism is, however, not limited to Kant's formulations. Whereas Kant's approach was directed at the conditions of concepts and experience, East Indian yogis were devoting their energy to the inner absence of all things meaningful that constituted, in their view, reality.

Along with the questions outlined thus far, there is one that dominates much of Africana philosophy and has become increasingly central since early modern times, namely, "What does it mean to be a human being?" Let us call the area of research associated with this question philosophical anthropology. Unlike anthropology, which is an empirical science, this area of philosophy examines problems raised by the human being as a subject of study. These problems include the difficulty of studying an object that is also the agent conducting the investigation. But more germane to our focus, philosophical anthropology is central in an area of thought that is dedicated to the understanding of beings whose humanity has been called into question or challenged in the modern era. The consequences of lost peoplehood, of denied humanness, are severe in that they lead to groups or kinds of people being treated as property (slavery), as waste to be eliminated (genocides, holocausts), as subhuman or animals (racism).

Returning to our initial question of the meaning of Africana philosophy, we have already defined Africana philosophy as an area of philosophical research that addresses the problems faced and raised by the African diaspora. Such an approach includes the centrality of philosophical anthropology. A reason for this focus is the historical fact of racism and colonialism in the modern era. Both phenomena led to the subordination of African peoples in the modern world. This degraded status involved political and

---

[28] These are well-known works by Kant. For commentary, see Ernst Cassirer, *Kant's Life and Thought*, trans. James Haden, introduction by Stephan Körner (New Haven, CT: Yale University Press, 1981).

social scientific claims that pushed down and defined such people as lesser human beings, if as human beings at all. A peculiar set of problems emerges from this historical circumstance which, as we will see, come to the fore in Africana philosophy. These include the problem of the relation of the categories "black," "African," and "reason," as well as discourses of African diasporic originality and imitation and the dynamics of Africana metaphilosophy. With regard to the last, there is a group of philosophers who see the fundamental questions of Africana philosophy to be prolegomena – that is, the conditions necessary for its possibility. (We see here the continued influence of Kant on modern philosophical thought.) Others, such as myself, have argued that Africana metaphilosophy faces the paradox that Africana philosophy is a living philosophy because many of its practitioners are willing to think beyond philosophy in ways that Kenneth Knies has characterized as "post-European science" or post-European philosophy.[29] The term I use in my own work, which will be discussed in the section on Africana phenomenology and existential philosophy, is a "teleological suspension of philosophy," which, paradoxically, generates new philosophy by going beyond philosophy.[30]

Africana philosophy, in taking modern concerns such as race, racism, and colonialism seriously, explores problems of identity and social transformation, of the self and the social world, of consciousness and intersubjectivity, of the body and communicability, of ethics and politics, of freedom and bondage, to name several. Although stated here in couplets, it should be borne in mind that these are not necessarily opposing dualities. Their distinctions are, however, crucial for many of the debates in the field. In addressing them, other, older questions come to the fore with new meaning.

In the area of philosophy of history, the past and present raise problems of interpretation. Is the past, for instance, a set of purely contingent

---

[29] See Lewis R. Gordon, "African-American Philosophy, Race, and the Geography of Reason," in *Not Only the Master's Tools: African-American Studies in Theory and Practice*, ed. Lewis R. Gordon and Jane Anna Gordon (Boulder, CO: Paradigm Publishers, 2005), pp. 3–50 and Kenneth Danziger Knies, "The Idea of Post-European Science: An Essay on Phenomenology and Africana Studies," in *Not Only the Master's Tools*, pp. 85–106.

[30] I discuss this concept in more detail in Lewis R. Gordon, *Disciplinary Decadence: Living Thought in Trying Times* (Boulder, CO: Paradigm Publishers, 2006), especially the introduction and ch. 1.

events without any overarching rationality or reason? Or, is the past a coherent movement of events whose eventual culmination is the resolution of all conflicts and contradictions? Although these questions are examined in Africana philosophy, there is also the question of how Africana philosophy is often excluded by racist attitudes toward its inclusion in the philosophical arena. And even when it is included, there is also the problem of retrospective inclusion. Putting aside the question of coherence in history, there is also the problem of whether Africana philosophy can simply be added to the history of ideas as currently constituted without seriously disrupting that field. And further, internal to Africana philosophy is the question of its own historical scope. Is it truly a peculiarly modern form of thought, as I asserted at the outset of this introduction? How coherent is it, for instance, to include ancient African thought in Africana philosophy when there was no reason for ancient Africans to have conceived of themselves as "African" in the first place? The analogue, as we have seen, would be "ancient European philosophy." There was, however, no such thing. There was properly "ancient Athenian," "ancient Ionian," "ancient Macedonian," or "ancient Roman," "ancient Sicilian," or "ancient Thracian" or "ancient Phoenician" philosophy. The same applies to ancient and medieval Asia. There was ancient Chinese and Indian philosophy, but there was no reason to regard them as Asian. Similarly, there was "ancient Egyptian/Kamitic," "Axumitic," and "Nubian" thought.

The "African" in our interpretation of ancient African thought must, then, be a modern imposition onto the past. This does not, however, mean that the cultural and historical foundations of the civilizations that have come to be known as "African" could not be those that we retrospectively consider by that name. We should, in other words, regard references to ancient African philosophy as similar to our use of the terms ancient Asian or ancient European philosophy. It is a term from the present that identifies a genealogical link to the past with the understanding that the term itself would be alien to those ancient civilizations.

These considerations of retrospective genealogical connections pertain, as well, to the history of the human species. Our species, *Homo sapiens sapiens*, evolved on the African continent about 220,000 years ago and then spread across the planet at least by 50,000 years ago. What this means is that, retrospectively, nearly all of the research on the near primordial ancient past is about peoples whom we would today call Africans, who eventually settled in the areas we now call Asia, Europe, and North and South America and came to be known as Asians, Europeans, and (Native) Americans.

We can, however, make the context of our discussion specific by focusing our discussion on the Latin word *Africanus*, which was already being used extensively by the Middle Ages. The origin of the word is uncertain. One story is that it was in honor of a black inhabitant of ancient Rome named Afer since the Romans referred to North Africa as *Africa terra* ("land of the Afri," which is the plural for Afer). This is an unlikely story for many reasons. First, it presupposes that the presence of blacks in Rome was an unusual occurrence, which does not match the facts.[31] What we would today call black people have with certainty inhabited the southern Mediterranean for at least 30,000 years since they were the original groups of *Homo sapiens* who migrated there and met the Neanderthals already living there.[32] Second, there is admittedly something very odd about naming an entire group of conquered people after one of its members. It makes more sense that the conquered would do that with regard to the conquerors, as the indigenous people of the Caribbean had done. For instance, the 1492 encounter between the Old World and the New World resulted in a new way of looking at an old relationship, since today we think more to Cristóbal Colón for the meaning behind the modern use of the word colony, in spite of its being coined by Edmund Burke (1729–1797). I have traced its etymological roots as follows: at least from the Greek *klon*, which means "member" or "limb," but also, without the accented "o," means rectum. The Latin word *colonus*, meaning farmer, from which we get colony, is related to the Greek word not only in appearance but also in the historic fact that, by the time of European feudalism, farmers were mostly serfs serving landlords, and before that, as today, farms produced food for the cities but were also parts of the whole. In other words, whether in Athens, Rome, or Constantinople, farms were the periphery from which food was brought to the center; they were, in Roman terms, within their dominion. When Colón realized that the largest New World island, Hayti, had neither East Indian resources nor gold, but that the debts

---

[31] See e.g. Frank M. Snowden, Jr., *Blacks in Antiquity: Ethiopians in the Greco-Roman Experience* (Cambridge, MA: Belknap Press, 1970) and *The William Leo Hansberry African Notebook*. Vol. II: *Africa and Africans as Seen by Classical Writers*, ed. Joseph E. Harris (Washington, DC: Howard University Press, 1981).

[32] See e.g. Charles Finch, III, *Echoes of the Old Darkland: Themes from the African Eden* (Decatur, GA: Khenti, 1991).

for his expeditions had to be paid by other means, he literally sought prof-
its from the blood and sweat of the indigenous people through agriculture,
which entailed farmers becoming settlers but with a new set of relations
since their proximity to the "center" was now remote. What is strange about
this situation is that the harbinger of this new period should have so fitting
a name.[33] After Columbus it was more likely that the conquering group
produced such a dubbing as a vain testament to themselves, as rendering
the conquered lands in their own image, as in the case of America, which
was named after Amerigo Vespucci (1454–1512) by Martin Waldseemüller
(c. 1470–c. 1522) in 1507.[34] This is not to say that the story is entirely impossible. We have, after all, already seen that the prevailing word Egypt has
its source in only a part of ancient Kamit. But, third, there seems to be
some etymological connection in the word that links it, unfortunately, to
the many negative stereotypes already underway by the Middle Ages and the
modern era. Although Afer was the Phoenician name of a group of indigenous people living near Carthage, based on the Phoenician word *afar*, which
means "dust," and became the Latin word for the lands on the southern side
of the Mediterranean, the word is also peculiarly related to those such as
"feral" (savage, wild), *ferris* (iron, which rusts). Remember that the people of
Africa did not – indeed, could not – refer to themselves as such since Phoenician and Latin, or even the possible Greek source *aphrike* ("without cold"),
were not from indigenous African languages, and, more, most had no reason to refer to themselves in continental terms since such an understanding
of the world did not at that time exist for most, save, perhaps, the Egyp-
tians/Kamites because of the Pharaoh Necho II's (c. 609–593 BCE) sending
an expedition of Phoenician ships around the continent in the seventh
century BCE.

---

[33] See C. L. R. James, *The Black Jacobins: Toussaint L'Ouverture and the San Domingo Revolution*,
2nd edn (New York: Vintage, 1989); Tzevan Todorov, *The Conquest of America: The Question
of the Other*, trans. Richard Howard (Norman, OK: University of Oklahoma Press, 1999)
and Enrique Dussel, *The Invention of the Americas: Eclipse of the "Other" and the Myth of
Modernity*, trans. Michael D. Barber (New York: Continuum, 1995) for discussion of this
transition. For discussion on Burke's impact on the history of colonialism see Seamus
Deane, *Foreign Affections: Essays On Edmund Burke* (South Bend, IN: Notre Dame University
Press, 2005).

[34] *The Cosmographiae Introductio of Martin Waldseemuller in Facsimile* (New York: United States
Catholic Historical Society, 1907, repr. 1969); a copy of the original 1507 text, published
in Strasbourg, is available in the New York Public Library.

There was already a connection between linguistic and cosmological organizations of life across the peoples of east Africa and those eventually known as the people of sub-Saharan Africa.[35] Those connections should be viewed as we use the terms "Latin" and "Germanic" and the more broad "Indo-European" to refer to those of Europe and western Asia. By the Middle Ages there was a growing notion of "Africa," and the impact of trade across the continent also brought with it an exchange of ideas, especially along Judaic, Christian, and Muslim lines of thought; it was around this time that a sense of a black diasporic people began to be formed because of the Arabic and East Indian slave trades, both of which continue to this day.[36] The Atlantic slave trade signaled the beginning of the "modern" black diaspora and philosophical writings born from that historical development. It is in this sense, then, that Africana philosophy originates from medieval and modern contexts.

[35] Finch, *Echoes of the Old Darkland*; see also Finch, "From the Nile to the Niger: the Evolution of African Spiritual Concepts," in *A Companion to African-American Studies*, ed. Lewis R. Gordon and Jane Anna Gordon (Malden, MA: Blackwell Publishers, 2006), pp. 453–75. See also Graham Connah, *African Civilizations: An Archaeological Perspective*, 2nd edn (Cambridge: Cambridge University Press, 2001) and, for a critical survey of recent debates on African civilizations, see Aaron Kamugisha, "Finally in Africa? Egypt, from Diop to Celenko," *Race and Class* 45, no. 1 (2003): 31–60.

[36] For a discussion of contemporary slavery see Kevin Bales, *Disposable People: New Slavery in the Global Economy* (Berkeley, CA: University of California Press, 1999).

Part I

Groundings

1 Africana philosophy as a modern philosophy

There is much debate over the meaning and moment of "modernity."[1] In most North American philosophical courses, modernity begins more with a whom than with a when, and that person is René Descartes. In some fields, such as political philosophy, the who sometimes refers to Niccolò Machiavelli, in whose thought could be found proto-modern ideas. And still others would begin with Thomas Hobbes (1588–1679). For the most part, the when of modernity in this sense arises approximately from the fifteenth into the sixteenth centuries. Other theorists of modernity argue that the modern should not be looked at in terms of a set of ideas by an individual thinker but a set of circumstances that form systems in which people think. Recall from our introduction that in the fifteenth century Christendom looked eastward for the center of the world, which was considered to be India.[2] Seeking a shorter route to the east by going westward around what was then thought to be a smaller planet, they encountered a world which challenged their previous point of center. With the Atlantic Ocean displacing the Mediterranean Sea as the leading place of maritime commerce, the center moved westward and northward in an expanding Christendom, and Europe came into being as the modern world. Christopher Columbus's landing in

---

[1] See e.g. Robert B. Pippin, *Modernism as a Philosophical Problem*, 2nd edn (Malden, MA: Blackwell Publishers, 1999); Walter D. Mignolo, *Local Histories/Global Designs: Coloniality, Subaltern Knowledges, and Border Thinking* (Princeton, NJ: Princeton University Press, 2000); Roxanne L. Euben, "Mapping Modernities, 'Islamic' and 'Western,'" in *Border Crossings: Toward a Comparative Political Theory*, ed. Fred Dallmayr (Lanham, MD: Lexington Books, 1999), pp. 11–38; and Frank Kirkland, "Modernity and Intellectual Life in Black," *The Philosophical Forum* 24, nos. 1–3 (1992–3): 136–65.

[2] See e.g. Enrique Dussel, *Beyond Philosophy: Ethics, History, Marxism, and Liberation Theology*, ed. Eduardo Mendieta (Lanham, MD: Rowman & Littlefield, 2003) and *The Invention of the Americas: Eclipse of "the Other" and the Myth of Modernity*, trans. Michael D. Barber (New York: Continuum, 1995).

1492 thus signaled more than a successful expedition. It signaled the birth of a new age.

Accompanying this new world and new age was also what Dussel calls its "underside," by which he means all the negative things that come along with its positive proclamations.[3] With discovery, there was conquest; with expansion, there was enslavement; with unprecedented wealth were poverty and starvation; with growing industry, there were (and continue to be) ecological disasters. Yet it cannot be denied that there are also peculiar ideas that mark modern thought. Many philosophers look to Descartes, for instance, because of his focus on epistemology as first philosophy, his exploration of scientific methodology, his conception of theoretical physics as a mathematical thematizing of a nature whose essence is "invisible," and more.[4] The use of naturalistic explanations instead of, say, faith-based ones that appeal to the Bible or the Qur'an, tends to stand out more in the modern age than in the age of scholasticism. But this case is clearly the story of Europe. The importance of Africa in the formation of modernity is absent save in the model of the transforming center offered by Dussel, the darker side of the Renaissance articulated by Mignolo, or the reminders of that complex history of trade inherited and reorganized by the Afro-Arabic and African world articulated by Cedric Robinson.[5] As Robinson reminds us:

> By the eighth and ninth centuries, Islam had come to dominate Europe's access routes to the precious metals, manufactures, silks, and textiles produced in Africa and Asia. Henri Pirenne, the Belgian historian (*Mohammed and Charlemagne*), had characterized this historical moment by declaring (in somewhat poetic terms) that by the eighth century, the

---

[3] Enrique Dussel, *The Underside of Modernity: Apel, Ricœur, Rorty, Taylor, and the Philosophy of Liberation*, trans. Eduardo Mendieta (Atlantic Highlands, NJ: Humanities International Press, 1996).

[4] See e.g. his *Discourse on Method*, in René Descartes, *Descartes' Philosophical Writings*, trans. and ed. Norman Kemp Smith (London: Macmillan, 1952).

[5] Dussel, *Beyond Philosophy*; Walter Mignolo, *The Darker Side of the Renaissance: Literacy, Territoriality, and Colonization*, 2nd edn (Ann Arbor, MI: University of Michigan Press, 2003); and Cedric Robinson, *An Anthropology of Marxism* (Aldershot: Ashgate, 2001). For more on the (Afro-) Islamic influence, see Albert Hourani, *Islam in European Thought* (Cambridge: Cambridge University Press, 1991). Afro-Islamic and other forms of African thought will come to the fore in the course of various discussions in this book, but an excellent – perhaps the best – contemporary compendium on this thought is *A Companion to African Philosophy*, ed. Kwasi Wiredu (Malden, MA: Blackwell Publishers, 2004).

Mediterranean had been transformed into a "Muslim lake." . . . Pirenne had argued that the Dark Ages were characterized by Islamic control over the seats of civilization and the routes of long-distance trade. And until mechanisms were found in Europe to open its doors to peoples of the book, European thought, too, was confined.[6]

Another model of modernity, premised upon the development of ideas, examines early modernizing philosophical thought on the African continent and its extensions into Iberia or al-Andalus, which was the Moorish name of that peninsula. Recall that the Moors were African Muslims who invaded Iberia in 711 and had conquered much of the peninsula by 732. The famed north African Ibn Rushd (1126–1198), also known by his Latin name Averroës, is a case in point. Rushd's place in the Western medieval canon led to a downplaying of his being a Moor. Although read in the West primarily as an interpreter of Aristotle, with whom he also shares some biographical similarity since Aristotle, as physician to the Macedonian royal family which led the conquest of Athens and expanded the Macedonian empire, was part of the conquerors of Athens as the physician Rushd was part of the Afro-Arabic conquerors of Iberia, his thinking contributed much to two important sets of ideas associated with modern thought. The first is that reason must be a mediator of conflicting interpretations of scripture; the second that reason should serve as a guide to conduct. In both instances, there is fallibility, as contrasted with ancient Platonic thought, where reason places us in contact with the eternal, immutable forms. For Plato, reason is not fallible; it is our appetites and spiritedness that are. The first idea of the mediating role of reason in conflict over scripture entails an environment of multiple interpretations of sacred texts, which emphasizes human agency in the process of scriptural interpretation. "The Word," in other words, loses claim to its clarity and absoluteness of meaning. Ibn Rushd argued that religion and philosophy need not be in conflict, in this regard, since the province of each, echoing Jesus's famous rendering unto Caesar's what is his and unto God what belongs to God, is different – God in the case of the former, reason in the case of the latter. This separation of religion and reason, and Ibn Rushd's insistence that reason should govern conduct, are

---

[6] Robinson, *An Anthropology*, p. 35. And for Henri Pirenne, *Mohammed and Charlemagne*, trans. Bernard Miall (New York: Barnes and Noble, 1956). See also *Golden Age of the Moor*, ed. Ivan Van Sertima (New Brunswick, NJ: Transaction Publishers, 1992).

heavily associated, as Mourad Wahba points out, with the European Enlightenment.[7] The reception accorded Ibn Rushd in the Islamic world (he was briefly labeled a heretic) reveals that his ideas partially belonged to a different time than the one in which he lived.

A similar argument has been recently made by Teodros Kiros about the Ethiopian philosopher Zara Yacob (1599–1692).[8] Like Ibn Rushd, Yacob centered reason in the process of interpreting scripture. But more, his method involved a process of searching called, in Amharic, *hasasa* or *hatata*. Kiros writes, "Central to this project is the idea that reason itself is incomplete without God's guidance."[9] The result is one of subjecting faith to critical self-examination. Crucial here is that critical self-examination of faith is not a threat to God but a presumption of the compatibility of faith with God. Kiros compares Yacob with Descartes for this reason: whereas medieval thought appealed to faith above reason, both men ultimately saw reason and God as consistent. This is a feature of the rationalist dimension of Enlightenment thought.

We may at this point ask about the relationship of these examples of modernist thinking to the historical reality of Africa. It is very difficult to write about what Africa was like during medieval times and the period of European expansion in the fifteenth century. Although all historical evidence reveals the contrary, much of the history of Africa has been conditioned in the Western academy by themes of "primitivism." The scale of the trade routes in ancient Africa through to the age of exploration, the great libraries located in such places as Timbuktu and ancient Songhai,

---

[7] Mourad Wahba, "Philosophy in North Africa," in Wiredu, *A Companion to African Philosophy*, pp. 149–60. See Averroës [Ibn Rushd], *Decisive Treatise & Epistle Dedicatory*, trans. with introduction and notes by Charles E. Butterworth (Provo, UT: Brigham Young University Press, 2001), and for a short biography and introduction, see Liz Sonneborn, *Averroes (Ibn Rushd): Muslim Scholar, Philosopher, and Physician of Twelfth-century al-Andalus* (New York: Rosen Central, 2006). By comparison, the Tunision born Ibn Khaldūn (1332–1406) is hardly known in the Western academy although his ideas have had even more impact on the organization of knowledge in the modern world than perhaps any thinker from this period. See Aziz Al-Azmeh, *Ibn Khaldūn in Modern Scholarship: A Study in Orientalism* (London: Third World Centre for Research and Publishing, 1981). See also Hourani, *Islam in European Thought*.

[8] Teodros Kiros, *Zara Yacob* (Trenton, NJ: Red Sea Press, 2004).

[9] Teodros Kiros, "Zara Yacob and Traditional African Philosophy," in Wiredu, *A Companion to African Philosophy*, p. 184.

and the cities that greeted Portuguese soldiers and traders along the coasts of Africa all suggest a very different Africa than the one that dominated after three hundred years of kidnapping away its most important resource: its people. What is more, the fallacy of reading the history of encounters between Europeans and Africans as commencing during the age of exploration contributes much to the misrepresentation of the history of both continents. (Black) Africans have always inhabited Europe and Asia, and (white) Europeans have always found their way onto the African continent. Their numbers were always smaller than the local populations, but they were sufficiently present to warrant their identification in written texts and works of art.[10] This could only have occurred in an environment of trade with a significant economy to support it, and in communities with regulations and agreements with other communities to ensure the safe movement of goods from one region to another, which, by the age of Muslim empires, stretched from the Atlantic Ocean to the Pacific with Arabic as its *lingua franca*.[11]

Sages, theologians, and legal scholars in Africa, in other words, were going through a process of intellectual reflection with their correlates in what we now know as European and Asia, with Europe playing the role of catching up, until catastrophe hit the African continent and disrupted its economies, governing bodies, and, consequently, its institutions of higher learning.[12] Modernity in Africa, then, became more a story of

---

[10] Witness some of the mummified remains of Bronze Age Europeans, such as the Xinjiang mummies, which are on display in the Urumqi museum, China, as well as the references and drawings in ancient materials in Egypt and references to blacks in European artifacts and writings. For discussion see e.g. J. P. Mallory and Victor H. Mair, *The Tarim Mummies: Ancient China and the Mystery of the Earliest Peoples from the West* (London: Thames & Hudson, 2000); Frank M. Snowden, Jr., *Blacks in Antiquity: Ethiopians in the Greco-Roman Experience* (Cambridge, MA: Belknap Press, 1970); *The William Leo Hansberry African History Notebook*. Vol. II: *Africa and Africans as Seen by Classical Writers*, ed. Joseph E. Harris (Washington, DC: Howard University Press, 1981); *African Presence in Early Asia*, ed. Runoko Rashidi and Ivan Van Sertima (New Brunswick, NJ: Transaction Publishers, 1985); and Charles Finch, III, M. D., *Echoes of the Old Darkland, Themes from the African Eden* (Decatur, GA: Khenti, 1991), especially chs. 1 and 5.

[11] See e.g. Hourani, *Islam in European Thought*, p. 11.

[12] Classic statements on the impact of the slave trade are Eric Williams's *Capitalism and Slavery* (Chapel Hill, NC: University of North Carolina Press, 1994) and Walter Rodney, *How Europe Underdeveloped Africa*, rev. edn (Washington, DC: Howard University Press, 1981), but the scale of cultural damage is rarely assessed. See Cheikh Anta Diop,

embodying the underside of which Dussel wrote. The thought of African thinkers became increasingly a form that lacked matter as millions of Africans were involuntarily shipped and distributed across the globe. Suddenly Africans who spoke and wrote of reason began to disappear as Africans. The half Berber St. Augustine (354–430 CE), for instance, eclipsed in ancient and medieval Western thought perhaps only by Socrates, Plato, and Aristotle in importance, simply became a great "Roman" philosopher and theologian in modern and contemporary scholarship, and subsequent thinkers ranging from those in present-day Morocco to present-day Mali, Chad, Libya, Egypt, and Ethiopia fell under the category of "Semitic" (and at times "Hamitic") in ways that mistakenly rendered them as "white" or "Asiatic," but, in each formulation, definitely outside of Africa as the "Afro-Semite" disappeared as a form of human classification. The unfortunate reality is that "mixed black" populations seem to have no place in the study of antiquity and medieval times, where the rule seems to be that the conquered people become identified in terms of the conquering community, except in the case of the Moors in the Iberian Peninsula and Mediterranean islands such as Sicily and Corsica. The image on the Corsican flag continues to be a dark-skinned Moor. Recall that the Moors were indigenous Africans of northwest Africa who were conquered by Muslims from the east, absorbed into the Islamic empire, and in turn became zealous messengers of Islam in their conquest of the western through central Mediterranean. In antiquity, and even earlier times, however, the problem is complicated further by the imposition of a border between northeast Africa and the Middle East or Asia Minor. The region is treated today as if such a border existed in ancient times. Part of that rationalization has been the construction of "Semitic people" as a racial category, a designation that does not match archaeological evidence. The term was first used in German as *semitisch* by August Ludwig von Schlözer (1731–1809) in 1781 to refer to the language groups of the Middle East, which include Hebrew, Arabic, Aramaic, Assyrian, and Armenian, and it was based on biblical genealogies where such people were supposedly descendants

Precolonial Black Africa: A Comparative Study of the Political and Social Systems of Europe and Black Africa, from Antiquity to the Formation of Modern States, trans. Harold J. Salemson (Westport, CT: L. Hill, 1987). A look at the efficiency costs of the rise of European hegemony has also been posed in a fresh way by Charles Mills's *The Racial Contract* (Ithaca, NY: Cornell University Press, 1999), which will be discussed in ch. 4, below.

of Noah's son Shem (Genesis 10:21–30).[13] The word is mediated by its Greek derivative *sēm*, although it is peculiarly similar to the Latin *semi*, meaning "half," which becomes illuminating when we consider the flaws behind the construction. Charles Finch offers the following critique of the term:

> [T]he Semitic type only begins to emerge at the end of the proto-historical period, between 5,000–4,000 BCE, as a result of the gradual inbreeding of the autochthonous Blacks of Western Asia with immigrating Indo-European types. These Blacks belonged to the Natufian culture whose remains, covering most of Western Asia, date back to 10,000 BCE . . . From what we know about the early migrations of Africans out of the continent to populate the rest of the Old World, there is nothing strange in this aboriginal presence in Western Asia. Western Asia is, after all, geographically adjacent to Africa and therefore a logical conduit through which Africans could migrate. The first cultures of Western Asia, especially those in the Fertile Crescent, arose out of the aboriginal black Natufians.[14]

Finch adds that

> The noted linguist, Joseph Greenberg, has . . . discarded as imprecise and illogical such familiar linguistic categories as "Semitic" and "Hamitic" in favor of a more inclusive category, which he termed "Afro-Asiatic." In Greenberg's opinion, this category was justified by the demonstrable affinities between the Semitic Hebrew, Arabic, Phoenician, Aramaic, and Amharic on the one hand and the northeast African group (formerly "Hamitic"), comprising Egyptian, Cushitic, Chadic, and Hausa on the other. According to Greenberg, the long-dead mother tongue of all these languages would have originated in the highlands of Ethiopia. What this means, in effect, is that the so-called Semitic languages are but branches of an original northeast African parent, of which Egyptian and Cushitic are "charter" members.[15]

---

[13] The source of this genealogy is Eichhorn's *Repertorium*, vol. VIII (published in Leipzig, 1781), p. 161. It is cited on p. 706 of vol. XIII of *The Catholic Encyclopedia: An International Work of Reference on the Constitution, Doctrine, Discipline, and History of the Catholic Church*, ed. Charles C. Herbermann, Edward A. Pace, Thomas J. Shahan and John J. Wynne (New York: The Encyclopedia Press and Robert Appleton Company, 1912).

[14] Finch, *Echoes of the Old Darkland*, p. 131.

[15] *Ibid.*, p. 134. See also J. H. Greenburg, "African Languages," in *Peoples and Cultures of Africa*, ed. E. P. Skinner (Garden City, NJ: Natural History Press, 1973), pp. 70–80.

Finch brings the argument to its conclusion: "The first Semites in history were in every way 'mulattos'; all that we have said up to now points ineluctably to this conclusion."[16] For our purposes, what is important is that this argument challenges the tendency to examine Africans in purist terms and in those where, when mixture is admitted, there is a tendency to write agency out of the role of Afro populations in the processes of cultural and, if the researcher prefers, racial amalgamations.

The clearly modern moment of Africana philosophy as we understand it today begins, however, with the conquest of the Americas and with the Atlantic slave trade. The European mapping of the coasts of Africa and Columbus's expedition to the Caribbean inaugurated the discourse on Africa. Although the medieval (white Germanic) Iberians referred to Africa as "the place of the Moors" or "the place of dark-skinned people," those ascriptions were made without a continental consciousness and the notion of an African diaspora. The rationalization of taking slaves from Africa, advanced and later rejected by Bartolomé de las Casas (1484–1566), the first ordained priest to visit the New World, was based on a logic that made the salvation of the indigenous peoples of the Americas more important than the servitude imposed on the Africans. Although following, with Bible in hand, Hernando Cortez (1460–1521) and other conquistadors, who established themselves by way of the sword, he saw that the baptizing of indigenous peoples may have offered their souls salvation but not their flesh, as the mounting heaps of bodies literally became confused with mountains as landmarks for docking ships. Las Casas was rightly outraged by the carnage he was witnessing in the newly conquered regions of the Caribbean and Central America. He appealed first to King Ferdinand (1452–1516), who had, as we have seen, with Queen Isabella (1451–1504), expelled the Jews and the Moors from Spain and had financed Columbus's voyages, and then Charles I (1500–1558) and Pope Paul III (1468–1549) to take action against the looming genocide.[17]

---

[16] Finch, *Echoes of the Old Darkland*, p. 135.

[17] Bartolomé de las Casas, *An account of the first voyages and discoveries made by the Spaniards in America. Containing the most exact relation hitherto publish'd, of their unparallel'd cruelties on the Indians, in the destruction of above forty millions of people. With the propositions offer'd to the King of Spain, to prevent the further ruin of the West Indies. By Don Bartholomew de las Casas, Bishop of Chiapas, who was an eyewitness of their cruelties. Illustrated with cuts. To which is added, The art of travelling, shewing how a man may dispose his travels to the best advantage* (London: J. Darby for D. Brown at the Black Swan and Bible without Temple-Bar, J. Harris at the Harrow in Little Britain, and Andr. Bell at the Cross-keys and Bible in Cornhil, 1699).

The Church's power stood, however, with the Crown on an edifice of great wealth that would be jeopardized by a decree abolishing forced servitude in the newly conquered territories. So it was decided by the Spanish authorities in 1517, with the influence of Las Casas's *Historia de las Indias* (1516), that forced labor would be drawn primarily from Africa, where there were tropical peoples who held no claim to the New World and whose darkness of skin, the growing logic suggested, reflected an absence, if not simply a darkness, of soul.[18] Such a position gained popularity, in spite of black participation, such as that of the navigator Pedro Alonso Niño (1468–1505), at the beginning of Spanish and Portuguese explorations and colonial efforts.

So began the Atlantic slave trade. Las Casas eventually renounced all slavery and devoted the rest of his life to its abolition, but his efforts were too late.[19] The thought and political efforts of the Spanish court historian Juan Ginés de Sepúlveda (1494–1573) prevailed.[20] He used Aristotelian notions of "natural slaves" and "natural masters" to support continued expansion through conquest and enslavement. The result was an epoch in which millions of people were shipped across the Atlantic Ocean to provide the labor that built the wealth of modern and contemporary European and North American countries. Often forgotten are the millions who died during the trip that became infamously known as the Middle Passage. The brutality of an industry premised upon naked greed was such that the ships packed human beings in layers on structures that afforded little movement for weeks at a time. The result was an unsanitary environment of sweat, urine, feces, and blood that dripped from the upper layers to the bottom amid the constant presence of scurrying rats, in turn infested by ticks and lice. Disease was rampant; and since only the minimum rations were afforded the enslaved, so was starvation. When the kidnapped were brought to the surface to stretch their legs, many jumped overboard; and there were occasions of revolt, some of which, as in the case of the *Amistad*,

---

[18] *Ibid.* See also Las Casas, *Short Account of the Destruction of the Indies*, introd. Anthony Pagden and trans. Nigel Griffin (New York: Penguin Classics, 1999) and Tzvetan Todorov, *The Conquest of America: The Question of the Other*, trans. Richard Howard (Norman, OK: University of Oklahoma Press, 1999).

[19] See Paul S. Vickery, *Bartolomé de Las Casas: Great Prophet of the Americas* (New York: The Newman Press, 2006).

[20] See Lewis Hanke, *All Mankind Is One: A Study of the Disputation Between Bartolomé De Las Casas and Juan Gines De Sepulveda in 1550 on the Intellectual and Religious Capacity* (Chicago, IL: Northern Illinois University Press, 1974).

were successful.[21] Retaliation was often brutal. Some reports included, as C. L. R. James recounted, slaves being butchered and their parts force-fed to the surviving "cargo."[22]

Although there were white slaves in the earlier period of the modern Atlantic trade, especially those who were convicted of crimes in Europe, enslaved as bounty by pirates, or who were indentured, the trade was mostly reserved for indigenous peoples and Africans in the entire New World by the eighteenth century.[23] The cultural reality that emerged in the countries whose coastlines faced the Atlantic became one of African enslavement and an increased logic of inferiority.

Accompanying such atrocities were great developments in European thought. The fifteenth century witnessed the toppling of the geocentric in favor of the heliocentric view of the solar system by Nicolaus Copernicus (1473–1543), which set much of the stage for the conceptual dimension of Columbus's achievement. (It should be borne in mind that the ancient Chinese, Egyptians, and Aztecs, just to name a few, were aware of the earth's spherical shape.) The sixteenth into seventeenth centuries had the spectacular achievements in physics of Galileo Galilei (1564–1642), René Descartes in physics, mathematics, and philosophy, and Francis Bacon in natural scientific methodology (1561–1626); and the seventeenth and eighteenth centuries boast achievements in mathematics (such as the differential calculus) and mechanistic physics by Gottfried Leibniz (1646–1716) and Isaac Newton (1643–1727), Adam Smith in economics (1723–1790), and in philosophy, David Hume (1711–1776), last of the "great triumvirate of British Empiricists" (which includes John Locke and Bishop Berkeley),

---

[21] See e.g. Walter Dean Myers, *Amistad: A Long Road to Freedom* (New York: Puffin, 2001), and for resistance and revolts on land, see e.g. Herbert Aptheker, *American Negro Slave Revolts* (New York: International Publishers, 1983) and Thomas Wentworth Higginson and James M. McPherson, *Black Rebellion: Five Slave Revolts* (New York: Da Capo, 1998).

[22] C. L. R. James, *The Black Jacobins: Toussaint L'Ouverture and the San Domingo Revolution*, 2nd edn (New York: Vintage, 1989), ch. 1, "The Property."

[23] See e.g. Claudia Durst Johnson, *Daily Life in Colonial New England* (Westport, CT: Greenwood Press, 2002) and Robert Davis, *Christian Slaves, Muslim Masters: White Slavery in the Mediterranean, the Barbary Coast and Italy, 1500–1800* (New York: Palgrave Macmillan, 2003). The British and Spanish brought Asian slaves – from China, India, and the Philippines – to the New World in the middle of the nineteenth century. See C. N. Le, "The First Asian Americans," *Asian-Nation: The Landscape of Asian America* (11 February, 2007): www.asian-nation.org/first.shtml.

Jean-Jacques Rousseau (1712–1778), and Immanuel Kant (1724–1804). In the North American colonies these developments were explored and advanced in their own right most notably by Benjamin Franklin (1706–1790), Thomas Jefferson (1743–1786), and Benjamin Banneker (1731–1806). Along with these developments in the sciences (and we could add the arts by including the great European novelists, poets, and composers of this period), a concerted effort to make similar achievements in the study of human beings also emerged. Hume, as is well known, had set out to offer a study of human nature on a par with the achievement of Newton in physics. And in the texts of many of these writers the contrasting terms in their study of the human being became the European white versus the African black.[24]

The inclusion of Banneker on this list reveals a reality that is emphasized in Africana intellectual history. That Banneker was a freed black whose contributions in the sciences – in mathematics, astronomy, meteorology, and architecture – rivaled those of Franklin and certainly surpassed Jefferson makes it appropriate to include him on the list of eighteenth-century Enlightenment thinkers. It reveals, as well, an aspect of Africana intellectual history that is an ongoing theme in the work of many of the philosophers we will examine. Africana thought is often accused of being of particular instead of universal significance. In response, as we will see, many Africana philosophers argue that such a conclusion would be in error because of the ironic inclusiveness of Africana thought. A legacy of modern colonialism and racism is that to articulate the set of problems and concerns of Africana thought one must engage the tradition that accompanied its emergence in the modern world. Africana thought always presupposes other kinds of thought, whereas European thought often denies the existence of those beyond its own. Africana thought is not against European thought but emerges along with it, although thinking in Africa preceded such activity in Europe by the mere fact that human beings have lived in Africa for many millennia more than they have lived on any other continent. But, more germane to the modern context, even Africana thinkers who avow a rejection of European thought often do so through specifying the thought

---

[24] This information can be found in any standard history of modern science, but see e.g. Philipp Frank, *Modern Science and its Philosophy* (New York: Collier Books, 1961). See also Fatimah Jackson, "Anthropological Measurement: The Mismeasure of African Americans," *Annals of the American Academy of Political and Social Science* 568 (2000): 154–71.

they reject, which means, in effect, offering knowledge of that tradition. This is, as we will see, a source of great debate in the postmodern and poststructural groups, who argue against Eurocentrism – the centering of European thought – but seem to do so by only evoking European thinkers.

For our purposes what is significant about the question of modernism is that it brought the human self as an object of study to center stage and along with it the problem of the human being that supports that self. The question that followed was that of the adequacy and scope of applying to the study of the human beings the methods developed for the study of natural phenomena. Although we have here looked briefly at two stories – one of those suffering under the yoke of European expansion and the other of those benefiting from the consciousness raised by such expansion – the consequence of philosophical anthropology is exemplified by both in the radically different perspectives raised by the Fanonian existential question, "In reality, who [and what] am I?"[25]

Africana philosophers, as we will see, are some of those who see the liberating aspects of thought among those who live this question from the underside of the modern world.

[25] Frantz Fanon, *The Wretched of the Earth*, trans. Constance Farrington (New York: Grove Press, 1963), p. 250. For discussion, see also Lewis R. Gordon, *Existentia Africana: Understanding Africana Existential Thought* (New York: Routledge, 2000), pp. 4–5.

2 Classic eighteenth- and nineteenth-century foundations

The question of slavery has been a constant concern of modern European thought. John Locke found it necessary to offer rationalizations for it in his *Second Treatise on Government*, and constant references to themselves as "slaves" struggling for their freedom occur even in the arguments used by the Founding Fathers of the American Revolution.[1] In philosophies of the modern era, then, we find the contradictory situation of arguments being offered against slavery by those who also depended on and offered arguments for the enslavement of others. This required great acts of self-deception and misrepresentation of history. Locke, for instance, argued that the procurement of slaves was permissible from a just war of self-defense against someone or some group who had violated a law of nature (for example, waging war against a fellow human being). In effect, his enslavement and the taking of his property (but not that of his wife and heirs) are the continuation of that war, in which the master is here read as protecting himself from the license of the enslaved. But since it is war, the enslaved does in fact have a right to struggle for his or her freedom since it is something that can be taken but not given away. Yet, under the supervision of the Earl of Shaftesbury (1632–1704), Locke wrote *The Fundamental Constitution of Carolina* in 1670, which permitted racialized slavery. How could this be justified when many of the enslaved of the Carolinas were kidnapped from communities

---

[1] John Locke, *Second Treatise on Government*, ed. C. B. Macpherson (Bloomington, IN: Hackett, 1980). For some recent Africana philosophical discussion of Locke's thought, see Bernard Boxill, "Radical Implications of Locke's Moral Theory: The Views of Frederick Douglass," in *Subjugation and Bondage: Critical Essays on Slavery and Social Philosophy*, ed. Tommy L. Lott (Lanham, MD: Rowman & Littlefield, 1998), pp. 29–48 and "A Lockean Argument for Black Reparations," *The Journal of Ethics* 7, no. 1 (2003): 63–91. On the US Founding Fathers conception of themselves as "slaves" to England, see Joe Feagin, *Racist America: Roots, Current Realities, and Future Reparations* (New York: Routledge, 2001).

in Africa that were not at war with any European nation – and certainly not the colony of Carolina?[2] Relatedly, how could war be used here when the circumstance was not a conflict between states but between traders and individuals who were not soldiers in conflict with them? As Jean-Jacques Rousseau (1712–1778) famously argued in *The Social Contract*, book I, chapter 4:

> Men are not naturally enemies, if only because when living in their original independence, they do not have sufficiently stable relationships among themselves to constitute either the state of peace or the state of war. It is the relationship between things, not between men, that constitutes war; and as the state of war cannot arise from simple, personal relations, but only from proprietary relations, private war between one man and another can exist neither in the state of nature, where there is no stable property, nor in the social state, where everything is under the authority of the laws . . . War is not, therefore, a relation between man and man, but between State and State, in which private individuals are enemies only by accident, not as men, nor even as citizens, but as soldiers; not as members of the fatherland but as its defenders. Finally, each State can have only other States, and not men, as enemies, since no true relationship can be established between things of different natures.[3]

Rousseau argued that once a soldier had surrendered, he or she was no longer a representative of a state in conflict with another state, and thus war could not stand as a legitimate ground for the enslavement of former soldiers. All that remained was an appeal to the right of conquest, which simply affirmed the right of the enslaved to seek sufficient force against servitude. If the war metaphor is pushed to its extreme as a right to massacre, the same counter argument of using might against the conqueror applies. As Rousseau concludes, "Thus, from whatever point of view things

---

[2] Another consideration is that Locke's philosophy makes human labor an important ingredient in the formation of property. In order for the things produced by slaves not to become their property or for even the bodies of the enslaved not to be their own requires either (1) making the enslaved African culpable for some deed that warrants the alienation of his or her liberty or (2) denying that the African is a human being. The latter would entail the African's inability to produce property or even to suffer alienation.

[3] Jean-Jacques Rousseau, *The Collected Writings of Rousseau*. Vol. X, *Social Contract, Discourse on the Virtue Most Necessary for a Hero, Political Fragments*, and *Geneva Manuscript*, ed. Roger D. Masters and Christopher Kelley (Hanover, NH: University Press of New England, 1994), pp. 135–6.

are considered, the right of slavery is null, not merely because it is illegitimate, but because it is absurd and signifies nothing. Those words *slavery*
and *right* are contradictory; they are mutually exclusive."[4]

Returning to Locke on Carolina and the subsequent history of the
American colonies, how, then, could the claim of slavery be anything but
metaphor when applied to the landed gentry and propertied classes of the
American colonies fighting against taxation from England? In effect, their
rationalization offered a counter argument that Rousseau did not anticipate
since his argument presumed the humanity of the enslaved. In the nineteenth century, this proviso became obvious in the *Dred Scott* v. *Sanford* (1857)
case where the United States Supreme Court ruled that blacks, whether
enslaved or free, could not be citizens of the United States and lacked a
standing before the court. Further, the court argued that Scott was property,
and that to honor his freedom would be to deny his master of his property.
His master, in other words, had standing before the law. In effect the ruling simply declared that blacks were not fully human beings. It offered a
way for white Americans to be consistently anti-slavery while favoring the
enslavement of blacks. The former is only wrong against human beings.[5]

Africana philosophy examines what emerges from the question "In reality
who and what am I?" when posed by those who were actually enslaved and
by those who lived the dubious status of a questioned humanity.

Anton Wilhelm Amo

The first recorded Africana thinker to take up those questions in the modern
world is Anton Wilhem Amo (1703–*c.* 1759), who was born in Awukena in the
coastal region of Axim in Ghana. He was brought as a slave to Amsterdam
by the Dutch East India Company at the age of four and was given as a
blackamoor gift to Duke Anton Ulrich von Braunschweig-Wofenbüttel (1633–
1714), who in turn gave Amo to his son, August Wilhelm (1662–1731), who
in 1708 christened him Anton Wilhelm.[6]

---

[4] *Ibid.*, p. 137.

[5] For more on the *Dred Scott* case, see Don E. Fehrenbacher, *The Dred Scott Case: Its Significance
in American Law and Politics*, new edn (New York: Oxford University Press, 2001).

[6] The discussion of Amo that follows is informed by the following works: *Anton Wilhelm Amo
Antonius Gvilielmus Amo Afer of Axim in Ghana: Translation of His Works* (Halle: Martin Luther
University, Halle-Wittenberg, 1968); *Readings in African Philosophy: An Akan Collection*, ed.

The literature on Amo is not clear about how he was formally freed from servitude by the duke, but it is certain that he was raised as a member of the duke's family and was afforded all the educational benefits thereof. Between 1717 and 1721, he studied at the Wolfenbüttel Ritter-Akademie, then from 1721 to 1727 at the University of Helmstedt, and then at the University of Halle, where he studied Latin, Greek, Hebrew, French, German, and Dutch before completing his studies with a degree in law in 1729 with a thesis entitled *Dissertatio inauguralis De Jure Maurorum in Europa* ("Inaugural Dissertation on the Laws of Moors [Blacks] in Europe," recently translated as "The Rights of Moors in Europe"). He then continued his studies at the University of Wittenberg, where he focused on philosophy, history, and medicine, and earned his doctorate of philosophy in 1734 with his dissertation published under the title *De humanae mentis apatheia* (available in English translation as *Of the Apatheia of the Human Mind, namely, the Absence of Sensation and the Faculty of Sense in the Human Mind and their Presence in our Organic and Living Body*).

Amo subsequently taught philosophy at Halle under his preferred name of Antonius Gvilielmus Amo Afer, where he became professor in 1736, and, in 1738, saw his second major work come to print, *Tractatus de arte sobrie et accurate philosophandi* ("Treatise on the Art of Philosophizing Soberly and Accurately"). In 1740 he moved to the University of Jena, but his tenure there was short lived as the political and intellectual climate changed in Europe. Catherine Reinhardt related the culmination of these changes in France, which was once more progressive than its northern neighbors:

> France's concerns with the racial dimension of the black and free colored population living on French soil gradually increased. Since the . . . laws were never properly enforced and a steady stream of black slaves continued to enter the country, King Louis XVI saw it necessary to enforce a new law in 1777 called *Police des Noirs*. As opposed to the previous two laws that applied to black slaves only, the *Police des Noirs* focused on all nonwhites. Entry into France was prohibited to all blacks and people of color regardless of their status as slaves or as freedmen . . . The number of blacks on French

Safro Kwame (Lanham, MD: University Press of America, 1995); William Abraham, "Anton Wilhelm Amo," in *A Companion to African Philosophy*, ed. Kwasi Wiredu (Malden, MA: Blackwell, 2003), pp. 191–9; and Kwasi Wiredu, "Amo's Critique of Descartes' Philosophy of Mind," in *A Companion to African Philosophy*, pp. 200–6.

soil had reached the limit of French acceptability and the authorities believed it necessary to stop their influx . . . The stringent *Police des Noirs* was to be a safeguard for the French population assuring – in the words of a government official – the "total extinction" of the "black species" in France.[7]

To make matters worse Amo's benefactors and protectors in the duke's family and at the University of Halle were all dead by then, after which he was subject to much racial insult, which included a play lampooning him in Halle. And the stage was being set for even the most influential philosophers of that century to be purveyors of a philosophical anthropology premised upon the inferiority of people from the tropics and the notion of natural superiority of white peoples of the north, in spite of an absence of empirical data beyond travel logs and adventure stories by sailors. It was contradictory for an empiricist such as David Hume to advance such claims as factual, without empirical evidence. Think as well of Kant, who treated the racial inferiority of blacks as a necessary consequence of adaptation to heat. The ugly side of the Enlightenment was, in other words, already becoming suffocating and dangerous, so Amo returned to Axim in 1747, where he found his birth siblings and was welcomed as a traditional doctor. He subsequently lived in the Dutch fort of San Sebastian, perhaps for his safety, where he eventually died.

Amo's biography already reveals several themes of Africana philosophy. The first is that when he had the opportunity to bring his thought to print, he wrote on the injustice of the slave trade and the treatment of blacks in Europe. He posed, in effect, the question of the inclusion of blacks in European society, a question that continued, as we shall see, in W. E. B. Du Bois's (1868–1963) formulation of twoness with regard to being both black and American.[8] On the other hand a former black slave Jacobus

---

[7] Catherine A. Reinhardt, *Claims to Memory: Beyond Slavery and Emancipation in the French Caribbean* (New York: Berghahn Books, 2006), pp. 34–5. She offers a larger account of this changed climate on pp. 23–58.

[8] The classic formulations of double consciousness, which will be discussed later, can be found in W. E. B. Du Bois, *The Conservation of the Races* (Washington, DC: The American Negro Academy, 1898); *The Souls of Black Folk* (Chicago: A. C. McClurg & Co., 1903); *Dusk of Dawn: An Essay Toward an Autobiography of a Race Concept* (New York: Harcourt, Brace & Co., 1940); and *John Brown* (Philadelphia: G. W. Jacobs & Co., 1909).

Capitein (1717–1747), who mastered several European languages and received theological training at the University of Leiden in 1742,[9] devoted his energy to defending slavery, on the grounds of its supposedly offering civilization and Christian salvation for Africans. There is, as well, in Amo's biography the complex question of naming. His life is one of being named and choosing his name. Notice, for instance, that he added the name Afer when he began teaching at Halle. No doubt Amo wanted to emphasize the significance of his Africanness, which by that point also meant his blackness, that he was an African professor teaching in a German university in the eighteenth century. An ongoing debate in Africana philosophy involves the acceptance or rejection of African and black designations. Amo may have found it important to assert his African identity in the effort to draw attention to the significance of his achievements. Third, there is his focus in his doctoral dissertation on a problem of human science – namely, the relationship of mind to body. There, he takes on Cartesian dualism. Descartes argued that the mind was distinct from the body because the latter was sensory, changing, and contingent but the former was linked to cogitation or thinking, which revealed essential or necessary invisible features of reality that were not sensible but comprehensible. Further, parts of the body could be destroyed while thinking continued intact. In thinking, we are linked to God, who thinks reality in its clarity and distinctness. Amo's response was not to reject the mind as metaphysical but to argue that the aspects of mind that feel and perceive made sense as a function of the body. The mind, in other words, must be living, and it could be so only by virtue of the body.

Amo's critique of Descartes suggests that he may have been drawing upon an Akanian understanding of the subject from his early years in what is today Ghana. Since he spoke Akan, the metaphysics of the language, so to speak, worked its way into his investigations of philosophy written in Latin. Kwasi Wiredu recently offered a discussion of Descartes that illustrates this point. The Akan would have a problem with the expression, "I think, therefore I am." He or she would be compelled to ask, "You are what? Where?" Wiredu explains:

[9] For discussion of Capitein's life and thought, see David Nii Anum Kpobi, *Saga of a Slave: Jacobus Capitein of Holland and Elmina* (Legon, Ghana: Cootek, 2001) and K. K. Prah, *Jacobus Eliza Johannes Capitein, 1717–1747: A Critical Study of an Eighteenth Century African* (Trenton, NJ: Africa World Press, 1992).

"Wo ho" is the Akan rendition of "exist". Without the "ho", which means "there", in other words, "some place", all meaning is lost. "Wo", standing alone, does not in any way correspond to the existential sense of the verb "to be", which has no place in Akan syntax or semantics. [Return], now, to "I think, therefore I am", and consider the existential component of that attempted message as it comes across in Akan. In that medium the information communicated can only be that I am there, at some place; which means that spatial location is essential to the idea of my existence. It is scarcely necessary to point out that this is diametrically opposed to Descartes' construal of the particular cogitation under scrutiny. As far as he is concerned, the alleged fact that one can doubt all spatial existences and yet at the same time be absolutely certain of one's existence under the dispensation of the *Cogito* implied that the "I", the ego, exists as a spiritual, non-spatial, immaterial entity. The incongruity of this sequence of thought, quite apart from any *non sequiturs*, must leap to the Akan eye. There is, of course, nothing sacrosanct about the linguistic categories of Akan thought. But, given the *prima facie* incoherence of the Cartesian suggestion within the Akan conceptual framework, an Akan thinker who scrutinizes the matter in his or her own language must feel the need for infinitely more proof of intelligibility than if s/he contemplated it in English or some cognate language.[10]

The differentiating cognate language here is Latin, and the connections suggest that Amo's location in Africana philosophy should not be limited to the fact of his origins; Africana philosophy was a living reality in his thought.

There is, as well, a pressing concern with philosophical methodology and metaphilosophy or a theory or philosophy of philosophy. The Africana philosopher in the Western world faces incredulity from a community of scholars many of whose most untalented members, with limited reasoning power are afforded more legitimacy than the most astute thinker who chooses to recognize the humanity of black subjects. It is a reality that continues in much of what is called today "professional philosophy."[11] The

---

[10] Kwasi Wiredu, *Cultural Universals and Particulars: An African Perspective* (Bloomington, IN: Indiana University Press, 1996), p. 141. Cf. also Wiredu, "Amo's Critique of Descartes' Philosophy of Mind," especially p. 203.

[11] See e.g. John Ayotunde Isola Bewaji, *Beauty and Culture: Perspectives in Black Aesthetics* (Ibadan, Nigeria: Spectrum Books, 2003), section 3.5, "The Professionalization of Philosophy: A Disadvantage and Disservice to Humanity," pp. 33–4.

Africana philosopher thus faces, as Frantz Fanon (1925–1961) later reflected, the neurotic situation of having to have faith in reason in a world in which, as he put it, "when I was present, it was not; when it was there, I was no longer."[12] The response of giving up reason is, however, unreasonable, especially for a philosopher. Again, in Fanon's words, "I would personally say that for a man whose only weapon is reason there is nothing more neurotic than contact with unreason," so the task becomes one of offering a conception of reason that will reveal the defects of the nay-sayers.[13] All this brings us to perhaps the most tragic meditation of Africana philosophy, at least in that dimension of it which reflects on the modern condition. Its concerns with the human subject and reason are connected to the guiding commitment and faith in the value of freedom. Amo's life could be read as a dialectical path in which his intellectual achievements made more acute the nature of his bondage and his realization of having to lay foundations for a promised land into which he and many others, like the proverbial Moses, never entered.

Quobna Ottobah Cugoano

The next, most provocative treatment of these questions explored by Amo is by Quobna Ottobah Cugoano (c. 1757–c. 1803). Born in the city of Ajumako, on the coast of Fantyn in Ghana, where he spent his childhood as a member of the house of the Fanti king Ambro Accasa, ruler of Ajumako and Assinie, Cugoano was kidnapped into slavery at about the age of thirteen while playing in the woods near his home. After suffering the horrors of the Middle Passage he was brought to Grenada, where he labored under the cruel plantation system. He was eventually purchased in 1772 by Alexander Campbell, who brought him to England where, as a result of a series of judicial decisions that effectively led to the outlawing of slavery in England, he became a Christian and adopted the name John Stewart and gained his freedom. He devoted his time to learning how to read and write, and his employment was as a servant for the famed painters Richard Cosway

---

[12] Frantz Fanon, *Black Skin, White Masks*, trans. Charles Lamm Markmann (New York: Grove Press, 1967), pp. 119–20.
[13] *Ibid.*, p. 118.

(1742–1821) and Maria Cosway (1760–1838). He became active in London's abolitionist community and wrote and published *Thoughts and Sentiments on the Evil and Wicked Traffic of Slavery and Commerce of the Human Species* (1787), a copy of which was sent to King George III of England (1738–1820) in an unsuccessful effort to enlist the royal family in the movement to abolish the Atlantic slave trade.[14] Not much is known about the rest of Cugoano's life after that, save the approximate date of his death.

Unlike Amo, Cugoano enjoyed no formal education. His book, however, reflects in its structure a feature of many subsequent texts in Africana thought. It belongs to no single genre but to a variety. It is autobiographical, exegetical, and philosophical. As we will see, some Africana philosophers, in their reflections on philosophical writing, argue that such an approach makes sense where the subject matter of bondage and racism demands a variety of techniques by which to get at the human subject that grounds the reflections. Others simply take the texts as autobiographical narratives with some philosophical insights. What is crucial for our purposes is that Cugoano took the time to develop full-fledged theories to support the arguments he made against slavery, and in doing so he offered some original contributions to philosophy.

To achieve his task, Cugoano first had to address the arguments advanced for slavery. Many of them appealed to an anthropological schema in which blacks were located at the level of beasts. Since he and the 20,000 other blacks living in England at the time exemplified the contradiction of such a thesis, it was clear that the claims of the opposition required making human beings into beasts instead of encountering them as such. Thus, Cugoano raises the question, "What is the character of men and women who would make their fellow human beings into beasts?" They would have to be both inhumane and inhuman. In effect their actions created a world in which a human way of living was absent. They were thus, in his words, "wicked." This argument, which in effect concludes that the racist and slave master commit an act against humanity, is one that recurs in Africana thought. It

---

[14] The text remains in print but under the title *Thoughts and Sentiments on the Evil of Slavery*, with an introduction by Vincent Carretta (London: Penguin Classics, 1999). The succeeding discussion has benefited from Paget Henry's "Between Hume and Cugoano: Race, Ethnicity and Philosophical Entrapment," *The Journal of Speculative Philosophy* 18, no. 2 (2004): 129–48.

is in Fanon's 1952 text, *Black Skin, White Masks*, when he argues that racism and colonialism attack the same subject: the human being.[15]

Cugoano then takes on David Hume, who not only claimed that there were no arts and sciences in Africa, but also that Africans did not object to slavery. Cugoano first rejects the factual basis of Hume's claim, which, as we have already seen, is ironic since Hume's main claim to fame in philosophy is as an empiricist. Recall that Cugoano lived in the home of the Fanti ruler Ambro Accasa. This experience offered him an understanding not only of day-to-day west African cultures of the eighteenth century but also of their political institutions. His report includes pointing out that they were communities with free subjects and that their military service was voluntary, a function of duty and respect, unlike the case of the mercenary armies of Europe. In short he presented direct experience (much of which has been subsequently verified by ethnographers) over Hume's hearsay. He then takes on the use of Hume's remarks to justify slavery. In effect, the argument relied on a suppressed premise that slavery is wrong. Thus, it does not make sense to use slavery to punish people for not rejecting slavery. How can people be improved morally by imposing an immoral practice on them?

Cugoano then addresses the dominating political theories of eighteenth-century England. By this time the rise of modern capitalism was in full swing in Europe and the Americas, and the political philosophies that offered conceptions of human beings premised upon a selfish human nature that required modern liberal states were dominant. These models relied on formulations of states of nature in which life was either "nasty, brutish, and short," as claimed by Thomas Hobbes in *Leviathan* (1660), or those requiring mediators in conflicts over property, as argued by John Locke in *The Second Treatise of Civil Government* (1690). Cugoano argued that life without the institutions that in the end support slavery was free and fulfilling and one in which natural rights were enjoyed. In short he argued that human beings could flourish naturally and that their dehumanization was caused by pernicious institutions of civil society and governing bodies that encouraged enmity among them.

---

[15] "All forms of exploitation resemble one another. They all seek the source of their necessity in some edict of a Biblical nature. All forms of exploitation are identical because all of them are applied against the same 'object': man" (Fanon, *Black Skin, White Masks*, p. 88).

The question is then raised, "Why is the 'natural' good?" Is not Cugoano here committing a fallacy, pointed out by Hume in *A Treatise of Human Nature* (1739–40), of ascribing an "ought" to an "is?"[16]

A central feature of Cugoano's discussion is that he is working within a framework in which, much like Descartes, there is a spiritual grounding of natural phenomena. Recall that for Descartes, mathematics, which exemplifies the essence of physical reality, for instance, is also God's thought. Cugoano makes a similar claim, but he makes explicit its theodicean dimension. The word "theodicy" is a conjunction of the ancient Greek words *theo* (god) and *dikê* (justice). It emerged through the problem of addressing the compatibility of a good, omnipotent, and omniscient god with the existence of evil and injustice. If God is all powerful, all knowing, and all good, why does God not do something about evil and rectify injustice? Traditional responses are of two kinds.[17] The first points to human limits in the face of God, as exemplified by the clichés "It is God's will" or "God only knows." In short, God can see what is ultimately good; human beings cannot; so evil and injustice only appear as such. The second is that God has granted humanity freedom, which means He must not interfere with human choices. Evil and injustice are functions of human agency. In other words, God remains good. Human beings, however, are a mixed affair. Whether these two arguments exonerate God or not has been a matter of debate for going on two millennia. Yet, as we will see, the problem of theodicy is of great significance in Africana philosophy.

Philosophy was not the only discipline involved in debates over slavery. Theologians also brought their interpretation of scripture to bear on the subject. That slavery was not consistently denounced in the Bible provided support for the slave masters, and many also appealed to the story of Ham, who was cursed for looking at his naked drunken father Noah, and claimed that Africans were his descendants. Others also advanced the bondservant

---

[16] David Hume, *A Treatise of Human Nature*, ed. (with introduction) Ernest C. Mossner (London: Penguin Classics, 1968), book III, part I, sec. 1, pp. 507–21, but especially p. 520. See also Hume's *An Enquiry Concerning the Principles of Morals*, new edn, ed. J. B. Schneewind (Indianapolis, IN: Hackett, 1983), which offers a more concise formulation.

[17] See St. Augustine, *The City of God*, trans. Marcus Doas, with an introduction by Thomas Merton (New York: Modern Library, 1950) and for an overview of the legacy of these arguments in Western theodicean thought see John Hicks, *Evil and the God of Love*, rev. edn (New York: Harper & Row, 1978).

argument based on Exodus 21:2–6, Exodus 22:1, 3, Deuteronomy 15:12–18, and Leviticus 25:44–6. These passages permitted the use of indentured servants (those who labor without pay in order to pay off debts), the decision to remain a slave after completion of initial servitude, the paying off of debt for a crime, and the enslavement of pagans. We should bear in mind that these are edicts of a people who themselves were, at least as told in the Hebrew Bible, slaves for more than five hundred years and did not want to return to their previous condition. Thus, it is no accident that we find a passage such as the following: "He who kidnaps a man, whether he sells him or he is found in his possession, shall surely be put to death" (Exodus 21:16), which is hardly compatible with modern slavery, the kind against which Cugoano was arguing. Consider, as well, Deuteronomy 23:15–16, which states: "You shall not hand over to his master a slave who has escaped from his master to you. He shall live with you in your midst, in the place which he shall choose in one of your towns where it pleases him; you shall not mistreat him." This passage suggests that the ancient Hebrews also saw their communities, in effect, as sanctuaries for runaway slaves while at the same time they were attempting to develop laws in which even those who had only their labor to offer could rectify wrongdoing through compensation.

Cugoano's response to theodicean arguments was to radicalize their foundations or go to their roots. If God is the underlying force of nature, what is God trying to say or illustrate through His words on earth – in fact, in all historical events? As Descartes argued that mathematics was the language in which God thinks nature, Cugoano went further and argued that reality itself was God's language:

> all the various things established, admitted, and recorded, whether natural, moral, typical or ceremonial . . . were so ordered and admitted as figures, types, and emblems and other symbolic representations, to bring forward, usher in, hold forth, and illustrated that most amazing transaction . . . of the salvation of apostate men.[18]

Every element of reality is but a word in this complex set of sentences, paragraphs, narratives that constitute God's providence. What this suggests

---

[18] Quobna Ottobah Cugoano, *Thoughts and Sentiments on the Evil of Slavery and Other Writings*, ed. with introduction and notes Vincent Carretta (New York: Penguin Books, 1999), p. 39.

is that there is nothing intrinsically evil in these elements but something whose illustration, in a broader context, is ultimately good. Blackness of skin, for instance, is not naturally evil but carries a spiritual message of salvation through having been linked to servitude. In similar kind slavery is but a word whose deeper meaning is the bondage suffered in sin versus the freedom offered by God on whose continued speaking or writing everything depends. "If there had been no evil and sin amongst men, there never would have been any kind of bondage, slavery, and oppression found amongst them."[19] Slavery, in other words, is an expression of sin. Since it behooves us to struggle against sin, we should fight against slavery.

One could imagine the many directions in which Cugoano's thought could be taken today. The field of semiotics (the study of signs and symbols), or even philosophy of language, as well as philosophy of religion and the area of theodicy, would benefit much from his thought. For example, the secularization (eliminating the spiritual, supernatural, and theological dimensions) of his theodicean argument poses some interesting conclusions. If nature is neutral but expressive as a language, then much of what we do as theorists of nature (scientists) or reality that includes nature (philosophers) is read phenomena. But more, in recognizing the absence of a redemptive goal, in fact any goal, would mean that justification for a historical event is misguided in natural terms. Such a search would stand outside of nature or the larger reality that includes nature, which means that to make it rely on that reality would entail a theodicy. It would mean ascribing an intrinsic justification for a reality that faced the contradiction of actions and people who stood outside of it. But this would also be a contradiction, since they too would have to be expressed, which means that they would have to be both internal and external to the language, which means that the logic for their denigration would eventually be contradictory.

For our purposes what is important here is that themes of the humanity of black subjects and what it means to be human, as well as confronting the contradictions of society and thought and the effort to develop a logic or method to address the broader reality implied by those contradictions, come to the fore. These are the ongoing features of Africana philosophy, and Cugoano, in this important work, is one of their pioneers.

---

[19] *Ibid.*, pp. 41–2.

From David Walker's *Appeal* to the founding of the American Negro Academy

The diasporic consciousness that emerged from the slave trade stimulated classic protest literature, primarily in the model of prophetic Christian condemnation of slavery and providential interpretations of the plight of black people. David Walker's *Appeal to the Colored Citizens of the World* (1829) is an instance.[20] Walker (*c.* 1796–1830) was a freed black from Wilmington, North Carolina, who had witnessed some of the cruelest instances of the brutality meted out against slaves. One infamous example was of a slave who was forced to beat his own mother to death. Walker eventually settled in Boston, Massachusetts, where he wrote his *Appeal*, in which he argued for slaves and all blacks to defend themselves and fight for their freedom even by violent means, and he excoriated the racist behavior of whites and argued for a separatist black nation, which made him a predecessor of separatist Black Nationalism. The banned work was distributed with the help of sailors who smuggled copies through southern ports. Slave holders in the South issued a $3,000 reward for Walker dead and a $10,000 one for him captured alive. He died in 1830 of undetermined causes, although there was speculation that he was poisoned.

Maria Stewart (1803–1879), a strong supporter of Walker, was born Maria Miller in Hartford, Connecticut. She married James W. Stewart in Boston in 1826, and was widowed three years later. Her inheritance was stolen through the fraudulent activities of white businessmen. She then moved from Boston to New York City, where she continued her education and became an outspoken critic of slavery, racism, and sexism. She eventually settled in Washington, DC. Stewart became a political activist and continued her public speaking. Her work includes "Religion and the Pure Principles of Morality, the Sure Foundation on Which We Must Build," which

---

[20] The pamphlet was published in Boston by David Walker in 1829 and remains in print. See e.g. David Walker and Henry Highland Garnet, *Walker's Appeal, With a Brief Sketch of His Life, and Also Garnet's Address to the Slaves of the United States of America* (New South Wales, Australia: Dodo Press, 2007). For discussion of Walker's life and thought see Peter P. Hinks, *To Awaken My Afflicted Brethren: David Walker and the Problem of Antebellum Slave Resistance* (University Park, PA: Pennsylvania State University Press, 1997). For more discussion of Walker in philosophical terms see Darryl Scriver, *A Dealer of Old Clothes: Philosophical Conversations with David Walker*, foreword by Daphne M. Rolle (Lanham, MD; Rowman & Littlefield, 2003).

was published in the abolitionist paper *The Liberator* in 1831.[21] In that work, among other things, she argued from a virtue perspective – that is, focusing on character – for the cultivation of talent in the struggle for recognition and respect.[22] She is known as the first African American woman to write a political manifesto and as one of the founding voices of black feminist thought, although her work defended a model of Christian virtue and European conceptions of womanhood that, as we shall see, affirmed the perspective of a black world that could only see itself through the eyes of whites.[23] In "Religion and the Pure Principles of Morality, the Sure Foundation on Which We Must Build," for instance, she beseeched her black readers to "Prove to the world, that / Though black your skins as shades of night, / Your hearts are pure, your souls are white." Let us call this theme of revealing a white soul in a black body worthy of recognition by the white world the dialectics of white recognition. It is a theme that, as we will see, stimulated much debate among blacks in the New World.[24]

Martin Delany (1812–1885), a free black born in Charlestown, Virginia, knew from his own experience that there was nothing about his dark

---

[21] Stewart's writings appear in a variety of anthologies. For a compilation of her writings and a discussion of her life, see *Maria W. Stewart: America's First Black Woman Political Writer: Essays and Speeches*, ed. Marilyn Richardson (Bloomington, IN: Indiana University Press, 1987). "Religion and the Pure Principles of Morality, the Sure Foundation on Which We Must Build" appears on pp. 28–42. See also *Black Women's Intellectual Traditions: Speaking Their Minds*, ed. Kristin B. Waters and Carol B. Conaway (Lebanon, NH: University of Vermont Press/University of New England Press, 2007).

[22] For more discussion, see Stefan Wheelock, "Toward a Poetics of Racial Slavery and the Body Politic: Maria Stewart and Radical Turns in early African-Atlantic Political Thought," in his *Reason and Slavery: African-Atlantic Political Writing in the Age of Revolution* (Jackson, MS: The University Press of Mississippi, forthcoming).

[23] Christian virtue, from the medieval Latin word *virtu*, often focused on virginity and chastity in women, which is much different from the Greek term *areté*, often translated as "virtue," which focuses on excellence of character. For discussion, see Alisdair MacIntyre, *After Virtue: A Study in Moral Theory*, 2nd edn (South Bend, IN: Notre Dame University Press, 1984). It should also be borne in mind, however, that the word *virtus* means strength and *virtû*, merit, which relates to contemporary, colloquial expressions such as those referring to one's "strengths" or asking whether a case has "merits."

[24] Frantz Fanon, for example, explored this phenomenon as a pathology in *Black Skin, White Masks* and Cornel West offers a critique of the dialectics of white recognition through what he calls the exceptionalist and assimilationist traditions in *Prophesy, Deliverance! An Afro-American Revolutionary Christianity*, anniversary edn (Louisville, KY: Westminster John Knox Press, 2002), pp. 72–80.

complexion that necessitated inferiority.[25] He assisted his family in teaching freed and enslaved blacks how to read and write, which was against the law in antebellum Virginia and the rest of the South. The Delany family had to flee to Chambersburg, Pennsylvania, in 1822, when their activities were discovered. By his twenties Delany had written a novel and many essays, founded two newspapers, *The Mystery* in 1842 and then *The Northern Star* in 1847, married Catherine A. Richards in 1843, and had acquired training, as an apprentice, in the clergy and in medicine. He, along with two other blacks, Isaac H. Snowden and Daniel Laing, Jr., had received medical training at Harvard University as matriculated students for the medical doctorate but were forced to leave because of protest by alumni who claimed that the conferring of the doctorate of medicine on Delany and the other two black students would ruin the value of their Harvard degree. The dean of the school, Oliver Wendell Holmes, Sr., oversaw the dismissal of the three black students.[26] Delany's response to this situation, faced by many before him and even more afterward, was that reason held no genuine sway over most whites and that the value of white supremacy trumped that of merit in white dominated societies. His experience and conclusion here portend a later reflection by Frantz Fanon: "The racist in a culture with racism is . . . normal. He has achieved a perfect harmony of economic relations and ideology."[27] Delany went on to practice medicine in Pittsburgh, Pennsylvania, and exemplified valor in a cholera epidemic in 1854, during which most of the white doctors fled, while he remained and organized a team of male and female nurses and provided medical care for the city. He worked as a school principal and continued writing

[25] For a compilation of Delany's writings, see Martin Robinson Delany, *Martin R. Delany: A Documentary Reader*, ed. Robert S. Levine (Chapel Hill: University of North Carolina Press, 2003). For studies of Delany's life, see Tunde Adeleke, *Without Regard to Race: The Other Martin Robinson Delany* (Oxford, MS: University of Mississippi Press, 2003) and Dorothy Sterling, *The Making of an Afro-American: Martin Robison Delany, 1812–1885* (New York: Da Capo, 1996).

[26] For more details on what happened at Harvard, see Louis Menand, *The Metaphysical Club: A Story of Ideas in America* (New York: Farrar, Stroux, and Giroux, 2001), pp. 7–9. There is not much available on Laing and Snowden, including their birth and death dates, but Menand mentions that Laing completed his studies at Dartmouth and Snowden studied privately with a surgeon at Massachusetts General Hospital.

[27] Frantz Fanon, *Toward the African Revolution*, trans. Haakon Chevalier, ed. Josèphe Fanon (New York: Grove Press, 1967), p. 40.

critical social commentary, in which he argued for the equal education of black women, the founding of a black nation in Central or South America, and criticized the hypocrisy of white abolitionists for their refusal to elect blacks among the ranks of their leadership. He then visited Liberia in 1859 and led expeditions into Yoruba Land in 1860, where he negotiated rights for the New World black settlements there. His efforts at organizing the emigration of blacks from the United States were abandoned, however, at the outbreak of the Civil War in 1861. Delany organized black troops in New England and persuaded President Lincoln in 1865 to let black troops fight in the South in order to encourage fellow blacks there to join the Union against the Confederacy. He eventually achieved the rank of major in the Union army, and after the war, he served as a trial justice in South Carolina before eventually moving to Xenia, Ohio, where he died from consumption.

Frederick Douglass (1818–1895) was a little younger than Delany and more disadvantaged at the outset.[28] A born slave, whose father was most likely his master, Douglass lived through the horrors of the system in Maryland, before standing up against a slave breaker and eventually escaping to New York where he became one of the main spokespersons of the abolitionist movement led by William Lloyd Garrison (1805–1879). Douglass wrote about his experiences as a slave in three autobiographies. He went to Ireland and then on to Scotland and England on the publication of the first, *Narrative of the Life of Frederick Douglass, an American Slave, Written By Himself* (1845), to avoid extradition to the South under the fugitive slave laws. Given the protections afforded his book under the copyright laws of the land, he was living the ironic situation of his text having more rights than he himself. Douglass's speeches in Europe drew large crowds and rallied much support for the abolitionists and brought his cause to the attention of some English benefactors who paid Hugh Auld, his former owner, and thereby manumitted him and enabled him to return to the United States as a freed man. He subsequently dedicated his life to journalistic, social activist, and government service,

---

[28] Douglass's writings are more easily accessed than any other African-American political and philosophical writer of the nineteenth century. See e.g. *The Life and Writings of Frederick Douglass*, ed. Philip S. Foner (New York: International Publishers, 1950). All of his narratives/autobiographies remain in print. For a collection of philosophical treatments of his work, see *Frederick Douglass: A Critical Reader*, ed. Bill E. Lawson and Frank M. Kirkland (Malden, MA: Blackwell, 1999).

which included his tenure as the minister-resident and consul-general to Haiti (1889–91).

Douglass's primary contribution to Africana philosophy is the theory of freedom implicit in his narratives and his radical egalitarianism. He defended the rights of women and was a known activist in the suffragette movement. His view of freedom emerged in several stages in his narratives, many of which foreground what was to come in the twentieth-century reflections of W. E. B. Du Bois, Richard Wright, and Frantz Fanon. Douglass argued, in his three biographies, that acquiring literacy in his youth had transformed him. It made him realize that literacy was not a uniquely divine ability of whites. This reminded him of his humanity and made more intense his realization of the scale of harm done to him and many others by slavery. His masters responded by intensifying their dehumanizing effort to affirm his bondage and thereby continue to make him into a slave. Although literacy offered a new understanding of slavery and freedom, Douglass also solicited the aid of supernatural forces, through the aid of a roots amulet from a fellow slave, to protect him. He eventually realized, however, that he could only claim his freedom through fighting for it, through risking his life. He resisted the slave breaker Covey, which led to a physical altercation in which Douglass defended himself without killing the man. To fight Covey at all was to risk death, as it was to allow Covey to live. As Paul Gilroy observed, "For [Douglass], the slave actively prefers the possibility of death to the continuing condition of inhumanity on which plantation slavery depends."[29] I have argued that this conflict can also be understood in existential philosophical terms.[30] Douglass's preference for the possibility of death is governed by his realization of the affirmation of life. The existential paradox here is that he must be willing to die in order to live. This was not a trivial matter under legalized slavery. The fight held within it a form of infinite resignation, where the slave had every reason to believe that his life was over while he was fighting for its continuation. The conflict was liberating. From that moment onward Douglass was able to plot his path to liberty, although he searched for his freedom for the rest of his life. In

---

[29] Paul Gilroy, *The Black Atlantic: Modernity and Double Consciousness* (Cambridge, MA: Harvard University Press, 1993), p. 63.

[30] Lewis R. Gordon, *Existentia Africana: Understanding Africana Existential Thought* (New York: Routledge, 2000), ch. 3, "Frederick Douglass as an Existentialist," pp. 41–61.

Douglass the distinction between liberty and freedom is crucial: the former is the absence of an impediment; the latter requires the conviction of self-worth, responsibility, and dignity in the face of death. Others could enable his liberty, as the patrons who later manumitted him attest, but only he could secure his freedom. Seizing one's freedom is something one is responsible for alone. Liberty is external; freedom is internal and constitutive of what one is or wishes to become.

The most influential member of this black intelligentsia in his time was Alexander Crummell (1818–1898).[31] Born a free black in New York City, he aspired to a career in the clergy. After study in abolitionist schools he petitioned in 1839 for admission to the General Theological Seminary of the Episcopalian Church. The seminary refused to admit black students, so, as did Delany with medicine, Crummell studied privately and became an ordained Episcopalian priest in 1844. While spending time in England raising funds to build a church for poor blacks, he enrolled in Cambridge University, where he earned a bachelors of arts degree at Queens' College in 1853. He then went to Liberia, where he became one of its most influential citizens as a clergyman and professor of intellectual and moral science at Liberia College. His views, which advocated the creation of a black Christian republic that combined the best of European culture with Western-educated black leadership, brought him into opposition with Liberia's elite in a debate that, as we will see in our discussion of recent African philosophy, continues – namely, concerns of politics and rule. After returning to the United States in 1873 he founded and became the head pastor of St. Luke's Episcopal church in Washington, DC, where Maria Stewart was among his parishioners, and he became well known as a political organizer and institution builder. He subsequently taught at Howard University (1895–7) and in 1897 founded the American Negro Academy. His contributions to Africana philosophy pertain, thus, both to his own ideas and his foresight in building institutions devoted to intellectual work.

Although primarily a religious thinker and moralist committed to the cause of black liberation, many of Crummell's views were conservative and

---

[31] Crummell's writings have been anthologized by Wilson Moses as Alexander Crummell, *Destiny and Race: Selected Writings, 1840–1898* (Amherst, MA: University of Massachusetts Press, 1992). See also Moses's historical study of Crummell, *Alexander Crummell: A Study of Civilization and Discontent* (Oxford: Oxford University Press, 1989).

at times reactionary, although in every case his position was based on foundations that seemed reasonable in his time, and in some cases still seem so to this day.[32] He was against the Marxist notion of a class struggle being applied to the United States, for instance, because, as he pointed out in "The Negro as a Source of Conservative Power," wage labor is not identical with slave labor. The white working-class of the nineteenth century was simply better off and had more opportunities – political and economic – than blacks of any class stratum. Oddly enough, he admitted in the same essay that such Marxist arguments made perfect sense for blacks: "If it were the *black* labour of the South I could easily understand it; and I could at once proffer my warmest sympathies. But as it regards *white* labour all the facts are against the theory."[33] He advocated, in his essay "The Black Woman of the South: Her Neglects and Her Needs," for the upliftment of black women, and even spoke of equality between women and men, but proposed a curriculum that consigned their role to that of "refined," literate housekeepers.[34] (It should be borne in mind that this was the position of most of the black female organizations at the time.) But perhaps most controversial are his views on the supremacy of Christianity, providence, black people, and the English language.

What is often overlooked in commentaries on Crummell is that his thought was also addressing concerns of social decay in the nineteenth century. This was, as is well known, a major concern of Friedrich Nietzsche (1844–1900), who, in such writings as *The Birth of Tragedy from the Spirit of Music* (1872), *On the Genealogy of Morals* (1887), and *Will to Power* (1901), saw European civilization as suffering a long, drawn-out condition of decadence and a loss of the vitality necessary, literally, to bring value to their values. An area born from such ideas was the philosophy of civilization.[35] Crummell, living the underside of North American civilization, saw its corrupt, contradictory,

---

[32] For critical assessments of Crummell, see e.g. K. Anthony Appiah, *In My Father's House: Africa in the Philosophy of Culture* (New York: Oxford University Press, 1992), ch. 1, and Josiah Ulysses Young, III, *A Pan-African Theology: Providence and the Legacies of the Ancestors* (Trenton, NJ: Africa World Press, 1992).

[33] Crummell, *Destiny and Race*, p. 237.   [34] *Ibid.*, pp. 220–3.

[35] For an example of philosophy of civilization that had a far more damaging effect on Africa than that attributed to Crummell by Appiah, see Albert Schweitzer, *Philosophy of Civilization*, trans. C. T. Campion (Buffalo, NY: Prometheus Books, 1987), where e.g. indigenous Africans are described as "childlike." See ch. 6, below, for discussions of this notion and its role in the rationalization of indirect rule in Africa.

and decadent sides. Like Nietzsche, he concluded that it was misguided to deny the naturalness of decadence, although, like Cugoano and Delany, he saw God as the spiritual force that supports nature. Peoples and their civilizations come and go. But Crummell's reading, unlike Nietzsche's, was to place providence into his philosophy of civilization. Subsequent Africana philosophers would reject this view for a variety of reasons that included their support of scientific secularism, existential rejections of the spirit of seriousness – the belief in objective, material values in the physical world – and the rejection of philosophy of civilization as an ethnocentric and at times racist enterprise. Crummell took for granted the demise and eventual extinction of non-black indigenous peoples as a function of their internal weakness, of their, in other words, decaying spirit. In "The Destined Superiority of the Negro," he defended blacks as superior to all other races on the grounds of their supposed capacity for imitation.[36] Blacks or, in the idiom of the times, Negroes, he argued, had an infinite capacity to adapt. That suggested, he further argued, that they would take on the features of civilizations necessary for their survival while retaining just enough of themselves to maintain their uniqueness. Seeing a future world dominated by Christianity and Europeans, Crummell, in effect, argued that blacks could, and indeed would, survive through adapting to that future as black Euro-Christians. Blacks, in effect, were the vitalistic, reproductive force made flesh in the human species. One could easily see how Crummell was turning upside down the social Darwinism of the times, whose greatest promoter, short of Darwin himself, was the biologist and social philosopher Herbert Spencer (1820–1903).[37] The "fitness" of whites, Crummell was suggesting, should not be judged by their domination at the moment of his reflections but by what the future held. White supremacy might, after all, only be a short chapter in the history of humankind. This too is an argument, as we will see, that recurs in Africana philosophy – particularly in the area of philosophy of economics and theories of decadence.

The significance of Crummell as an institution builder cannot be overestimated. The biographical sketch I provided only touches on some highlights. As stated, this aspect of his work is important to mention because he built

---

[36] Crummell, *Destiny and Race*, pp. 194–205, but especially pp. 200–2.

[37] See e.g. Herbert Spencer, *The Study of Sociology* (New York: D. Appleton and Co., 1874) and *Spencer: Political Writings*, ed. John Offer (Cambridge: Cambridge University Press, 1993).

intellectual institutions as well, of which we shall here consider just one: the American Negro Academy.

Crummell saw the advancement of knowledge as vital for civilization itself. Thus, he had at least two aims when he founded the American Negro Academy, which he wanted to call the African Academy. The first was to create an alternative to the high-profiled, white-appointed representatives of black communities in the United States, whom he called "Leaders for Revenue."[38] For Crummell, the task of black intellectuals was a mission, a calling, which he saw jeopardized by such purely market-oriented opportunists. Although the peculiarity of the circumstances of race and racism bring a unique dimension to Crummell's concern, the situation of philosophers with a calling admonishing rhetoricians and for-profit intellectuals, as found in Plato's condemnation of the sophists, continued in Crummell's time, as it does today. His second reason is exemplified in the first paragraph of the constitution and by-laws of the American Negro Academy, which he composed:

> This Academy is an organization of Authors, Scholars, Artists, and those distinguished in other walks of life, men of African descent, for the promotion of Letters, Science, and Art; for the creation, as far as possible, of a form of intellectual taste; for the encouragement and assistance of youthful, but hesitant, scholarship; for the stimulation of inventive and artistic powers; and for the promotion of the publication of works of merit.[39]

The words "men of African descent" were literal. Although there were prominent African-American women intellectuals at the time who included Anna Julia Cooper (1858–1964), Ida B. Wells-Barnett (1862–1931), Mary Church Terrell (1863–1954), and the many participants in the Black Women's Club Movement born at the founding of the National Association of Colored Women (NACW) in 1896, Crummell's leadership brought with it no sense of the role of women as intellectuals. This notion of black womanhood was not a view that was held only among black male leaders of the time. As already pointed out, it was the prevailing view of many black female organizations and their publications. Magazines included *The Woman's Era*,

---

[38] Moses, *Alexander Crummell: A Study of Civilization and Discontent*, p. 258.
[39] *Ibid.*, p. 365.

which was geared toward a mixed-race middle-class aspiring for recognition in terms of the most elite models of womanhood. Many argued for female "delicateness" and "refinement," offered by European society, and nearly none of them took seriously the plea of former slave women for alternative conceptions of femininity exemplified by those who came from the fields such as Sojourner Truth (also known as Isabella Baumfree, 1797–1883). This high-culture view of womanhood was not the position shared by all black male leaders from the century. Frederick Douglass is a well-known example, but Martin Delany, who is attacked by Anna Julia Cooper in *A Voice from the South* as sexist, was actually the one who insisted, in his September 6, 1848 speech in Cleveland, Ohio, on black female equality at all levels – especially in professional intellectual work.[40]

Still, in spite of such shortcomings, the American Negro Academy provided a context for the exploration of ideas for a stellar group of black male intellectuals at a time when even for those who had academic posts, the message that the education of blacks should focus on only practical needs or vocational training for the darker lower classes, and a mimicking of elite European society locked in the dialectics of white recognition for the "colored" or mixed-race communities prevailed. They included perhaps the most famous black intellectual of the modern era, W. E. B. Du Bois (1868–1963), the educator and conservative Booker T. Washington (1856–1915), the poet Paul Laurence Dunbar (1872–1905), lawyer, songwriter, playwright, historian, and political activist James Weldon Johnson (1871–1938), historian Carter G. Woodson (1875–1950), philosopher and critic Alain Locke (1886–1954), bibliophile and historian Arthur Schomburg (1874–1938), and lawyer, journalist, and political activist Archibald H. Grimke (1849–1930). It was in this association that the arguments brewing from the eighteenth century through to the nineteenth century took new form and set the groundwork for twentieth-century Africana philosophy.

---

[40] Anna Julia Cooper, *The Voice of Anna Julia Cooper: Including A Voice From the South and Other Important Essays, Papers, and Letters*, ed. Charles Lemert (Lanham, MD: Rowman & Littlefield, 1998). For the women's club movement, see Barbara Ryan, *Feminism and the Women's Movement: Dynamics in Social Movement Ideology and Activism* (New York: Routledge, 1992), and for a collection of black feminist writings that include several of the prominent writers from the club movement, see *Words of Fire: An Anthology of African-American Feminist Thought*, ed. Beverly Guy-Sheftall with an epilogue by Johnnetta B. Cole (New York: The New Press, 1995).

Two Caribbean men of letters: Anténor Firmin and George Wilmot Blyden

The Caribbean played a complex role in the development of Africana thought. First, it was the place in which modern capitalist expansion was inaugurated in 1492. Second, the movement of people and, as a consequence, ideas was rapid in that constellation of islands and continental shores, and with it came to the fore many of the anxieties of modern life and thought. And third, it was the place of profit and experimentation that affected a great many of the aspirations and hopes of nations in the Atlantic and subsequently the rest of the world. The impact of the cultivation of sugar is a case in point. It is difficult today to imagine how much of a luxury a teaspoon of sugar once was. That it became part of the everyday life of Europeans while there was merciless, enslaved toil on sugar-cane fields across the Caribbean changed the consciousness of even the most "rude" European. Sugar was a commodity that literally made their lives sweet.[41]

But such joys were interrupted on many occasions, the most significant of which was the very bloody Haitian revolution in 1804, in which black slaves demanded their rights to their past freedoms and access to the sucrose of modern life, especially since they had already tasted too much of its bitter fruit. In its effort to suppress the revolution, which included such brutal tactics as attempting to butcher every black over the age of twelve, France had to sell off portions of its colonial holdings, which included Louisiana. The result was the expansion of the United States, the reduction of France, and the contradictory historical event of the French Revolution calling for freedom and brotherhood while devoting considerable energy to defending slavery and denying the exemplification of modern freedom in black bodies. Fear of the revolution inspiring slaves across the New World produced levels of collective neurosis: maps of the Caribbean for a time did not include Haiti, which, no doubt, had a profound effect on the study of geography and history in the region. President Thomas Jefferson, one of the authors of the American Declaration of Independence, imposed sanctions on the island,

---

[41] For a detailed history, see Eric Williams, *Capitalism and Slavery*, with a new introduction by Colin A. Palmer (Chapel Hill, NC: University of North Carolina Press, 1994). This work was originally published in 1944. Williams, as is well known, after teaching as a professor of history at Howard University, became the first prime minister of independent Trinidad.

which resulted in a blockade in which access to international commerce was not granted until a ransom of several hundred million gold crowns was paid to the United States government in the 1820s. This payment contributed to Haiti's future as the most poverty-stricken nation of the New World, and a history of US occupation, constant pillaging of its institutions of national finance, and reigns of brutal dictators.[42]

Although the Haitian revolution established the first black republic, slave revolts were a constant feature of life in the region. The island of Jamaica had so many in the seventeenth and eighteenth centuries that the British chose to negotiate with the former slaves, known as Maroons, led by an Ashanti woman affectionately called "Granny Nanny," for control of the coasts while the Maroons controlled much of the inner countryside.[43] Added to all this was the fact that the slaves vastly outnumbered the whites in the Caribbean. On some islands whites comprised less than 10 percent of the population. The result was the preservation of a great array of African practices and customs by the majority population and, in many instances, a more fluid crossing of racial lines. This was the context for the emergence of the two final contributors to nineteenth-century Africana thought that we will discuss in this chapter.

Anténor Firmin (1850–1911) was born in Haiti during the forty-sixth year of its independence. His life in many ways brings to the fore the side of the Haitian revolution that is not often written about in the constant stream of denunciations of its history: there was much innovation as the former slaves experimented and attempted to build what they knew was a beacon of hope for enslaved people worldwide. Firmin's entire education was in Haiti. He studied at the Lycée National du Cap-Haitien and the Lycée Pétion in Port-au-Prince. He chose law as his profession and became a successful politician, which took him to Paris in 1883 as a diplomat. He was invited to join the Anthropology Society in Paris in 1884, where he was appalled at the racist anthropological theories espoused by his colleagues in the face of his presence as their clear contradiction. Although more serious in their

---

[42] For more detailed discussion, see C. L. R. James, *The Black Jacobins: Toussaint L'Ouverture and the San Domingo Revolution* (New York: Vintage, 1989) and Sibylle Fischer, *Modernity Disavowed: Haiti and the Cultures of Slavery in the Age of Revolution* (Durham, NC: Duke University Press, 2004).

[43] For more discussion, see Karla Gottlieb, *The Mother of Us All: A History of Queen Nanny, Leader of the Windward Jamaican Maroons* (Trenton, NJ: Africa World Press, 2000).

methodological approaches than the extremely popular Count Arthur de Gobineau's *Essai sur L'Inégalité des Races Humaines* (1853–5) [*Essay on the Inequality of Human Races*], their conclusions revealed clear convergence with that racist diatribe – the supposed superiority of the Aryan race; the innate inferiority of the Negro; the search for a polygenic account of the emergence of different races, in effect, a collapse of race into species differentiation; and more.[44] De Gobineau's text was translated into several other European languages, which included five editions in German, and is included in the Oxford Library of French Classics.[45] The influence of de Gobineau's work brings home one of the features of modern civilization that is the brunt of much criticism in Africana philosophy: influence in the white world is not a function of being correct, truthful, or excellent – it is a world unfortunately that often asserts its superiority through the luxury of rewarded mediocrity.

The logic of the situation begged as many questions as it was supposed to answer. The existence of Firmin could easily be rationalized by his white colleagues into the logic of exceptionalism, where he achieved as an exception to the rule but would fail as an instance of it. Firmin's response was to write his own account of race in direct response to de Gobineau. The result was *De L'égalité des Races Humaines* (1885) [*The Equality of Human Races*].[46] The scale of Firmin's achievement in that work, and its near absence of attention save for specialists in the Afro-Francophone world, is perhaps one of the great travesties of the impact of racism on the history of ideas. Nearly every contemporary debate in race theory and Africana philosophy is touched upon in an insightful way in that tome of more than a century past. Firmin returned to Haiti in 1888, where he eventually became foreign minister in 1891, when he successfully prevented the United States from acquiring the Môle of St. Nicolas, the deep-sea harbor in which Columbus first entered the island. The incident led to the US ambassador, Frederick Douglass (who acted from being insulted by his white countrymen who refused to recognize a black ambassador), being relieved of his post, and Firmin was held in ill repute for even going through the negotiations in the first place. He was made

---

[44] Gobineau's text was published in Paris and a recent version in English is *The Inequality of Human Races*, preface by George L. Mosse (New York: H. Fertig, 1999).

[45] See Carolyn Fleuhr-Lobban's introduction to Anténor Firmin's *The Equality of the Human Races: A Nineteenth Century Haitian Scholar's Response to European Racialism*, trans. Asselin Charles (New York: Garland, 1999), pp. xi–l.

[46] The work was published in Paris by Librairie Cotillon.

Minister of Paris in 1900 under the Simon government in Haiti, which considered him a political threat. Among his efforts was his attendance at the First Pan-African Congress in London, where he met W. E. B. Du Bois and Anna Julia Cooper, as Haiti's representative. He eventually returned to Haiti at the head of what became known as the Firmin insurgency of 1902. This was an effort, described by Carolyn Fleuhr-Lobban and Asselin Charles, "to reform government institutions, advocate the engagement of foreign capital interest in the Republic, and reduce the role of the army in Haiti."[47] The effect was disastrous. As Fleuhr-Lobban and Charles relate:

> The Firminist insurgency amounted to civil war and its bent on military takeover appeared inconsistent with Firmin's disdain for the "ignorant" militarists he despised. The foreign press, the diplomatic community, and the international Pan-African Association insisted that Firmin lay down his arms. A call for the United States intervention would have meant another violation of Firmin's strongly held principle against foreign domination; in fact the US maintained strict military neutrality during the civil war, as did England and France. With greater strength in the north Cap Haitien region the movement was eventually overwhelmed by political forces in Port-au-Prince.[48]

The event led to Firmin seeking exile in the island of St. Thomas. He continued writing on social and political matters, especially pan-Africanism and pan-Caribbean politics, before dying shortly after another attempt to secure his leadership of Haiti in 1911.[49]

This synopsis of Firmin's life reveals the struggles he faced to effect his politics, which placed him in the tradition of black republicanism, exemplified by commitment to a domination-free society governed by non-arbitrary laws, as the following quotation attests:

> The wish I formulate for the people of my race, wherever they may live and govern themselves in the world, is that they turn away from any thing that smacks of arbitrary practices, of systematic contempt for the law and for freedom, and of disdain of legal procedures and distributive justice. Law, justice, and freedom are eminently respectable values, for they form the

---

[47] Fleuhr-Lobban and Charles, "Introduction," *The Equality of the Races*, p. xli.   [48] *Ibid.*

[49] For a discussion of his writings during this period, see J. Michael Dash, "Nineteenth-Century Haiti and the Archipelago of the Americas: Anténor Firmin's Letters from St. Thomas," *Research in African Literatures* 35, no. 2 (2004): 44–53.

crowning structure of the moral edifice which modern civilization has been laboriously and gloriously building on the accumulated ruins of the ideas of the Middle Ages.[50]

Firmin's dream of non-arbitrary laws was not realized. The subsequent history of Haiti became one stained by the leadership of brutal dictators, most of whom were placed in power or supported by the United States. An additional result is the absence of peaceful transitions of leadership. The coup is the dominating method.

Although Firmin wrote *The Equality of the Human Races* as a scientist, and defended a positivist conception of science, which he claimed was in the spirit of August Comte (1798–1857), his achievement in the text is also a magnificent example of philosophical anthropology and philosophy of human science. There is not enough space here to provide a detailed account of his thought, but an illustration by way of his critique of Kant should provide an indication of his importance to philosophy. He begins with a reflection on method. One cannot study the human being as one would ordinary natural objects, he argues, because the human being is a contradictory subject. "Man can lower himself to the lowest depths of ignorance and complacently wallow in the muddy swamps of vice, yet he can also rise to the resplendent heights of truth, goodness, and beauty."[51] Philosophers and scientists have attempted to resolve these contradictions by developing overly formalized idealistic theories of the human or subjective reductive naturalistic ones. To illustrate his point, Firmin argues that Kant's moral philosophy (formal, transcendental idealism) illuminates his anthropology more than his *Pragmatic Anthropology*. In the former, Kant separates moral philosophy from what he calls moral anthropology, where the former is rational and the latter is simply empirical. This division leads Kant to use the term anthropology in a way that is very different from the scientists of his day, who regarded it as the natural study of the human being. Kant regarded their work as properly "physical geography," and his theory of human difference is, in many ways, a geographical theory of intelligence. Hegel, Firmin argues, is an heir to Kant in this regard, since he too sees race ultimately as geographical. In effect, Kant and Hegel were engaged in a form of geographical idealism.

Yet as the scientists criticized the philosophers for their idealism, they failed to see the errors of their naturalistic reductionism. The scientists of

---

[50] Firmin, *The Equality of the Human Races*, p. lvii.   [51] *Ibid.*, p. 3.

the eighteenth century simply presupposed that the human being could be studied in the same manner as plants, other animals, and other natural phenomena. What is missing in their analysis, Firmin argues, is an understanding of the implications of social life. Natural history must give way, then, to a form of unnatural history since the human being makes his or her own history. The human being, as Firmin proposes, emerges in a human world, which leads to anthropology as "the study of Man in his physical, intellectual, and moral dimensions, as he is found among the different races which constitute the human species."[52] Although Firmin refers to the "different races," it is important to notice that he adds "which constitute the human species." His criticism of his colleagues is that they sought, in their effort to articulate a great distance between the Caucasian and Negro, to advance a theory of species differentiation instead of racial differentiation. Racial differentiation could only make sense for members of the same species. To advance his case Firmin took on many of the racist claims propagated by mainstream naturalists of his day, such as those against race mixing. The fertility of mixed-race offspring dispels the notion of species difference. As well the claims of polygenesis – that whites and blacks evolved from completely different animal ancestors – are a variation of the species difference argument, which is not only proven wrong by racial mixture, but also by the fact that contemporary versions of each group are manifestations of even older mixtures. Here, Firmin's argument precedes much of what was to be found in critical race theory by the second half of the twentieth century.

What should also be noticed is that although Firmin allied himself with the positivist science of his day, his thought clearly transcends positivist reductionism. For instance, he focused on the historical question of classification not in terms of individuals, although he offers analyses of their thought, but in terms of systems of knowledge. He understood, and was in fact explicit, about the limits involved in constructing anthropology and of how the orders of knowledge of the nineteenth century were in fact constructing the very subject they had set out to study. Readers familiar with the thought of Michel Foucault (1926–1984) will easily recognize Firmin's reflection as in stream with an archaeology of knowledge and its role in the constitution of subjects of inquiry, and more, that he recognized the role

---

[52] *Ibid.*, p. 10.

of racial impositions on the subject matter and the underlying investments involved in geography and natural history meant that he was aware of the genealogical organization of thought on human subjects. His understanding of social life and the question of moral imposition or the impact of rules on the organization of human subjects meant, as well, that he was a precursor in the area of philosophy of social science which examines problems of the constitution of social reality. Firmin understood, in other words, that, as Alfred Schutz (1899–1959) later pointed out in his *Phänomenologie des inneren Zeitbewusstsein* (1928) [*Phenomenology of the Social World*], social life is an achievement, not a determined reality.[53] This made him a precursor, as well, of social constructivism, but his version is rooted in a very thick conception of history.

Firmin also introduced a concept in Africana thought that was later taken up by the Guyanese revolutionary Walter Rodney (1942–1980) – namely, the concept of underdevelopment.[54] Firmin writes throughout the text of what he calls the "regeneration of the black race." By this, he means that it was not the natural condition of blacks to be in an inferior position to whites, and that the actual history of blacks in Africa was much different from what had been perpetrated by eighteenth- and nineteenth-century Eurocentric writings on Africa and the Caribbean. He offers a history of ancient Africa that predates the writings of the Senegalese Cheikh Anton Diop.[55] The Europeanizing and Asianizing of ancient Egypt are instances of the exceptionalist rule, whereby an ancient African nation (or group of nations) is literally taken out of Africa because of an analytical reduction of civilization into things European and Asian. That the history of Africa was one of

[53] Alfred Schutz, *Phenomenology of the Social World*, trans. George Walsh and Frederick Lehnert, with an introduction by George Walsh (Evanston, IL: Northwestern University Press, 1967); for commentary, see Maurice Natanson, *Anonymity: A Study in the Philosophy of Alfred Schutz* (Bloomington, IN: Indiana University Press, 1986) and Lewis R. Gordon, *Fanon and the Crisis of European Man: an Essay in Philosophy and the Human Sciences* (New York: Routledge, 1995), ch. 3.

[54] See Rodney, *How Europe Underdeveloped Africa*.

[55] See e.g. Cheikh Anta Diop, *Civilization or Barbarism: An Authentic Anthropology*, trans. Yaa-Lengi Meema Ngemi, ed. by Harold J. Salemson and Marolijn de Jager (Brooklyn, NY: Lawrence Hill Books, 1991); *The African Origin of Civilization: Myth or Reality*, trans. Mercer Cook (New York: L. Hill, 1974); and *Precolonial Black Africa: A Comparative Study of the Political and Social Systems of Europe and Black Africa, from Antiquity to the Formation of Modern States*, trans. Harold J. Salemson (Westport, CT: L. Hill, 1987).

a rapid change and spiraling degeneration during the slave trade suggested that a process of underdevelopment led to the question-begging situation of black inferiority. This is what Rodney ultimately argued in his classic work *How Europe Underdeveloped Africa*.

The concept of regeneration brings to the fore a problem that we have touched upon in the introduction regarding European self-perception. A consequence of modern historicism is the notion of the European never really having a primitive past. It is an analytical notion in which when Neanderthals, for instance, are discovered to have been white, the discussion of their intelligence shifts and a greater effort to articulate it and their humanity unfolds in the research.[56] In short, a white primitive becomes an oxymoron, and in effect, the ascription of intelligence functions retroactively from the present to the past and returns to the present. Whites thus function as the *telos*, as the aim, of the human species. It is, in effect, the reassertion of an old logic, namely, Aristotelianism, where there is a search for the aim of living phenomena.[57] Darwinism, properly speaking, should not make any teleological claims. But social Darwinism falls into this trap, and the logic from race to racism follows.[58] The concept of regeneration suggests that the past was not one of any human race being inferior to another but that historical forces came into play to subordinate, by force, some groups of human beings over others. The concept of regeneration suggests that every individual member of each group of human beings, as living creatures, is in a generative process to achieve his or her potential, but that that potential is not a metaphysical external prime mover. It is what individuals in each group may strive for in the absence of domination. We see here the basis of Firmin's republicanism.

---

[56] One could chronicle this progression in the *Journal of Human Evolution* or Neanderthal reports in the journal *Science*, but fine summaries are provided in the BBC News, World Edition, "Neanderthals 'Mated with Modern Humans'" (April 21, 1999): see website: http://news.bbc.co.uk/2/hi/science/nature/323657.stm and "Neanderthals 'Had Hands Like Ours'" (March 27, 2003): see website: http://news.bbc.co.uk/2/hi/science/nature/2884801.stm.

[57] Cf. Aristotle's *Physics* and *On the Generation of Animals*, as well as his *Metaphysics* and *Nicomachean Ethics*, for instances of Aristotelian teleological models of reality, reproduction, and human action.

[58] See Benjamin Farrington's taking even Darwin to task for this error in his exposition of Darwinism and critical evaluation of social Darwinism in Farrington's *What Darwin Really Said* (New York: Schocken Books, 1996).

A scholar of great repute from the Caribbean island of St. Thomas, Virgin Islands, George Wilmot Blyden (1832–1912) is often thought of more in relation to Martin Delany and Alexander Crummell than to Anténor Firmin. Like Delany and Crummell he was precocious and had attempted to complete his formal education in the United States but was rejected on the basis of his race. He decided to emigrate to Liberia, where he continued his studies on his own and eventually became principal of the Alexander High School in Monrovia (1858) and then a professor at the Liberian College (1862–71). Blyden served as a statesman between Liberia and Sierra Leone for most of his career. He was secretary of state in Liberia (1864–6), led expeditions from Sierra Leone to various areas of west Africa while editing the *Negro*, the first pan-African journal in west Africa. He eventually served as Liberia's ambassador to Britain and France, and as president of Liberia College and served for a time as minister of native affairs in Lagos, Nigeria, before settling in Freetown as the director of Muslim education, where he died in 1912.[59]

Blyden's work was more social scientifically focused in the areas of linguistics, history, and sociology. His insights along the way offered much for the philosophy of culture. For instance, he was critical of the Crummellian project of christianizing Africa, arguing, in *African Life and Customs* (1908), that it was much easier to change a people's theology than their religion.[60] Crummell saw the effort to change the normative basis of how people lived as having a damaging effect, although one could engage them at the level of rational reflection on the implications of their customs and thoughts. Central in this regard is his study of the Muslim populations of western Africa, where he observed the difference between the impact of Christianity and Islam on blacks. The former, he concluded, had a negative effect of demanding subservience in the psychic and social life of blacks, which he considered demoralizing, whereas the latter afforded more dignity since it was more aligned with traditional African conceptions of self-assertiveness. With regard to modernization, he was a pioneer of the view that modernization need not only be European and that it was possible to develop a distinctively African form of modernity.

[59] For more details on Blyden's life and thought see Hollis Lynch, *Edward Wilmot Blyden: Pan-Negro Patriot, 1832–1912* (Oxford: Oxford University Press, 1970).

[60] Blyden, *African Life and Customs* (Baltimore, MD: Black Classics Press, 1994). The work was originally published by the *Sierra Leone Weekly News*.

Conclusion

The eighteenth and nineteenth centuries were periods in which much pioneering work emerged in Africana thought, some of which was explicitly philosophical and some more an example of social criticism with philosophical implications. Recurring themes are (1) the centrality of philosophical anthropology in the intellectual battle against racism and colonialism; (2) the problem of modernization and the meaning of civilization in theorizing human reality; (3) the importance of freedom and liberation as subjects of philosophical reflection; (4) the significance of identity questions of classification and addressing dualisms of superiority and inferiority in studying the human species; (5) the emancipating significance of knowledge and the lived reality of its contradictions; (6) the weight of history in the formation of human identity; and (7) the importance of metaphilosophical reflections on method and thought itself. Many individuals contributed in one way or another to some if not all of these problems. Some were clergymen and women, who considered the place of human beings in the wider cosmos, and others were black nationalists seeking a future in which to exist as black need not entail being homeless. We now turn to the more familiar themes of African-American, Afro-Caribbean, and African philosophies, over which the term Africana is the contemporary rubric.

Part II

From New World to new worlds

3 Three pillars of African-American philosophy

Our discussion of nineteenth-century Africana philosophy has been, in effect, a discussion of the foundations of African-American philosophy. African-American philosophy is an area of Africana philosophy that focuses on philosophical problems posed by the African diaspora in the New World. Although there is some controversy over the term "African American" to refer specifically to the convergence of black people in the New World continents and regions of the modern world, let us use that term since it is the one most used by philosophers in the field.[1] Thus by African-American philosophy let us then mean the modern philosophical discourse that emerges from that diasporic African community, including its francophone, hispanophone, and lusophone forms. To articulate the central features and themes of the thought from that intellectual heritage, I would like to begin by outlining some of the thought of the three greatest influences on many (if not most) in the field – namely, Anna Julia Cooper, W. E. B. Du Bois, and Frantz Fanon.

Anna Julia Cooper and the problem of value

The life of Anna Julia Cooper (1858–1964) defies belief.[2] She was born a slave, from her father and master George Washington Hayward and his slave, her

---

[1] This is an issue I have discussed in a variety of forums. For now, the reader is encouraged to consult the discussions of these terms that emerge in part I of *Not Only the Master's Tools: African-American Studies in Theory and Practice*, ed. Lewis R. Gordon and Jane Anna Gordon (Boulder, CO: Paradigm Publishers, 2006). See also Frank Kirkland, "Modernity and Intellectual Life in Black," *The Philosophical Forum* 24, nos. 1–3 (1992–3): 136–65 and Corey D. B. Walker, "Modernity in Black: Du Bois and the (Re)Construction of Black Identity in *The Souls of Black Folk*," *Philosophia Africana* 7, no. 1 (2004): 83–95.

[2] The biographical section of this summary is informed by Charles Lemert, "Anna Julia Cooper: The Colored Woman's Office," in *The Voice of Anna Julia Cooper, Including "A Voice*

mother, Hannah Stanley Hayward, in Raleigh, North Carolina and went to school shortly after the ratification of the Thirteenth Amendment to the US Constitution, which outlawed slavery except for inmates. She was still a child during these events, but took so well to her studies at St. Augustine's Normal School and Collegiate Institute for Free Blacks that she was teaching mathematics to high school students before reaching the age of puberty. Education became her profession for the rest of her life. She was briefly married around the age of nineteen (her exact age was uncertain because of the absence of a birth certificate) to George Cooper, and marriage unfortunately required her to cease teaching, but George Cooper died within two years of the marriage. Cooper never remarried but resumed teaching. She adopted several children throughout the course of her long life, five of whom were the children of her half brother. She spent most of her life in Washington, DC, where, after achieving her bachelor's and master of arts degree from Oberlin College in 1887, she taught at the M Street High School, which became the Laurence Dunbar School for Negroes and Native Americans. She defied convention there by providing the students with an education in the humanities and sciences, which prepared them to go on for liberal arts degrees at some of the nation's most competitive colleges and universities. The general position, advocated by Booker T. Washington (1856–1915), founder of the Tuskegee Institute, was that black youths should receive vocational training. Cooper was outspoken in her rejection of this view, and it soon led to her being attacked by the infamous "Tuskegee machine" of Washington supporters. She was maligned in the DC papers supportive of Washington, which accused her of sexual indiscretion with one of her adopted children. The result was her being fired (non-renewal of her contract) from her post of principal of the school in 1906.

Cooper's response was to teach college courses at Lincoln University in Missouri. She resumed her principalship at the M Street High School in 1912 until her retirement in 1930. In 1915 she commenced part-time graduate study in Romance languages at Columbia University, but had to leave the

from the South" and Other Important Essays, Papers, and Letters, ed. Charles Lemert and Esme Bhan (Lanham, MD: Rowman & Littlefield, 1998), pp. 1–43, and Cooper's autobiographical reflections from *A Voice from the South*. Cooper's doctoral dissertation was translated and edited by Frances Richardson Keller as *Slavery and the French and Haitian Revolutionists. L'Attitude de la France a l'égard de l'esclavage pendant la Révolution* (Lanham, MD: Rowman & Littlefield, 2006).

program because of its one-year residency requirement in New York City, which she could not fulfil because of her parental and teaching duties. She resumed her doctoral studies a decade later at the Sorbonne, which she was able to do while working in the United States since that institution did not have a residency requirement, and earned her doctorate in comparative literature by writing a thesis on the Haitian Revolution entitled "L'Attitude de la France a l'égard de l'esclavage pendant la Révolution."

Cooper did not make much of her activist work, but she is perhaps most known in that arena as one of the organizers of the first Pan-African Congress, which took place in 1901 in London, and for her feminist writing and her work in education. She is without question the most sophisticated thinker on what is known today as black feminist thought from the late nineteenth century into the early twentieth century. Yet, in spite of her achievements, Cooper's intellectual influence emerges more from the last quarter of the twentieth century onward. Thus, although the first forty years of her life were spent in the nineteenth century, her ideas belong more to the debates of the twentieth and twenty-first. African-American philosophy also came to the fore as an area of inquiry in the last quarter of the twentieth century, and so did the set of questions to which Cooper's thought became more relevant than in her own times.

Cooper's most influential work is her book *A Voice from the South*.[3] In that work she articulated the argument that continues to resonate in much black feminist thought, namely, that black women must become agents of their own future, and that much of the health of their community rests on their shoulders because of the burdens they are forced to carry. This argument is advanced through her theory of worth, which she issues in response to racist arguments against the value of black people. The antiblack racist argument is that the absence of black contribution to civilization suggests that humankind could do well without black people. Cooper's response was that worth was a function of what an individual produced in relation to that which was invested in him or her. She pointed out that very little was invested in blacks, and even less in black women. Yet what blacks have produced is enormous. There is not only the slave labor used to build much of the Americas, but also the innovations and strides of black communities under enormously handicapped conditions. By contrast, the amount

---

[3] See Lemert and Bhan, *Anna Julia Cooper*, pp. 51–196.

invested, socially and economically, in the production of whites, especially white men, for their achievements is so costly that it diminishes their over-all worth. Although some achieve much more than was invested in them, more consume than produce. This argument, from her essay "What Are We Worth?"[4] enabled her to advance the importance of a black feminist agenda through the claim that, internal to black communities, much more was invested in black men than black women, but that black women pro-duced more in relation to such investments than did black men because of being laborers who also bore children. In effect, she formulated an effi-ciency theory of human worth. The effects of this theory can be seen today in much black feminist thought, especially the womanist forms, although, unlike Cooper, many of the contemporary theorists have substituted "most oppressed" in the formulation.[5] Cooper, like Marx, was in fact working with a model of alienation that did not require the category of oppres-sion, although subjugation and correlates with slavery were hallmarks of their thought.

Cooper's contributions in education also related to her efficiency theory of value. She saw how her students were able to perform with an education in the humanities and sciences. The exclusion of such students from the wider communities of learning meant that those who were ultimately less valuable were given the opportunity to contribute. For her this meant that the overall potential of education was, in effect, being lowered by racism since genuine competition was being handicapped. One could think of her argument in terms of sports. In the past blacks were kept from competing with whites in sports. The claim was that they were not capable of such competition. Today, it has become more difficult to imagine the reverse: white athletes who can genuinely compete with black ones. Cooper's argu-ment is that a similar phenomenon awaits all aspects of social life; the limitations on performance are more artificial, and one does not really know what communities can contribute unless they have the opportunity to do so.

Cooper's argument has within it an element found in the thought of Friedrich Nietzsche. According to Nietzsche, worth and health are intimately

---

[4] *Ibid.*, pp. 161–87.
[5] See e.g. Jacquelyn Grant, *White Women's Christ and Black Women's Jesus: Feminist Christology and Womanist Response* (Atlanta, GA: Scholars Press, 1989).

related. A healthy individual or community is one that can best handle adversity. Thus, the argument goes, those who are benefiting from an absence of adversity are in fact less healthy than those who have had the experience of overcoming it. We see here a return of the conclusion from Alexander Crummell, that blacks have a reason more for pride than shame in their history, for they are truly a community that has been tested and have been not only able to survive, but also to make contributions of their own to humankind.

W. E. B. Du Bois and the problem of double consciousness

Born in Great Barrington, Massachusetts, W. E. B. Du Bois (1868–1963) is known among Africana academics as the "dean of African-American schol-ars." He is the best known and most written about Africana thinker. He wrote three autobiographies, scores of books, and subsequent biographies and studies have been written on him, many of which have been more obsessed with placing him under the rubric of either a major European thinker or an American and European social movement.[6] Du Bois, how-ever, was a pioneer whose innovations actually placed him in a class by himself. He studied philosophy while an undergraduate at Harvard Univer-sity and, although a gifted student, was discouraged by the independently

---

[6] See e.g. David Levering Lewis, *W. E. B. Du Bois: Biography of a Race, 1868–1919* (New York: H. Holt & Co., 1993); *W. E. B. Du Bois: The Fight for Equality and the American Century, 1919–1963* (New York: H. Holt & Co., 2000); David Levering Lewis (ed.), *W. E. B. Du Bois: A Reader* (New York: H. Holt & Co., 1995); Daniel Agbeyebiawo, *The Life and Works of W. E. B. Du Bois* (Accra: Stephil Print, 1998); Samuel W. Allen, *A Personal Interview of W. E. B. Du Bois* (Boston: Boston University, 1971); William L. Andrews, *Critical Essays on W. E. B. Du Bois* (Boston: G. K. Hall, 1985); Herbert Aptheker, *W. E. B. Du Bois and the Struggle against Racism in the World* (New York: United Nations, 1983); Bernard W. Bell and Emily Grosholz (eds.), *W. E. B. Du Bois on Race and Culture: Philosophy, Politics, and Poetics* (New York: Routledge, 1996); Joseph P. DeMarco, *The Social Thought of W. E. B. Du Bois* (Lanham, MD: University Press of America, 1983); Arnold Rampersad, *The Art and Imagination of W. E. B. Du Bois* (New York: Schocken Books, 1990); and Adolph Reed, Jr., *W. E. B. Du Bois and American Political Thought: Fabianism and the Color Line* (New York: Oxford University Press, 1997). And this is only to name a few. In 2000, *The Annals of the American Academy of Social and Political Science* devoted its March issue of volume 56 to a reprint of and collection of critical essays on his article "The Study of Negro Problems." See also Luc Ngowet's *Phénoménologie de la liberté. Introduction à l'ontologie de W. E. B. Du Bois* (Paris: forthcoming). All this is just a fragment of the work on Du Bois and his thought.

wealthy William James (1842–1910) from pursuing a career in philosophy on the grounds that he could better serve his race through working in the discipline of history. He took James's advice. While studying for the doctorate in history, he also studied in Berlin, since the German universities were considered the premier institutions of the age. His work qualified him for the Dr. Econ. degree at the University of Berlin, which was awarded to him in his later years.[7] After returning to the United States and achieving his doctorate in history, Du Bois embarked on a career that touched nearly every aspect of US academic and political life. In spite of his credentials, he was never hired as faculty at a predominantly white university. He taught first at Wilberforce University and then, after conducting a major ethnographic study in the city of Philadelphia for the University of Pennsylvania, taught at Atlanta University before embarking on a career in public life that included co-organizing the Niagara Movement, the National Association for the Advancement of Colored People, and the first Pan-African Congress, as well as editing *Crisis* magazine, becoming an organizer in international peace movements, and eventually joining the US Communist Party and emigrating from the United States to Ghana, where he died one day before the famous Civil Rights March on Washington, DC, in August 1963. His writings and ethnographic work spanned the scope of many fields and, in the case of sociology, literally created urban ethnography and many of the theoretical foundations of US sociology. Since our concerns are primarily philosophical, I will simply focus on his contribution in that area.

The importance of W. E. B. Du Bois to the study of blacks and the development of black thought in the New World is that he outlined most of the important themes of this area of inquiry since the 1890s. If there is any doubt, a consultation of nearly every text in the field will reveal his influence.[8] Although many concepts have been generated by the work of Du Bois,

---

[7] He had completed his studies early and was denied being awarded the degree because of the objection of one committee member on the ground that he was not in study a sufficient number of years for this prestigious degree. See David Levering Lewis, *W. E. B. Du Bois: Biography of a Race, 1868–1919* (New York: Holt, 1993) and *W. E. B. Du Bois: The Fight for Equality and the American Century, 1919–1963* (New York: Holt, 2000).

[8] A search through anthologies and journals in black studies will reveal just that. For a sample, see *A Companion to African-American Studies*, ed. Lewis R. Gordon and Jane Anna Gordon (Malden, MA: Blackwell, 2006); *The African American Studies Reader*, ed. Nathaniel Norment, Jr. (Durham, NC: Carolina Academics Press, 2001); *Africana Studies: A Disciplinary Quest for Both Theory and Method*, new edn, ed. James Conyers (Jefferson, NC: McFarland & Company, 2005).

I should like here simply to focus on two that have been of great influence on twentieth-century and contemporary Africana thought.

Du Bois recognized that the question of black people was of philosophical importance. He formulated it at first subjectively, in *The Souls of Black Folk* (1903), by asking how it feels to be a problem and, since addressed to a black person, to be black.[9] Though seemingly banal, the question was of great importance since in one sweep it brought an ontological and a methodological problem to the fore. To admit that black people can feel anything was to acknowledge the presence of an inner life with a point of view. Such acknowledgment is crucial for the building of communication, public exchange, and, as one climbs the lists of ascriptions, humanity. The question, then, signals the being of blacks as a human mode of being. But this question of being required explanation or, as Du Bois eventually formulated it, meaning. This question of the relationship of meaning to being enabled Du Bois to pose the classic social-theoretical problem of explanation in the face of freedom: how can one explain (that is, utilize a discourse premised upon determined criteria) a free being (who, in other words, challenges and often transcends determined criteria)?[10] The methodological significance of the question can be understood through the lens of his earlier empirical work on blacks in Philadelphia, that studying black people was not like studying other peoples.[11] Because society presumed blacks to live outside of the framework of peoplehood, their study required breaking through the veil imposed against their humanity. In "The Study of the Negro Problems" he made this clear in terms of the challenges it posed to positivistic science.[12] The methodological implication of the question is, thus, that people should be studied as human beings; but what do we do when the humanity of a group is challenged? We need, in other words, to find a way to study black people without black people becoming problems-in-themselves.

---

[9] The work first came to print in Chicago by A. C. McClurg. References here are to *The Souls of Black Folk*, with introductions by Nathan Hare and Alvin F. Poussaint, revised and updated bibliography (New York: Signet Classic/New American Library, 1969).

[10] See also e.g. W. E. B. Du Bois, "Sociology Hesitant," *boundary 2*, 27, no. 3 (2000): 37–44.

[11] W. E. B. Du Bois, *The Philadelphia Negro: A Social Study*, with an introduction by Elijah Anderson (Philadelphia, PA: University of Pennsylvania Press, 1996).

[12] W. E. B. Du Bois, "The Study of Negro Problems," *The Annals of the American Academy of Political and Social Science* 11 (1898): 1–23. Reprinted in *The Annals of the American Academy of Political and Social Science* 56 (2000): 13–27.

The question of problem-people also raises a theodicean question.[13] Recall that the term is from the conjunction of the Greek words *Zdeus* (which became *deus*, *theus*, and then *theo*) and *dikê* (justice) – the term "theodicy" refers to God's justice or the justice of God. It is an area of inquiry in which one attempts to find an account of the compatibility of an all-good and all-powerful God in a world marked by injustice and evil. Theodicean problems emerge, as the works of John Hick in *Evil and the God of Love* and Kwame Gyekye in *An Essay on African Philosophical Thought* have shown, from any system of thought in which God or a perfect set of gods are the source both of being and value.[14] Most theodicean arguments defend God's goodness as compatible with God's omniscience and omnipotence through an appeal either to our ignorance of God's ultimate plan for us all or through an appreciation of the freedom endowed on us by God. In the first instance, the conclusion is that things only appear bad because serving God's purpose is ultimately good. In the second, injustice and evil are our fault because they are consequences of our free will, which is, in the end, a good thing. In either formulation, God is without culpability for evil and injustice. In the modern age theodicy has paradoxically been secularized. Whereas God once functioned as the object, the rationalization, and the legitimating of an argument, other systems have come into play, such as systems of knowledge and political systems, and they have taken up the void left by God. The clear system of knowledge is modern science and the modes of rationalization it offers. Political systemic rationalization avers an intrinsic goodness and justice of the given political system. We thus see here the persistent grammar of theodicy even in an avowedly secular age. In the context of modern attitudes toward and political treatment of black people, a special kind of theodicean grammar has, however, asserted itself. The appeal to blacks as problem-people is an assertion of their ultimate location outside the systems of order and rationality.[15] The logic is straightforward: a perfect

---

[13] Here is one of the many instances to which I referred in ch. 2.

[14] John Hick, *Evil and the God of Love*, rev. edn (New York: Harper & Row, 1978) and Kwame Gyekye, *An Essay on African Philosophical Thought: The Akan Conceptual Scheme*, rev. edn (Philadelphia, PA: Temple University Press, 1995), pp. 123–8.

[15] For more discussion, see also Nahum Dimitri Chandler, "Originary Displacement," *boundary 2* 27, no. 3 (2000): 249–86; Lewis R. Gordon, *Existentia Africana: Understanding Africana Existential Thought* (New York: Routledge, 2000), ch. 4, "What Does It Mean to be a Problem?"; and Eleni Varikas, *Les rebuts du Monde: Figures du paria* (Paris: Éditions

system cannot have imperfections. Since blacks claim to be contradictions of a perfect system, the imperfection must either be an error in reasoning (mere "appearance") or lie in black people themselves. Blacks become rationalized as the extraneous evil of a just system.

The formation of such systems and their theodicean rationalizations leads to the construction of insiders and outsiders. The "outside" is an invisible reality generated, in its invisibility, as nonexistent. The effect, then, is that a new link with theodicy emerges and the result is the rationalization of people who are inherently justified versus those who are not necessarily people and thus could never be justified under the principles of the systems that form both. The result is, as Du Bois famously observed, the splitting of worlds and consciousness itself according to the norms of US society and its contradictions. He first addresses this conflict as one of "twoness" in which the Negro, as blacks were characterized then, struggled with being part of a Negro nation while trying to become part of the American nations; is, in other words, a Negro American possible?[16] The problem was that "American" was persistently defined as "white" in North America and the rest of the Americas.

Du Bois then rearticulates the relationship of blacks to politics and knowledge in the modern world in *The Souls of Black Folk* and in the section on white folks in *Darkwater* through the lived reality of double consciousness. Discussion of this concept is vast in the secondary literature on Du Bois, which I will not outline here.[17] Instead, I should like simply to focus on the coextensivity of the concept. It manifests itself, in other words, in several

Stock, 2007). Jane Anna Gordon offers development of this insight in her book *Why They Couldn't Wait: A Critique of the Black–Jewish Conflict Over Community Control in Ocean-Hill Brownsville, 1967–1971* (New York: Routledge/Farmer, 2001) and in her essays "Some Reflections on Challenges Posed to the Social Scientific Study of Race," in *A Companion to African-American Studies*, pp. 279–304; "Double Consciousness and the Problem of Political Legitimacy," in *Not Only the Master's Tools: African-American Studies in Theory and Practice*, ed. with introduction by Lewis R. Gordon and Jane Anna Gordon (Boulder, CO: Paradigm Publishers, 2006), pp. 205–26; and "The Gift of Double Consciousness: Some Obstacles to Grasping the Contributions of the Colonized," in *Postcolonialism and Political Theory*, ed. Nalini Persram (Lanham, MD: Lexington Books, 2007), pp. 143–61.

[16] See W. E. B. Du Bois, *The Conservation of the Races* (Washington, DC: Negro Academy Press, 1898).

[17] For a survey of some of these discussions, see Ernest Allen's "On the Reading of Riddles: Rethinking Du Boisian 'Double Consciousness,'" in *Existence in Black: An Anthology of Black Existential Philosophy*, ed. with introduction by Lewis R. Gordon (New York: Routledge,

ways. The first, negative version is of the psychological formation of the self. There, one's self-image is entirely a function of how one is seen by others. The black self becomes, from this interpretation, a white point of view; it is as seen through the eyes of whites. Another version of double consciousness emerges from the double standards of citizenship, where the black individual who is born in a white and even light-skinned, black-majority society discovers that he or she is not fully a citizen, or at least is not treated as or taken seriously as a citizen, by virtue of being racially designated black.[18] Why is being black treated as antipathetic to being an American (in all the Americas) or a European? Although posed in the New World context and in Europe, the question can be extrapolated to Asia and, ironically, Africa. For although there are blacks in Asia, and there have always been dark-skinned people in Asia, the designation of blackness emerges more in Papua New Guinea and Australia through a process that erases the presence of blacks in the rest of Asia and in the Pacific.[19] With regard to Africa, the extension of problematized membership is ironic because there have been and continue to be (black) Africans who do not consider themselves to be black. The lived reality of many Ethiopians was, for instance, one of becoming black. That they are aware of a black identity either imposed upon them or within

---

1997), pp. 49–68. See also Sandra Adell's *Double Consciousness/Double Bind* (Urbana, IL: University of Illinois Press, 1994), Elijah Anderson and Tukufu Zuberi's commemoration issue of *The Annals of the American Academy of Social and Political Science* (March 2000), and Nahum Dimitri Chander, "The Souls of an Ex-White Man: W. E. B. Du Bois and the Biography of John Brown," *CR: The New Centennial Review* 3, no. 1 (2003): 179–95.

[18] This is the question posed, as well, by Paul Gilroy to himself and fellow British blacks in *The Black Atlantic: Double Consciousness and Modernity* (Cambridge, MA: Harvard University Press, 1993). I write "an American society" since blacks in other American societies face the same question except in those countries that are considered black ones such as Jamaica, Haiti, Antigua, and the Bahamas. For them, there is no contradiction between being black and Jamaican, Haitian, Antiguan, or Bahamian. For discussion, see *Latin@s in the World-System: Decolonization Struggles in the Twenty-First Century US Empire*, ed. Ramón Grosfoguel, Nelson Maldonado-Torres, and José David Saldívar (Boulder, CO: Paradigm Publishers, 2005) and *The Other African Americans: Contemporary African and Caribbean Immigrants in the United States*, ed. Yoku Shaw-Taylor and Steven A. Tuch (Lanham, MD: Rowman & Littlefield, 2007). And for European racism against Third World immigrants, see also Paul Hockenos, *Free to Hate: The Rise of the Right in Post-Communist Eastern Europe* (New York: Routledge, 1994).

[19] For discussion, see Talib Y. and F. Samir, "The African Diaspora in Asia," *UNESCO General History of Africa*, vol. III, ed. M. El Fasi; *African Presence in Early Asia*, ed. Runoko Rashidi and Ivan Van Sertima (New Brunswick, NJ: Transaction Publishers, 1985); and Charles Finch, *Echoes of the Old Darkland: Themes from the African Eden* (Decatur, GA: Khenti, 1991).

their ranks means that they, too, face a form of double consciousness; but what makes theirs different is the question of the nation they consider normative. Since they do consider themselves African but see a contradiction between being black and African, the category may here be subverted or demand a different logic than the ones that occupy such African countries as South Africa (where white supremacy has a documented history). Within philosophical circles, the problem becomes more acute since the argument here is that "black" is not indigenous to African cultural identity.[20]

The epistemological dimension of double consciousness emerges from the mainstream approaches to the study of black people. The prevailing view in most disciplines of human study is to treat white people as the standard or norm. The effect is to make whites function as the standard of the real, and as a consequence, knowing or studying only whites becomes the equivalent of studying humanity. In effect, whites become "universal" and non-whites "particular." Since blacks are human beings, this means that their relation to this logic is a constant encounter with a false universal. This means that the black world is more linked to truth than the white world because the black world realizes that the domain over which truth claims can appeal is much larger than the white world, as universal, is willing to allow, admit, or see. All this leads to a phenomenological problem of perception. That double consciousness is a form of consciousness already makes it rich with phenomenological significance. Phenomenology examines reality as constituted by consciousness, where consciousness is understood in its intentional or directed form as always having to be of something. The consciousnesses that manifest themselves in double consciousness are (1) consciousness of how mainstream society sees itself (dominant "reality") and (2) consciousness of its contradictions (subaltern reality). Since to see both is to see the dialectical relationship constitutive of truth, then the first by itself must manifest a form of consciousness that hides itself.

In *Black Reconstruction in America*, Du Bois brings these questions of social contradictions to the study of US history, which, as told by historians who treated black inferiority as axiomatic, was a rationalization of white

---

[20] For discussion, see e.g. V. Y. Mudimbe, *The Invention of Africa: Gnosis, Philosophy, and the Order of Knowledge* (Bloomington, IN: Indiana University Press, 1988) and Nkiru Nzegwu, "Colonial Racism: Sweeping out Africa with Mother Europe's Broom," in *Racism and Philosophy*, ed. Susan E. Babbitt and Sue Campbell (Ithaca, NY: Cornell University Press, 1999), pp. 124–56. We will return to this problem in the chapter on African philosophy below.

supremacy and the curtailment of freedom.[21] The period of reconstruction was an opportunity for history to move forward with a broadening of opportunities available for every human being in the country that was poised to assume world leadership. That project was destroyed by the creation of US apartheid or Jim Crow, and served as a counter case to notions of history as progress. The doubled contradiction here is that a form of anti-freedom, white supremacy and a new kind of capitalism that deepened inequalities worldwide was being touted by the mainstream as progress. Du Bois thus showed that although history was indeed dialectical, it was not necessarily, as Hegel had argued, a resolving, unfolding dialectic of increased freedom. In effect, Du Bois, argues Susan Searls-Giroux, offers an explanation for why movements of increased freedom lead to greater struggles against their elimination in the modern world, namely, that the underlying logic of racism as its governing anthropology, anxiety, and theodicy occludes critical reflection on human possibilities. Du Bois, Searls-Giroux further argues, offers a philosophy of critical historical analysis that can be foundational for a critical pedagogy for radical democratic freedom.[22]

Although there is much more that can be said about Du Bois's thought, our main point, as seen in our discussion of eighteenth- and nineteenth-century Africana philosophical thought, is exemplified here: Du Bois places the philosophical anthropological problem at the forefront with the normative one. We must ask what it means not to be a problem, what kinds of social forces are required for such a transformation, and what kinds of reflection and study are needed to articulate such possibilities.

Fanon's critique of failed dialectics of recognition

Some Africana philosophers have had an impact across the entire spectrum of the field, as did most of the eighteenth- and nineteenth-century

---

[21] W. E. B. Du Bois, *Black Reconstruction in America: 1860–1880* (New York: Atheneum, 1992), originally published in 1935.

[22] Susan Searls-Giroux, "Reconstructing the Future: Du Bois, Racial Pedagogy and the Post-Civil Rights Era," *Social Identities* 9, no. 4 (2003): 563–98, and especially 591–6. See also Reiland Rabaka, *W. E. B. Du Bois and the Problems of the Twenty-First Century: An Essay on Africana Critical Theory* (Lanham, MD: Lexington Books, 2007) and Corey D. B. Walker, *Between Transcendence and History: Theology, Critical Theory, and the Politics of Liberation* (forthcoming), for a developed discussion of the critical theoretical dimensions of Du Bois's thought.

figures discussed in chapter 2.[23] The influence of Frantz Fanon (1925–1961) on African-American, Afro-Caribbean, and African thought is so vast that he counts as one such figure.[24] Although he was Du Bois's junior by nearly sixty years and was outlived by Du Bois by two years, the international impact of their thought was of near equal weight, although Du Bois left many more writings to study. I will discuss Fanon here and then reintroduce him in the next chapters as his role in the development of thought in those regions unfolds.

Fanon left us an extraordinary legacy that includes his being one of the canonical figures of African-American philosophy and one of the actual parents of postcolonial philosophy.[25] There is a paradox in Fanon's being a contributor to any kind of philosophy. This is because, as he reflected in the fifth chapter of *Black Skin, White Masks*, "Reason" had a nasty habit of taking flight whenever he entered a room. Since philosophy is, as Karl Jaspers observed, a long hymn to reason, it follows that it too took flight.[26] Yet Fanon never lost faith as he encountered the paradox of needing it to

---

[23] For a more elaborate discussion of Fanon's thought, see Lewis R. Gordon, "Through the Zone of Nonbeing: A Reading of *Black Skin, White Masks* in Celebration of Fanon's Eightieth Birthday," *The C. L. R. James Journal* 11, no. 1 (2005): 1–43, and Nigel C. Gibson, *Fanon: The Postcolonial Imagination* (Cambridge: Polity Press, 2003).

[24] Like Du Bois, there is a vast secondary literature on Fanon and autobiographical material available. See e.g. Renate Zahar, *Frantz Fanon: Colonialism and Alienation, Concerning Frantz Fanon's Political Theory* (New York: Monthly Review Press, 1974); Irene Gendzier, *Frantz Fanon: A Critical Study* (New York: Vintage, 1974); Alice Cherki, *Frantz Fanon: A Portrait*, trans. Nadia Benabid (Ithaca, NY: Cornell University Press, 2006); *Rethinking Fanon: The Continuing Dialogue*, ed. Nigel Gibson (Amherst, NY: Humanity Books, 1999); and *Fanon: A Critical Reader*, ed. Lewis R. Gordon, T. Denean Sharpley-Whiting, and Renée T. White (Oxford: Blackwell Publishers, 1996).

[25] Although postcolonial literary studies focus more on Edward Said, the author of *Orientalism* (New York: Routledge, 1978), in addition to Gayatri Spivak, author of "Can the Subaltern Speak?" and Homi Bhabha, author of *The Location of Culture* (London: Routledge, 1994), all three reveal much debt to Jacques Derrida and Michel Foucault, both of whom in turn have genealogical links to Frantz Fanon, although the presuppositions of Fanon's thought are different from theirs in that he makes explicit the question and process of decolonization. For discussion see Ato Sekyi-Otu, *Fanon's Dialectic of Experience* (Cambridge, MA: Harvard University Press, 1996) and Gibson, *Fanon: The Postcolonial Imagination*.

[26] "Philosophy through the millennia is like one great hymn to reason – though it continually misunderstands itself as finished knowledge, and declines continually into reasonless understanding," Karl Jaspers, *Philosophy of Existence*, trans. Richard F. Grabau (Philadelphia, PA: University of Pennsylvania Press, 1971), p. 60.

fight against its failures, as we observed in the introduction of this book. He knew, in the end, that his relationship with reason, which he characterized with the capital "R" ("Reason"), required taking it off of its pedestal so that it would not stand in reality's way with false truths of completeness or universality. He thus, in spite of Reason, found a form of reason through which his philosophical reflections emerged. Let us call those reflections anti-colonial philosophy.

Fanon, like Du Bois, was guided by the challenge of freedom and the constraints placed on searching for it in the modern world. His aims led to what I call a teleological suspension of philosophy.[27] By that, I mean that the kind of reason Fanon was fighting against led its practitioners to believe in its absoluteness. When philosophy becomes absolute or "deontological," it loses its own sense of purpose and becomes, like the universal in Søren Kierkegaard's *Fear and Trembling*, below the realm of faith.[28] Since an absolute is higher than a universal, that form of reasoning collapses upon itself by attempting to become greater than itself. But such an attempt would be teleological, and in Kierkegaard's case, the teleological movement involves reaching out to God. Ironically, such reaching out brings one back to the ethical, since God is not evil, and in this sense, one has ironically become more ethical by being willing to transcend ethics for its own sake.[29] Fanon understood that philosophy could best be salvaged by our willingness to transcend it.

Fanon's thought should, however, be understood in terms of the theoretical context from which he was arguing. There are themes in his thought that place him along the genealogical line of thinkers emerging from the ideas of Jean-Jacques Rousseau. One of them is the distinction between liberty and freedom. In the tradition of Anglo-analytical philosophy, and in fact in most Anglo societies, this distinction is difficult to understand. That is

[27] See Lewis R. Gordon, *Disciplinary Decadence: Living Thought in Trying Times* (Boulder, CO: Paradigm Publishers, 2006). See also the fifth chapter of Lewis R. Gordon, *Fanon and the Crisis of European Man: An Essay on Philosophy and the Human Sciences* (New York: Routledge, 1995).

[28] Søren Kierkegaard, *Fear and Trembling* and *Repetition*, ed. and trans. with introduction and notes by Howard V. Hong and Edna H. Hong (Princeton, NJ: Princeton University Press, 1983); see the section "Is There a Teleological Suspension of the Ethical?"

[29] Cf. Calvin O. Schrag, "Note on Kierkegaard's Teleological Suspension of the Ethical," in his *Collected Papers: Betwixt and Between* (Albany, NY: State University of New York Press, 1994), pp. 27–32.

because that tradition focuses almost entirely on liberty. One should think of liberty as what one is able to do without constraints. Liberty, as we saw in our discussion of Frederick Douglass, is something we share with other animals. It is about the presence or absence of constraints. Freedom, however, is about how a human being makes choices and takes responsibility for those choices. Freedom could, then, be manifested even where there is very limited liberty. It is connected, as well, to the virtues (or vices) that one may exemplify in the face of the options available in a given situation. Freedom is always, as well, about being an adult. Children have liberty, but they have little freedom. This is because they are responsible for only some (and, when too young, none) of their choices. There is a dialectical implication to this distinction. One could, for example, in acquiring maximum liberty lose one's freedom. If, for instance, all is permitted, one cannot coherently be responsible for what one has done. This dialectical feature is also ironic. It suggests that we can at times lose by winning and win by losing. Sometimes, one can best fight back by not fighting at all.

The second distinction is between the will in general and the general will. Rousseau argued that any society founded upon the consent of the people faces the possibility of that consent as a majority or a consensus. The mere majority is a function of the will in general. That is where people meet in a self-interested way, with no one necessarily considering the interests of others. In effect, it is a contingent collection of interests, with one interest having more numbers in its support than the others. The general will, however, is not about a collection of interests but about the interest of the collective. It is about the interest of the society, where everyone is understood as a valued member. It involves reason, where one reflects on the overall good, whereas the will in general simply requires rationality or figuring out what is within one's self-interest or how to get what one wants.[30]

The distinction between liberty and freedom is the genealogical source of Fanon's philosophy of human science and social theory, and the distinction

[30] See the classic discussion in Rousseau's *Social Contract*, book II, ch. 3, included in his *The Collected Writings of Rousseau. Vol. IV: Social Contract, Discourse on the Virtue Most Necessary for a Hero, Political Fragments, and Geneva Manuscript*, ed. Robert D. Maters and Christopher Kelly, trans. Judith R. Buh, Roger D. Masters, and Christopher Kelly (Hanover, NH: Dartmouth College / University Press of New England, 1994), pp. 147–9.

between the will in general and the general will is exemplified in much of his political thought.

Fanon has offered several other key foundational concepts. Here are three. The first is sociogenesis. By that, Fanon means that which is created or constructed by the social world. For Fanon, as for most existential phenomenologists, the social world is an achievement of intersubjectivity, which is always a function, at least in our world, of human activities. We can refer to Fanon as an existential phenomenologist because of the forms of arguments he makes, but more historically, he studied with Maurice Merleau-Ponty (1908–1961) during his years at Lyons, and Jean-Paul Sartre (1905–1980) and Karl Jaspers were among his sources of inspiration during his studies at the *lycée*.[31] The existential dimension is connected to Fanon's commitment to agency. He rejects structuralist readings of human beings, and he also rejects those that reduce the human being simply to a mechanistic organism. He wants the human being to be what he calls actional, which requires a world of meaning. A behavioral model locks the human being at the level of a series of effects. Action requires the addition of an "inside," of understanding what is intended. For example, a hand in contact with a shoulder is a behavior that could have many meanings when understood as an action. It could mean, "Wait!," "Listen!," "Are you OK?" or be a gesture of affection. And more dramatic, biologically functioning is a behavior, but living (which is also an interpretation of the French use of the word *existence*) is a meaningful activity.[32] Fanon's work, in this regard, could be considered a fight against nihilism, a goal sought by oppressors for the minds of the oppressed; it is a goal for them to lose meaning, for them to lose faith in alternatives, and for them eventually to give up on the possibility of positive

---

[31] For an updated biography with discussion of Fanon's education see Alice Cherki, *Frantz Fanon: A Portrait*, trans. Nadia Benhabid (Ithaca, NY: Cornell University Press, 2006), especially pp. 15–16.

[32] This central theme of existential philosophy can be found in nearly every existential thinker, including those as varied as Albert Camus and Keiji Nishitani; but it is also a theme in much psychoanalytical work and in the philosophy of culture. For a recent example of the former, connected to Fanon, see Kelly Oliver, *The Colonization of Psychic Space: A Psychoanalytical Social Theory of Oppression* (Minneapolis, MN: University of Minnesota Press, 2004) and for a classic statement of the human world as one of meaning see Ernst Cassirer, *An Essay on Man: An Introduction to a Philosophy of Human Culture* (New Haven, CT: Yale University Press, 1962).

change. Without meaning, their lives would be as the mechanism of things, of tools.

Another concept is epistemological colonization at the methodological level. Here Fanon advances the demand for radical self-reflective thought. Without such a requirement, colonizing forces could move from the focus of discussion to infecting the mode of presenting thought itself. If methods have been colonized, then the outcomes of inquiry could become affirmations of colonialism. We see Fanon's phenomenology coming to the fore here, for what is this form of critique but a suspension of methodological claims, of making method itself an object of inquiry whose ontological status must be suspended? We can call this the Fanonian phenomenological reduction.

And third, Fanon offers his own approach to psychoanalysis through the introduction of a discourse on failures. Here he is being phenomenological, psychoanalytical, and dialectical. The phenomenological point pertains to the study of human beings, which he says in the second chapter of *Black Skin, White Masks*, is not identical to botany and mathematics – namely, natural science and analytical or deductive systems. It is psychoanalytical because it raises questions of what is repressed by the declaration of failure. It is not, after all, a concept that makes sense as a feature of nature or being-itself without appealing to a form of ancient teleological naturalism such as one finds in Aristotle.[33] Nothing intrinsically fails. It simply is. That failure is a function of the human world means that it must be connected to notions of meaning and purpose. Fanon's point is that we should not simply dismiss failures but try to understand them; we should try to learn both about what failure signifies and what it means to us who interpret it as such. And finally, it is dialectical because it involves examining contradictions, wherein learning constitutes the forward movement or consequence of such an engagement. Fanon offers several contributions to philosophy from these premises, the most notable of which is the advancement of postcolonial philosophy itself.

The sociogenic analysis is the first contribution. It offers much for philosophy of liberation since the movement from bondage to liberation would

---

[33] Aristotelian teleology emerges in a variety of his works, but for this discussion *On the Generation of Animals* offers an excellent portrait.

make no sense without the subjects of liberation being able to affect the social world in which their identities have been forged. At the heart of sociogenesis is the foundation of what today is often called "constructivity." For construction to occur something has to be able to change from one form to another. The point about social meaning, however, is that although the change may not necessarily be biophysical or simply physical, it is paramount that the change is meaningful. In short, Fanon announces the relationship between meaning and the constitution of forms of life, and that a central role of liberation thought is the reconfiguration of concepts, including those through which practice can become praxis or freedom-constituting activity. The addition of freedom raises the question of the distinction between freedom and liberty. If freedom is a function of meaning, and if human beings, as meaning-constituting subjects, are the manifestations of freedom, what, then, is coherent about bondage? The argument here suggests a dialectical movement as follows: bondage is an imposition on freedom/human beings with the aim of creating nonhuman physical objects – namely, animals that could obey complex commands. The reassertion of the humanity of such beings is their call for liberation, which requires the coordination of freedom and liberty. Thus, the dialectic becomes movements from freedom to bondage to liberation. The middle stage requires more than a curtailment of liberty since the goal is also to make the subject give up on freedom.

Although the social world is paramount, a danger in the social world is the subordination of the individual to futile conditions of meaning. One example is the dialectics of recognition. Fanon argues that it is futile for colonized and racially oppressed peoples to seek their liberation through seeking recognition from their colonizers and racial oppressors. In doing so, they will be caught in a logic that props up their oppressor as the standard of human value. Fanon often speaks of this in terms of narcissism, where there is a demand for a deceiving mirror image. It is an effort to force the oppressor to become one's mirror, and the effort would require making oneself identical to the oppressor. The situation is a failure on two levels. First, it is a lie. As long as the oppressor is the standard, then the demand for recognition leads to acts of imitation, of never being the standard. Second, its achievement would logically increase the world of oppressors, unless everyone achieved such a status, which would render oppression meaningless except as a search for those to oppress. It would, in other words, also be neurotic.

In *Black Skin, White Mask* Fanon shows that the sciences of the human being offered by the West offer the pretense of universality and a problematic claim to ontology. Appealing to sociogenesis he shows that the colonial condition displaces each of these sciences by imposing their limits. Take, for example, Lacanian psychoanalysis. The role of men and women is displaced in the colonial setting, where there are men of color who seek recognition from white men. Thus, one could not properly say that concepts of lack and castration only produce sexual identities and roles as ontologically basic. A black man seeking affirmative words of white recognition in the hope of escaping blackness could only be explained by the social forces that intervened. In effect Fanon is advancing an argument first introduced by W. E. B. Du Bois in *The Souls of Black Folk*, which is that blacks often emerge as a problem at the epistemological and political levels. Because the systems lay claim to ontological validity, there must be something wrong with those who do not "fit" them. Such people become "problems." Du Bois's and Fanon's point is that there is nothing intrinsically wrong with such people. There is something wrong with the social systems in which they live. Think, for instance, of trying to figure out why one's slave is "unhappy." It is the aim of creating "happy slaves" that is problematic. In fact one could argue that the resistance of blacks and indigenous people to such a form of assimilation is healthy. But still there are cases in which ordinary explanations of the unhappiness of subjects of color fail, simply because the mechanisms of explanation require not addressing the notion of a sociogenic explanation. And therein awaits much error.

Fanon also demonstrated the limits of the Self–Other dialectic in colonial and racialized environments. That dialectic is properly an ethical one. At its heart is the possibility of symmetry – the Self that sees another as Other is also seen by that other Self as its Other. In short there is a Self–Other and Other–Self relation in which reciprocity shines. But colonial and racist settings only set that relationship as one between colonizers or members of the dominating race. Because the colonized and racially denigrated experience the Self–Other relationship with each other and do not have the imposition of the master's inferiority on them (otherwise, he or she would not be "master"), then they could imagine the master as another human being or at least one who thinks he or she is more. But the problem is that the colonizer/master does not encounter another human being in the lower depths. Thus for him or her there is no possibility of an equal relationship between those beings and his- or herself. The relations for the colonizer/master, then, are Self–Other and non-self-and-non-others. Literally, there is no one there, only "things" that stand apart from the world of the colonizers and are racially inferior. As a matter of praxis, then, decolonizing struggles and those against racial oppression do not begin on ethical but on peculiarly political premises of constructing a genuine Self–Other relationship through which ethical relations can become possible. A problem that emerges, however, is that politics also requires the elevation of those who are "nothings" to the level of "people." The struggle here, then, is a conflict with politics as an aim through which ethical relations can emerge. The dialectic, echoing the one on liberation, becomes one from war or violence to politics to ethics. A more stable, humane environment is needed, in other words, for ethical life.

The critique of presuming the presence of a Self–Other dialectic leads to a critique of normative political theory. For such theory, most represented by modern liberalism, the claim is that it is about theorizing what should be, but the thought in fact presupposes the very political reality it needs to construct for its condition of possibility. To put it differently, for those who rule, ethics needs to precede politics since it presupposes an already just and humane, although often hidden, environment as the *de facto* context of its inquiry into what ought to be. Those who are oppressed regard the appeal to ethics as begging the question of the relevance of good will and argue for the need to shift the conditions of rule, to engage in politics, before addressing an ethics. Failure to do so would have the conservative consequence of preserving the colonial and racist condition. And worse, one may discover at the end of a political process that some oughts are no longer viable; they face no chance, in other words, of any longer becoming a lived reality.

From the previous two arguments Fanon argues that the sociogenic problem is that there is no coherent notion of normality for colonized and racialized subjects. To repeat, the goal of colonialism is the achievement of the "happy slave," a condition that is, patently, abnormal.

Fanon also argues, from his critique of prioritizing ethics, that decolonization is a violent phenomenon. This is so because ethics, in such efforts, has been suspended. Where ethics is suspended, all is permitted. And in that sphere of permissiveness is violence. What is more, because the consent of the oppressed has been rendered irrelevant, then the process becomes, in their lived reality, one of violation or an unjust ushering in of the future.

These ideas, wedded to some of the Rousseauian premises mentioned above, inform Fanon's social and political theory.[34] This makes sense, as well, because of the genealogical political line from Rousseau through to Kant, Hegel, Marx, and on to Sartre in the European tradition and its manifestations in the Caribbean from the Haitian revolution through to Anténor Firmin, C. L. R. James (1901–1989), Aimé Césaire, and, in the conjunction of the two lines, Fanon. Consider the distinction between the will in general and the general will. Fanon makes the distinction, in *Les Damnés de la terre* (1961), between nationalism and national consciousness. The former involves members of ethnic groups collapsing into the interests of their community over all others, and its logic, premised upon sameness, has a sliding scale infinitesimally to the self. At the end, nationalism and self-interest follow the same logic, and the result is the will in general – just a matter of which collective of interests will prevail over other collectives of interests by sheer number. But national consciousness always transcends selfishness. This is not to say that it must erase the individual. It is to recognize that an individual makes no sense outside of such a social world and that a social world makes no sense without distinct individuals. Together, they are demanded by Fanon's argument to make a transition from instrumental rationality to reflective reason, from thinking only about hypothetical means to reflecting on valued ends.

Fanon's postcolonial social and political philosophy then comes to the fore in his discussion of the leadership that emerges through processes of decolonization. He argues that those who are most suited for the process of decolonization are not necessarily (and often not so) suited for the process of postcolonization. Whereas the dialectic in colonialism is between colonizers and colonized, what follows is not postcolonialism but neocolonialism where the leadership fails to build the infrastructure of the nation (national consciousness). Instead, capital becomes the mediation of

---

[34] For more on this connection, see Jane Anna Gordon and Neil Roberts (eds.), *Creolizing Rousseau: A Symposium*, special issue of *The C. L. R. James Journal* (Fall 2007).

relationships between former colonizers and the new state. The new dialectic, then, is between the so-called "postcolonial bourgeoisie" and the people. The actual dialectic of anti-colonial struggles for Fanon, then, is a movement from colonialism to neocolonialism to postcolonialism.

Finally, but not exclusively, Fanon argues that the task of the theorist is to formulate new concepts by and through which, in a dialectical critique, the people could struggle forth to construct a new humanity or their liberation.[35]

The works of Cooper, Du Bois, and Fanon have stimulated many movements in Africana philosophy, but in no place has their combined influence been more stark than in North America, where they generated several philosophical movements, to the discussion of which let us now turn.

---

[35] Fanon brings the connections between his text and *L'Internationale* (1871), the poem by Eugène Edine Pottier from which the title, *Les damnés de la terre*, is drawn and which parallels the conclusion. Observe the first line of the first stanza, *"Debout, les damnés de la terre"* ("Arise, damned of the earth!"), and the last four lines of the sixth, *"C'est la lutte finale / Groupons-nous, et demain / L'Internationale / Sera le genre humain"* ("It's the final struggle / Let's gather, and tomorrow / The International / Will be humankind"). Fanon's treatment is not imitation but reformulation through evocation since his version transcends the reductionism of a proletariat-only politics. His intervention was mediated by thought on revolution in the Africana context, which included the Haitian poet Jacques Rouman's adaptation of the poem, in his book of verse *Bois-d'ébène* (Port-au-Prince, Haiti: Imp. H. Deschamps, 1945). The translations are mine.

4 Africana philosophical movements in the United States and Britain

Africana philosophy in North America and Europe is primarily a tale of struggles in the United States and Britain. Although there is a contingent whose academic credentials were acquired at Canadian universities, no Africana philosophical movement has developed there. The creative work in the anglophone world is read through the lens of the United States, which is often presupposed by the term "African America." I will therefore focus this discussion on African America in dialogue with Britain. It should be borne in mind that the thought discussed in this context is multinational, which is a continued legacy from the nineteenth century. The approaches include pragmatism and prophetic pragmatism, analytical philosophy, Afro-feminism, Afrocentrism, Afro-postmodernism, Afro-poststructuralism, African-American existentialism and phenomenology.

There is much debate over the genealogical location of African-American pragmatism. Because of their association with William James, perhaps the most vociferous proponents of all the classical US pragmatists, W. E. B. Du Bois and Alain Locke (1886–1954) are often associated with pragmatism. It was my contention in the section on Du Bois that he was an independent thinker whose focus on consciousness suggests a more phenomenological and dialectical reading than is often afforded in the pragmatist tradition, which focuses more on experience. Some scholars contend that Du Bois had a pragmatist strain in his efforts at historical social transformation, as Cornel West argues.[1] A problem with this view, however, is that it would make all of the Africana philosophical tradition pragmatic since one of the elements outlined in chapter 3 is the quest for liberation through historical social transformation. Recall that we had identified elements of

---

[1] Cornel West, *The American Evasion of Philosophy: A Genealogy of Pragmatism* (Madison, WI: University of Wisconsin Press, 1989).

(1) philosophical anthropology, (2) liberation and social transformation, and (3) reflective critique on the role of reason itself and its relation to the first two as its themes.

Alain Locke, in similar kind, addressed these elements in the course of his career. A native of Philadelphia, he studied philosophy at Harvard and became the first African-American Rhodes scholar. Although the scholarship offered a right of admission to the colleges at Oxford, five refused him on racial grounds. A then new college, Hertford College, admitted him, and he went on to study in Berlin and then, after teaching as an assistant professor of English and philosophy at Howard University, returned to Harvard where he achieved his doctorate in philosophy in 1918. His dissertation, advised by Ralph Barton Perry (1876–1957), was entitled "Problems of Classification in Theory and Value." Locke had wanted to work with his mentor Josiah Royce (1855–1916), whom he admired for, among other things, being the only major white academic philosopher of his day to have written a critique of racism, but Royce had died while Locke was preparing his prospectus.[2] Locke was also awarded a full professorship in philosophy at Howard University in 1918 and subsequently became chairperson of that department until his death in 1954. His contributions were primarily institutional, although his philosophical ideas stand in their own right. Institutionally the majority of African Americans who studied philosophy or the African Americans with whom they had studied philosophy had some relationship with him. But more, he is perhaps best known for his work on aesthetics and culture, and most notably for his leadership in what became known as the Harlem Renaissance. The spirit of this movement was exemplified in his important essay "The New Negro," which became the introduction to the famous anthology that bore its name.[3] That association has led to Locke being known more as a cultural critic than a philosopher.

[2] For Josiah Royce on racism, see his *Race Questions, Provincialism, and Other American Problems* (New York: Macmillan, 1908), and for recent discussion of that work see Dwayne Tunstall, *Encountering Josiah Royce's Ethico-Religious Insight* (New York: Fordham University Press, forthcoming). For a short biography of Alain Locke see Leonard Harris's "Introduction," in *The Philosophy of Alain Locke: Harlem Renaissance and Beyond*, ed. Leonard Harris (Philadelphia, PA: Temple University Press, 1989), pp. 1–27. Harris is also at work on a full-length biography of Locke for the University of Chicago Press.

[3] Alain Locke (ed.), *The New Negro: Voices of the Harlem Renaissance*, introduced by Arnold Rampersad (New York: Touchstone, 1992). The essay "The New Negro" appears on pp. 3–18. The anthology was originally brought to print in New York in 1925 by Albert and Charles Boni Inc.

Locke's views on philosophical anthropology, social transformation, and philosophical reason can be found in his writings on value and on race. In his essay "Values and Imperatives," he argues that the quest for value-free conceptions of human phenomena is futile because it demands using as a proper venue for human activities a world in which human beings cannot actually live. Although Locke is often interpreted by Locke scholars in terms of pragmatism, especially since he was in dialogue with such pragmatists as John Dewey (1859–1952) and Sidney Hook (1902–1989), it is nevertheless striking that he built his analysis from a rejection of notions of disembodied consciousness.[4] Given the situating of the body as a point of departure Locke was critical of monistic and absolutist views of values. Instead he defended a form of pluralism through which human beings worked out their differences in an active negotiation of political life and cultural creativity.[5] Such cultural pluralism would be a constant reminder of human diversity, and in that regard of the possibility of living with difference instead of against it. Locke's emphasis on culture and community is perhaps connected to the Hegelian phenomenological thought of his mentor, Josiah Royce.[6] For Hegel, Royce, and Locke it was incoherent to speak of the isolated, individual human being. The human being must be understood through the community in which he or she lives, and that community is not locked in a permanent set of values but a living, dialectically evolving one.

Prophetic and other recent forms of African-American pragmatism

Alain Locke's view of thinking through living, dialectically transformative social roles is later taken up by Cornel West in his philosophy of prophetic pragmatism. This philosophy, according to West, finds its inspiration in the historically informed thought of John Dewey. West articulates Dewey's

---

[4] See "Values and Imperatives," in Harris, *The Philosophy of Alain Locke*, pp. 31–50. For recent essays on Locke as a pragmatist, see *The Critical Pragmatism of Alain Locke*, ed. Leonard Harris (Philadelphia, PA: Temple University Press, 1999).

[5] See e.g. "Pluralism and Intellectual Democracy," "Cultural Relativism and Ideological Peace," and "Pluralism and Ideological Peace," in Harris, *The Philosophy of Alain Locke*, pp. 41–66, 67–78, and 95–102.

[6] See e.g. Josiah Royce, *The Religious Aspect of Philosophy* (Boston, MA: Houghton Mifflin, 1885), *The World and the Individual* (Gloucester, MA: Peter Smith, 1976), *The Philosophy of Loyalty* (Nashville, TN: Vanderbilt University Press, 1995).

intellectual genealogy from the period of classical pragmatism, which Dewey shared with Charles Sanders Peirce (1839–1914) and William James. Had West also included Dewey's influences prior to his association with pragmatism he would have had to contend with the foundations of Dewey's thought in Hegel's as well through his mentor at the Johns Hopkins University, George Sylvester Morris (1840–1889), and the work of Dewey and Morris at the University of Michigan, which engaged the work of Hegelian idealism, especially through the thought of the British philosopher Thomas Hill Green (1836–1882). Dewey was not yoked to Hegelian idealism, of which he became a critic, but there are elements of Hegel's thought such as a focus on individuals in community and the dynamic potential of dialectical inquiry that remained. In effect, then, both Locke and West (by way of Dewey) show European genealogical links to Hegel, although, as we shall see, that relationship is not as determinative as it might at first appear.

West argued, following Richard Rorty (1931–2007), who in turn was following Jacques Derrida, that philosophy is a special kind of writing.[7] In the United States such philosophical writing, West insists, is pragmatism, because it is supposedly the kind of avowed position that unfolds from philosophical writings that are supposedly indigenous to the nation. In *Prophesy, Deliverance!*, he advocates African-American philosophy as a conjunction of pragmatism with Marxism and prophetic Christianity.[8] Since African Americans are Americans, it follows, he argues, that they must engage America's indigenous philosophy. Since, as well, the problems faced by African Americans are social and historical, then the critical, socially engaged and historical work of Deweyan pragmatism, as opposed to the more abstract kinds, will be useful to African Americans. An objection could be raised here that West presents a rather distorted image of Deweyan pragmatism, for Dewey wrote on as many abstract themes as he did concrete and social historical ones. He wrote books on logical thinking, for instance, and his work on experience and science could rival his "abstract" contemporaries. Dewey, however, did call for a "reconstruction" of philosophy and

---

[7] See such books by Richard Rorty as *Philosophy and the Mirror of Nature* (Princeton, NJ: Princeton University Press, 1980) and *Contingency, Irony, and Philosophy* (Cambridge: Cambridge University Press, 1989).

[8] Cornel West, *Prophesy, Deliverance! An Afro-American Revolutionary Christianity*, anniversary edn (Louisville, KY: Westminster John Knox Press, 2002).

for its relevance in human affairs under the rubric of what he first called "experimentalism" and then "instrumentalism," his name for his brand of pragmatism, which gives credence to West's interpretation of his work.[9] Marxism, West argues, is pertinent to a revolutionary Afro-American philosophy of liberation because of its egalitarian ethic and commitment to the fight against poverty and capitalist exploitation, both of which are crucial to the upliftment of black populations. Prophetic Christianity brings both pragmatism and Marxism together in its critical stand against power echoed from the lives of ancient Hebrew prophets and exemplifies West's focus on an Afro-American revolutionary Christianity.

I have argued in "The Unacknowledged Fourth Tradition" that West is in fact appealing to more than three sources of African-American philosophy.[10] He argues in *Prophesy, Deliverance!*, for example, that a viable philosophy must present resources in the struggle against dread, despair, and disease, none of which are pragmatist, Marxist, or prophetic Christian but clearly existentialist formulations, which, in his citations, he acknowledges in explicit appeals to Søren Kierkegaard and Anton Chekhov (1860–1904).[11] But more, in his discussion of traditional black responses to antiblack racism, after revealing the flaws in the exceptionalist, assimilationist, and marginalist traditions, he advances what he calls the African-American humanist tradition, which he sees in jazz music and in such authors as Ralph Ellison (1913–1994) and James Baldwin (1924–1987). His articulation of these responses reveals an independent black intellectual tradition, although West does not acknowledge this in the course of his argument.[12] More, that he defends the black humanist tradition as a viable means of resistance and resource

[9] See e.g. John Dewey, *Essays in Experimental Logic* (Chicago, IL: University of Chicago Press, 1916); *How We Think* (Boston, MA: D. C. Heath & Co., 1910); *Logic: The Theory of Inquiry* (New York: Holt, 1938); and *Reconstruction in Philosophy*, enlarged edn with a new introduction by the author (Boston, MA: Beacon Press, 1948).

[10] See Lewis R. Gordon, "The Unacknowledged Fourth Tradition: An Essay on Nihilism, Decadence, and the Black Intellectual Tradition in the Existential Pragmatic Thought of Cornel West," in *Cornel West: A Critical Reader*, ed. George Yancy (Malden, MA: Blackwell Publishers, 2001), pp. 38–58.

[11] See *Prophesy, Deliverance!* and *The Cornel West Reader*, new edn, ed. Cornel West (New York: Basic Civitas Books, 2000).

[12] This philosophical tradition is well documented in the work of Leonard Harris, George Yancy, Tommy Lott, and John Pittman. See *Philosophy Born of Struggle: Afro-American Philosophy since 1917*, ed. Leonard Harris (Dubuque, IW: Kendall/Hunt, 1983), which appears in a radically different second edition in 2000; (George Yancy (ed.), *African American*

for creative explorations of liberating possibilities raises questions of the necessity of the Marxist and prophetic Christian pragmatist foundations of his argument, especially since the one he ultimately defends as the most viable response is a predominantly secular humanist position embodied by Ralph Ellison and many jazz musicians (although the category of secular might be stretched here, given our earlier discussion of theological and religious grammars). Jazz musicians such as Duke Ellington and John Coltrane are so clearly informed by their spiritual outlooks on the world, which was strongly Afro-Christian in the lives of both men, that West's main point may not be affected by this criticism.[13] By the end of the book, West defends his case for the religious community through averring the rhetorical genius of a set of brilliant black preachers as sites of inspiration. And in his later work, as Marxism drops by the wayside, one finds a form of trenchant US Americanism coming to the fore.[14] In effect, West's prophetic pragmatism increasingly collapses into a form of optimistic Americanism, in which the best of American values await their fruition.

Prophetic pragmatism is not the only recent form of pragmatism. Leonard Harris, for instance, has built his pragmatism on the thought of Alain Locke. For Harris the central task has been to articulate a theory of social identities on which Locke's theory of cultural pluralism can be built.[15] As

---

Philosophers: 17 Conversations (New York: Routledge, 1998)); and Tommy L. Lott and John P. Pittman (eds.), *A Companion to African-American Philosophy* (Malden, MA: Blackwell Publishers, 2003).

[13] See e.g. James H. Cone, *The Spirituals and the Blues: An Interpretation*, reprint edn (Maryknoll, NY: Orbis Books, 1992). See also Cone's student Josiah Ulysses Young, III, *A Pan-African Theology: Providence and the Legacies of the Ancestors* (Trenton, NJ: Africa World Press, 1992) and, of course, Howard Thurman, *Deep River and the Negro Spiritual Speaks of Life and Death* (Richmond, VA: Friends Press, 1990).

[14] This is the path taken from *The American Evasion of Philosophy: A Genealogy of Pragmatism* (Madison, WI: University of Wisconsin Press, 1989) through to *Race Matters* (Boston: Beacon Press, 1993) and most recently, *Democracy Matters: Winning the Fight Against Imperialism* (New York: Penguin, 2004). For a criticism of this path, see "The Unacknowledged Fourth Tradition," in *Cornel West: A Critical Reader* and Nelson Maldonado-Torres, "Toward a Critique of Continental Reason: Africana Studies and the Decolonization of Imperial Cartographies in the Americas," in *Not Only the Master's Tools: African-American Studies in Theory and Practice*, ed. Lewis R. Gordon and Jane A. Gordon (Boulder, CO: Paradigm Publishers, 2006), pp. 51–84. Cf. also Clarence Sholé Johnson, *Cornel West and Philosophy* (New York: Routledge, 2002).

[15] Harris makes this case over the course of a series of essays. See, especially, his preface to *The Critical Pragmatism of Alain Locke*, pp. xi–xxv; his afterword to *The Philosophy of Alain Locke*, "Rendering the Subtext: Subterranean Deconstructive Project," pp. 279–89.

well, most recently pragmatism has emerged in African-American political religious thought, cultural criticism, and race theory. Victor Anderson
and Paul C. Taylor, for instance, have advocated cultural criticism, in the
pragmatist vein, as a way of addressing contemporary problems of citizenship faced by African Americans.[16] This question of citizenship is also taken
up by Eddie Glaude, Jr., whose work offers an integration of Dewey's and
African-American thought to form, in effect, a historical cultural epistemology through which sites of uncertainty are defended through a rejection of *a priori* responses to social problems.[17] The main object of Glaude's
criticism is messianic African-American politics, which he regards as a
form of politics that has enmeshed discussions of social transformation
of the lives of black Americans into a model shackled by the search for
black representation, often in the form of a charismatic leader, without
the infrastructural conditions for social change.[18] According to Glaude,
messianic politics, by which he means black politics of the 1960s, does
not fit the subsequent "post-soul" moment. What is needed, Glaude concludes, is political imagination, which, he argues, means being attuned
to what actually makes a difference in the lives of people in the contemporary world. This politics requires dealing with the tragic, and often
absurd, dimensions of the world we live in, which Glaude refers to as a
world governed by the blues. The blues do not emerge here as a sexy
dimension of a serious work in social criticism but as the core of what

---

[16] Victor Anderson, *Against Ontological Blackness* (New York: Continuum, 1999) and *Pragmatic
Theology: Negotiating the Intersection of an American Philosophy of Religion and Public Theology*
(Albany, NY: State University of New York Press, 1999); and Paul Taylor, *The Concept of Race*
(Cambridge: Polity, 2004). For a critical discussion of Anderson's work, see Lewis R. Gor-
don, *Existentia Africana: Understanding Africana Existential Thought* (New York: Routledge,
2000), pp. 145–52.

[17] Eddie S. Glaude, Jr., *In a Shade of Blue: Pragmatism and the Politics of Black America* (Chicago,
IL: University of Chicago Press, 2007).

[18] This is an argument that speaks to the entire black diaspora, as witnessed by E. Franklin
Frazier's exploration of it in *Black Bourgeoisie: The Book That Brought the Shock of Self-
Revelation to Black America* (New York: The Free Press, 1997), originally published in Paris,
France by Librairie Plon in 1955 as *Bourgeoisie noire* and translated into English by Fra-
zier and published by the Free Press in 1957, and Fanon's trenchant criticism of the
postcolonial bourgeoisie in *The Wretched of the Earth*, trans. Constance Farrington, with
a preface by Jean-Paul Sartre (New York: Grove Press, 1963) and, more recently, trans.
Richard Philcox, with a foreword by Homi Bhabha and preface by Jean-Paul Sartre (New
York: Grove Press, 2004). We will look at this theme in subsequent chapters of this book,
so I will only raise it here.

it means to be sober in the face of life's travails. It is, in other words, an adult sensibility to social problems. Although he does not characterize it this way, which is my formulation from the black existential tradition, he ultimately regards pragmatism as a mature engagement with social reality.

Tommy Shelby has also advanced the pragmatist argument both against and for black solidarity. While rejecting the form of black solidarity that would entail a loyalty among blacks for each other over all others, he advocates what he calls "pragmatic solidarity," which is the kind that is used in the fight against antiblack racism. This form of solidarity does not exclude the participation of non-blacks.[19] And working from a pragmatist perspective, Anna Stubblefield has argued for a conception of race as referring to aggregates that function more like families, people with a common connection, although having variation over time, while building the case for an ethics of racial justice through arguing against prioritizing ontological claims about race.[20]

I should here like to make several criticisms of the pragmatist project, especially prophetic pragmatism. The thesis that pragmatism is the indigenous philosophy of the United States and the earliest American philosophy is, quite simply, false. Philosophy existed in North American thought more than a century before either the lectures of Ralph Waldo Emerson (1803–1882) in Cambridge or Peirce's writings on clarifying ideas. The error comes from treating only secular or naturalistic thought as properly philosophical. The thought of Jonathan Edwards (1703–1758) is an early instance of reflection on problems of existence in the North American colonial context, as George Cotkin has shown.[21] And along with Edwards, we could ask about the thought of black, brown, and red religious thinkers on subjects ranging from metaphysics to ethics or on problems of philosophical anthropology in light of colonization and racialized slavery.[22] Further, it

---

[19] See Tommie Shelby, *We Who Are Dark: The Philosophical Foundations of Black Solidarity* (Cambridge, MA: Harvard University Press, 2005).

[20] Anna Stubblefield, *Ethics Along the Color Line* (Ithaca, NY: Cornell University Press, 2005).

[21] See George Cotkin, *Existential America* (Baltimore, MD: Johns Hopkins University Press, 2003). See also Leonard Harris, Scott L. Pratt, and Anne Waters (eds.), *American Philosophies: An Anthology* (Malden, MA: Blackwell, 2001), which offers a richer conception of American philosophical thought than those offered by most scholarship on this subject.

[22] See e.g. Corey D. B. Walker, *Between Transcendence and History: Theology, Critical Theory, and the Politics of Liberation.* For Native American thought, see e.g. Wub-E-Ke-Niew,

is not only the characterization of the American in African American that needs interrogation, but also the African. Prophetic pragmatists write as though Christianity were the only religious resource for reflection available to African Americans. That approximately 30 percent of slaves brought from Africa to the New World were Muslim, that there are Afro-Jewish communities, and that the Nation of Islam can attest to effective recruitment among the black underclass and prison populations suggest that Christianity does not stand as the only option except for people who are believing Christians or those scholars who can only see black Americans in Christian terms.[23] There are, as well, secular blacks to consider. This question of the identity of African Americans makes it all the more crucial to ask why the African in African American is not added to Cornel West's triumvirate of pragmatism, Marxism, and prophetic Christianity. After all, even where religious, most African Americans practice some form of creolized African version of the European and Middle Eastern religions to which they adhere.

The question of creolization raises the additional task of formulating a more accurate depiction of African Americans since they are, perhaps, one of the most mixed racial groups in the New World. Moreover, since African Americans were never sedentary but instead always a migrating population as a consequence of persecution and poverty, the black groups that make up African America should be understood in terms of the constant flow back and forth through the Caribbean and South America

---

We Have the Right to Exist: A Translation of Aboriginal Indigenous Thought: The First Book Ever Published from an Ahnishinahbaeo Jibway Perspective (New York: Black Thistle Press, 1995); Vine Deloria, *God Is Red: A Native View of Religion* (Golden, CO: Fulcrum Publishing, 1994); Lewis Hanke, *Aristotle and the American Indians* (Bloomington, IN: Indiana University Press, 1959); and Robert Allen Warrior, *Tribal Secrets: Recovering American Indian Intellectual Traditions* (Minneapolis, MN: University of Minnesota Press, 1995).

[23] For further explorations of Islam and the category of the Afro-Arab, see Allan D. Austin, *African Muslims in Antebellum America: Transatlantic Stories and Spiritual Struggles* (New York: Routledge, 1997) and Ronald A. T. Judy, *(Dis)Forming the American Canon: African-Arabic Slave Narratives and the Vernacular*, with a foreword by Wahneema Lubiano (Minneapolis, MN: University of Minnesota Press, 1993). The literature around Jews is mired by a tendency to erase the existence of Afro-Jews in ways that are not as sustainable in Islam because of the strong international appearance of darker Islamic communities such as those found today in north and central Africa. For the North American context, see Walter Isaac, "Locating Afro-American Judaism: A Critique of White Normativity," in Lewis R. Gordon and Jane Anna Gordon (eds.), *A Companion to African-American Studies* (Malden, MA: Blackwell Publishing, 2006), pp. 512–42.

and Africa. Oddly enough, in spite of the many criticisms unleashed by pragmatist philosophers against the unity of the term, black seems to encompass this diasporic group more than the terms "Afro-American" and "African American."[24] But finally there is the pragmatist preference for criticism over grand theory. Prophetic pragmatism draws much from postmodern poststructural thought, in which theory is rejected as a master narrative. Only criticism remains. The problem with this view, however, is that this argument is advanced in the service of liberation and social transformation. It entails, literally, building the future only on a negative relationship with the present and the past. Ironically, the classical pragmatists would support this criticism since they not only engaged in social criticism but also constructed new ideas on which to build the future.

Black feminist and womanist thought

The question of building a future is strongly focused on in African-American feminist thought, whose genealogical foundations are from at least two primary sources. The first is the thought of Anna Julia Cooper and the public intellectual work of women, particularly black women, such as Sojourner Truth (Isabella Baumfree) and Maria Stewart from the early nineteenth century to women such as Mary Church Terrell and Ida B. Wells-Barnett (1862–1931) at the beginning of the twentieth century. I use the expression "black feminist thought" because much of this area of research has been antipathetic to the idea of a black feminist philosophy. Here, the task has been to articulate the lives of black women as a critique of racism and sexism and as inspiration for the construction of an ethics or politics of social transformation in which racism and patriarchy are destroyed in the interest of a feminist future. This line first took three paths. The first

[24] This is a point on which even conservative blacks agree. See John McWhorter, "Why I'm Black, Not African American," *Los Angeles Times* (September 8, 2004): manhattan-institute.org/html/_latimes-why_im_black.htm. See, as well, Sylvia Wynter's defense of the term in her essay "On How We Mistook the Map for the Territory, and Re-Imprisoned Ourselves in Our Unbearable Wrongness of Being, of *Désêtre*: Black Studies Toward the Human Project," in Gordon, *Not Only the Master's Tools*, pp. 85–106. Cf. also Corey D. B. Walker, "Rethinking Race and Nation for a New African American Intellectual History," *Black Renaissance/Renaissance Noire* 4, nos. 2/3 (2002): 173–86.

was through the groundbreaking anthological work of novelist and literary scholar Toni Cade Bambara (1939–1995), who presented a collective of black women's debates on feminism in the context of the Black Arts movement, which was influenced by the Black Power movement of the 1960s, where the goal was to produce art that would empower and therefore play its role in the liberation of black people.[25] The second was through the thought of philosopher and cultural critic Angela Y. Davis, whose ideas were first inspired by Marxism and the Frankfurt school critical theory and then through developments in British cultural studies.[26] The continued theme in Davis's work has been the fight against slavery, which, in the Marxist tradition, takes different forms in society. Her work shows the connection between black female subordination and such institutions as prisons.[27] The third, postmodernist line emerged through the writings of bell hooks (Gloria Watkins), whose work brought the question of black women's lives into postmodern feminist theory and whose writings on pedagogy and cultural criticism advocated, as did Cornel West, a more postmodern genealogical approach to problems in African-American thought.[28] We could call this genealogical line from Cooper and black women public intellectuals the "secular line" since the main mode of argumentation does not rely on religious or theological premises.

The second primary source is theological. Although its proponents often refer back to the religious speeches by black women, such as those of Sojourner Truth and Maria Stewart, the main source of theoretical work has been the Black Theology of James Cone and the cultural criticism of the novelist and essayist Alice Walker. Cone had argued that a symbolic reading

[25] See Toni Cade Bambara (ed.), *The Black Woman: An Anthology*, reprint edn, introduced by Eleanor W. Traylor (New York: Washington Square Press, 2005). (This work was originally published by New American Library in 1970.)

[26] Angela Y. Davis, *Women, Race, and Class* (New York: Vintage, 1983) and *The Angela Y. Davis Reader*, ed. Joy Ann James (Oxford: Blackwell Publishers, 1998).

[27] See e.g. Angela Y. Davis, *Abolition Democracy: Beyond Prisons, Torture, and Empire – Interviews with Angela Davis*, ed. Eduardo Mendieta (New York: Seven Stories Press, 2005) and for some discussion, Neil Roberts's review of that work in *Souls* 8, no. 3 (2006): 78–80.

[28] bell hooks/Gloria Watkins, *Ain't I a Woman? Black Women and Feminism* (Boston, MA: South End Press, 1981); *Feminist Theory from Margin to Center* (Boston, MA: South End Press, 1984); *Black Looks: Race and Representation* (Boston, MA: South End Press, 1992); *Teaching to Transgress: Education as the Practice of Freedom* (New York: Routledge, 1994).

of the Bible, especially Exodus and the Gospels, would reveal that Jesus could not be represented today by white power but by Black Power or the struggles of black people against white oppression.[29] By arguing that sexual oppression must be added to the argument, theologians such as Jacquelyn Grant and Katie Canon were able to contend that Jesus today would be best symbolized by black women, that is, people who suffer from sexism and racism.[30] This argument took a dialectical path through the thought of Alice Walker, who argued that part of black women's fight against oppression is to assert themselves as women.[31] By this, she meant that the racial and sexual subordination of black women designated them as children, making assertion of their adult status a form of transgression – what in the vernacular is known as being "uppity" or "womanish" when referring to black girls. Walker transformed this term into "womanist" and "womanism," calling for women of color to center each other in their lives. What emerges here is a challenge to the old Victorian lady iconography that affected the thought of Maria Stewart and the Club movement. Sojourner Truth's famous speech at the Women's Rights Convention in Akron, Ohio, in 1854, becomes the appropriate exemplar:

> That man over there says that women need to be helped into carriages, and lifted over ditches, and to have the best place everywhere. Nobody ever helps me into carriages, or over mud puddles, or gives me any best place, and ain't I a woman? . . . I have plowed, and planted, and gathered into barns, and no man could head me – and ain't I a woman? I could work as much and eat as much as a man (when I could get it), and bear the lash as well – and ain't I a woman? I have borne thirteen children and seen most all sold off to slavery and when I cried out with my mother's grief, none but Jesus heard me – and ain't I woman?

[29] See James Cone, *Black Theology and Black Power* (New York: Seabury Press, 1969); *A Black Theology of Liberation* (Philadelphia, PA: Lippincott, 1970); and *God of the Oppressed* (New York: Seabury Press, 1975).

[30] Jacquelyn Grant, *White Women's Christ and Black Women's Jesus: Feminist Christology and Womanist Response* (Atlanta, GA: Scholars Press, 1989); Katie Geneva Cannon, *Katie's Canon: Womanism and the Soul of the Black Community* (New York: Continuum, 1995).

[31] Alice Walker, *In Search of Our Mothers' Gardens: Womanist Prose* (San Diego: Harcourt Brace Jovanovich, 1983). See also *You Can't Keep a Good Woman Down* (New York: Harvest Books, 1982).

Ironically, although the womanist argument was not itself a theological one, it was primarily embraced by black women theologians, especially lesbian theologians, who took the dialectics of oppression into the fight against homophobia.[32] As we see, the movements here are twofold. First, they are semiological. The project is to read the symbols of the primary sacred texts to reveal the message of liberation. The second is a search for an identity that correlates with the symbols followed, and this identity eventually took the form of a standpoint from which the rest of the arguments flowed. In short, the black woman (heterosexual in some cases, lesbian or bisexual in others) became the object and subject of liberation and, eventually, its source.

The secular and theological lines converged in the thought of Patricia Hill Collins and Joy Ann James. Collins argued that the proper method for black feminist thought was engagement with postmodern thought and standpoint epistemology.[33] Postmodernism offered the rejection of an essentialism that centered patriarchy and racism. Without such centers there is no basis for rejecting black women's perspectives on the world. Such perspectives, she argues, when focused on questions of liberation and social change, should be called the black feminist standpoint. The logic of this argument is similar to that of the Afrocentric scholar Molefi K. Asante's appeal to needing one's own standpoint or center from which to build one's relationship with the rest of the world.[34] Collins claims that this standpoint leads to supporting the set of values articulated by the black secular and womanist movements. Joy Ann James also builds her argument on black women's standpoints, but she historicizes the argument to focus on the kinds of politics and the feminism they foster. In other words for James black feminism is not a singular politics but a multitudinous one, with right-wing, conservative, liberal,

---

[32] This outcome of this dialectic has its opposition within black feminist theology. See e.g. Cheryl J. Sanders, "Sexual Orientation and Human Rights Discourse in the African-American Churches," in Saul Olyan and Martha C. Nussbaum (eds.), *Sexual Orientation and Human Rights in American Religious Discourse* (New York: Oxford University Press, 1998), pp. 178–84. Sanders argues against the notion of black female Christians endorsing the lesbian dimensions of womanist theology.

[33] See Patricia Hill Collins, *Black Feminist Thought: Knowledge, Consciousness, and the Politics of Empowerment*, rev. 10th anniversary edn (New York: Routledge, 2000).

[34] See Molefi K. Asante, *The Afrocentric Idea*, rev. edn (Philadelphia, PA: Temple University Press, 1998), which will be discussed shortly.

and radical left perspectives.[35] Like Collins, however, she is antipathetic to essentialist discourses, but James extends her criticisms to centrism as well. As a result, she is critical of Collins's centrism, which, she argues, leads to a depoliticization of black women's lives because it eliminates plurality on the one hand, and provides the basis for a formulation of "black women as the new talented tenth" on the other. In her book *Shadowboxing* James argues that she prefers narrative models as opposed to critical theoretical and philosophical ones in the service of social transformation.[36] What is consistent with Collins's work here is James's preference for cultural criticism. Collins's contribution, however, is that she places the question of developing a black feminist epistemology at the forefront of the debate, which raises the possibility of moving from black feminist thought to black feminist philosophy.

This question of articulating a black feminist or womanist philosophy has been taken up by Renee McKenzie, an Episcopalian priest, who argues that a black feminist philosophy is possible through developing a logic that can address the oppositions raised by exclusive, disjunctive approaches.[37] Womanism, she argues, faces the problem of being both an ethics and a politics. The problem is that ethics focuses on the individual in ways that transcend politics, while a failure to respond to the political context will leave black women stuck in a world without movement. Here we see a convergence of Cooper, Du Bois, and Fanon, for McKenzie is arguing that a consequence of the modern world is that the normative, liberal approach of prioritizing ethics has a politically conservative consequence since it preserves through failing to address the fact that different groups of people do not live with equal normative weight in the society. A politics of social transformation is needed, in other words, to enable the ethical appearance of once subordinated individuals. Thus ethics finds itself in conflict with liberation politics. McKenzie approaches this question through the resources of existential phenomenology, which is discussed below. Her response to the

---

[35] See Joy Ann James, *Transcending the Talented Tenth: Black Leaders and American Intellectuals*, with a foreword by Lewis R. Gordon (New York: Routledge, 1997).

[36] See *Shadowboxing: Representations of Black Feminist Politics* (New York: St. Martin's, 1999).

[37] Renee McKenzie, "A Womanist Social Ontology: An Exploration of the Self and the Other Relationship in Womanist Religious Scholarship" (Philadelphia: Temple University Dissertation in Philosophy of Religion, 2005), and "A Womanist Social Ontology," *Newsletter on Philosophy and the Black Experience* 6, no. 1 (2006): 7–9.

face-off is to argue that a dialectical logic of both-and is needed, which she argues can converge in the embodied, seemingly contradictory movements of a womanist philosophy.

The variety of approaches in black feminist thought/philosophy brings us back to the question of approaches to philosophy. For instance, only three of the aforementioned black feminist theorists had direct training in philosophy – Davis, James, and McKenzie. Davis's approach was through critical theory; James's was through prophetic pragmatism and European continental social and political philosophy; and McKenzie's was through existential phenomenology.[38] Yet, with the exception of McKenzie, it is clear that in black feminist thought, as with prophetic pragmatism, post-modernism has functioned paradoxically as a dominating narrative of anti-domination, and its defense of social transformation only in negative terms raises the same set of criticisms against postmodernist approaches stated earlier, namely, that they do not offer ideas on which to build the future but instead only criticisms of what is wrong with present and past ones.

Although their numbers are still small, the community of black feminist professional philosophers continues to grow. Jennifer Lisa Vest, Anika Mann, and Kathryn Gines are three women who are part of this growing community. Jennifer Vest is a poet and philosopher whose work focuses on the intersection of Native American and Africana philosophy. She also is a Seminole Indian who challenges notions of singular identities.[39] Mann works in the area of ethics.[40] And most related to the work of Renee McKenzie, Gines's work is in the area of black existential philosophy.[41]

---

[38] There is an Afro-Latina feminist existential phenomenological line, which I will return to below. I do not include it here because it has less of a relationship with womanism, although the proponents do engage the Latin American philosophy of liberation.

[39] See e.g. Jennifer Lisa Vest, "Critical Indigenous Philosophy: Disciplinary Challenges Posed by African and Native American Epistemologies" (Berkeley, CA: University of California Doctoral Dissertation in Ethnic Studies, 2000) and "The Promise of Caribbean Philosophy: How it Can Contribute to a 'New Dialogic' in Philosophy," *Journal of Caribbean Studies* 33, no. 2 (2006): 3–34.

[40] See e.g. Anika Maaza Mann, "Sartre's Ethics of the Oppressed," *Philosophy Today* 49, no. 5 (2005): 105–9; Robert Bernasconi and Anika Maaza Mann, "The Contradictions of Racism: Locke, Slavery, and the Two Treatises," in Andrew Valls (ed.), *Race and Racism in Modern Philosophy* (Ithaca, NY: Cornell University Press, 2005).

[41] See e.g. Kathryn T. Gines, "Fanon and Sartre 50 Years Later," *Sartre Studies International* 9, no. 2 (2003): 55–67.

None of these women's work belongs in a single box, and neither does the work of many of the women in Africana philosophy who preceded them.

Afrocentrism and Afrocentricity

Ironically, Patricia Hill Collins's standpoint epistemology also shares much with Afrocentrism, which is often confused with Afrocentricity, a movement that many of her proponents oppose but which stands as one of the most controversial yet influential challenges to African-American thought.[42] The confusion emerges from the fact that proponents of Afrocentricity refer to themselves as Afrocentric, which unfortunately means that their work is mistaken for, as many of them have protested, Afrocentrism, which, they further argue, presents itself as a centrism along with Eurocentrism but with a black face.[43] Although the genealogy of Afrocentricity points through a variety of historians and social theorists such as Harold Cruse (1916–2005), Kwame Nkrumah (1909–1972), and Kwame Ture (formerly Stokley Carmichael, 1941–1998), back to the foundations of black nationalism in the nineteenth century, the most influential representatives of Afrocentricity are Maulana Karenga (previously Ron Everett) and Molefi Keti Asante (formerly Arthur Lee Smith, Jr.).

Karenga is most known internationally as the founder (in 1966) of Kwanza, which is celebrated by millions of people of African descent worldwide after the Chanukah and Christmas holidays, and as the founder

---

[42] See e.g. Clarence E. Walker, *We Can't Go Home Again: An Argument about Afrocentrism* (New York: Oxford University Press, 2001) and William D. Hart, "The Rival Narratives of Black Religion," in Gordon and Gordon, *A Companion to African-American Studies*, pp. 476–93. The main focus of their attack is the work of Molefi K. Asante. Their criticisms are based primarily on Asante's work of the 1980s and early 1990s. For two recent formulations, see Molefi Kete Asante, *Race, Rhetoric and Identity: The Architecton of Soul* (Amherst, NY: Humanity Books, 2005) and *An Afrocentric Manifesto: Toward an African Renaissance* (Cambridge: Polity, 2008).

[43] See Molefi K. Asante, *The Afrocentric Idea* and *An Afrocentric Manifesto*. In the latter volume Asante argues that Patricia Hill Collins conflates Afrocentrism with Afrocentricity, and he points out that she has even argued, in *From Black Power to Hip Hop: Racism, Nationalism, and Feminism* (Philadelphia, PA: Temple University Press, 2006), that Afrocentrism was one of the foundations of Black Studies. Asante takes her to task on this claim by pointing out that Afrocentricity emerged in the 1970s, nearly a decade after the founding of Black Studies programs in the late 1960s.

of US.[44] The term "US" is not an acronym.[45] It simply represents black populations fighting against antiblack oppression. This path of resistance is inspired by what Karenga calls the Kawaida philosophy, which Karenga develops out of the ideas of traditional African communities such as the Zulus, the Yorùbá, and, in more antiquated times, the *Ma'at* of the Egyptians.[46] Karenga's focus is on liberation and social transformation, but his arguments are informed by a philosophical anthropology of cultural appropriateness and a critique of Western rationality through the reconstruction of classical African thought. His own philosophical contribution rests on advancing ethics as the *philosophia prima*. Such a priority, he argues, does not lead to the radicalizing of individuality, such as one finds in Anglo-liberal ethics, but to an obligation outward into a thick conception of historical responsibility. This means, for Karenga, a community-oriented philosophy whose obligations extend across the ages.[47]

Asante's work, on the other hand, emerged through the field of communications, and his theoretical work in communicology led to his

[44] See Scott Brown, *Fighting for US: Maulana Karenga, the US Organization, and Black Cultural Nationalism*, foreword by Clayborne Carson (New York: New York University Press, 2003). Karenga earned two doctorates – one in history and the other in philosophy, with a specialization in ethics.

[45] It is sometimes confused with the expression "United Slaves," but Karenga and Asante reject referring to black people as "slaves." They prefer the expression "enslaved" to signify an imposition instead of a disposition. See *The Afrocentric Idea*.

[46] On the question of contemporary Africana philosophy's relation to traditional African philosophy, see Kwame Gyekye's *An Essay on African Philosophical Thought: The Akan Conceptual Scheme*, rev. edn (Philadelphia, PA: Temple University Press, 1995) and Paget Henry, *Caliban's Reason: Introducing Afro-Caribbean Philosophy* (New York: Routledge, 2000), ch. 1, "The African Philosophical Heritage." See also Tsenay Serequeberhan, *Our Heritage: The Past in the Present of African-American and African Existence* (Lanham, MD: Rowman & Littlefield, 2000).

[47] Maulana Karenga has written many books, but see, most recently, *Maat: The Moral Ideal in Ancient Egypt – A Study in African Ethics* (Los Angeles, CA: University of Sankore Press, 2006), hardback edition published in 2004 by Routledge, and "Philosophy in the African Tradition of Resistance: Issues of Human Freedom and Human Flourishing," in Gordon and Gordon, *Not Only the Master's Tools*, pp. 243–72. In these works Karenga argues for building a thick conception of ethical life on resources offered from the ancient Egyptian concept of *Ma'at*, which means truth, law, justice, and order in the universe. The goddess who also bears that name symbolizes the term. She wears a crown with a huge ostrich feather and she stands on a stone platform or foundation exemplifying stability. In Egyptian/Kamitian mythology, Ma'at would weigh the heart of the deceased to determine his or her fate in the afterlife.

critical engagements with postmodern rhetorical techniques. Like Collins and Karenga, Asante argues for African cultural resources against antiblack oppression. But he stresses the question of agency more than most standpoint theorists.[48] For him, the question is that of the agency of African people in history. In his criticism of postmodernism, for example, he argues that postmodernists often forget that African people were also contributors to modernity. It is not, in other words, that they were passively "made" by the modern world but that they were more involved in a dialectical struggle the consequence of which is the modern era.[49] Drawing primarily upon the thought of Cheikh Anton Diop, Asante argues for the importance of building on the resources of African classical civilization, the exemplar of which is ancient Egypt or Kemet (his preferred spelling for Km.t) and its genealogical foundations from its southern (for those ancient peoples "upper") instead of eastern and northern ("lower") neighbors.[50] In agreement with Karenga, Asante takes the standpoint argument to the question of language itself and advocates not only a thorough grounding in African history but also for the liberating force of speaking and writing in African languages. In a recent essay he refers to such research and the disciplinary construction of African *logoi* as "Africology."[51] Finally, for Karenga and Asante, the encounter that created the term "African American" was not simply one in which a new phenomenon occurred but instead a misleading one – namely, the notion of the black or the African American as other than the African. Asante makes this point through his rejection of "dialect," or even "creole," and argues, instead, that what is known as "Ebonics" or "black speech" is in fact an African language, and that embedded in that language are the resources of black resistance to racial oppression.[52]

---

[48] See e.g. Asante, *The Afrocentric Idea*, p. 41.

[49] *Ibid.*, p. 9. Cf. also Clarence J. Munford, *Race and Civilization* (Trenton, NJ: Africa World Press, 2003) for a similar but more detailed discussion from the field of history.

[50] Asante, *The Afrocentric Idea*, pp. 11, 21.

[51] *Ibid.*, 19–20 and Molefi Kete Asante, "Sustaining Africology: On the Creation and Development of a Discipline," in Gordon and Gordon, *A Companion to African-American Studies*, pp. 20–32.

[52] Asante, *The Afrocentric Idea*, pp. 46, 68–91, and part II, which is a theory of African communicology as a discourse of resistance and freedom. For more on the linguistic dimensions of this argument within the Afrocentric movement see Ama Mazama, *Langue et identité en Guadeloupe. Une perspective afrocentrique* (Pointe-à-Pitre, Guadeloupe: Editions Jasor, 1997). And for a discussion of Ebonics in a related, but not Afrocentric

Criticisms of Afrocentricity and Africology, often couched, as we have seen, in a conflation of these terms with Afrocentrism, abound. One criticism is that it is ironically an African-American philosophy, since most Africans in Africa do not subscribe to Afrocentric philosophy. This criticism is often a tit-for-tat type of attack since Afrocentrics regularly produce continental Africans who do subscribe to their philosophy. But more, the criticism asserts itself without entertaining the internal conditions of the Afrocentrics' argument. In other words, it begs the question of who is authentically an African. Thus, if we concede the terms of the Afrocentric position, it is an intellectual movement that is located in a strange place in this chapter, because Afrocentrics (as opposed to Afrocentrists) do not claim to belong in African-American philosophy but in African philosophy. Another criticism is the notion of African *logoi*, given the argument about language. In effect the appeal should not be to a Greek term for a concept, whose origin simply means to put things in an order. This criticism applies more to the Africology designation than that of Afrocentricity, for the latter ultimately makes the question of a *logos* secondary to that of a foundation, ground, or the notion of centeredness, which is not identical with centrism, articulated in the concept of *djed*, which refers to the pillars representing stability exemplified in ancient Kemetic/Egyptian mythic life as the backbone of the god Osiris. Relatedly, the kinds of arguments on which these cultural and structural appeals rest have clear roots in Kantianism.[53] To avoid this, the logic of the African in negative terms is required, where the goal becomes eliminating European elements. But such a path would become reactionary, as Fanon learned in his engagements with *Négritude*, where the African became defined in opposition to the European; the result would be the problem of irrationalism as a form of rationality, a *logos*, in

way because of the focus on black as opposed to African, see the work of the linguist Geneva Smitherman in such works as *Word from the Mother: Language and African Americans* (New York: Routledge, 2006) and *Talkin that Talk: African American Language and Culture* (New York: Routledge, 1999).

[53] See our discussion of Kant in the introduction of this book. The standpoint argument suggests necessary and sufficient conditions for the emergence of a liberated black consciousness, the result of which is the notion of an African transcendental subject. For discussion of transcendental subjects and subjectivity, see David Carr, *The Paradox of Subjectivity: The Self in the Transcendental Tradition* (New York: Oxford University Press, 1999).

other words, of anti-*logos*.[54] Lucius T. Outlaw, Jr., takes this concern to the methodological level:

> Much of the difficulty plaguing Asante's methodological efforts is due to his over-reliance on "Eurocentric" as a tool for making certain critical distinctions. This notion is much too blunt, and much too loaded with complicated and complicating semantic weightings of notions of raciality and ethnicity, to do the fine-grained work called for without especially deft handling when attending to epistemological and methodological matters. By way of his training, and his own continuing self-education notwithstanding (note his discussion of Husserlian phenomenology . . .), Asante has not yet cultivated sufficient deftness of understanding and articulation with regard to epistemological matters. Moreover, too often his distinguishing matters as either being European or African is simplistic; and frequently he bequeaths to the possession of Europeans what cannot rightly be claimed to be the property of or patented by any particular people, such as the important norm of "objectivity" in knowledge production. Ironically, in this way Asante participates in the very Eurocentric project of hegemonic appropriation against which he continues to struggle so valiantly.[55]

In many ways, the ideas and problematics of Afrocentricity are, in the end, heavily contingent on modernity. Asante admits this when he reminds us that African peoples contributed to the formation of the modern world. Unlike the postmodernists, however, who articulate their positions almost entirely in the negative, Afrocentrics avow a positive path, but that path is almost entirely in terms of the past. The philosophical and social transformative challenge then becomes the existential problematic of whether one could ever "return," as a living ethic, to one's cultural past.[56]

African-American analytical philosophy

We find a different situation when we turn to African-American and Afro-Canadian analytical philosophy. I will simply refer to them as African

---

[54] See Frantz Fanon, *Black Skin, White Masks*, trans. Charles Lamm Markmann (New York: Grove Press, 1967), ch. 5.

[55] Lucius T. Outlaw, Jr., "'Afrocentricity': Critical Considerations," in Lott and Pittman, *A Companion to African-American Philosophy*, p. 63.

[56] We will return to Afrocentricity in our discussion of African-American existential philosophy in this chapter.

American since Canada is part of North America and because most, if not all, Afro-Canadian analytical philosophers teach in the United States. It is my hope that this circumstance will have changed shortly after the publication of this book, but I am not optimistic. The designation "analytical philosophy" also poses some difficulty in the Africana philosophical context. This is because, although nearly all African-American philosophers have had some contact with analytical philosophy, many African-American philosophers consider what they do to transcend the analytical–continental rubric. Thus, there are only a small handful who outright identify themselves as "analytical philosophers." This group nevertheless stands among the most influential members of the field, regardless of philosophical persuasion.

African-American analytical philosophy is, basically, the application of Anglo-analytical philosophy to the study of black problems, most significantly those that are a function of the impact of race and racism on the lives of black people.[57] The major exemplars of this approach are Kwame Anthony Appiah, Bernard Boxill, Tommy Lott, Howard McGary, Bill Lawson, Rodney Roberts, Adrian Piper, John Pittman, Laurence Thomas, Charles Mills, Naomi Zack, and Rainier Spencer. Appiah is best known for his work on race and racism.[58] Race, he argues, is not scientifically valid and thus "racialism," which requires the belief in races, should be rejected. He refers to race as "fictitious." Racism is of two kinds – extrinsic and intrinsic. Extrinsic racism is the use of (spurious) evidence in support of one's racial beliefs or to advocate the superiority of one race over another. Intrinsic racism appeals to the group itself as the basis of those beliefs. Thus, an intrinsic antiblack racist or an intrinsic white supremacist believes that blacks are inferior because they are blacks and whites are superior because they are whites. Because of his rejection of race, Appiah rejects notions of natural or intrinsic divisions between human beings and thus endorses cosmopolitan liberalism, although he rejects international federalism, which, at least, means that he

---

[57] Because of the focus on race and racism, a valuable, more detailed philosophical introduction to this approach can be found in Paul C. Taylor, *Race: A Philosophical Introduction* (Cambridge: Polity, 2004).

[58] See especially K. Anthony Appiah, "Racisms," in David Theo Goldberg (ed.), *The Anatomy of Racism* (Minneapolis, MN: University of Minnesota Press, 1990), pp. 3–17; *In My Father's House: Africa in the Philosophy of Culture* (New York: Oxford University Press, 1992); and *Color Conscious*, with Amy Gutmann (Princeton, NJ: Princeton University Press, 1996).

accepts divisions of nations and the inequalities that follow from this form of political theory, although he argues for rich nations assisting poor ones.[59]

Bernard Boxill explores issues of social justice and respect for blacks through critically engaging the work of John Rawls (1921–2002) and offering close readings of the work of classic figures such as John Locke, Jean-Jacques Rousseau, and Frederick Douglass.[60] Boxill argues against colorblind notions of social justice since that would require ignoring the existence of an identifiable group who has suffered historic and present racial discrimination. Looking into the past, blacks have been discriminated against in a way that has placed whites at an advantage. Looking into the future, the maintenance of such an advantage would constitute an injustice. Thus, social justice requires acting upon remedies that would both respond to the past and contribute to the construction of a more just future. Tommy Lott also works through classic Anglo figures such as Thomas Hobbes and John Locke, but he writes more through the resources of African-American writers such as W. E. B. Du Bois and Anna Julia Cooper, as well as some thinkers in the European continental tradition such as Jacques Derrida and Michel Foucault, through whom he advances his constructivist view of race.[61] Howard McGary has examined topics ranging from affirmative action to reparations and the role of violence in struggles for social change.[62] Bill Lawson, in similar kind,

---

[59] K. Anthony Appiah, *Cosmopolitanism: Ethics in a World of Strangers* (New York: W. W. Norton, 2006).

[60] See Bernard Boxill, *Blacks and Social Justice*, rev. edn (Lanham, MD: Rowman & Littlefield, 1992).

[61] See Tommy Lee Lott, *The Invention of Race: Black Culture and the Politics of Representation* (Malden, MA: Blackwell, 1999). See also his very influential essay "Du Bois on the Invention of Race," in *African-American Perspectives and Philosophical Traditions*, ed. with introduction by John Pittman (New York: Routledge, 1997), pp. 166–87, and his essay "Patriarchy and Slavery in Hobbes's Political Philosophy," in *Philosophers on Race: Critical Essays*, ed. Julie K. Ward and Tommy L. Lott (Oxford: Blackwell Publishing, 2002), pp. 63–80.

[62] See Howard McGary, *Race and Social Justice* (Oxford: Blackwell, 1999); "On Violence in the Struggle for Liberation," in *Existence in Black: An Anthology of Black Existential Philosophy*, ed. Lewis R. Gordon (New York: Routledge, 1997), pp. 263–72; "Alienation and the African-American Experience," in Pittman, *African-American Perspectives and Philosophical Traditions*, pp. 282–96; "Racial Integration and Racial Separatism: Conceptual Clarifications," in Harris, *Philosophy Born of Struggle*, pp. 199–211; "The Black Underclass and the Question of Values," in *The Underclass Question*, ed. with introduction by Bill E. Lawson, foreword by William Julius Wilson (Philadelphia, PA: Temple University Press, 1992); and, with Bill E. Lawson, *Between Slavery and Freedom: Philosophy and American Slavery* (Bloomington, IN: Indiana University Press, 1992).

has explored issues ranging from affirmative action to the notion of an underclass, and black music, especially jazz. Underlying Lawson's thought, however, is a concern for what the constant reversals on each success means for the historical understanding of justice and liberation for blacks. Echoing Cornel West's worry of the nihilistic threat, Lawson wonders whether "disappointment" must be the normative expectation behind every black effort at social transformation.[63]

The nihilistic threat is also faced in the effort to expand analytical philosophical treatments of justice beyond debates on distribution. Rodney Roberts argues that rectificatory justice should also be considered.[64] A crucial aspect of justice is the articulation of injustice and the kinds of responses suitable to it. Roberts in effect addresses a problem that emerges at a more profound level of philosophical work. On the one hand, there is the subordination of social and political philosophy into a form of pseudo-economics, where even in writing style many such philosophers have a tendency to imitate the disciplines of economics and law. This tendency leads to a focus on philosophy as a matter of representing only a dominant point of view since the power of distribution is already in the hands of the haves instead of the have-nots. Injustice, however, cuts across all segments of the population, and the dynamics involved in what kinds of injustice are rectified versus those that are not bring to the fore the question of equality, at least in terms of justice itself. Roberts argues for a conception of social justice that brings dominated and oppressed groups into the picture as a necessary condition of justice instead of as a peripheral concern of dominating groups.

Roberts's contention that injustice is a necessary condition for reflecting on justice leads to his rejection of placing a statute of limitations on injustice.[65] In many ways this argument enables him to examine questions of reparations in the American context since there is great reluctance to respond to the injustices waged against blacks in the United States. The main case study is slavery, but there are many other instances to consider.

---

[63] See Bill E. Lawson on "On Disappointment in the Black Context," in *Existence in Black*, pp. 149–56; see also, with McGary, *Between Slavery and Freedom*.

[64] Rodney C. Roberts, "Justice and Rectification: A Taxonomy of Justice," in *Injustice and Rectification*, ed. Rodney C. Roberts (New York: Peter Lang, 2002), pp. 7–28.

[65] Rodney C. Roberts, "The Morality of a Moral Statute of Limitations on Injustice," *The Journal of Ethics* 7, no. 1 (2003): 115–38.

Recall that W. E. B. Du Bois's *Black Reconstruction in America, 1860–1880* provides the best study of how an added injustice was placed on the effort to establish a just social order in the United States following the Civil War. The undermining of freedom for the former slaves and the black freedfolk, solidified by the court opinions and legislation that culminated in the 1896 sanctification of Jim Crow and the reign of terror of such groups as the Ku Klux Klan that dominated that period well into the 1940s and instances of mob lynching and the decimation of the infrastructures of many black civic and economic institutions, to name but a few examples, raises the question of injustice and rectification well into the present. Think, as well, of the number of blacks incarcerated for crimes they did not commit or those whose punishment was far more severe than those of whites for the same offenses. Such a history raises the question of why there is so much resistance to making amends with black Americans versus other groups.

In his article "Why Have the Injustices Perpetrated against Blacks in America Not Been Rectified?" Roberts's response is that the problem rests in the conception of who or what constitutes a "we" in any theory of justice. Rawls, for example, builds his theory of justice on the social contractarian model of an original position in which each of "us" must think through what principles will work given "our" values.[66] In later essays, Rawls argues that his theory is political, not metaphysical, by which he meant that it was not an appeal to a transcendental "us" or "we" but actual, say, Anglo-Americans. But herein is the problem, which was raised by Du Bois as well more than a century ago: the African American is treated as outside the category of "us," in spite of being a product of America. Although other groups may have been discriminated against for a time, most have been absorbed into the American "us" except for indigenous Americans and black Americans. Here, we see how African-American philosophy is crucial for a contemporary analysis of justice, since it is able to articulate the doubled dimensions and contradictions of a society's self-conceptions. Roberts queries whether the "us" condition of ethics and justice is a viable option for

---

[66] Rodney C. Roberts, "Why Have the Injustices Perpetrated against Blacks in America Not Been Rectified?" *The Journal of Social Philosophy* 32, no. 3 (2001): 357–73. For Rawls, see his *A Theory of Justice* (Cambridge, MA: Harvard University Press, 1971); *Political Liberalism* (New York: Columbia University, 1993); and *The Law of Peoples* (Cambridge, MA: Harvard University Press, 1999).

rectification considerations for blacks and indigenous peoples. If not, then a more radical conception of how ethics works in the face of difference is needed for a full-scale, versus partial, theory of justice.

Adrian Piper's work in Africana philosophy focuses primarily on the relevance of Kant to the study of xenophobia, although one could argue that her work as a performance artist needs to be studied as part of her contribution to the field. In effect, she addresses the themes of philosophical anthropology, social transformation, and the metacritique of reason through resources of Kant's thought, mediated by her mentor John Rawls's American liberal emendations, and those of art and cultural criticism, especially with regard to representations of the self and challenges raised by Humean and Kantian conceptions of rationality.[67]

Laurence Thomas has applied his analytical skills to the study of slavery and anti-Semitism and to concepts of moral respect and recognition. In his book *Vessels of Evil*, he offered a comparative study of racialized slavery and the Holocaust in which he argued against the comparison of the two because of the difference of exigency and temporal compression involved in each.[68] Slavery, he argued, did not have genocide as its purpose, but the sole goal of the Holocaust was genocide.[69] The critic could respond, however, that Thomas's argument works if and only if slavery is divorced from antiblack racism. Antiblack racism, it could easily be shown, has an ultimate objective of genocide or at least is an ongoing effort toward such a goal; Abdul R.

[67] See Adrian Piper, "Xenophobia and Kantian Rationalism," in Pittman, *African-American Perspectives and Philosophical Traditions*, pp. 188–232; and "Adrian M. S. Piper," in Yancy, *African American Philosophers*, pp. 49–71. Piper has produced an enormous amount of artistic work and writings on art and social criticism. See e.g. *Talking to Myself: The Ongoing Autobiography of an Art Object* (Bari: Marilena Bonomo, 1975), available in its entirety in *Voices Today's Visions: Writings by Contemporary Women Artists*, ed. Mara Witzling (New York: Universe Publishing, 1994), pp. 268–308; *Decide Who You are* (New York: Paula Cooper Gallery, 1992); *OUT OF ORDER, OUT OF SIGHT, Selected Writings*, vols. I and II (Cambridge, MA: MIT Press, 1996); "Passing for White, Passing for Black," *Transition* 58 (1992): 4–32; "The Joy of Marginality," *Art Papers* 14, no. 4 (1990): 12–13; "Self-Portrait Exaggerating My Negroid Features," *The Twentieth Century Art Book* (New York: Phaidon, 1996), p. 396; "Selected Funk Lessons: A Page Project by Adrian Piper," *Artforum* 22, no. 5 (1984): 64; "A Tale of Avarice and Poverty," *WhiteWalls* 15 (1987): 70–81; "Political Self Portrait #2 (Race)," *Heresies 2: Third World Women* 4 (1979): 37–8.

[68] Laurence Mordekhai Thomas, *Vessels of Evil: American Slavery and the Holocaust* (Philadelphia, PA: Temple University Press, 1993).

[69] *Ibid.*

JanMohamed recently characterized it as a form of terror of which the effect was the creation of death-bound subjects.[70] More recently Laurence Thomas has argued that the discussion of the racism of Kant (and, by implication, other modern European philosophers) fails to deal with the main thrust of their argument, which is that full citizenship should not be available to people who are not fully mature.[71] In other words, if blacks were as Kant believed them to be, his position was a perfectly reasonable one to hold. In effect Thomas's work places Fanon's argument from the essay "Racism and Culture," in *Toward the African Revolution*, that racism embodies a form of rationality, possibly even reasonableness, in an analytical philosophical context.

Charles Mills, who is also a contributor to Afro-Caribbean analytical philosophy, has taken a different tack in his work, which focuses on subjecting liberal social contract theory to a form of immanent critique. The modern world, he argues, is not marked by a value-neutral social contract on which modern capitalism and its accompanying values (or lack thereof) have been built but instead premised on a racial contract through which white supremacy has been constructed.[72] The constellation of agreements over the period from Columbus's voyages to the formation of the slave trades and the conquest of indigenous lands to the period of high colonialism of Africa and Asia in the nineteenth century coalesce in this racial contract. In effect Mills poses a challenge to what is known as ideal social contract theory, which posits consent under hypothetical conditions freed of the world's contingencies. Even that purely formal, ideal world of consent is governed by the realities of conceptualization in the actual world, where value-neutral views of the human being or even purely formal rational beings are affected by white normativity. Thus, ideal theory is, in this view, another way of saying theory whose consequence is white-centric. The question posed by Mills's work is the viability or hopelessness of ideal theory. Although he does not make it explicit we see in Mills's work the return of the problem of double consciousness since the contradictions of liberal social contract theory, at least as advanced by John Rawls and Robert Nozick (1938–2002), come to the

---

[70] Abdul R. JanMohamed, *The Death-Bound-Subject: Richard Wright's Archaeology of Death* (Durham, NC: Duke University Press, 2005).

[71] See Laurence Thomas, "Moral Equality and Natural Inferiority," *Social Theory and Practice* 31, no. 3 (2005): 379–404.

[72] See Charles W. Mills, *The Racial Contract* (Ithaca, NY: Cornell University Press, 1997).

fore in its claims to universality in the face of its historical particularity.[73] Mills argues for working through analytical liberal political theory because it is the dominating philosophical approach in the US academy and the one that has an audience with policy makers in the United States. Articulating a theory of justice that is attuned to the historical contractual injustices may be the most viable route for the social transformative aspect of African-American philosophy to take.

And finally, though not exhaustively, there are Naomi Zack and Rainier Spencer. Zack builds her work on Appiah's rejection of race, but she advances the position in a more radical form. For her, to endorse anything that is false is morally wrong, and thus since race is, given Appiah's argument, false, it is wrong to maintain or use race concepts. Zack argues, moreover, that within the framework of US treatments of race and racism whites must be pure and blacks are defined by the "one drop rule," which requires proof of a single black ancestor even a few generations back. From such a view, black and white mixed-race people are supposedly logically raceless.[74] It is not clear in her work what Native Americans, northeast Asian immigrants, and a variety of other groups and their mixtures are in the American system, although she has edited a volume in which these issues are explored by other authors.[75] Black identification seems to be the problematic concern of her work, which in her essay "Race, Life, Death, Identity, Tragedy and Good Faith" she compares to identifying with ancestors who were prison convicts. It would be irrational and perhaps wrong to identify with such ancestors, she argues, and in similar kind one should not identify with blacks (an oppressed race).[76] Spencer also explores problems of mixture and race and

---

[73] The literature on Rawls and Nozick is vast, but most ultimately point to the following two, now classic works in liberal political philosophy: John Rawls, *A Theory of Justice*, rev. edn (Cambridge, MA: Belknap Press of Harvard University Press, 1999), original version 1971, and Robert Nozick, *Anarchy, State, and Utopia* (New York: Basic Books, 1974).

[74] These ideas are in Zack's book *Race and Mixed Race* (Philadelphia, PA: Temple University Press, 1994). She has continued this course of argumentation through several subsequent works, including *Bachelors of Science: Seventeenth-Century Identity, Then and Now* (Philadelphia, PA: Temple University Press, 1996) and *Philosophy of Science and Race* (New York: Routledge, 2002).

[75] See *American Mixed Race: The Culture of Microdiversity*, ed. Naomi Zack (Lanham, MD: Rowman & Littlefield, 1995).

[76] Naomi Zack, "Race, Life, Death, Identity, Tragedy and Good Faith," in Gordon, *Existence in Black*, pp. 99–110. Criticisms of Zack and Appiah can be found in Lewis R. Gordon, *Her*

advocates a rejection of the race concept, but he offers an iconoclastic critique of Zack and much recent work on mixture by arguing, for instance, that mixed-race and multiracial studies suffer from a contradictory set of aims.[77] On the one hand, they challenge the tenability of race and its impact on American society. On the other, they present a case for their inclusion in the US racial order. These projects, he argues, are not compatible since the truth of the first destroys the basis for the second, but even if they were so, there are other contradictions at the heart of the multiracial formulations of mixture offered by many scholars in the field. He points out that discussions that examine black–white mixture often fail to acknowledge the already mixed dimension of African Americans. By posing mixture against black Americans, such advocates are in fact posing multiraciality against multiraciality. In effect, they would have to create a conception of "purity" that erases mixture within one group as the basis of determining mixture for a preferred group, in this case offspring with a white parent. There are also logical problems of descent, which make, in effect, an offspring genetically connected to a parent from which she or he is considered ontologically different. Is not, in other words, a black offspring of a white parent no less genetically connected to that parent than to the black one? Yet the ontological racial divide makes the offspring radically different from the white parent but the same as the black one. Spencer offers historically informed theoretical challenges to the field by exemplifying consistency in his constructivism through his constantly reminding the reader that just as social identities come into being, they can also cease to continue. What, in other words, will be the organization of human identities in the future will be a function of the kinds of critical questions and social and political conditions that come to bear on their meaning and being. In this sense he is building upon what, as we have seen, Frantz Fanon called sociogenesis – how the social world produces identities.

Majesty's Other Children: Sketches of Racism from a Neocolonial Age (Lanham, MD: Rowman & Littlefield, 1997) and *Existentia Africana*. See also David Theo Goldberg, *Racist Culture* (Oxford: Blackwell, 1993) and *Racial Subjects: On Writing Race in America* (New York: Routledge, 1997). Cf. also Albert G. Mosley, "Are Racial Categories Racist?" *Research in African Literatures* 28, no. 4 (Winter 1997): 101–11.

[77] See Rainier Spencer, *Challenging Multiracial Identity* (Boulder, CO: Lynne Rienner, 2006) and *Spurious Issues: Race and Multiracial Identity Politics in the United States* (Boulder, CO: Westview, 1999).

Although very fruitful in the analysis of the terms and concepts used in debates on such problems, such as "race," "black," "respect," and "social justice," the analytical approach faces several limitations already identified by our discussion of Du Bois and Fanon, the most crucial of which is the presumption of the validity of interpretation within the dominant system – what in Foucauldian language we might call "the dominant philosophical episteme" as presently constituted. Philosophical thinking is, however, greater than the application of a precluded method. It requires dealing with the idiosyncrasies of reflection that enable method and thought to be subject to evaluation. This is Du Bois's and Fanon's insight into the study of what it means to be problems and the importance of taking seriously the illustrative potential of contradictions and failures. Put differently, African-American philosophy should also offer a critique of its own foundations. Could not the racism that many African-American analytical philosophers encounter in the philosophy profession, for example, also be a function of a philosophy that refused to recognize race in the first place?[78] The response could be that their work is such a corrective, but the response that many black analytical philosophers encounter from white analytical philosophers is that to engage race at all leads to excommunication from the analytical world. The work of Charles Mills and Rodney Roberts raises this problem. In Mills's thought the racism in dominant philosophical circles is acknowledged. It is Rodney, however, who raises the problem at the level of the humanity of black folk. Logic calls for a standard the core definition of which excludes black folk. We see here the continued relevance of Fanon's critique of strategies premised upon the dialectics of recognition.

---

[78] See e.g. Charles Mills, *Blackness Visible: Essays on Philosophy and Race* (Ithaca, NY: Cornell University Press, 1997), and Leonard Harris, "'Believe It or Not' or the Klu Klux Klan and American Philosophy Exposed," *Proceedings and Addresses of the American Philosophical Association* 68, no. 5 (1995): 133–7. Harris's point is that if the Ku Klux Klan had in fact created American philosophy, it would look exactly the way it did in 1995. It is not, by the way, that white analytical philosophers are any more racist than white European continental ones, but that the cases are many. In addition to Mills's and Harris's accounts, see e.g. Paget Henry's "Afro-American Studies and the Rise of African-American Philosophy," in Gordon and Gordon, *A Companion to African American Studies*, pp. 223–45. My own experience includes departments, analytical and continental in persuasion, that objected to my (and that of even white philosophers who do work on race) inclusion on the grounds that I would "attract too many black people."

African-American and Afro-British European continental philosophy

The African-American, Afro-Canadian, and Afro-British European continental wing faces similar challenges as the analytical one. That area of thought consists of the application of arguments offered by the European continental tradition to the study of African-American, Afro-Canadian, and Afro-British problems. Similar to the situation of the analytical philosophers, there is virtually no presence of Africana representation in European continental philosophy in the Canadian academy. Pioneers of the continental approach include Lucius T. Outlaw, Jr., who advocated engagements with Frankfurt school critical theory and Derridian deconstruction; Robert Bernasconi, who has offered Levinasian and "later" Sartrean readings of black invisibility and humanism; Roy Martinez, who attempted a Heideggerian reading of black existence; Paul Gilroy, whose recent work on nationalism, fascism, racism, and colonial longing is explored through the resources of Frankfurt school critical theory; and Rozena Maart, who has been working on an integration of Black Consciousness, deconstruction, and psychoanalysis through the thought of Fanon, Biko, Derrida, Freud, and Lacan.[79] There

---

[79] See Lucius T. Outlaw, Jr., *On Race and Philosophy* (New York: Routledge, 1996) and *Critical Social Theory in the Interests of Black Folks* (Lanham, MD: Rowman & Littlefield, 2005), and the Italian British philosopher Robert Bernasconi's "Casting the Slough: Fanon's New Humanism for a New Humanity," in *Fanon: A Critical Reader*, ed. Lewis R. Gordon, T. Denean Sharpley Whiting, and Renée T. White (Oxford, Blackwell Publishers, 1966), pp. 113–121; "Heidegger's Alleged Challenge to the Nazi Concepts of Race," *Appropriating Heidegger*, ed. James E. Faulconer and Mark A. Wrathall (Cambridge: Cambridge University Press, 2000), pp. 50–67; "Kant and Blumenbach's Polyps: A Neglected Chapter in the History of the Concept of Race," in *The German Invention of Race*, ed. Sara Eigen and Mark Larrimor (Albany, NY: State University of New York Press, 2006), pp. 73–90; "Kant as an Unfamiliar Source of Racism," in *Philosophers on Race: Critical Essays*, ed. Julie K. Ward and Tommy L. Lott (Oxford: Blackwell, 2002), pp. 145–66; "Politics beyond Humanism: Mandela and the Struggle against Apartheid," in *Working Through Derrida*, ed. Gary B. Madison (Evanston, IL: Northwestern University Press, 1993), pp. 94–119; Paul Gilroy, *Against Race: Imagining Political Culture Beyond the Colorline* (Cambridge, MA: Belknap Press, 2002) and *Postcolonial Melancholia* (New York: Columbia University Press, 2006); Rozena Maart, *The Politics of Consciousness, the Consciousness of Politics: When Black Consciousness Meets White Consciousness*, 2 vols. (Guelph, Canada: Awomandla Publishers, 2006); Ronald A. T. Judy, "Fanon's Body of Black Experience," in Gordon et al., *Fanon: A Critical Reader*, pp. 53–73, and "Kant and Knowledge of Disappearing Expression," in Lott and Pittman, *A Companion to African-American Philosophy*, pp. 110–24; and Roy Martinez,

are others, as well, who are associated with European continental thought beyond its mere application, particularly in race theory, such as David Theo Goldberg, Judith Butler, Drucilla Cornell, Robert Gooding-Williams, Linda Martín Alcoff, Frank Kirkland, Cynthia Willett, A. Todd Franklin, Jaqueline Renee Scott, Renee McKenzie, Kathryn T. Gines, Robert Birt, Paget Henry, and, given my engagements with European thinkers such as Hegel, Marx, Husserl, Jaspers, Sartre, Schutz, and Foucault, some of my own work.[80] The primary criticism of the application of European continental philosophy

Kierkegaard and the Art of Irony (Amherst, NY: Humanity Books, 2001) and Roy Martinez (ed.), *The Very Idea of Radical Hermeneutics* (Amherst, NY: Humanity Books, 1997). There are other African-American philosophers who engage European continental thinkers, and they do not necessarily do so as an application of the European thinker's thought. See e.g. *Critical Affinities: Nietzsche and the African-American Experience*, ed. Todd Franklin and Renee Scott (Albany, NY: State University of New York Press, 2006). And in similar kind, although more from the literary vein, see *"Race," Writing, and Difference*, ed. Henry Louis Gates, Jr. (Chicago, IL: University of Chicago Press, 1986) and Judy, *(Dis)forming the American Canon*, where Kant, Foucault, and Derrida are informative but not necessarily conclusive.

[80] The works by this list of thinkers are manifold. Some of David Theo Goldberg's books have already been cited; Judith Butler's emerges through her critique of identity and more explicitly in her engagement with Frantz Fanon in her essays, "Endangered/Endangering: Schematic Racism and White Paranoia," in *Reading Rodney King, Reading Urban Uprising*, ed. Robert Gooding-Williams (New York: Routledge, 1993), pp. 15–22, and "Violence, Non-Violence: Sartre on Fanon," in *Race after Sartre*, ed. Jonathan Judaken (Albany, NY: State University of New York Press, 2008). Butler's books also offer much for poststructural approaches to this area of thought. See e.g. Judith Butler, *Gender Trouble: Feminism and the Subversion of Identity* (New York: Routledge, 1990), recently reprinted as a Routledge Classic (2006); *Bodies That Matter: On the Discursive Limits of Sex* (New York: Routledge, 1993); *Antigone's Claim* (New York: Columbia University Press, 2002); *Undoing Gender* (New York: Routledge, 2004); and *The Judith Butler Reader*, ed. Sarah Salih and Judith Butler (Malden, MA: Blackwell, 2004). Drucilla Cornell has written many works, but see especially *The Philosophy of the Limit* (New York: Routledge, 2000) and *Moral Images of Freedom: A Future for Critical Theory* (Lanham, MD: Rowman & Littlefield, 2007). For Gooding-Williams, see *"Look, a Negro!: Philosophical Essays on Race, Culture and Politics* (New York: Routledge, 2005), and *Zarathustra's Dionysian Modernism* (Palo Alto, CA: Stanford University Press, 2001); Linda Martín Alcoff, *Visible Identities: Race, Gender, and the Self* (New York: Oxford University Press, 2006); Frank Kirkland, "Modernity and Intellectual Life in Black," in Pittman, *African-American Perspectives and Philosophical Traditions*, pp. 136–55; "Enslavement, Moral Suasion, and Struggles for Recognition: Frederick Douglass's Answer to the Question – 'What Is Enlightenment?'" in *Frederick Douglass: A Critical Reader*, ed. Bill E. Lawson and Frank M. Kirkland (Malden, MA: Blackwell, 1999), and his co-edited anthology, with D. P. Chattopadhyaya, *Phenomenology, East and West: Essays in Honor of J. N. Mohanty* (Dordrecht, Netherlands: Kluwer, 1993). Cynthia Willett's

to African-American problems is quite simply that it is Eurocentric and thus suffers from the same problems as the mere application of Anglo-analytical philosophy. I do not see how such an argument could be sustained against the approach of engaging but not reducing the thought to European continental philosophy, since it lacks the requisite centering of European thought as thought. But within their ranks there are great differences between scholars who see their work as primarily textual and those who do not.

The textualists tend to endorse some form of Afro-postmodernism and Afro-postmodern poststructuralism. These approaches face some of the criticisms of prophetic pragmatism. The main thrust of Afro-postmodernism is a radical anti-essentialism, which leads to the rejection of all "master narratives," and leaves no alternative for intellectual work but that of textual or cultural criticism. This is a function of the anti-foundationalism of the postmodernist turn. Yet the question emerges of how one can build new ideas through a commitment to criticism only. Would not the only creative options be that of style or technique? Even where one shows that an argument is logically flawed, one cannot, in this view, take that conclusion as a consequence with any bearing on reality. There are some ironic results of all this. First, the turn to postmodern criticism has produced a body of literature, what Cornel West referred to as philosophical writings, which constitutes a philosophy (or philosoph*ies*). Is this not an imposition of a master narrative (philosophy) over these texts? If this is so, would not, then, the notion of an Afro-postmodern philosophy be a contradiction of

work in the field pertains to her connecting poststructural feminism and the Hegelian dialectics of recognition with the thought of Fredrick Douglass, in such works as *Maternal Ethics and Other Slave Moralities* (New York: Routledge, 1995) and *The Soul of Justice: Social Bonds and Racial Hubris* (Ithaca, NY: Cornell University Press, 2001). Kathryn Gines's work includes "The Ambiguity of Assimilation: Commentary on Eamonn Callan's 'The Ethics of Assimilation,'" in *Symposia on Gender Race and Philosophy* 2, no. 2 (2006) and "Sartre and Fanon: Fifty Years Later," in *Sartre Studies International* 9, no. 2 (2003). Robert Birt's work includes his essay "Existence, Identity, Liberation," in *Existence in Black*, ed. Lewis R. Gordon and *The Quest of Community and Identity: Critical Essays in Africana and Social Philosophy*, ed. Robert E. Birt (Lanham, MD: Rowman & Littlefield, 2002). Paget Henry's work will be discussed in more detail in Afro-Caribbean philosophy, but the importance of the European continental tradition is obvious in his canonical book, *Caliban's Reason: Introducing Afro-Caribbean Philosophy* (New York: Routledge, 2000). My own work is referenced more under the discussion of Africana existential phenomenology, which concludes this chapter.

terms? And if so, would not the turn to postmodern critique mean, then, the abrogation of philosophy? These questions lead to more unsettling ones. For instance, postmodernism is marked by strong anti-humanist commitments (since humanism is, after all, a form of centered narrative). Yet there is no black philosophical text, as I have been arguing since the introduction of this book, that lacks an appeal to some kind of humanism or to the humanity of black people, often defended in the form of a philosophical anthropology. The obvious reason for this is that these texts are being written by people whose domination is marked by their dehumanization; it would be contradictory for them to fight for a humanity that they must reject.

The impact of postmodern criticism, wedded to at least the language of textual (Derridian deconstruction) and genealogical (Foucauldian) poststructuralism has been such that certain themes have come to dominate discussions of race, gender, sexual orientation, and class, and they often have the effect of closing off further thinking on the subject. Examples here include ascriptions of "binary analysis," "essentialism," and the noncontextual presumption of and often demand for symmetry. Binaries are rejected as binaries in this discourse, which means, paradoxically, that there must be something essentially wrong with binaries. This is supposedly an anti-essentialist critical perspective. Why must binaries be outlawed in an analysis? Binaries persist in many settings where they are not only accurate ascriptions but also productive. The computers on which most of us write our criticisms would not function without binary operations, and even more, thought makes no sense without the ability to make distinctions at any moment between what is and is not. But more, an is and is-not structure is not necessarily a binary one, as Aristotle pointed out more than two millennia ago in his *Metaphysics*, since the possibilities that constitute is-not are infinite and those that constitute "is" may be finite.

A similar criticism applies to anti-essentialism. First, it collapses into a form of essentialism. It essentializes the use of essence by making any appeal to essence "essentialist." This is, however, an error in reasoning, since one could easily develop a theory of essence without making essence an imposed necessity on all of reality or even over a single subject. The confusion emerges here, as Ernst Cassirer pointed out in his philosophy of symbolic form, in the presumption of Aristotelian substance as the underlying core of essence. It is to presume that the essence of a thing must somehow be inside the thing.[81] Taking even the anti-essentialist's own discursive arguments seriously requires presenting essence as an external, organizing narrative that constitutes the meaning of (and again, not *in*) a thing and the essence itself could be understood in terms of a thing-itself. This subtle difference presents a form of constructivist view of essence that is not essentialism. This view of essence, shared also by Husserlian phenomenologists, does not eliminate contingency from the world.[82] To conflate the essence of a thing into the substance of a thing is a function of not distinguishing between areas of knowledge in which generality rules with accuracy but without exactitude. Think, for instance, of mathematics and the natural and theoretical sciences versus the social sciences and the humanities. Identification of phenomena in the former requires working by rules whose underlying subject matter has no exceptions (laws), while those in the latter always have exceptions. The error is to make the exception the rule and the rule the exception.

There are many aspects of social life over which we make fairly accurate predictions and assessments, but it would be irresponsible, as so many critics have shown, to claim that we make foolproof associations.[83] Those general moments are not ones of collapsing into essential*ism* but simply descriptions that are communicable because thematic.[84] Although many

---

[81] See Aristotle's *Categories* and *Metaphysics*. For Cassirer's critique, see *Substance and Function and Einstein's Theory of Relativity*, trans. William Curtis Swabey and Marie Collins Swabey (Chicago, IL: Open Court, 1923). See also S. G. Lofts, *Ernst Cassirer: A "Repetition" of Modernity*, foreword by John Michael Krois (Albany, NY: State University of New York Press, 2000) and Sebastian Luft, "Cassirer's Philosophy of Symbolic Forms: Between Reason and Relativism – a Critical Appraisal," *Idealistic Studies* 34, no. 1 (2004): 25–47, especially p. 29.

[82] Classic formulations of this argument emerge in Husserl's work from his *Logical Investigations*, 2 vols., trans. J. N. Findlay (London: Routledge, 2001; originally published in 1901) onward, but see especially *Ideas Pertaining to a Pure Phenomenology and a Phenomenological Philosophy*, 2 vols., trans. F. Kersten (The Hague: Nijholt, 1983), and for discussion see Lewis R. Gordon, *Fanon and the Crisis of European Man: An Essay on Philosophy and the Human Sciences* (New York: Routledge, 1995), ch. 3.

[83] These criticisms go back to Max Weber and many other social theorists of the late nineteenth century, and they return in Alisdair C. MacIntyre, *After Virtue: A Study in Moral Theory*, 2nd edn (South Bend, IN: Notre Dame University Press, 1984). For an account in Africana philosophy, see Lewis R. Gordon, *Fanon and the Crisis of European Man* and *Disciplinary Decadence: Living Thought in Trying Times* (Boulder, CO: Paradigm Publishers, 2006).

[84] This observation is, by the way, shared by the hermeneuticists. See e.g. Hans Gorg-Gadamer, *Truth and Method*, 2nd rev. edn (New York: Continuum, 1989), and Paul Ricœur,

postmodernists, in the wake of Jacques Derrida's discussion of *différance*, searched for incommunicable terms, the true logic of such a turn is that in principle incommunicability should pertain as well to the self posing concepts to the self. The structure of such a proposal should be such that the moment it is posed to another, it is not communicated, which applies, as well, to the self posed to the self as other. In every moment of posing of the self as other is an implicit appeal to others through whom and with whom to communicate.[85]

A result of this turn to incommunicability is a strange notion of a politics of resistance premised upon the search for the hidden and the enigmatic. Wahneema Lubiano problematized this turn in her foreword to Ronald A. T. Judy's *(Dis)Forming the American Canon*, when she queried Judy's argument that *Ben Ali's Diary*, a work by an Afro-Arabic American slave, resists epistemic subjugation (through philosophy, philology, canon formation, historical, and other forms of Western disciplinary readings):

> in the case of Judy's argument for ben Ali, that particular narrative –
> resistant to decipherability – might also resist gendering. If this is so, I want
> to hear it said, see it written. And then perhaps a reader might take up the
> argument . . . is mystery an epistemological politics?[86]

The notion of mystery as a politics requires its appearance. Politics is peculiarly social; it is premised upon communication, exchange, persuasion, in a word, appearance. If anything, mystery is more suited for an anti-politics. A similar argument could be made for its status as an epistemological category. Where mystery works is at a semiological level, as a trace of the absent or absence, where diagnosis or the question of an ethical relation to

From Text to Action, trans. Kathleen Blamey and John B. Thompson (Evanston, IL: Northwestern University Press, 1991).

[85] See Jacques Derrida, *The Margins of Philosophy*, 2nd edn, trans. Alan Bass (Chicago, IL: University of Chicago Press, 1985). An obvious affinity of this criticism is Wittgenstein's famous rejection of private language arguments. See Ludwig Wittgenstein, *Philosophical Investigations*, 3rd edn, trans. G. E. M. Anscombe (Englewood Cliffs, NJ: Prentice Hall, 1958), paragraphs 269 and 275. And finally, a version of this argument appears in the thought of Jean-Paul Sartre: see *Transcendence of the Ego: An Existentialist Theory of Consciousness*, trans. and annotated with an introduction by Forrest Williams and Robert Kirkpatrick (New York: Noonday Press, 1960). Cf. also Gordon, *Existentia Africana*, and ch. 4.

[86] Wahneema Lubiano, "Foreword," in Judy, *(Dis)Forming the American Canon*, p. xxiii.

knowledge emerges. Mystery stimulates anxiety for some, the need to disclose for others, and there are those who may delight in it as an aesthetic experience. Eventually, the question is raised, Is this not a form of response to oppression that counsels problem people, as Du Bois would formulate it, to become more problematic by simply being out of the system's reach? What is this but a textual, theoretical reformulation of the conclusion of Ralph Ellison's *Invisible Man*, where the protagonist drains energy from the city without being seen? His resistance, in many ways, may be his own folly.[87]

We find a similar problem of reasoning in postmodern notions of symmetry. To work, the arguments must not assert an *a priori* commitment for or against asymmetry or symmetry since this would impose a necessity (supposed essentialism) on the result. Either must be examined as *ex post facto* descriptions in an argument.[88] If an asymmetry is asserted prior to its concrete manifestation, the appeal would be to an *a priori* asymmetry. One could claim that it is not a necessary asymmetry but an arbitrary or contingent one, but if that is so, the modal question of whether that is a necessary arbitrariness or not would not have emerged. The case of symmetry is very similar. Although there is an injunction against binaries, symmetrical assertions abound in places where there is a claim of difference. For example, nowhere is this more evident in African-American philosophy than in some black feminist writings. On the one hand, there is the authors' claim that black women's lives are fundamentally different from black men's and should be focused on even to the exclusion of black men. But when black men are discussed as fundamentally different from black women, the criticism such authors offer is that there is a wrongful exclusion of black women.[89] The first claim could only be defended through admitting

---

[87] Ralph Ellison, *Invisible Man* (New York: Vintage, 1990).

[88] The source of this argument is Hume's critique of causation in *A Treatise of Human Nature*, ed. with introduction by Ernest C. Mossner (London: Penguin Classics, 1969), book I, part III, especially secs. III, XIV, and XV. Hume faced the problem of the absence of an empirical basis of his appeal to empiricism.

[89] A case study of this phenomenon is the literature on Frantz Fanon as sexist. For a genealogy and discussion of this literature see T. Denean Sharpley-Whiting's *Frantz Fanon: Conflicts in Feminisms* (Lanham, MD: Rowman & Littlefield, 1998), and see also Lewis R. Gordon, "Through the Zone of Nonbeing: A Reading of *Black Skin, White Masks* in Celebration of Fanon's Eightieth Birthday," *The C. L. R. James Journal II*, no. 1 (2005): 1–43.

an asymmetry. The second claim could only maintain the asymmetry if, and only if, the added claim was made that the first can exist independently of the second, but it cannot be the case the other way around. Put differently, a discussion of black men entails a discussion of black women, but one of black women does not entail any of black men.

One approach to the problem of presumed symmetry in a theoretical model that outlaws presumptions is to appeal to the social constructivity of the asymmetry to begin with. If, however, the asymmetry is socially constructed, it does not follow that the symmetry must not have been constructed, which means, then, that constructivity cannot be used as an invalidating premise. If, in other words, asymmetry is only a social creation, what, then, is symmetry? If we assert, as well, the social constructivity of symmetry, then a prior neither-nor must be the case. We are left, then, with a premise whose set cannot have any members for the sake of validity. But then a new necessity is imposed, namely, the logic of the empty set, from which anything can be validly generated. The upshot is that postmodern anti-essentialism goes nowhere since the denial of essentialism does not ensure anti-essentialism. Admission of having made essentialist claims does not amount to an affirmation or rejection of essentialism. In short, for the criticism to have an impact, it must displace or reject grounding any argument, but such a rejection would itself be a criterion that grounded the process of "ungrounding." Paget Henry makes a similar criticism of a cherished concept of poststructural anti-essentialist modes of inquiry – namely, "undecidability" – when he writes:

> To the extent that post-structuralists engage in discursive activity, the privileging of the undecidable middle functions as a center of discourse construction. As such a center, a new metaphysics of difference and undecidability develops around it. This metaphysics soon establishes its own distinct binaries and polarities. These develop around the prioritizing of language as the carrier of the site of the undecidable middle. As such language acquires a unique discourse constituting value in relation to other discourse-constituting factors such as the economic, the political, the factual or the event. From these hierarchies will follow patterns of inclusion and exclusion as well as prescription for rejecting and accepting specific socio-historical projects. In short, the undecidable middle brings into being a new metaphysics and the possibilities of new discourses, but human discourses nonetheless. As a result, this entire epistemic constellation of the

semiotic middle is as much in need of justification as polar centered discourses [i.e., binary oppositions] and their metaphysical foundations [essences].[90]

We are thus faced with our second, underlying concern of Africana philosophy – namely, that of liberation and social transformation – what Henry in the above quotation referred to as "socio-historical projects" – returning with the query: can African-American and Afro-British philosophy afford to sacrifice reality in its pursuit of such a goal?

Cedric Robinson's anthropology of Marxism

The pragmatist response to this question of reality involves, as we have seen, historically situated social criticism. This response has often converged with the African-American and Afro-British Marxist traditions, where reality is seen in materialist terms. Many proponents of that tradition have resisted offering a new theory of Marxist philosophy. The exceptions include Du Bois, Fanon, the Trinidadian C. L. R. James (1900–1989), whose work we will briefly examine in chapter 5, the early Stuart Hall, the early Cornel West, and Cedric Robinson.[91]

Du Bois and Fanon have received considerable attention in this book thus far. Although Hall's contributions are not primarily philosophical, his work brought the thought of the Italian Marxist Antonio Gramsci (1891–1937) to bear on cultural politics in Britain through his leadership of the Centre for Contemporary Cultural Studies at the University of Birmingham. Focusing on Gramsci's theory of hegemony, which explores how consent is manufactured, Hall transformed Marxist critiques of ideology through what was in effect a cultural expansion of the phenomenological theory of constitutionality to argue that people are the producers of the culture they consume. The

---

[90] Paget Henry, "C. L. R. James and the Orthodoxies of John McClendon and David Scott: a Review Essay," *The C. L. R. James Journal* 13, no. 1 (2007): 285–6.

[91] For Stuart Hall, see *Stuart Hall: Critical Dialogues*, ed. David Morley, Kuan-Hsing Chen, and Stuart Hall (New York: Routledge, 1996). The most influential intellectual and political treatment of African-American Marxism is Cedric J. Robinson's classic work *Black Marxism: The Making of the Black Radical Tradition*, reissued edn, with a foreword by Robin Kelley (Durham, NC: University of North Carolina Press, 2005), which was originally printed in London in 1983 by Zed Press. See also Robinson's *Black Movements in America* (New York: Routledge, 1997).

phenomenological theory of constitution argues that meaning is created as if already existing. It poses the active dimension of human subjects in the formation of structures, but it does not treat those structures as easily transformed. The theme of the relationship between agency and structure is at the heart of the concept, and although Hall does not articulate his work in those terms, his approach challenges reductionistic views of extreme agency versus extreme structure. Both affect each other. As an innovation in Marxism, Hall's approach rejects the simple model of a bourgeoisie that simply dictates its values to a passive proletariat. The correlate with race is the rejection of a structural whiteness that simply dictates its values to a passive blackness locked in the first stage of Du Boisian double consciousness.

West, as we have seen, drew upon Gramsci as well, but he also sought compatibility between Deweyan pragmatism and Marxism, which he attempted to fuse in a form of writing inspired by Derridian deconstruction as read by Richard Rorty. Robinson, however, turned to Foucauldian poststructuralism to offer an archaeology of the contradictions of historical Marxism and liberalism as peculiarly bourgeois orders of knowledge that created a polar, dualistic, oppositional conception of man in the form of a class struggle that placed gender and race, and consequently all women and people of color, as epiphenomenal and, thus, at the periphery.[92] By drawing upon premodern foundations of socialist thought, Robinson argues that market economics as formulated by modern liberalism and Marxism produced, as the "ferment of a *civilization*, rather than the simple products of a particular event," a false dilemma by limiting the drama of modern manifestations of agency as a conflict between the bourgeoisie and the proletariat, in effect making agents appear solely as capitalist and industrial workers.[93]

Marx and Engels were able to achieve this false anthropology, Robinson argues, through articulating a conception of intellectual history that drew upon resources from Greek antiquity and then hopped over the Middle Ages into the modern era, where the market became the center of economic analysis. The general view that there was no economic theory proper in antiquity was a function of the examination of society offered by Plato and

---

[92] Cedric J. Robinson, *An Anthropology of Marxism* (Aldershot, Hampshire: Ashgate, 2001). For the main poststructural influence, see Michel Foucault, *The Order of Things: An Archaeology of the Human Sciences*, trans. Alan Sheridan (New York: Vintage, 1973).

[93] See e.g. Robinson, *Black Marxism*, p. 2.

Aristotle in which ethics became a focus of practical life in a form that covered over the measures of wealth and the ongoing function of material sustenance in Athenian society – namely, the governing dynamics of the household manifested by women and slaves. The subsequent reduction of economic theory to concerns of production, demands, prices, and alienation revealed a focus on the relations of a growing bourgeois class and the form of labor most capable of being absorbed into it at the expense of the many other organizations of people in modern life to whom wealth tended not to be distributed. As with antiquity, what is missing here is the significance of the elision of women and slaves as central concerns of political economy.

Robinson then argues that in the Middle Ages, by contrast, the effort to make Christianity a feature of everyday life led to conflicts with the governing groups through a demand for a redistribution of wealth in concert with Christian egalitarianism. The imperfect history of these struggles took a variety of forms, where discussions of a more rigorous egalitarianism included discourses on the human that included women, indigenous peoples, and slaves. A crucial dimension of this conflict is that it unfolded within the framework of theological and religious axiology. Marx's attack on religion is well known, and his tendency to draw from the secular intellectuals in his interpretation of history rendered such thinkers as Luis de Molina (1535–1600), Francisco Suárez (1548–1617), and the debates over slavery and war in the thought of Bartolomé de Las Casas (c. 1474–1566), Juan Ginés de Sepúlveda (1494–1573), Francisco de Vitoria (c. 1483–1546), and Domingo de Soto (1494–1560), and the radical socialist thought of Marsilius dei Mainardini, also known as Marsilius of Padua (c. 1275/1280–1342), in a word, invisible to the course of materialist history. Added to this are all the people who are historic foci of Christian socialism, such as Marx and Engels's hated lumpen-proletariat, whom they refer to as the "dangerous class," who are "the social scum, that passively rotting mass thrown off by the lowest layers of old society," and the vast category of people subsumed under the category of poor and indigent. They are condemned to "decay and finally disappear in the face of Modern Industry . . ."[94]

"By evacuating radical medieval philosophy from socialism's genealogy," Robinson objects,

---

[94] Karl Marx and Friedrich Engels, *Manifesto of the Communist Party*, in *the Marx-Engels Reader*, 2nd edn, ed. Robert C. Tucker (Princeton, NJ: Princeton University Press, 1978), p. 482.

Marx privileged his own ideological rules of discursive formation, providing a rationale for distinguishing the a [*sic*] scientific socialism concomitant with the appearance of capitalist society from the lesser ("utopian") and necessarily inadequate articulation of socialism which occurred earlier. So doing, he deprived his own work of the profound and critical insights exemplified in Marsilius's writings. Both the ancients and his own immediate predecessors, for instance, contributed to an inferior, more ambiguous, and misogynist consciousness of female liberation to that constituted in medieval radicalism.[95]

In stream with Foucault, Robinson concludes that Marxism was part of the episteme that it criticized, that it was, in effect, bourgeois science. "That and related discourses of bourgeois political economy," he concludes,

> were directly implicated in the legitimation of slave economies, slave labor and racism. Democracy, too, fueled by centuries of popular resistances, had acquired its better champions among medieval socialists. Notwithstanding their keen appetites for history, Marx and Engels had chosen to obliterate the most fertile discursive domain for their political ambitions and historical imaginations. Possibly even less troubling for them, they displaced a socialist motivation grounded on the insistence that men and women were divine agents for the fractious and weaker allegiances of class.[96]

Marxism and other forms of bourgeois political economic science thus offer a conception of reality that, given Robinson's critique, literally limits what one is able to see. In this regard, the black radical tradition stands, along with feminist theory, not as an addendum to Marxism, but as, literally, part of the rest of the world manifested by its blind spots. We see here, in effect, a return of the dialectical dimension of the double consciousness argument and more, for Robinson's aim is a critique in the sense of attempting to bring out the antinomies and limitations of a theory in the interest of its ultimate aims. Since liberation is the ultimate aim of struggles against exploitation, Marxism must be subjected to a metacritique even if that means, while appreciating its inspiration toward radical efforts at social transformation, going beyond it.[97] Robinson's classic work *Black Marxism* thus stands as part of his effort to offer such a critique. We see, as well, in Robinson's work the themes that have been

---

[95] Robinson, *Black Marxism*, p. 138.   [96] *Ibid.*, pp. 138–9.   [97] Cf. *ibid.*, pp. 156–7.

serving as the leitmotif of the Africana tradition: he offers a philosophical anthropology in the interest of liberation in the service of which he subjects both to a metacritique of its presuppositions and reason. Reality here, then, is historical in a way that brings to the fore the underside of history.

African-American existential philosophy, phenomenology, and their influence

The question of reality is also taken up by African-American existential philosophy and African-American phenomenology. Since I know of no African-American phenomenology that is not also part of African-American existential philosophy, I will discuss them together, although in theory they are analytically distinct.

As in the other forms of African-American thought, African-American existential thought addresses the ongoing motif of black problems. The word existence comes from the Latin expression *ex sistere*, which means to stand out or to emerge. "To exist" literally means to emerge from indistinction or insignificance or, simply, to appear. The word today is most often associated with being, but its etymology, especially as it is used in French, suggests to live and to be. Conception is the beginning of one's existence and death is its end, although one could continue, so to speak, in the memory of others. To exist to oneself in the sense of living is to become fully aware of being alive and what that signifies. To exist at all is to appear to some consciousness, even if that means from one's point of view.

Paget Henry has shown that problems of existence were struggled with in precolonial Africa in the form of the human being's relation to forces and beliefs of predestination in the face of an unfolding future.[98] Each human being is expected to seek out his or her unique "calling" in life, a view which places much agency or responsibility in individuals linked to a broad community of elders, ancestors, deities, and an ultimate being, as attested to by Kwame Gyekye in his study of the conceptual scheme of the Akan, who were among the West African groups whose descendants were kidnapped and brought to the New World.[99] In most African cosmological systems the

---

[98] Paget Henry, "African and Afro-Caribbean Existential Philosophies," in Gordon, *Existence in Black*, pp. 11–36.

[99] See Gyekye, *An Essay on African Philosophy*.

past has greater ontological weight than the present, and the future has none since it has not yet occurred.[100] The classic existential claim that we are what we have done, which makes much of who we are to be something in the making, unfolds; however, here there is the difference of the promised self to achieve. A crucial feature of this view is that this promised self does not exist but is instead sought. The failure to achieve one's calling simply means a miserable life, and its achievement an alignment with things that will make one happy. But the crucial point, as far as existential notions of freedom are concerned, is that no one and nothing else could make those choices for the agent; the choices are not, in other words, determined.

The enslaved and freed Africans that came to the New World eventually created creolized cultures with the indigenous people of America, Asian migrant workers and indentured servants, and Europeans. This convergence created new problems of existence that included but were not limited to racialized slavery and antiblack racism.

To some extent we have already been examining early formulations of black existential thought in our discussions of the thought of eighteenth- and nineteenth-century Africana philosophers. The centrality of such problems as the meaning of being human, the concept of freedom, and the limits of rationality are longstanding existential themes. They are evident in the work of some of the most influential writers in African-American literature, whose genealogy from the writings of Phillis Wheatley (1753–1784, black inner life) and James Weldon Johnson (1871–1938, alienation) came most explicitly to the fore in the writings of Richard Wright (1908–1960), who articulated the situation of the black subject in antiblack society. A situation, as argued by Jean-Paul Sartre and Simone de Beauvoir (1908–1986), refers to what emerges from human encounters, which they describe as a conflict of freedoms.[101] Such encounters often generate meanings that the agents do not necessarily intend. This is so in Wright's short stories, as

---

[100] This view of time has created some controversy in the interpretation of some communities, as we will see in our discussion of African philosophy. But for now standard texts include, in addition to Gyekye's, John Mbiti's *African Religion and Philosophy*, 2nd enlarged and rev. edn (Oxford: Heineman, 1990); Benjamin C. Ray, *African Religions: Symbol, Ritual, and Community*, 2nd edn (Upper Saddle River, NJ: Prentice Hall, 2000).

[101] See Jean-Paul Sartre, *Being and Nothingness: A Phenomenological Essay on Ontology*, trans. Hazel V. Barnes (New York: Washington Square Press, 1956) and Simone de Beauvoir, *The Ethics of Ambiguity*, trans. Bernard Frechtman (New York: Citadel, 2000).

Kathryn T. Gines has argued, but it is best known through his novels.[102] In *Native Son* the protagonist Bigger Thomas finds himself in a serious situation when he helps his white employer's drunken daughter to her bedroom after chauffeuring her and her boyfriend round Chicago and realizes that he, with her in his arms, is at risk of being "discovered." Wright articulates the relationship between choice and options for those who are denied normality, those who find themselves constantly thrown into situations they would prefer to have avoided. He outlines many of the classic existential problems of freedom and responsibility that follow. In "How Bigger Was Born," his famous introduction to the 1940 edition of *Native Son*, he argues that US society "makes" Bigger Thomases, people who, in attempting to assert their humanity, become its troublemakers as society attempts to force them back into "their place" while holding them responsible for their actions. Wright is able both to criticize a system for what it does to people while recognizing the importance of responsibility, even under unjust systems, as a necessary condition for human dignity and maturity. In his last novel, *The Outsider*, this theme is explicitly made through the anti-hero, Cross Damon, who finds himself incapable of experiencing responsibility because he lives in a world that inhibits his development into a man. His greatest fear is realized when he dies confessing a feeling of "innocence" after having killed several people.[103] Wright has had an impact on nearly every subsequent aspect of black existential thought, as we will see in the course of this discussion.

Another theme that comes to the fore in literary black existential thought is invisibility, a subject that has become almost synonymous with Ralph Ellison.[104] Here, black invisibility is a function of hypervisibility. It is a form of being what Frantz Fanon called a phobogenic object, an object that stimulates anxiety. Ellison laments the madness faced by educated blacks, who naively expect their achievements to entail their inclusion (visibility) instead of heightened exclusion (invisibility) in the United States, for they live in a social world in which they exemplify the "impossible." Baldwin brings such questions to interracial, bisexual, and sexually open settings and looks at

---

[102] See Kathryn T. Gines, "Existentialism and Exile: The Philosophical Legacy of Richard Wright," presented at the Eastern Division American Philosophical Association Meetings held in Washington, DC (December 2006).

[103] See Richard Wright, *Native Son* (New York: Harper & Row, 1960) and *The Outsider* (New York: Harper & Row, 1960).

[104] See Ellison, *Invisible Man*.

the question of suffering as a struggle to defend the possibility of genuine human relationships. I add "sexually open" since the characters in Baldwin's work often resist fixed sexual identities.[105] The question of invisibility takes on a unique form, as well, in the novels of Toni Morrison, particularly her inaugurating work, *Bluest Eye*. There, Morrison brings out the peculiarity of notions such as "ugliness" and "beauty" that dominate women's lives in general but black women's in a profound way through expectations of mimesis. The expectation that black women will copy white females' appearance subordinates their lives since all imitations are ultimately inauthentic. They live by a standard that they can never meet. This theme of inauthenticity is taken to another level when she writes of bad "mixture" in a world that bridges the gaps between adults and children the consequence of which is molestation and incest, mixtures that, in stream with Ellison, produce madness.[106] More recently, in *Freedom in the Dismal*, Monifa Love brings many of these existential themes together through a provocative exploration of the meaning of freedom in the midst of very limited options.[107] I have here offered but a glimpse of the work of the literary African-American existentialists since the focus of this study is philosophical. They are touched upon here because a feature of existential thought is its challenge to disciplinary boundaries. To have not mentioned the literary figures would be a misrepresentation of this area of thought. Yet although the literary figures explore these existential themes with evocative force, the questions they have raised take on added dimensions when considered through theoretical reflection.

More recently, black existential thought has manifested itself in the writings of academics from a variety of fields ranging from philosophy to communications. Although we have explored his ideas in terms of prophetic pragmatism, Cornel West has, for example, also extended pragmatism to

---

[105] The classic instance is James Baldwin,' *Another Country* (New York: Vintage, 1993). For discussion see Guy Mark Foster, "Love's Future Structures? The Dilemma of Interracial Coupling in Postwar African American Literature" (Providence, RI: Brown University Dissertation in English, 2003) and Jean-Paul Rocchi, "James Baldwin. Ecriture et Identité," (Paris: University of Paris IV-Sorbonne Dissertation in Literature, 2001).

[106] Toni Morrison, *The Bluest Eye* (New York: Holt, Rinehart, and Winston, 1970). For more discussion, see Gary Schwartz, "Toni Morrison at the Movies: Theorizing Race through *Imitation of Life* (for Barbara Siegel)," in Gordon, *Existence in Black*, pp. 111–28.

[107] Monifa Love, *Freedom in the Dismal: A Novel* (Kaneohe, Hawaii: Plover Press, 1998).

draw upon existential influences, as I suggested in pointing out the impact of Kierkegaard and Chekov on his writings, into existential pragmatism. His continued motifs of dread, despair, death, disease and, in his most popular work, nihilism provide additional support.[108]

The phenomenological approach also has roots in the thought of Du Bois and Fanon. Since phenomenology is premised upon taking seriously the role of consciousness in the formation of meaning, Du Bois's turn to the examination of double consciousness and the varieties of race consciousness, as well as his subsequent work on the formation of historic consciousness and its importance in processes of social transformation, is one instance. Fanon's work is phenomenologically rich; as we have seen, his insight on method, that it, too, must be evaluated through critical, decolonizing investigations, and his work on recognition make sense only within a phenomenological framework.[109]

African-American phenomenology was formerly inaugurated in the American academy in the form of an existential phenomenology in the late 1960s, however, in the thought of William R. Jones.[110] Such work was soon followed by Lucius T. Outlaw, Jr.'s effort to articulate a hermeneutics of black experience through engaging the thought of Alfred Schutz and Charles Johnson's examination of African-American writing through the thought of Martin Heidegger.[111] The subsequent work of the first two of these three philosophers is of enormous influence. In *Is God a White Racist?*

---

[108] See Cornel West's *Race Matters*, which includes his very influential essay "Nihilism in the Black Community." He returns to the theme of nihilism, as well, in *Democracy Matters*.

[109] There is the added consideration that Fanon studied with one of the great French phenomenologists in the Husserlian tradition, Maurice Merleau-Ponty. See Alice Cherki's *Fanon: A Psychological Biography*, trans. Nadia Benabid (Ithaca, NY: Cornell University Press, 2006).

[110] See William R. Jones's dissertation, "On Sartre's Critical Methodology" (Providence, RI: Brown University Philosophy of Religion Dissertation, 1967).

[111] Lucius T. Outlaw, "Language and the Transformation of Consciousness: Foundations for a Hermeneutic of Black Culture" (Boston, MA: Boston College Doctoral Dissertation in Philosophy, 1972) and Charles Johnson, *Being and Race: Black Writing since 1970* (Bloomington, IN: Indiana University Press, 1988), which was also his doctoral dissertation in philosophy at the State University of New York at Stony Brook. The Heideggerian line has not had many adherents. Independent explorations include the work of Roy Martinez, and the very creative addition of Heideggerian discussions of death in relation to the struggles of Frederick Douglass and Richard Wright in Abdul R. JanMohamed's *The Death-Bound-Subject: Richard Wright's Archaeology of Death* (Durham, NC: Duke University Press, 2005).

Jones argued that the history of modern Christianity raised the problem of theodicy; God, it seems, has not been on the side of black people.[112] This raises a problem for Black Theology, which, through the writings of such luminaries as Howard Thurman and James Cone, argued that the Bible should be interpreted as offering a story of liberation for black people.[113] Jones argued that since the evidence does not support that thesis, the only way to avoid the problem of a black-hating God was to pose the question of liberation as a function of human history.[114] He advocated the route of secular humanism, where human beings take responsibility for the course of history. Jones's subsequent work has been devoted to developing a theory of oppression that would render the course of liberation more coherent, and, in the tradition of Crummell, he has been instrumental in building the infrastructure for African-American philosophy in the wider academy. It was Jones, for instance, who made the case for formal, academic African-American philosophy in the 1970s and the co-founding of the Committee on the Status of Blacks in Philosophy in the American Philosophical Association.[115] In similar kind Outlaw's *On Race and Philosophy* focused on struggles against racism, the need for black-affirming environments, the development of an anti-racist philosophy, and the construction of Africana philosophy.[116] Johnson's efforts turned toward creative writing, where he is mostly known as an award-winning novelist. His inaugural work in philosophy, which he characterized as "a phenomenology of black writing," addressed the anxiety of the black writer who struggles through crises of identity in search of liberation often in the form of a "mythical home."[117] Drawing upon Karsten

---

[112] William R. Jones, *Is God a White Racist?*

[113] For a concise discussion of this movement, see James Cone, "Black Theology as Liberation Theology," in *African American Religious Studies*, ed. Gayraud S. Wilmore (Durham, NC: Duke University Press, 1989), pp. 177–207.

[114] For additional discussion of this view, see Roy D. Morrison, II, "Self-Transformation in American Blacks: the Harlem Renaissance and Black Theology," in Gordon, *Existence in Black*, pp. 37–48. Morrison (1926–1995) was primarily a philosopher of science who taught at Wesleyan Theological Seminary. His magnum opus was published just before his death: *Science, Theology, and the Transcendental Horizon: Einstein, Kant, and Tillich* (Atlanta, GA: Scholars Press, 1994).

[115] See William R. Jones, "Crisis in Philosophy: The Black Presence," *Proceedings and Addresses of the American Philosophical Association*, 47 (1973–9), and "The Legitimacy and Necessity of Black Philosophy: Some Preliminary Considerations," *The Philosophical Forum* 9, nos. 2–3 (1977–1978): 149–60.

[116] Lucius T. Outlaw, *On Race and Philosophy* (New York: Routledge, 1996).

[117] Johnson, *Being & Race: Black Writing since 1970*, p. 8.

Harries's theory of kitsch as a flight into a form of self-confidence in an effort to evade the precarious dimensions of self-consciousness offered by modernity, Johnson argued, for instance, that

> Like fascist art in Germany during the 1930s, Negritude – all Kitsch – is a retreat from ambiguity, the complexity of Being occasioned by the conflict of interpretations, and a flight by the black artist from the agony of facing a universe silent as to its sense, where even black history (or all history) must be seen as an ensemble of experiences and documents difficult to read, indeed, as an experience capable of inexhaustible readings.[118]

That the criticism negates any black perspective *qua* itself as a legitimate one brings to the fore the recurring problem of black intellectual production in a world in which the generative or normative grammar of such activity is, in a word, "white." This whiteness functions, although not made explicitly so, as axiomatic, which means that it evaluates instead of receiving interrogation. In effect, as self-justified, it becomes both its source and recipient of its emplacement or "home," the result of which is a moribund assessment of the black condition.

The theme of homelessness brings us back to the thought of Molefi Asante, whose work appears, as an heir of Negritude, to be a prime target of Johnson's criticism. Although Afrocentricity stands as its own philosophy, its emphasis has strong existential overtones. For instance, the argument that African peoples should claim historical agency and that such a project cannot be waged on unstable foundations, where stability is here taken as locating one's home in Africa, is synchronous with Johnson's diagnosis, even though Johnson and Asante take radically different positions on the possibility and place of "home." Asante insists that his claims are cultural, not racial, but that homelessness is a function of rejecting the continued survival of a transgeographical home – namely, African cultures – carried down through the ages in the people who are also known as black people in the modern world.[119] An affirmation of that culture requires education, where the claim is that freed minds will lead to emancipated communities. Where Afrocentricity departs from existential philosophy, however, is ironically on this very question of the relation of thought to action. The logic of

---

[118] *Ibid.*, p. 20, and Karsten Harries, *The Meaning of Modern Art* (Evanston, IL: Northwestern University Press, 1968), p. 158.

[119] He is explicit about this in *The Afrocentric Idea* and *An Afrocentric Manifesto*.

the argument requires, in effect, an act of conceptualization that precedes existence, and this is because of the requirement of stability. The argument forecloses what a person of African descent is to be by focusing more on his or her past than future; in fact, it formulates the African's future *in* the past. Johnson's criticism looms. To be fair to Asante, however, it should be borne in mind that it is not his goal to transform Afrocentricity into an existential philosophy. But more germane here, it should also be considered that the argument could easily be transformed into an existential one through first rejecting the notion of a human nature that occludes human possibility and then arguing for a philosophical anthropology that, in giving primacy to agency and freedom, makes culture more of a context than a determinism. If this is his meaning, Afrocentricity would not only be correctly read in existential terms but also be able to offer this appeal as a response to Johnson's challenge of constructing open instead of closed texts. I do not think Asante would object to this consideration.

A criticism that could be made of Johnson's conception of the black writer at the precipice of kitsch is that it ironically fails to articulate the existential situation of at least the black American writer as a black living in America. The imposition of racism is more than a question of homelessness. It is also, as Abdul JanMohamed argues in his study of Richard Wright, a form of living with the threat of death constitutive of a unique form of subjectivity, which he calls "the death-bound-subject."[120] Richard Wright, for instance, was not a writer struggling for recognition at a distance from the lived reality of being black in the modern world. His writings reveal, JanMohamed argues, that he was part of a tradition that

> reveals itself as an amazing archive of knowledge about the destructive effects of terroristic coercion and the means and effort required to resist and, indeed, triumph over such coercion . . . [T]his tradition of African American *literary* meditation about the death-bound-subject evinces a fascinating transformation – from relatively "impersonal" meditations of the early slave narratives, such as those of Harriet Jacobs and Douglass, to progressively more "subjective" presentations of the same fundamental experiences. This gradual shift, in which Wright occupies an important

---

[120] See JanMohamed's *The Death-Bound-Subject: Richard Wright's Archaeology of Death*. Cf. also Joyce Ann Joyce, *Richard Wright's Art of Tragedy* (Iowa City, IA: Iowa University Press, 2001).

median point, reaches its climax generally in the work of Toni Morrison and most particularly in *Beloved*, which, by focusing so relentlessly and unsentimentally on an instance of infanticide that is fueled by undeniable maternal love, raises that aporetic structure of the death-bound-subject to its excruciatingly painful and profoundly illuminating climax.[121]

As JanMohamed further reminds us: "It is important to emphasize that in the racialized relations between whites and blacks in the South nothing short of the absolutely *total* subservience of blacks was, in practice, demanded and, most important, policed by the threat of death."[122] Subjection here is externally imposed by the social and historical realities of antiblack racism, but as an external imposition, it lacks the internal essential features of self-closure of which Johnson offers a critique.

Fanonian themes of sociogenesis, failures of the dialectics of recognition, and interrogation return here. Recall Fanon's locating the kinds of subjectivity racism generates in the social world, and that, among its many consequences, is the collapse of whole groups of people into the zone of nonbeing, outside of the ethical sphere of dialectical dynamics between self and other, with the condition of living the reality of denied humanity. JanMohamed acknowledges this connection by concluding his study with a reflection on choice from Fanon, who was also a friend of Richard Wright:

> I find myself suddenly in the world and I recognize that I have one right alone: That of demanding human behavior from the other.
> One duty alone: That of not renouncing my freedom through my choices.[123]

The most explicitly detailed phenomenological lines were inaugurated in 1995, with the publication of *Bad Faith and Antiblack Racism* and *Fanon and the Crisis of European Man*, and through a series of articles during the same decade by the Afro-Latina philosopher Linda Martín Alcoff, brought together and revised as *Visible Identities: Race, Gender, and the Self*.[124] The first

---

[121] JanMohamed, *The Death-Bound-Subject*, pp. 3–4. This observation could also apply to black religious existential reflection on death-bound subjectivity, as found in the thought of Howard Thurman, *Deep River and the Negro Spiritual Speaks of Life and Death* and *Disciplines of the Spirit* (Richmond, IN: Friends United Press, 1963).

[122] JanMohamed, *The Death-Bound-Subject*, p. 7.

[123] The quotation is from p. 229 of *Black Skin, White Masks*, and it is included on p. 300 of JanMohamed's study.

[124] Lewis R. Gordon, *Bad Faith and Antiblack Racism* (Amherst, NY: Humanity Books, 1999), originally published in 1995 by Humanities International Press in the New Jersey

two works offered phenomenological descriptions of what were called "coextensive" dimensions of bad faith, where embodied and institutional forms of consciousness hide from themselves, which facilitates a world that is antipathetic to constructing critical norms of evidence addressing the complex interplay between intersubjectivity or "social reality." In effect, racism involves making groups of human beings into things that they are not, and antiblack racism is a form of such activity. But more, there are implications of being able to deny reality, being able to live falsehoods, and these, it was argued, have an impact on the challenges faced in human studies. For what can be made of such an inquiry when the theorist is in bad faith? This question is taken up in *Fanon and the Crisis of European Man*, where the problem of studying human beings under colonial conditions, where the very process of producing knowledge has been colonized by the kinds of rationality and rationalizations that support it, comes to the fore. This work introduces what became known as Africana existential phenomenology, postcolonial phenomenology, or, more recently, decolonial phenomenology through addressing the Du Boisian problematic of "problem people" and the Fanonian demand of a decolonized methodology. The text shows, for instance, that crises are functions of human communities denying their agency in the formation of human problems; that the effort to transform such problems requires a conception of history that allows for agency in history instead of only the historical agent; that although human study cannot be an exact science, it can be a coherent and rigorous one, which means that the effort to articulate a subject of liberation is possible; that the logic of human value has tragic dimensions because of the maturation process required for its own evaluation; that struggles for liberation make no sense without the emergence of a livable everyday as an ordinary form of life; and that the role of disciplines in the construction of human subjects is always limited by the possibility of disciplinary decay or "disciplinary decadence." These ideas are expanded in other works through analyses of how this approach exemplifies the phenomenological self-reflective movements of not presuming its method, but to function properly as such, it must

Highlands, and *Fanon and the Crisis of European Man*. I have already cited *Visible Identities* in the brief discussion of Afro-European continental philosophy. Alcoff is here referred to as "Afro-Latina" so as to bring to the fore the dimensions of her work that deal with the complexity of race and populations who can sometimes "pass," to which I will return at the end of this chapter.

commit an act of "ontological suspension" or suspension of one's ontological commitment, the correlate of which in Husserlian phenomenology is bracketing or parenthesizing the natural attitude.[125] This means, then, that this form of phenomenology is able to look at what it means to be a problem instead of simply what it is to be a problem. The separation of meaning from being here enables one to suspend the seriousness of the value-category of blackness and in that stroke takes seriously the distinction of having problems versus being them.

The question of decolonizing method comes to the fore in the redundancy of the term postcolonial phenomenology. For phenomenology requires not only suspension of ontological commitments, but also those commitments connected to the evaluation and means of going about making commitments. Such a turn pushes the inquirer up against whatever limits he or she may face. This means that even the method is subject to a suspension, which disables a colonizing episteme's or order of knowledge functioning as a legitimating process. The point is perhaps most stark in the case of logic. A proper self-critical phenomenological investigation requires suspending the legitimating and ontological force of logic itself because even logic must be subjected to a process of legitimation if it is to be accepted; the very notion of "evidence," in other words, must be made evidential. Ironically, this means taking reality seriously without placing a false domain or circle around it. The Fanonian demand of not assuming one's method is, then, in this sense, also a phenomenological one. These arguments lay foundations for what perhaps appears to be the first systematic Africana philosophy to have emerged since the eighteenth century. Systematic is not here meant as a closed "system," as one finds in Hegel, but instead a view of philosophy and reality that comes out of the Africana themes of philosophical anthropology, liberation, and metareflection. One of the main premises of this philosophy is that there is an incompleteness at the heart of all self-evaluating, living reality because reality is simply greater than anyone who attempts to evaluate it, and that reason, as the exemplar of this incompleteness, is broader than rationality. The effort to make rationality govern reason, to make reason maximally consistent, to make the part greater than the whole, is an effort to place the cart before the horse. This misguided logic leads to an effort to take the human (incompleteness) out of human phenomena, to construct a kind of anti-human world of completely law-governed things.

---

[125] See e.g. Gordon, *Her Majesty's Other Children, Existentia Africana*, and *Disciplinary Decadence.*

Since incompleteness is at the origin of human ways of life, the problems of bondage and colonization are not only external but also internal – they require closing off the options available for meaningful ways of life; one form of such erasure is "epistemic closure," where knowledge functions as a colonizing force.[126] The assertion of epistemology as first philosophy in the modern age exemplifies another dimension of such a force – namely, the goal of asserting a form of rationalism over reason. The value of ontological work, of re-examining and taking heed of the importance of reality, takes a new form, then, in the effort to free reason from the yoke of reductive rationality.

The argument about incompleteness also enables a critique of the kinds of reductionism that lead to conceptions of the human as a being completely governed by structural impositions on the one hand and those of the human being as radically free of such forces on the other. Human life is contextualized by structure, but it is not completely determined by it. Structure, which here can also be interpreted as "options," sets the context for choices, which unfold the ongoing meaning and values of a particular human being's story and the collective one of humankind. The interplay of structure and choices manifested by the relationship with them both produces and is produced by "subjects," which can be read through the phenomenological theory of constitution as passive–active modes of production. The subject is, in other words, produced and produces itself and other kinds of things at the same time.

Postcolonial Africana phenomenology also sees blackness as a dialectical limit of imposed whiteness, in which the theme of closure is its main motif. Du Bois's concept of double consciousness, extended phenomenologically, can be understood as a thesis on the dialectics between false reality and its contradictions. White supremacy and antiblack racism are values asserted on reality with additionally false notions of universals and particulars. Themes of incompleteness and freedom militate against such notions. That an understanding of that absolute reality cannot be a closed notion means that new concepts are needed through which to understand the unique dynamics of living beings and how the social world renders them replaceable and "irreplaceable."[127] And more, drawing upon the work of

---

[126] See Lewis R. Gordon, *ibid.* and *Fanon and the Crisis of European Man*.

[127] See e.g. Lewis R. Gordon, "Irreplaceability: An Existential Phenomenological Reflection," *Listening: A Journal of Religion and Culture* 38, no. 2 (2003): 190–202.

Frantz Fanon, it is an error to structure blackness in terms of white recognition, which is a reassertion of dependency and colonialism. Instead, the goal is to transcend the dialectics of recognition itself through a focus on engagements and creative negotiation of the world of meaning as constituted by the social world. The social world is the reality by which human beings live meaningfully, but it is not all of reality since the fact of death makes every human being aware that reality both precedes and exceeds the moment of human emergence. This is even more realized in the experience of the birth and loss of a loved one. There, one witnesses the supervening continuum of reality. This analysis reached across the African diaspora under the rubric of Africana existential philosophy.

Like Cornel West, Africana existential philosophy as manifested in *Her Majesty's Other Children, Fanon and the Crisis of European Man, Existentia Africana,* and *Disciplinary Decadence* regards nihilism as a fundamental problem of our time but concludes that it is symptomatic of a process of a greater social decay. This decay affects the construction and production of knowledge. When decadent, knowledge becomes deontological and stagnant; life and thinking require a "teleological suspension" of disciplinary commitments, where disciplines must be transcended for the sake of reality.[128]

Alcoff's *Visible Identities* offers a fairly comprehensive treatment of two visible identities that continue to have enormous impact on the outcome of people's lives: gender and race. One need not actively exhibit them to experience social responses premised upon them. Although a simple thesis, the sophistication with which Western societies have manifested their anxieties over these identities sets the stage for Alcoff's critical study. She studies not only gender and racial identities but also the study of these phenomena. The word "identity" has its etymology from the fourteenth-century French *identité*, which in turn is from the Latin *identitatem* (which refers to "sameness," abstracted from *identidem*, meaning "over and over"). The etymology has a bearing on much of the philosophical debate over the concept.

Alcoff begins the text by arguing that human beings negotiate identities by seeking some "mark" by which they are made manifest. We can think here of the complex, mythopoetic history of marks in many civilizations, and especially more germane here is the impact of the biblical rationalization

---

[128] For critical discussions of Gordon's work see e.g. *The C. L. R. James Journal* (fall 2007) and Drucilla Cornell, *Moral Images of Freedom*, pp. 105–35.

of the curse of Ham on so many generations of dispossessed peoples against whom it has been issued; or perhaps Kant's discussion of the darkness of the navel as a sign of impurity and its spreading out across some people into the darkness of their skin.[129] Visibility, Alcoff argues, is a fundamental dimension of gender and racial identities. The significance brought to visible phenomena varies, she argues, through time, i.e. it is sociologically and historically affected. The problem is thus not about "seeing" or "identifying" but about what is brought to such activity. Some critics argue that the relationship between seeing and seeing-as-bad is symbiotic, that the identities are constructed because they are supposedly generated by problematic conditions.[130] But here, I suspect, a process of diagnosis, as Nietzsche might have it, may be in order, where the critic's motivation is not necessarily to clarify.

The concept of identity is rejected by its critics while they often do so through a sleight of hand in which they advance their favored identity. This is especially so on the left, where "class" is usually privileged. There is also a liberal attack on identity, as exemplified by Arthur Schlesinger's liberal polemic, in which he defends the melting-pot ideology of homogeneity in the interest of a supposedly strong United States that brings everyone, ultimately, together under a single American ideal. The flaws of this argument are manifold: it claims to reject identity by asserting a supposedly supervening one, and it does not address the tendency of that identity to be normatively white. Political arguments, Alcoff contends, attack identity politics as exclusionist and antipathetic to freedom. Although she does not formulate it as such, the situation offered by these arguments is a neurotic one. We are asked not to exclude others while being encouraged to reject their imposition on whom or what we are. Here we see an argument similar to Cedric Robinson's on philosophical anthropology, which we

---

[129] Works abound, but see, e.g., *Stain Removal* (forthcoming) by Jerry Miller, who offers some insightful treatment of this subject in his discussions of Kant and Nietzsche. To this, I should like to add that there is something peculiarly Protestant about the discussion of identity in the modern age. I am thinking here of Max Weber's reflections on Calvinism in *The Protestant Work Ethic and the Spirit of Capitalism*, trans. Talcott Passons, with an introduction by R. H. Tawney (New York: Scribner, 1958). There is a search for an inner quality that would determine one's salvation, a search for something "inside" of us that makes us who and normatively what we are (e.g. "the saved" or the "damned").

[130] Some of this was discussed earlier in the section on analytical philosophy and race, especially with regard to the work of Naomi Zack.

discussed earlier, except that whereas he focused on the question of "man," Alcoff turns to philosophical treatments of the self, which she examines in the thought of a variety of Western philosophers; but we will here only examine her discussion of Judith Butler since it illustrates Alcoff's existential phenomenological critique well and will enable us to summarize her thoughts on gender and race.

The philosophical criticism exemplified in Butler's thought appeals to the etymology of the word "identity," which refers, as we have seen, to being the same. In asking the existential question "Who or what am I?" one in effect raises the question of an object with which one is identical, in one account, or the same, in another. In other words, "that is who or what I am." Alcoff offers a genealogy of various philosophical discussions of this in terms of the metaphysical presuppositions of emanating substance as a permanent essence (Aristotelianism) versus socially conditioned interpretation or narratives. Butler, Alcoff contends, is caught in the foundational fallacy of complete autonomy and ahistoricism. The problem with complete or radical autonomy is that it requires a conception of the person in which choosing an identity is interpreted in a way that requires each of us to be godlike in our acts of naming. It calls for, in other words, the materializing power of words. Alcoff takes issue with Butler over what could be called the dialectics of recognition that follow from being an object of such activity, which is located in Butler's thought as the oppressive force of interpellation (of being as named or identified by others). Alcoff's criticism is that Butler sets up a straw man argument through a misrepresentation of what should be expected from human identities. An interpellation is, in other words, never really exhaustive.[131] This is not to say that the search for recognition can never be oppressive. It can be so when it is at the level of standards of the self that are used to evaluate another set of standards of the self, as Toni Morrison showed so well in *The Bluest Eye*. To say, for example, that blacks are expected to be white is not to claim that the identity of the initial black individual is exhausted by the designation "black." It is about the normative status of the group to which that person may be linked in a series of significations that lead to a set of social relations in which not being white is treated as a normative flaw.[132]

---

[131] Alcoff, *Visible Identities*, p. 78.   [132] *Ibid.*, pp. 81–2.

Alcoff then moves on to philosophical and social theoretical explanations of how actual identities are formed. She works through Western hermeneutics and phenomenological accounts (the behavioral accounts already presuppose an epiphenomenal status to identity) and concludes that

> the Western hermeneutic and phenomenological traditions as well as Mead's social psychology [are] seriously deficient, not because they assume the justification of our existing beliefs but because they tend to portray our situation as if it were coherent, monocultural, and internally consistent in all respects.[133]

Alcoff defends more heterogeneous or mixed approaches to the study and conceptions of the self. She does not mean by this that her work should be read as "non-Western," but that it is part of a Western tradition that is a consequence of a more creolized understanding of the world as broader than those presented in the image of the self offered by traditional Western philosophy. This means that her existential philosophy, as with other Africana existential philosophy, articulates the contradictions that reveal the particularization of Western civilization. In other words, her message is that there is a broader story of the self to be told, and to tell it requires active engagement with the resources of knowledge that would expand the epistemological discussion into taking seriously the impact of geopolitical regions beyond the Occident.

Alcoff's discussion of gender and race thus calls for attempting to think outside of the proverbial box. Think of debates over the coupling of gender and race. They have a symbiotic relationship in our philosophical anthropology. No "race" lacks a gender or vice versa. There are differences, however, about their social constructivity. Although Alcoff admits this, she does not make the following consideration. There is an odd etymological link between "sex" and "science" in the Latin infinitive *secare* (to cut, to divide), which in turn has roots in the Hebrew *crethi*, derived from the root *carath* (to cut) and ancient Egyptian/Kamitian *crethi* and *kotket*.[134] One could argue, for example, that the link with sex and science is such that contemporary criticisms

---

[133] *Ibid.*, p. 124.

[134] See the Academy of St. Louis, *Transactions of the Academy of Science of St. Louis*, vol. I. *1856–1860* (St. Louis, MO: George Knapp and Company, 1860), p. 534. *Crethi* referred to royal armies in ancient Egypt/Kamit, which were split into two classes.

of it may be tantamount to searching for a form of biology without reproduction. Alcoff comes to this theme through her discussion of cultural and poststructural feminism, especially regarding the problem of interpellation posed by Butler. Alcoff argues, in effect, for a standpoint account ("positionality") attuned to the openness of the category for future alteration.[135] Such a view does not reduce women exclusively to the reproductive capacities of most women, but it does not reject this aspect of a woman's life either. Her claim is that one should take seriously the weight of the social world in how women are formed and how they negotiate that formation, and that that world should not be treated as completely independent of physical reality. Moreover, she contends, the "problem is not the absence of content for the category 'women' but an overabundance and inconsistency of content, given the multiple situations in which women find themselves in various cultures."[136]

Some critics might object that this argument is a reintroduction of essentialist claims. Alcoff responds by taking on the debate over essentialism and anti-essentialism, which, she argues, was ultimately premised on how to articulate the heterogeneity of women without emptying the concept "women."[137] It is easy to provide an account of essence that does not collapse into homogeneity. What is more difficult is to articulate a metaphysical conception of gender without homogeneity, substance, and determinism. Judith Butler famously argued for the performance of gender (and, eventually, sex) as its expression, which Alcoff points out is not free of metaphysical implications as found in such process metaphysics as those of Spinoza, Bergson, and Whitehead.[138] Alcoff concludes with arguing for a phenomenological treatment of lived bodies as lived-experience and a hermeneutics of the horizons available to such bodies, for which she turns to the study of race. She begins with the genealogical and archaeological poststructural accounts of race as a function of modern classification practices. Arguments about racial nominalism or eliminativism and racial essentialism fail to deal with how race is actually lived in the social world.[139] Alcoff prefers working through contextualism, where race is "socially constructed, historically

---

[135] Alcoff, p. 149.   [136] Ibid., p. 152.   [137] Ibid., p. 155.

[138] Ibid., p. 157. For Butler's thought on identity, especially gender identity, see e.g. *Gender Trouble*; *Bodies That Matter*; *Undoing Gender*; and *Giving and Account of Oneself* (New York: Fordham University Press, 2005).

[139] Alcoff, *Visible Identities*, p. 182.

malleable, culturally contextual, and reproduced through learned perceptual practices."[140] This approach should be articulated at both the objective (macro) and subjective (micro) levels. The rest of the analysis here is informed by Merleau-Ponty's and Frantz Fanon's phenomenology of embodied perception in intersubjective relations. She adds how a white normative social field is presumed, and that, in at least the US context, there is an expected limit on the identification of racial dynamics. A legitimate space is presumed by many whites and anti-race people of color to be one in which race is invisible. What this means is that a space without people of color is considered a "nonracial" one, and as the numbers of, say, blacks grow to a point where they are noticed, the space is transformed. The presence of color, especially black, brown, and red, signifies a chain of meanings regardless of the actions of the people designated as colored, and the meaning of the space, as racialized, collapses into pathology; the development is, in other words, treated as a disaster.[141]

The demand for the invisibility of race is what the call for colorblindness is about. Alcoff points out that the attack on visual perception fails to account for its being one among other forms of sensing, and that the socialization of perceptual processes could work their way through all the senses. What she does not say here, but we may wish to consider, is that a general presupposition is that a future may come in which there will be no races and hence, supposedly, no racism. Aside from arguments through which racism could exist without races, we could add that the presupposition of races disappearing is highly specious. If anything, the evidence suggests a future with a proliferation of races. If we take racialization seriously as a social phenomenon, however, we should admit that we do not really know what identities will emerge in the future and what they might mean.

The main criticisms of Africana existential phenomenology are from several angles. For critics who cannot see phenomenology as anything other than a European enterprise, the charge of Eurocentrism is unleashed. For those who reject the idea of non-discursive dimensions of reality, a reassertion of discursive, even textual, idealism would be their retort. For

---

[140] *Ibid.*

[141] For elaboration of this argument, see Jane Anna Gordon and Lewis R. Gordon, *Of Divine Warning: Reading Disaster in the Modern Age* (Boulder, CO: Paradigm Publishers, 2008).

instance, Butler could respond to Alcoff's appeal to non-discursive dimensions of experience with what she said in her now classic work, *Gender Trouble*:

> Within philosophical discourse itself, the notion of "the person" has received analytic elaboration on the assumption that whatever social context the person is "in" remains somehow externally related to the definitional structure of personhood, be that consciousness, the capacity for language, or moral deliberation. Although that literature is not examined here, one premise of such inquiries is the focus of critical exploration and inversion. Whereas the question of what constitutes "personal identity" within philosophical accounts almost always centers on the question of what internal feature of the person establishes the continuity or self-identity of the person through time, the question here will be: To what extent do *regulatory practices* of gender formation and division constitute identity, the internal coherence of the subject, indeed, the self-identical status of the person? To what extent is "identity" a normative ideal rather than a descriptive feature of experience?[142]

Here we encounter a problem similar to that of asking what, in Kantian terms, *noumena* look like. Butler, in effect, questions whether one can say anything about the non-discursive without drawing it into a discursive schema as meaningful, and, even more, that to defend identity as Alcoff does reveals an investment or normative commitment more than a description of reality. In response Alcoff could argue that "description" is, as well, normatively loaded and that at least in her case, she is admitting what her investments in identity are – namely, that there are actual people whose lives are affected by and through such identities.[143] A similar round of debates follow from philosophers who reject any reference to "consciousness" and intentionality, the former of which is included in Butler's list of problematic assumptions. But a difference with consciousness is that much depends on the interpretation of consciousness. Some existential phenomenologists, such as Jean-Paul Sartre and Maurice Merleau-Ponty, reject the view that consciousness rests

---

[142] Butler, *Gender Trouble*, p. 16.

[143] For a similar response, see Tracey Nicholls, "Dominant Positions: John Coltrane, Michel Foucault, and the Politics of Representation," *Critical Studies in Improvisation / Études critiques en improvisation* 2, no. 1 (2006), http://journal.lib.uoguelph.ca/index.php/csieci/article/view/87.

"in" anything and as "whole."[144] There is a meeting here of the existential phenomenologists, the poststructuralists, and the critical theorists. Butler and Gilroy, for instance, argue that the constitution of the self is premised upon, echoing Freud, loss. Characterized as melancholia, the loss on which identity and subject formation are based haunts projects of the self. The existential phenomenologists agree with this thesis, although they advance it through discourses of negation and incompleteness. All moments of emergence are premised upon separation.

Still, other critics of existential phenomenology, while agreeing with the melancholic aspect of appearance, could consider an appeal to social reality to be to a second-order form of reality. I do not, however, see how such philosophers would avoid begging the question of the real and the less real, especially since their assertion presupposes its communication; in other words, the distinction between first- and second-order realities does not offer what their proponents want, which is the notion of the "really real" over other kinds of reality. It is not that social reality is less real. It is governed by different resources through which we negotiate our relationship with the world or, in this case, each other. And finally, although not exhaustively, there are those who reject the entire existential phenomenological enterprise because they see it as an instance of another "grand narrative." This objection is a variation of the normative ideal diagnosis. I will not add responses to these criticisms here, since I have already discussed them in various forms throughout this text and have done so in other places.[145] Instead, let it be said that such philosophical debate is crucial and healthy for the continued growth of the field.

Today there is a growing group of existential phenomenological Africana philosophers. One set consists of some of the contributors to *Existence in Black: An Anthology of Black Existential Philosophy* (1997). More recently, the

---

[144] See e.g. Jean-Paul Sartre, *The Transcendence of the Ego: An Existentialist Theory of Consciousness*, trans. and annotated with introduction by Forrest Williams and Robert Kirkpatrick (New York: Hill and Wang, 1991); Maurice Merleau-Ponty, *The Visible and the Invisible*, trans. Alphonso Lingis (Evanston, IL: Northwestern University Press, 1969); and see also Lewis R. Gordon, *Bad Faith and Antiblack Racism, Fanon and the Crisis of European Man, Existentia Africana, Disciplinary Decadence*, and "Irreplaceability." See also Sara Ahmed, *Queer Phenomenology: Orientations, Objects, Others* (Durham, NC: Duke University Press, 2006) for a treatment of phenomenology in stream but not necessarily in line with Butler's thought.

[145] See Gordon, *Bad Faith and Antiblack Racism*.

philosopher of education Stephen Haymes has built upon black existential phenomenology in his study of the pedagogical practices of slaves and discourses of memory. For Haymes, slavery, racism, and colonialism were also traumatic events that literally "dismembered" a group of people. The goal of liberation for him is more than the struggle for freedom but also the effort to re-member, to put oneself together. The philosopher Clevis Headley has also taken up this question of trauma, which he has explored through essays on black aesthetics and race theory. Marilyn Nissim-Sabat has integrated this approach into her brand of Husserlian phenomenology to examine problems in psychoanalysis, gender theory, and racism.[146] Gail Weiss has also offered a series of works exploring the intersection of gender and race through the thought of Simone de Beauvoir and Frantz Fanon, whereas Ellen K. Feder has worked through a phenomenology of the body in creative explorations of Foucault's work on gender and race.[147] As well, Kathryn Gines has offered an existential defense of race where she argues for retention of the concept even with the elimination of racial oppression.[148] Anika Mann has brought existential phenomenology in a conversation with feminist standpoint epistemology.[149]

Although posing a challenge to phenomenology in the 1980s and 1990s, phenomenological research in feminist and queer studies continues to grow

[146] See her forthcoming book, *Neither Victim Nor Survivor: Thinking toward a New Humanity*, ed. Carolyn M. Cusick and Michael R. Paradiso-Michau, with foreword by Lewis R. Gordon (Lanham: Lexington Books, 2009).

[147] See Gail Weiss, "Freedom, Oppression and the Possibilities of Ethics for Simone de Beauvoir," *Simone de Beauvoir Studies* 18 (2001–2): 9–21; "'Politics Is a Living Thing': The Intellectual's Dilemma in Beauvoir's *The Mandarins*," in *The Contradictions of Freedom: Philosophical Essays on Beauvoir's "The Mandarins*," ed. Sally Scholz and Shannon Mussett (Albany, NY: State University of New York Press, 2005); *Body Images: Embodiment as Intercorporeality* (1999); and her forthcoming *Indeterminate Horizons: Re-Figuring the Grounds of "Ordinary" Experience*; and Ellen K. Feder, "The Discursive Production of the 'Dangerous Individual': Biopower and the Making of the Racial State," *Radical Philosophy Review* 7, no. 1 (2004); "The Dangerous Individual('s) Mother: Biopower, Family, and the Production of Race," *Hypatia* 22, no. 2 (2007): 60–78; and *Family Bonds: Genealogies of Race and Gender* (New York: Oxford University Press, 2007).

[148] Gines, "Sartre and Fanon: Fifty Years Later," and "From Political Space to Political Agency: Arendt, Sartre, and Fanon on Race and Revolutionary Violence" (Memphis, TN: Philosophy Doctoral Dissertation, University of Memphis, 2003).

[149] Anika Mann, "Ethics from the Standpoint of Race and Gender: Sartre, Fanon and Feminist Standpoint Theory" (Memphis, TN: University of Memphis Philosophy Dissertation, 2004).

in creative directions. There is Jacqueline M. Martinez's *Phenomenology of Chicana Experience and Identity*, which offers a phenomenology of the communication of race, gender, and sexuality.[150] David Fryer has engaged similar issues in his work on "post-humanism," which he sees as challenging closed forms of normativity. He has conjoined queer theory with Africana phenomenology to construct a genealogy of African-American queer studies in which he argues that anti-essentialism obfuscates the lived-experience of queer folk and that phenomenology offers a way of studying such a reality through its parenthesizing or suspending of normativity.[151] In the UK Sara Ahmed has also brought innovation to the study of queer theory and to phenomenology through her analysis of orientation, of how spatial orientation is lived and affects social relations as in the significance of queerness as a form of getting out of line.[152] In so doing she transforms the adjectival reading of "queer" into an activity exemplified in the infinitive "to queer." That orientation, to use her language, has profound disciplinary effects. It reveals how the avowedly non-philosophical can generate the philosophical:

> Perhaps my preference for such queer turnings is because I don't have a disciplinary line to follow – I was "brought up" between disciplines and I have never quite felt comfortable in the homes they provide . . . Disciplines also have lines in the sense that they have a specific "take" on the world, a way of ordering time and space through the very decisions about what counts as within the discipline. Such lines mark out the edges of disciplinary homes, which also mark out those who are "out of line." I write this book [*Queer Phenomenology*] as someone who does not reside within philosophy; I feel out of line even at the point from which I start. It is a risk to read philosophy as a non-philosopher.[153]

My response to Ahmed, given the argument I have made in *Disciplinary Decadence*, is that it is the non-philosopher who often produces new philosophy. That is because most philosophers are not willing to transcend philosophy, which ossifies the discipline. The philosophers who are willing

---

[150] Jacqueline M. Martinez, *Phenomenology of Chicana Experience and Identity* (Lanham, MD: Rowman & Littlefield, 2000).

[151] David Fryer, "African-American Queer Studies," in Gordon and Gordon, *A Companion to African-American Studies*, pp. 305–29.

[152] Sara Ahmed, *Queer Phenomenology*; see also her article, "Orientations: Toward a Queer Phenomenology," *GLQ: A Journal of Lesbian and Gay Studies* 12, no. 4 (2006): 543–574.

[153] *Ibid.*, p. 22.

to let it go, so to speak, to not worry about philosophy transcend philosophy in a paradoxically philosophical way. This "letting it go" is a phenomenologically rich notion, as we have seen argued by David Fryer. Ahmed's work brings into sharp focus the queer dimension of an act that manifests itself through its loss, its deviation. Ahmed works through her inquiry by way of deviation. One of them is her reading of the philosophical table, of literally how philosophers orient themselves to their place of work:

> My writing takes detours, turns, and moves this way and that . . . I turned toward the table quite by chance. Once I caught sight of the table in Husserl's writing, which is revealed just for a moment, I could not help but follow tables around. When you follow tables, you can end up anywhere. So I followed Husserl in his turn to the table, but when he turns away, I got led astray. I found myself seated at my table, at the different tables that mattered at different points in my life. How I wanted to make these tables matter![154]

Ahmed's play on words, "tables matter," unfolds in a complex series of twists, turns, deviations (her form of phenomenological movements) as she articulates her critique of the metaphysics of form and matter, wherein tables offer the trace of both. A wooden table is transformed matter, but its function orients us (to work, to eat, to drink, to talk, to distance, to hide, to sit at, to belong), and orienting ourselves through such thought enables us "to consider the history of 'what appears' and how it is shaped by histories of work."[155]

The teleology of form often demands a linearity of movement. Motion, however, is formed through the body. Drawing upon reflections from Fanon's famous example of casually reaching across his table for a cigarette, Ahmed points out the subterranean levels of orientation:

> Where phenomenology attends to the tactile, vestibular, kinesthetic, and visual character of embodied reality, Fanon asks us to think of the "historic-racial" scheme, which is, importantly, "below it." In other words, the racial and historical dimensions are beneath the surface of the body described by phenomenology, which becomes, by virtue of its own orientation, a way of thinking the body that has surface appeal . . . For Fanon, racism "interrupts" the corporeal schema. Or we could say that "the

---

[154] *Ibid.*   [155] *Ibid.*, p. 43.

corporeal schema" is already racialized; in other words, race does not just interrupt such a schema but structures its mode of operation.[156]

Echoing Alcoff, Ahmed argues

The "matter" of race is very much about embodied reality; seeing oneself or being seen as white or black or mixed does affect what one "can do," or even where one can go, which can be redescribed in terms of *what is and is not within reach.* If we begin to consider what is affective about the "unreachable," we might even begin the task of making "race" a rather queer matter.[157]

The understanding of actions and options comes to the fore in each of these phenomenological approaches, where the triumvirate of an anthropology (orientation), social transformation (deviation), and metacritique (queering) come to the fore in a philosophy of metastability. In similar kind Kenneth Knies has built upon the disciplinary critique offered by this form of phenomenology to articulate a theory of what he calls "post-European science," which refers to

actual disciplines and ways of thinking that have recently achieved institutionalization within the US academy, such as Africana Studies, Ethnic Studies, Latin American Studies, and postcolonial theory . . . [T]hey contain an animating *telos* that point toward a radical rethinking of theory itself, a rethinking capable of drawing science beyond a myopic closure that we will call "European."[158]

This transcending movement, Knies concludes, requires fending off

our natural tendency toward the geography of the globe. The periphery of Europe, like Europe itself, is primarily a spiritual shape, not a region one could localize on a map. It is a periphery that cuts right through Europe's geographical center: It encompasses humanity that stands at the edge of European Man's self-centering as *a priori* standard. This periphery is thus an under-periphery, the counterpart to Europe's understanding of its own height.[159]

---

[156] *Ibid.*, pp. 110–11.   [157] *Ibid.*, p. 112.

[158] Kenneth Knies, "The Idea of Post-European Science: An Essay on Phenomenology and Africana Studies," in Gordon and Gordon, *Not Only the Master's Tools*, p. 85.

[159] *Ibid.*, pp. 103–4.

The concept of an "under-periphery" resists neat polar logic of a margin and center, which is a central concern of Africana philosophy.

We have now come to the conclusion of our discussion of Africana philosophy in North America and its dialogue with thought in Britain. In each movement, the difficulty of articulating the subjects, strategies, and reflective evaluation posed challenges that expand the meaning of philosophical work. The concluding existential phenomenological line and its deviations explore the intersection of Africana existential phenomenological and European thought without the subordination of the former in terms of the latter. It is, in this respect, a deviation from the norm. One of the most influential recent developments from this turn is Paget Henry's historicist existential phenomenological work *Caliban's Reason*, which stands among the canonical work in Afro-Caribbean philosophy, to which we shall now turn.

5   Afro-Caribbean philosophy

Afro-Caribbean philosophy is a subset of Africana philosophy and Caribbean philosophy. We have already defined Africana philosophy as the set of philosophical reflections that emerged by and through engagement with the African diaspora. By Caribbean philosophy is here meant philosophy from the region and on the unique problems of theorizing Caribbean reality.

The etymology of the word "Caribbean" points to the Caribs, a group of Native peoples, in addition to the earlier arrived Taínos or Arawaks, among others, living in the region at the time of Columbus's landing in what is today the Bahamas. The term "cannibal" also has its roots in Carib, and the name "Caliban," which refers to the rapacious villain in Shakespeare's *Tempest*, is also a variation of that word. "Taínos" and "Arawaks" were not the names of the earlier people. European archaeologists in the first half of the twentieth century called them such. As we will see, the etymology of cannibal betrays the colonial logic that rationalizes much that happened there, and that logic contextualizes the philosophy as well.[1]

Afro-Caribbean philosophy is a form of philosophy rooted in the modern world that takes the question of modernity as one of its central concerns. It is modern because the Caribbean itself is a modern creation. Although the indigenous people preceded the modern world, the convergence of modernity with the African diaspora, marked by the consequence of European expansion, slavery, and genocide, transformed theirs into the New World.

---

[1] This history can be found in many standard accounts of the region. See e.g. Jan Rogonzinski, *A Brief History of the Caribbean: From the Arawak and Carib to the Present* (New York: Plume, 1999). See also Walter Mignolo, *The Idea of Latin America* (Malden, MA: Blackwell Publishers, 2006) for a portrait of how the Latinization of the region played a role in the suppression of its indigenous and black dimensions in the service of white-through-mixed emergent classes and their correlative politics.

Afro-Caribbean philosophy consists of the philosophical meditations on the question of African presence in the Caribbean and the modern questions of blackness raised by that presence. The latter, however, raise additional questions since "blackness" is, as Frantz Fanon points out near the end of his introduction in *Black Skin, White Masks*, "a white construction."[2] By this, he means that the people who have become known as black people are descendants of people who had no reason to have regarded themselves as such. As a consequence, the history of black people has the constant motif of such people encountering their blackness from the "outside," as it were, and then developing, in dialectical fashion, a form of blackness that transcends the initial, negative series of events. Again, paraphrasing Fanon, this time from *A Dying Colonialism*, it was whites who created the concept of the Negro, but it was the Negro who created the concept of Negritude.[3]

As we have already seen in our introduction and first chapter, although other groups have been categorized as "Negro" and "black" in the modern world in such places as Australia and the Polynesian islands, it is the descendants of the people kidnapped and enslaved from the coasts of the Atlantic and along the Arabic and East Indian trade routes who are most commonly linked to those terms. Thus, when Las Casas began his reflections on the New World predicament of indigenous peoples and the demand for cheap labor, the categories were already being formed as those to be inherited by generations into the present. It should be borne in mind, however, that these early formulations did not necessarily refer to the crystallized reductive notions of blackness that dominated racial consciousness from the nineteenth to twenty-first centuries. After all, the early, founding moments were also those of a complex war of hybrid populations. Recall that in January 1492 King Ferdinand and Queen Isabella had managed to drive the Moors out of Iberia, but that achievement was not regarded as the end of that war of several hundred years, and the expectation of its continuation meant that the age of exploration was also the continuation of, in the minds of the Spaniards being formed out of Christendom, their reconquering Christian

---

[2] Frantz Fanon, *Black Skin, White Masks*, trans. Charles Lamm Markmann (New York: Grove Press, 1967), p. 14. Markmann translates the passage "white artefact," but the word in the original French was "construction" (*une construction du Blanc*). See Fanon, *Peau noire, masques blancs* (Paris: Editions du Seuil, 1952), p. 11.

[3] Frantz Fanon, *A Dying Colonialism*, trans. Haakon Chevalier, with introduction by Adolfo Gilly (New York: Grover Press, 1965), p. 47.

land from the Islamic and Jewish world, a world marked in the Qur'an by "red" and "black" designations for the people of Africa and the Middle East. Ironically, then, modern colonialism was founded by a kind of conquest premised upon the elimination of one kind of colonialism in favor of another. This fact is no doubt a lesson that many efforts at decolonization in the twentieth century did not learn from the past. How many instances could deny an allegiance to a prior conquest? Crucial from the story of a Germanic early medieval past driving out an Afro-Semitic presence inaugurating modern expansion, then, is for us to understand that there is a history of the formation of modern blackness that is missing in many contemporary discussions. The Muslim, Jewish, Christian as well as Berber, Arabic, and other north African dimensions of the societies that became known as Portugal and Spain should be understood through the collisions they subsequently had with the indigenous peoples of the Americas. That hybrid population in the midst of war in the Mediterranean came to the New World expecting to meet a mediating red and brown Arabic community that stood between them and India, and that misunderstanding forged a philosophical anthropology marked as much by orthodoxy and infidels as by expectations of meeting friends and foe in the dynamics of war. Such expectations and fears guided as well the age of exploration from the Mediterranean along the costs of Africa, a continent that, given the demographics of the Mediterranean communities, they knew a bit more of than is presented in historical narratives that lay claim to ignorant adventurers. That so much of central Africa was located along trade routes that extended from the west to the eastern coasts of the continent meant that at least various forms of Arabic stood as the *lingua franca* between groups of African indigenous peoples, in addition to the creolized languages they used for trade such as, eventually, Swahili.

Caribbean philosophy, then, was already being formed by the reflections of these early encounters of so many divergent communities, and in its core, it was as it had to have been: a reflection on "man" through a robust realization of human difference and similarity – in short, philosophical anthropology. The profound divisions that occurred over time between the various groups, however, led to a phenomenon of denied interiority to the subjugated populations, to the point of there being a single narrative of reality as the perspective of domination. In effect, indigenous and black perspectives suffered the loss of their ability to appear.

A powerful "reappearance" of black reality in the New World took the form of predominantly black anti-slavery revolutionaries honoring indigenous peoples by restoring at the beginning of the nineteenth century the Taínos name of Ayiti (Haiti) to the Spanish-named island of Hispaniola. This was perhaps the first great act of interpellative resistance in the modern world, where naming and force met under an assertion of right. The significance of the Haitian revolution for the study of political responsibility has yet to be studied and theorized. It challenged the North American and European powers to come to terms with a responsibility that they have refused to accept into the twenty-first century. If we could imagine a situation in which all the communities enslaved by the European nations were able to rise up and vanquish their enslavers the following thought experiment may be worth considering from Karl Jaspers's *The Question of German Guilt*, which appeared in the original German as *Die Schuldfrage* (The Guilt Question).[4] The connection between *Schuld* (blame) and *Schule* (school) is revealing here since guilt also offers the prospect of learning. The text has been titled in English as *German Guilt* because Jaspers was addressing what his fellow Germans should learn and understand as they faced accounting for their actions and those of the German government in World War II. The expansion of this concept in this thought experiment through the Haitian revolution brings us to the question of modern guilt. Although not made explicit as formulated here, it is what haunts many discussions of slavery, colonialism, and racism in the modern world.

Jaspers famously outlined four dimensions of guilt with correlative responsibilities. The first was political, the second legal, the third moral, and the fourth metaphysical. He argued that the first is held by citizens; the second by individuals or conspirators; the third by individuals toward themselves; and the fourth between ourselves and God. Liability, properly understood, pertains to legal responsibility. Political responsibility, on the other hand, is not only held by government officials, but also faced by citizens in situations of defeat or vanquishment. In effect Jaspers argued that a government should behave in a manner that provides a good argument for mercy from the victorious. A cruel and unjust government, one that tortures and destroys the vanquished, forfeits any right to a limit on force when the tides have turned. Since the citizens are responsible for their government

---

[4] Karl Jaspers, *The Question of German Guilt*, with new introduction by Joseph W. Koerski, SJ, trans. E. B. Ashton (New York: Fordham University Press, 2000).

it is they who face the consequences of what it owes others at moments of defeat.

The Haitian revolution stimulated a discomfiting question, which is that of the responsibility borne by citizens of countries who profited from racialized slavery and other kinds of exploitation whose consequence was the radical dehumanizing of populations of people across the globe. Today, that question is known as the reparations debate over slavery. The Haitian revolution is a peculiar chapter in the history of this debate, since it was Haitian citizens who were forced to pay so-called "reparations" to the governments that engineered their previous enslavement. In effect, by placing the cart before the horse, by making those whose human rights were violated pay debts to their violators, the story of Haiti is one of a deferment of coming to terms with global responsibilities.

The question of modern guilt is broad in scope. Jaspers argued that it is citizens who must be responsible for the acts of their government for good reason. Without that or some similar constraint, the scope of responsibility would reach across all time to everyone in the universe to every-when to the point of a near Platonic form of responsibility. The metaphysical in the ascription was not accidental. In contemporary society, the requirement of "citizen" need not be the model since there are countless ways in which one benefits from the government to which one may be responsible without such a designation. But the example becomes flawed when there are people who do not have options over where they live. The enslaved people who founded Haiti through fighting against slavery had no alternative as citizens in Hispaniola because citizenship was not available to them as slaves. They faced the dynamics of violence that Fanon identified in *The Wretched of the Earth*, where the system offered nearly no options through which they could appear as human beings. The upsurge of asserting their humanity, as systemically illegitimate, made them violent, whether they actually harmed any one or not. The response of the colonizing nations, which was to deny the humanity of the revolutionaries and to disavow the legitimacy of their struggle as one of what Jaspers calls right (what should be defended even with force), means that the grammar of enslavement continued without rectification, and it has, in fact, become more rigorous, as Kevin Bales has shown, through a proliferation of enslaved people on a global scale today.[5]

---

[5] See e.g. Kevin Bales, *Disposable People: New Slavery in the Global Economy* (Berkeley, CA: University of California Press, 1999).

The debate on who is responsible, then, is, at least in Jaspers's analysis, one that needs to be addressed to the citizens of first world governments. How they would like to have been treated had the tables been turned and they were at the mercy of the colored nations of the world, where right is called upon to intervene on right, is the continued question. It is not an entirely arrested one, as we now see in the anxious reflections in the first world at the growing global power of, for example, China and India. The moral dimension is personal and the metaphysical one is too broad, but the complex series of treaties that comprise international law and the specific political possibility of a vanquished or at least prostrated citizenry raises the matter of accounts to be settled by citizens of, whether they fought for or against, a government whose behavior has been very bad.

As we saw in our second chapter, one of the greatest intellectual efforts to articulate the humanity and dignity of the people affected by such political irresponsibility in the eighteenth and nineteenth centuries is Anténor Firmin's *The Equality of the Races*.[6] I will not here repeat the details of our discussion in the second chapter except to recall that Anténor Firmin's life, as we saw, exemplified a side of the Haitian revolution that is not often written about in the constant stream of denunciations of its history: there was much innovation as the former slaves experimented and attempted to build a beacon of hope for enslaved people worldwide, even though conflicts developed among them that duplicated certain forms of social inequality. An anti-reductionist, Firmin investigated classifications as systems of knowledge whose consequences included the production of human subjects. He was a pioneer in the human sciences. His methodological innovations included the advancement of an archaeology of knowledge and the role of racial impositions on the subject matter. These underlying investments, he argued, involved the confusion of a geography with an anthropology.[7] And finally, though not exclusively, his concept of regeneration brought to the fore a problem of modern historiography, namely, the notion that the European *qua* European lacks a primitive past, which raises the question of

[6] Anténor Firmin's *Equality of Human Races: A Nineteenth Century Haitian Scholar's Response to European Racialism*, trans. Asselin Charles, with an introduction by Carolyn Fleuhr-Lobban (New York: Garland Publishers, 2000). For a more detailed discussion, see ch. 2 above.

[7] For comparison, see the section on the modern episteme in Michel Foucault's *The Order of Things: An Archaeology of the Human Sciences*, trans. Alan Sheridan (New York: Vintage, 1973).

the isomorphic use of "primitive" with dark peoples. In effect, he showed that the primitive was a modern construction.

Firmin's ideas, however, fell upon deaf ears. This was so primarily because of the strategic isolation of Haiti by the United States and its allies. For Firmin's thought to have "appeared" beyond the borders of Haiti required the Haitian people themselves to have appeared beyond the stereotypes and disavowals, poignantly analyzed by Sibylle Fischer, of their humanity.[8] How could such thought have its day in a world that could only see such people as violent, rapacious usurpers in ragged clothing with pitchforks and torches held high?

The next great effort at Afro-Caribbean appearance was no doubt through the political genius and the grand effort of Jamaican-born Marcus Mosiah Garvey (1887–1940). After traveling through the islands in his adolescent years, he was struck by the seeming universal status of blacks at the lowest level of each society.[9] After spending time in London, he was invited to the United States by Booker T. Washington in 1916, but Washington had died by the time Garvey arrived. He stayed in the United States and was so successful in organizing the black masses that he was for a time the most influential individual among the people of the black world. He founded the Universal Negro Improvement Association and African Community League under a program of race pride and economic self-reliance. An extraordinarily gifted speaker with an understanding of the organizing force of spectacles, Garvey understood that black populations needed symbols that represented possibility in their lives in addition to the material infrastructures he was arguing for. Since there are many studies of Garvey's life that chronicle his conflict with W. E. B. Du Bois and his eventual arrest in 1925 for tax evasion and his deportation from the United States in 1927, I will not get into the details of those matters here. What is crucial is that along the way Garvey set the framework for a form of Black Nationalism of a prophetic and philosophical kind. The prophetic side came from his political argument that black

---

[8] See Sibylle Fischer, *Modernity Disavowed: Haiti and the Cultures of Slavery in the Age of Revolution* (Durham, NC: Duke University Press, 2004).

[9] For discussions of Marcus Garvey's life and thought, see Tony Martin, *Race First: The Ideological and Organizational Struggles of Marcus Garvey and the Universal Negro Improvement Association* (Dover, MA: Majority Press, 1986); Rupert Lewis, *Marcus Garvey: Anti-Colonial Champion* (Trenton, NJ: Africa World Press, 1988); and *Garvey, His Work and Impact*, ed. Rupert Lewis and Patrick Bryan (Trenton, NJ: Africa World Press, 1991).

liberation rested upon the liberation of the African continent from colonialism. Prophesying the emergence of a royal liberator in Ethiopia, Garvey became the major prophetic figure for what became Rastafari in Jamaica. That movement came into being at the crowning of Emperor Tafari Makonnen in 1930, the avowed 111th emperor in the succession from King Solomon in Ancient Judea. Ras (Amharic for "King") Tafari ("to be feared") adopted the name Haile Selassie ("Might of the Trinity") on that occasion, and some of the followers of Garvey in Jamaica regarded those series of events to be the fulfillment of prophecy in the Hebrew Bible of the coming of the Messiah. The name they adopted, Rastafari, is Haile Selassie's title and name, and their subsequent philosophical and religious thought has had an enormous impact on the representation of black pride to this day.[10]

Garvey's philosophical thought focused on the affirmation of the black self. For Garvey it was crucial for black people to value themselves, but this thought was linked to his political philosophy, where such value was not simply at an individual level but required, as well, a nation through which such value could emerge as historical. In short, black pride required black nationhood. The question of the liberation of the African continent and the role to be played by the many ethnic groups returned, but the concept of nation advanced here undergirds the many ethnicities through the concept of race. In other words, the African states had to be founded on the black nation (racially understood), which, given Garvey's argument, was diasporic.

The next crucial moment of black intellectual appearance in the Caribbean was the return of Aimé Césaire (1913–) to the island of Martinique in 1939 and the publication in 1947 of his classic *Cahier d'un retour au pays natal* ("Return to My Native Land").[11] Although there were other Caribbean writers exploring similar themes at the time, what was unique about Césaire was that the stage he inaugurated was immediately seen in the Caribbean itself as also a Caribbean contribution to a pan-African chorus.

---

[10] Discussions abound, but see especially J. Owens, *Dread* (Kingston, JA: Sangsters, 1976) and Barry Chevannes, *Rastafari: Roots and Ideology* (Syracuse, NY: Syracuse University Press, 1994) and (ed.), *Rastafari and Other Caribbean World Views* (New Brunswick, NJ: Rutgers University Press, 1998).

[11] Aimé Césaire, *Notebook of a Return to My Native Land: Cahier d'un retour au pays natal*, trans. Mireille Rosello with Annie Pritchard, introduction by Mireille Rosello (Newcastle upon Tyne: Bloodaxe Books, 1995). For discussion, see Gregson Davis, *Aimé Césaire* (New York: Cambridge University Press, 1997).

Trinidadian-born C. L. R. James (1904–1989), for instance, had produced *The Black Jacobins*, his classic 1938 study of the Haitian revolution, in the United States, and it took time for the text to be understood as a contribution to Caribbean historical thought instead of only its history within a stream of "universal history." The disavowal of James as a thinker meant that it took until the near end of his long life for his thought to be read as such. Most studies of Marxism in the Western academy, including those that purport to focus on its twentieth-century innovators, were oblivious to James until pioneering work in literary and cultural studies conditioned his appearance beyond his small group of loyal followers from the British, US, and Caribbean labor movements.[12] James's writings were predominantly works in Marxism and what could later be called Afro-Caribbean Marxism or, as Paget Henry characterizes it in *Caliban's Reason*, Afro-Caribbean historicism, although James wrote on nearly every aspect of modern political thought.[13] His Marxist writings were primarily anti-Stalinist in his support of Trotskyism and then pan-Africanist in his attack on "state capitalism," which is how he regarded the Soviet Union. James's intellectual contributions consisted of his continuous production of oppositional histories and diagnoses of political phenomena through which he articulated his notion of "the creative universal," which, he argued, manifested itself in the resilience of the working classes and the peasantry.[14] An additional insight of James is his metatheoretical work on the problem of the relationship which thought has to history. A fundamental problem of twentieth-century Marxism, he argued, was that it fell behind the movement of world history. A difficulty with studying James's work, as with many other Africana thinkers, is that he straddled multiple dimensions of the triumvirate of philosophical anthropology, liberation, and critical reflection.[15] This affords his thought much

---

[12] For discussion from a broad spectrum of authors, see e.g. *C. L. R. James: His Life and Work*, ed. Paul Buhle (London: Allison & Busby, 1986).

[13] Paget Henry, *Caliban's Reason: Introducing Afro-Caribbean Philosophy* (New York: Routledge, 2000), pp. 51–6.

[14] James was perhaps the most prolific of all Caribbean social theorists. *The C. L. R. James Reader*, ed. Anna Grimshaw (Oxford: Blackwell Publishers, 1992) offers James's thought in his own words and provides an extensive bibliography of his writings, pp. 427–44.

[15] Although many books have been written on James, nuance is brought to his theoretical work, especially his studies of Hegel, in B. Anthony Bogues's *Caliban's Freedom: The Early Political Thought of C. L. R. James* (London: Pluto, 1997) and for his philosophical historicism, see Henry's *Caliban's Reason*, pp. 47–67.

freedom from the decadence of disciplinary reductionism. This has not, however, deterred some scholars from attempting to characterize him in terms
that clearly do not fit.[16]

Aimé Césaire and Suzanne Césaire had returned to Martinique after
playing their role, along with Léopold Senghor (1906–2001) and Léon Gontian Damas (1912–1978), in the development of what Aimé Césaire coined
Négritude, whose basic tenet was to affirm being black and being proud of
it or, in other formulations, the articulation of a uniquely African personal-
ity.[17] In his essay "West Indians and Africans," Fanon testified to the "scandal" created by Césaire, a dark-skinned Martinican, expressing pride instead
of shame in his appearance.[18] "What indeed could be more grotesque,"
Fanon recalled, "than an educated man, a man with a diploma, having
in consequence understood a good many things, among others that 'it was
unfortunate to be a negro,' proclaiming that his skin was beautiful and that
the '*big black hole*' [Africa] was a source of truth."[19] Césaire's thought, most
exemplified in his poetry, argued for positive black identification with Africa
and for an aesthetics that subverted the notion of white Eurocentric/white
superiority over the African/black.

Césaire had an extraordinary impact, as we saw in the previous chapter on African-American philosophy, especially through the effect he had
on perhaps the greatest Afro-Caribbean thinker – Frantz Fanon. I will not
focus in detail on Fanon's biography since he is unquestionably the best

[16] For an effort to sublate James's thought into a more narrow and unfortunately sectarian
conception of Marxist-Leninism, see John H. McClendon, III, *C. L. R. James's "Notes on
Dialectics": Left Hegelianism or Marxism-Leninism?* (Lanham, MD: Lexington Books, 2004)
and for an examination of him as a nationalist essentialist see David Scott, *Conscripts
of Modernity: the Tragedy of Colonial Enlightenment* (Durham, NC: Duke University Press,
2004). For criticisms of reading him in these terms, see Paget Henry, "C. L. R. James and
the Orthodoxies of John McClendon and David Scott: A Review Essay," *The C. L. R. James
Journal* 13, no. 1 (2007): 275–89.

[17] See e.g. Davis, *Aimé Césaire* and Shireen K. Lewis, *Race, Culture, and Identity: Francophone
West African and Caribbean Literature and Theory from Negritude to Créolité* (Lanham, MD: Lex-
ington Books, 2006). For more historical examinations of Negritude see Lilyan Kesteloot,
Black Writers in French: A Literary History of Negritude (Washington, DC: Howard University
Press, 1991); T. Denean Sharpley-Whiting, *Negritude Women* (Minneapolis, MN: University
of Minnesota Press, 2002).

[18] Frantz Fanon, *Toward the African Revolution: Political Essays*, ed. Josèphe Fanon and trans.
Haakon Chevalier (New York: Grove Press, 1967), p. 21.

[19] *Ibid.*, pp. 21–2.

known Afro-Caribbean thinker and the one on whom the most number of biographies have been written.[20] The short version is that he fought in the French Resistance in Word War II, returned to Martinique briefly after the war, and then went to France to study psychiatry (with Francois Tosquelles, 1912–1994) and philosophy (with Merleau-Ponty). As the head of psychiatry at Blida-Joinville Hospital (now Frantz Fanon Hospital) in Algeria, he developed a series of revolutionary innovations in humanistic psychiatry and challenged the "primivitist" school of psychiatry that was influential in the study of colonized subjects at the time. He eventually joined the Algerian National Liberation Front in the Algerian war but died from pneumonia while seeking treatment for leukemia in Bethesda, Maryland.

The impact of Fanon's thought on Afro-Caribbean philosophy cannot be underestimated. Nearly all its central concerns for the rest of the twentieth century came from his work. Although for a time he was more known for his thought on decolonization and postcolonization in *The Wretched of the Earth*, the problematics he raises in *Black Skin, White Masks* have now come into their own in Africana philosophy.[21] To summarize our discussion in the previous chapter, Fanon takes on in *Black Skin, White Masks* the theme of Prospero and Caliban through raising the question of epistemological colonization. He argues that race and racism are functions of the social world, but that that world often hides its own dependence on human agency. He also challenges the ethical system that dominates modern thought – namely, liberalism and its promise of assimilation of all human subjects. Fanon points out that many black people attempt to enter that sphere of recognition in good faith only to find a distorted image thrown back at them in the form of an alien and alienated subject. Whether through the resources of language, sexual and other forms of intimate relationships, or the constitution of dream life, the black self struggles to enter the dialectics of recognition, in which the white world serves as the standard for supposedly truly human modes of being. The dialectics of recognition means that blacks stand in a strange relation to theoretical work such as philosophy, whose idol is Reason

---

[20] See e.g. David Caute's *Frantz Fanon* (New York: Vintage, 1970); Irene Gendzier, *Frantz Fanon: A Critical Study* (New York: Pantheon Books, 1973); and Alice Cherki, *Frantz Fanon: A Portrait*, trans. Nadia Benabid (Ithaca, NY: Cornell University Press, 2006).

[21] Frantz Fanon, *The Wretched of the Earth*, trans. Constance Farrington (New York: Grove Press, 1963). The original French, *Les Damnés de la terre*, was published in 1961, and *Peau noir, masques blancs* (*Black Skin, White Masks*) appeared in 1952.

itself. They face the phenomenon of Reason taking flight whenever blacks enter the equation. Fanon also challenges several influential tropes in the study of race and racism. The first is the Self–Other dialectic. For Fanon, colonialism and racism placed whole groups of people below that dialectic, which means that they could only live dialectically with each other. At the interracial level of black and white, racism offers no such dialectic. There is, simply, such a relation between whites, but beyond whites with each other there is neither self nor others. In short, the human minimum is denied by systems of colonization and racism.

The result of Fanon's analysis was that one could not simply apply the Western human sciences to the study of racialized colonial subjects. Their logic often broke down. Lacanian psychoanalysis, for instance, did not work for the Martinican subject because both the Martinican female and the Martinican male sought recognition from white males, which, in effect, meant that Martinican males did not exist as Lacanian men. How could this be so if sex were to be ontologically basic, as presupposed by psychoanalysis? Fanon showed that colonialism – a social phenomenon – intervened and disrupted the patriarchal order of Lacanian categories. He showed the same for Hegelian categories, in which the master also seeks recognition, but this is not the case in the racialized schema faced by Afro-Caribbean subjects. Fanon showed that the resources of language faced similar limitations. The semiotic limits occurred in the regional transcendence of "blacks." In short, the Afro-Caribbean often attempted to master the colonizing language in order to transcend racial difference, but he or she often found the contradictions emerging from such mastery itself: (1) there seemed no way to be black *and* a master of the colonial language yet (2) there being blacks who seemed to have mastered it meant that there was something wrong with those blacks. They had, in other words, illicit use of licit grammar and words.[22] The structure was, in other words, deeply neurotic, but it was so on the level of a lived reality of constant failure. Thus, Fanon raised the question of an Afro-Caribbean philosophy as one that posed a philosophical anthropology premised upon the need to formulate an alternative social

---

[22] As we saw in our discussion of African-American philosophy, this is a major problem of the textualist tradition. It is also a feature of what Paget Henry calls the "poeticist tradition," since that one is also textualist. See Henry, *Caliban's Reason*, especially pp. 104 and 257.

world. His hopes for such a development rested on his existential commitment to contingency. There were, and continue to be, as he cautioned in his introduction to *Black Skin, White Masks*, people who could not be found in his book.

Ironically, although Fanon wrote those reflections in 1952, *Black Skin, White Masks* was not immediately recognized in the Caribbean. In France, it was somewhat of a scandal since the official French view was that there was no racial discrimination there and that French colonialism offered, in effect, colonial subjects access to the (French) universal.[23] That argument supported French leadership in another avowed project of supposed resistance through the formation of a "Latin" universal, namely, Latin America.[24] But in the islands the process of decolonization began to reach through the Anglophone, Francophone, and Hispanophone colonies in ways that brought the question of black emancipation to the table of international affairs as many African nations gained independence. Crucial in this regard was the Cuban revolution in 1959. For Fidel Castro placed, among his objectives, the question of racial justice at its forefront since the overwhelming number of poor Cubans, especially those that worked the sugar-cane fields, were black.[25] This does not mean, however, that it was such a concern that stimulated the revolution. Brian Meeks argues, for instance, that although race is often brought up with regard to the struggles in Cuba, what precipitated the revolution was not race but a conflict between Cuban elites, where younger generations were blocked under previous regimes from their expected right to inherit state power.[26] The treatment of blacks became an *ex post facto* consideration of world revolutionary struggle. Added to these developments in

[23] See Cherki, *Frantz Fanon*.

[24] For more on this history, see Walter Mignolo, *The Idea of Latin America* (Malden, MA: Blackwell Publishers, 2006). See also Nelson Maldonado-Torres, "Toward a Critique of Continental Reason: Africana Studies and the Decolonization of Imperial Cartographies in the Americas," in *Not Only the Master's Tools: African-American Studies in Theory and Practice*, edited by Lewis R. Gordon and Jane Anna Gordon (Boulder, CO: Paradigm Publishers, 2006), pp. 51–84, for the struggle for historical appearance in the region.

[25] See e.g. Lisa Brock and Otis Cunningham, "Race and the Cuban Revolution: A Critique of Carlos Moore's 'Castro, the Blacks, and Africa,'" *Cuban Studies* 21 (1991) | www.afrocubaweb. com/brock2.htm.

[26] See Brian Meeks, *Caribbean Revolutions and Revolutionary Theory: An Assessment of Cuba, Nicaragua and Grenada* (Kingston, Jamaica: University of the West Indies Press, 2001), pp. 49–60.

the 1960s was the growing discourse of underdevelopment as a new stage of colonial assertion or "neo-colonialism," which meant that black emancipation gained a new formulation through more historical-minded scholars and activists. Central among them was Guyanese Marxist historian Walter Rodney (1942–1980), whose *How Europe Underdeveloped Africa* (1972) and earlier pamphlet *Grounding with My Brothers* (1969) brought a fusion of historical themes under a new stage of Afro-Caribbean historical consciousness in the notions of underdevelopment and lumpen-proletariat politics of social transformation through Rastafari.[27] Orthodox Marxism argued that the proletariat – working-class consequences of industrialism – held the universal dimensions of the next stage in the ineluctable movement of history.[28] A problem for Third World peoples was what to do in places where there was no infrastructural development, where there was no industrial working class. The response from orthodox Marxism amounted to telling colonized and racialized subjects to wait for their turn.[29] In effect, the response of James in *Black Jacobins*, Fanon in *The Wretched of the Earth*, and Rodney was to offer alternative models of revolution with shared premises but different conclusions. They were reinvigorating dimensions of the liberation project that were derailed, as Cedric Robinson argued, by orthodox Marxism.[30] Revolution in the Third World required a different logic because of racial oppression. In other words, the struggle that was being waged from the Afro-Caribbean was not simply a matter of class membership but human existence. Thus, the place of philosophical anthropology and the logic of recognizing "lumpen" populations took a more central role in that context. The Rastafari movement, with its symbols of recognizing "natural" blackness such as dread locks and cultural links with music and rituals around marijuana ("ganja") that led to direct conflicts with the Jamaican (and other Caribbean) governments, brought these questions to the fore.

---

[27] Walter Rodney, *How Europe Underdeveloped Africa*, with a postscript by A. M. Babu (Washington, DC: Howard University Press, 1982) and *The Groundings with My Brothers*, with an introduction by Richard Small and a new introduction by Omawale (London: Bogle-L'Ouverture, 1975), originally published 1969.

[28] See Karl Marx and Friedrich Engels, *The Communist Manifesto* (London: Penguin Classics, 2002), originally published in 1848.

[29] See e.g. Jack Woddis's attack on Fanon in *New Theories of Revolution: A Commentary on the Views of Frantz Fanon, Régis Debray and Herbert Marcuse* (New York: International Publishers, 1972).

[30] Cedric J. Robinson, *An Anthropology of Marxism* (Aldershot, Hampshire: Ashgate, 2001).

Afro-Caribbean thought for most of the 1980s was heavily locked in discussions of political economy and history. A change developed in the 1990s, however, when African-American academic philosophy began to gain influence on African-American studies in North American universities. African-American academic philosophy began to formulate a set of problematics that conjoined the world of black public intellectuals with those of academic professionals. A group of Afro-Caribbean intellectuals, whose work was affected by mixtures in the United States, Canada, and the countries of the Caribbean, followed. Some of them were predominantly Caribbean in their orientation, and others were predominantly US black or Afro-Canadian in their upbringing. In effect, this was similar to what was happening at the same time in black popular culture, where Caribbean musicians, vinyl aficionados, dancers, and poets fused along the Hispanophone and Anglophone Caribbean with North American black Anglophone culture. The Committee on Blacks in the American Philosophical Association at first consisted of such a matrix: blacks from the United States and Canada and those from Puerto Rico, Jamaica, and Barbados met in the 1980s and 1990s under one racial rubric ("black") to discuss philosophical issues most relevant to them. The early meetings of that group were primarily through the intellectual identities of Anglo-analytical philosophy and American pragmatism. It is perhaps safe to say that the two exemplars of those models by the early 1990s were Bernard Boxill (Barbadian) in terms of the former and Cornel West (United States) in terms of the latter. Ironically, the committee itself was originally organized in the late 1970s by William R. Jones (United States), who inaugurated his career with a dissertation, as we have seen, on Jean-Paul Sartre's philosophical anthropology and who developed his own brand of humanism which served as a foundation of that stage of black existential and phenomenological philosophy. Others in that group included Lucius Outlaw (critical theory and phenomenology), Howard McGary (analytical philosophy), and Leonard Harris (pragmatism) from the southern, west coastal, and mid-western United States respectively. By the mid-1990s, that group included Charles Mills (Jamaican analytical philosopher trained in Canada), Robert Gooding-Williams (US-born specialist in European continental philosophy and nineteenth-century American philosophy), Naomi Zack (US-born proponent of "mixed race" and analytical philosophy but with existential sympathies). That was the context in which my work appeared in 1993, at first through a series of presentations and articles, and then in 1995 through the publication of *Bad Faith and Antiblack Racism* and *Fanon and the Crisis of European Man*. Crucial here, however, was also the work of organizing the US history of African-American philosophy through the interviews and anthologies put together by George Yancy (US-born and a specialist in American and European philosophies). All of this posed the question of whether such a correlate could emerge in the Caribbean context.

Much was happening at the same time in Caribbean literature through such writers as the Barbadian George Lamming, whose contribution to Anglo-Caribbean existentialism was simultaneous with Fanon's in the Francophone Caribbean, the Guyanese Wilson Harris, whose concerns of consciousness place him in the phenomenological wing, the Cuban-born Jamaican Sylvia Wynter, who represents the poststructural development, and the Antiguan Jamaica Kincaid, formerly Elaine Cynthia Potter Richardson, whose novels and essays raise the question of the political-geography of the "island" dimension of Afro-Caribbean consciousness.[31] As well, there was a sociological wing of writers thinking through questions of freedom and consciousness, although they were not working in concert. The work of Trinidadian-born Oliver Cox (1901–1973) examined race through an innovation of Marxism in his argument about the proletarianizing of a race and Jamaican-born Orlando Patterson raised the historical Hegelian formulations, but no writer exemplified commitment to the philosophical dimension of the sociological wing more than the Montserrat-born Antiguan Paget Henry, who took on the editorship of the *C. L. R. James Journal* in the late 1980s.[32] Henry had already made a name for himself as the father of Antiguan political economy in his classic work *Peripheral Capitalism and Development in Antigua* (1985), and his co-edited *C. L. R. James's Caribbean* (1992)

---

[31] See e.g. George Lamming, *In the Castle of My Skin*, with an introduction by Richard Wright (New York: Collier, 1970), originally published in 1952; Wilson Harris, *Palace of the Peacock* (London: Faber and Faber, 1960) and *Selected Essays of Wilson Harris: The Unfinished Genesis of the Imagination*, ed. with an introduction by Andrew Bundy (London: Routledge, 1999); Sylvia Wynter, *The Sylvia Wynter Reader*, ed. B. Anthony Bogues (Kingston, Jamaica: Ian Randle, forthcoming); and *After Man, Towards the Human: Critical Essays on the Thought of Sylvia Wynter*, ed. B. Anthony Bogues (Kingston, Jamaica: Ian Randle, 2005); and Jamaica Kincaid, *A Small Place*. The list of books by these writers is too long to cite here.

[32] For Oliver Cromwell Cox, see *Race*, 50th anniversary annotated edn of *Caste, Class, Race* (New York: Monthly Review Press, 2000), and for Orlando Patterson, see *Slavery and Social Death* (Cambridge, MA: Harvard University Press, 1982) and *Freedom* (New York: Basic Books, 1991).

had served as an exemplary fusion of Black British cultural studies and Caribbean historicism.[33] Under his editorship of *The C. L. R. James Journal*, the historicist dimension of that journal began to explore developments in African and African-American philosophy. It was, however, the publication of *Bad Faith and Antiblack Racism* that signaled a decision for Henry to delve more deeply into philosophy at the level of embedded work in the sociology of philosophy, which, in this case, meant doing philosophy instead of simply studying it.[34]

As we saw in the last chapter, *Bad Faith and Antiblack Racism* was one of the books that announced the existential phenomenological wing of African-American and Afro-Caribbean philosophy.[35] The text argued that a renewed reflection on the role of the theorist in the study of race and racism was necessary, and this reflective movement raised the question of bad faith. The reality of bad faith meant that any philosophical anthropology faced its own metastability, by which is meant that the thought itself as an object of consciousness placed it outside of an identity relationship with itself. This meant, further, that any reflective human endeavor always encounters its own incompleteness. For Henry this meant that the question of black consciousness was being posed and, with that, the question of the black self. Moreover, *Bad Faith and Antiblack Racism* argued that the historicist turn was limited in that it reflected only part of the problem. Colonialism and racism were not only matters of historical events; they were also questions about the constitution of new kinds of beings. In other words they raised new, ontological problems and problematics. Henry's historicism up to that point took the form of a fusion of the archaeological poststructuralism of Michel Foucault and the Marxist historicism of C. L. R. James. In both, however, he found it difficult to find an Afro-Caribbean self, although he experienced otherwise at the level of lived reality. The existential phenomenological posing of the

---

[33] Paget Henry, *Peripheral Capitalism and Underdevelopment in Antigua* (New Brunswick, NJ: Transaction Publishers, 1985).

[34] Lewis R. Gordon, *Bad Faith and Antiblack Racism* (Amherst, NY: Humanity Books, 1999), originally published in the Atlantic Highlands, NJ, by Humanities International Press in 1995.

[35] I belong to all the wings of Africana philosophy and have worked with Africana intellectuals globally. The Caribbean dimension of Africana philosophy has grown through my writings on Frantz Fanon and Africana Francophone and Hispanophone thought and through my teaching courses at the University of the West Indies at Mona, Jamaica.

creation of new kinds of beings and of how they live the consciousness of who or "what" they are offered the possibility of analyzing such subjects. That *Bad Faith and Antiblack Racism* and *Fanon and the Crisis of European Man* saw the thought of Frantz Fanon as foundational for this stage of African-American and Afro-Caribbean thought and, combined, those texts played their part in the case for the now canonical place of Fanon in postcolonial and Caribbean studies led Henry to thinking through the categories of his organization of Afro-Caribbean thought.

The results of Paget Henry's research came to the fore in the benchmark year of 2000. There, Afro-Caribbean philosophy was marked by the publication of Henry's *Caliban's Reason: Introducing Afro-Caribbean Philosophy* and my *Existentia Africana: Understanding Africana Existential Thought*, which, although not explicitly on Afro-Caribbean philosophy, is a contribution to that area by virtue of its being heavily informed by the thought of Frantz Fanon.[36] I will here focus on *Caliban's Reason*, however, since it is the text that placed this stage of Afro-Caribbean philosophy into its current schema, and I have already provided a discussion of *Existentia Africana* in the previous chapter.

The title *Caliban's Reason* points to the ongoing theme of Shakespeare's *Tempest* as the primary metaphor of modern colonization and racialization. Here, however, we see the theme of double consciousness made explicit and expanded in the Caribbean context. First, there is the form of double consciousness in which one sees oneself only through the eyes of others. For Caliban, this is reality through Prospero's eyes. In Eurocentric scholarship, reality is solely a function of what is understood through European perspectives. So, an Afro-Caribbean that subscribes to that view will only see his or herself through Eurocentric eyes that regard the Caribbean as marginal at best and, at worst, primitive or inferior. That, argues Henry, was the way most Caribbean intellectuals saw themselves. There is, however, another stage of double consciousness, where Caliban realizes the contradictions of the world as presented by Prospero. In that stage, Caliban is able to issue a critique of Eurocentrism and pose the possibility of seeing the self beyond the negative versions constructed by European modernity. This form of double consciousness involves recognizing how the Caribbean self (Caliban) was misrepresented. But this representation does not mean

---

[36] Henry, *Caliban's Reason*, and Lewis R. Gordon, *Existentia Africana: Understanding Africana Existential Thought* (New York: Routledge, 2000).

reinscribing Prospero's normativity; it does not, that is, require showing that Caliban is "as good as" Prospero. It requires understanding the problems of a Prospero-centered logic in the first place. Henry's response, then, is not to deny the achievements of European thought. His response is to demand examining the contributions from Africa, as well as the indigenous American and Asian worlds.

Raising the question of the intellectual contributions of the Afro-Caribbean to Caribbean life brought Henry in a tradition that goes back to Césaire. By raising this question, he brought to the table of ideas a different understanding of Africa in the Caribbean. There, Henry argues that what Africans brought to the New World were their unique visions of time and the distribution of values. Concerns of predestination governed (and still governs) the lives of many traditional African societies. The existential problematic thus focuses on problems of agency and human-centered action. How were these concerns affected by colonialism, slavery, and racialization?

Henry argues that a repression of the African self arose in the historical process of its dehumanization. Afro-Caribbean philosophy therefore faces an important mission: the liberation of the Afro-Caribbean self from the yoke of its dehumanization. Such a task is twofold. First, it takes the form of the constructive arguments for such self-recognition. Second, it involves the historical reconstruction of the intellectual history of such efforts. *Caliban's Reason* takes on both tasks, although most of the text does so through presenting a careful discussion of the variety of thinkers and ideas that comprise the body of Afro-Caribbean thought. The presentation is through a taxonomy of what Henry considers to be the major groups of Afro-Caribbean philosophy: (1) the historicists and (2) the poeticists. The former are primarily concerned with problems of social change and political economy. The latter celebrate the imagination with a focus on the conceptions of the self as represented by literature and poetry. Prime examples of historicists for Henry include Frantz Fanon, C. L. R. James, and his followers, who include the Antiguan public intellectual and social critic Leonard Tim Hector (1942–2003).[37] The poeticist wing includes Wilson Harris and Sylvia Wynter. The

---

[37] Tim Hector was Antigua's most prominent dissident intellectual. He was the editor of the newspaper *Fan the Flame*, in which he juxtaposed journalism with commentary on the intellectual scene in the Caribbean. See *The C. L. R. James Journal*'s (2004) commemoration issue on his life and thought.

categories are not meant to be exclusive, however, so there are historicist contributions by poeticists and vice versa. Fanon and Wynter, as well as the Martinican Edouard Glissant, for instance, both made historical and poetic contributions.[38] Wilson Harris's call for the primacy of the imagination in the Caribbean is also linked to his Hegelian-like notion of a supra-consciousness over and through all living things, which, although poetic, is claimed also to be historical. Henry then examines how different movements in the Afro-Caribbean were affected by these categories. One model that seems to defy this schema was African-American professional philosophy and its impact on the development of Afro-Caribbean philosophy. Many of the problematics formulated by African-American philosophy are faced in Afro-Caribbean philosophy. For instance, in his discussion of prophetic pragmatism, whose chief proponent is US-born Cornel West, Henry points out that a major shortcoming is the failure to recognize the African dimensions of the hybrid "African American." It is as if the African American were born in North American modernity without an African continued presence and an African past. Henry points out the importance of the phenomenological turn in Africa-American philosophy, which raises the question of the unique forms of consciousness posed by African America. To that he adds the value of a historicist dimension to phenomenological treatments of the meaning of African America, one that historicizes the African and other dimensions, and the importance of such an approach to the study of the constitution of the Caribbean self. Another category is Afro-Caribbean analytical philosophy or what he sometimes calls Afro-Caribbean "logicism." There, through the work of Bernard Boxill and Charles Mills, he sees the Afro-Caribbean proponents of logical analysis of language.[39] Related to the analytical group, he also examines what he calls "the linguistic turn" in Afro-Caribbean thought, whose chief proponents are UK-born of Guyanese-descent Paul Gilroy's Birmingham school form of cultural studies and Jamaican-born David Scott's Foucauldianism, wherein there is the poststructural appeal to the basis of

---

[38] Edouard Glissant is also known as the chief architect of the Creolité movement. See *Caribbean Discourses*, trans. with an introduction by J. Michael Dash (Charlottesville, VA: University of Virginia Press, 1989).

[39] Bernard Boxill, *Blacks and Social Justice*, rev. edn (Lanham, MD: Rowman & Littlefield, 1992) and Charles Mills, *The Racial Contract* (Ithaca, NY: Cornell University Press, 1998). See also Paget Henry, "African-American Philosophy," in *A Companion to African-American Studies*, pp. 223–45.

the self in the linguistic or, perhaps more accurate, discursive formations of modern societies.[40] Henry argues that this turn leads to a form of linguistic structuralism that evades the inner life or lived reality of the peoples of the region. The problem of language, after all, is central for the philosophical enterprise. The body of literature he explores, for instance, constitutes the discourse through which Afro-Caribbean life and problems can be understood. Yet, Henry argues at the close of the text, there are unresolved historical questions in the Caribbean that could benefit from a dialogue between the poeticists, who demand a role for political imagination, and the historicist demand for social change. But more, Henry raises there and later in a series of articles the crucial role of transcendental reflection in Caribbean philosophy.[41] By transcendental, he means the move from poetic interpretation and historicist examinations of temporality to the self-reflective analysis of preconditions and conditions of possibility. In short, Afro-Caribbean phenomenology, in addition to its historical and poetic dimensions, raises the question of Afro-Caribbean transcendentalism. For Henry, this means taking seriously the question of creolization in the Caribbean, where sources of transcendentalism are offered not only in the phenomenological writings from the 1990s and since 2000, but also much earlier, through the elements offered by the Indo-Caribbean tradition and its creolization with Africa and Europe.[42] As well, the clear role of double consciousness in Caribbean thought requires an explicit engagement with the work of W. E. B. Du Bois and its relevance to the Caribbean in the form of what Henry calls "potentiated double consciousness," the form of double consciousness that transcends the first stage mired in a failed dialectics of recognition.[43]

---

[40] Paul Gilroy, *The Black Atlantic: Modernity and Double Consciousness* (Cambridge, MA: Harvard University Press, 1993) and *Against Race: Imagining Political Culture beyond the Color Line* (Cambridge, MA: Belknap Press, 2002), and David Scott, *Refashioning Futures: Criticism after Postcoloniality* (Princeton, NJ: Princeton University Press, 1999) and *Conscripts of Modernity: The Tragedy of Colonial Enlightenment* (Durham, NC: Duke University Press, 2004).

[41] See Paget Henry, "Between Naipaul and Aurobindo: Where Is Indo-Caribbean Philosophy?" *The C. L. R. James Journal* 8, no. 1 (2002-3): 3-36, and "Wynter and the Transcendental Spaces of Caribbean Thought," in *After Man, Towards the Human*, ed. B. Anthony Bogues, pp. 258-89.

[42] *Ibid.*

[43] See especially Henry's article, "Africana Phenomenology: Its Philosophical Implications," *The C. L. R. James Journal* 11, no. 1 (2005): 79-112.

Henry's call for the Indo-Caribbean element raises the question of whether all facets of Caribbean life can be integrated into a theory of creolization. Migrating to the Caribbean as indentured servants and cheap laborers after the eradication of the slave trade in the British empire in the nineteenth century, the majority of the East Indian population came from the poorest communities of India and other parts of the empire. They eventually developed an unusual status within the racial hierarchies of the region. Known primarily through the pejorative "coolie," these populations were, until very recently, located on the bottom economic rung with blacks. They were, however, at times denigrated by the black population in a complex mixture of disdain and desire. The political economy of the Caribbean meant that "coolies" were lowly, but the aesthetic tastes of the region, especially in black communities, placed a premium on straight hair and facial features that provided Indo-Caribbeans with a commodity in the processes of amalgamation and upward mobility. The result is that nearly all of the black middle-classes, at least in the Anglophone regions, have some East Indian ancestry. The transcendental explorations that Henry poses are then culturally mediated by those who are entrusted with their preservation. The "coolie" communities were more Hindu than Muslim in the Caribbean, which meant that the lived reality of migration posed additional considerations beyond the travails of servitude. As Brinda Mehta observes in her study of Indo-Caribbean women writers, "The Indian women who braved the treacherous waters of the Atlantic – the *kala pani* – were dissatisfied with their continued state of marginalization and oppression in India."[44] The impact those early marine migrations had on the consciousness of those early waves of East Indians must be considered in a theory of the formation of the Indo-Caribbean self. Writes Mehta:

> According to Hindu belief, the traversing of large expanses of water was
> associated with contamination and cultural defilement as it led to the
> dispersal of tradition, family, class and caste classifications and to the
> general loss of a "purified" Hindu essence. *Kala pani* crossings were initially
> identified with the expatriation of convicts, low castes and other
> "undesirable" elements of society from the mainland to neighbouring
> territories to rid society of any visible traces of social pollution; those who
> braved the *kala pani* were automatically compromising their Hinduness.[45]

[44] Brinda Mehta, *Diasporic (Dis)locations: Indo-Caribbean Women Writers Negotiate the* Kala Pani (Kingston, Jamaica: University of the West Indies Press, 2004), p. 4.

[45] *Ibid.*, p. 5.

It would at first seem that a compromised Hinduness invites creolization, but the result, argues Mehta, has been a reasserted purity that resists submergence in the waters of creolization: "The creolization of Indian women was consequently seen as an infraction likened to the Hindu taboo of crossing the *kala pani*."[46] But more, creolization offers a conception of mixture that elides the conceptions of mixture, along with the unique anxieties, brought by Indian migrants who were constantly placed in geographical and social proximity with Afro-Caribbeans. The Indo-Caribbean term *dougla*, Mehta argues, is an understudied concept in this regard.

> While douglas have often been referred to as racial half-breeds or "ethnic bastards" in national discourses on citizenship by both Indians and blacks in Trinidad and Guyana, this group has also been subjected to a particular silencing in the political imaginary of these countries. Fetishized for their alterity by serving as visible reminders of a prior taboo, the mixing of black and Indian bloodstreams, dougla in-betweenness has often been a source of derision, alienation, misperception and social rejection.[47]

The complicated social question here is the extent to which the philosophical resources for struggling with religious and cultural taboos also played their role in the formation of Indo-Caribbean identities. There is the question, as well, of whether such resources meet in douglas as an Afro-Indo mixture, where West African predestination and Hindu taboos negotiate (if not battle) for psychic and cultural space. How, in other words, can anxieties over the self be negotiated when the source of disdain is not colonial imposition but internal criteria for illicit being?

These questions have been undertheorized, but they illustrate the generative potential of Henry's call for Indo-Caribbean reflection in Afro-Caribbean or Afro-Indo-Caribbean – in effect, *dougla* – philosophy. There is, as well, the presence of the sea. Surrounding those on the islands, facing those at the South American coasts, is the vast reminder of an illicit act, one which, recounting our earlier thought on metaphysical responsibility, brings the question of transcendental resources of resistance to the fore.

There have been an array of writings from a new generation of philosophers, social and political theorists, and cultural and literary critics since

---

[46] *Ibid.*, p. 7.

[47] *Ibid.*, p. 14. For a poignant portrait of some of these Afro-Indo liaisons in the context of the southern United States (a region that is Caribbean in many ways), see *Mississippi Masala* (1991), a film written by Sooni Taraporevala and directed by Mira Nair.

2000. These writers have expanded the meaning of the Caribbean philosopher to take on its historic legacy of the Caribbean writer, whose goal is a set of issues that include philosophy but is not limited to it. Such theorists include the philosopher Clevis Headley (Barbadian), the political theorists B. Anthony Bogues and Neil Roberts (Jamaican), the philosopher Gertrude James Gonzalez de Allen (Puerto Rican), the philosopher and religious thinker Nelson Maldonado-Torres (Puerto Rico), the literary and cultural theorist Claudia Milian Arias (El Salvador), the philosopher and classicist Patrick Goodin (Jamaican), the philosopher Mickaella Perina (Martinican), as well as a group of African philosophers who have joined the discussion such as Nigerian-born Nkiru Nzegwu, Ayotunde Bewaji, Lawrence Bamikole, and Tanzanian-born Aaron Kamugisha, as well as the great Ghanaian philosopher Kwasi Wiredu, whose analytical-pragmatist writings are also now being read in the Caribbean context, and the Kenyan philosophers D. A. Masolo and Frederick O'Chieng Odhiambo.

Asians and Asian Americans contributing to Africana Caribbean philosophy include the East Indian literary scholar Brinda Mehta and the Chinese American scholar Lisa Lowe. There are also scholars from Eastern Europe such as the philosopher Natalja Mićunović (Serbia) and the philosopher and literary theorist Alexis Nouss (Romania). These discussions have been taking place in a series of conferences since the late 1990s. These meetings take place annually at the University of the West Indies at Mona, Jamaica, under the title *Caribbean Reasonings*, and as The Cave Hill Philosophy Symposium at the University of the West Indies at Cave Hill in Barbados. An institution that organizes conferences through all the Caribbean is the Caribbean Philosophical Association, whose motto is "Shifting the Geography of Reason." There is also a growing community in Afro-Latin Caribbean philosophy. These scholars include Nelson Maldonado-Torres, Gertrude James Gonzalez de Allen, Claudia Milian Arias, Jorge Garcia (Puerto Rican), Jorge Gracia (Cuban), and Linda Martín Alcoff (Panamanian), among others.[48] Maldonado-Torres has

---

[48] See Linda Alcoff, *Visible Identities: Race, Gender, and the Self* (New York: Oxford University Press, 2006); Jorge Gracia, *Hispanic/Latino Identity: A Philosophical Perspective* (Malden, MA: Blackwell, 2000); Claudia Milian Arias, "New Languages, New Humanities: The 'Mixed Race' Narrative and the Borderlands," in *A Companion to Racial and Ethic Studies*, ed. David Theo Goldberg and John Solomos (Malden, MA: Blackwell, 2002), pp. 355–64, "Playing with the Dark: Africana and Latino Literary Imaginations," in Gordon and Gordon, *A Companion to African-American Studies*, pp. 543–68; and "Studying New World Negro

been the most active in developing this aspect of Afro-Caribbean philosophy and in taking the Fanonian side to a new dimension into what he calls a "post-continental" philosophy.[49] Here, Maldonado-Torres raises the question of the differences between the kinds of consciousness developed for continental formulations versus those governed by the logic of islands. He also raises questions of going beyond such logics at the linguistic levels as well as the regional levels – especially in terms of how one formulates the notion of "America" and the "Americas" – in the constitution of liberated selves. Maldonado-Torres, through the work of the Lithuanian Jewish philosopher Emmanuel Levinas and the Argentinean philosopher, historian, and theologian Enrique Dussel, also raises the question of ethics in Caribbean anti-colonial struggles.[50] Unlike Fanon's and my work, which questions the role of ethics under colonialism, Maldonado-Torres has attempted to reconcile ethics with postcolonial liberation.[51] To Maldonado-Torres's work we could also add Linda Martín Alcoff's, which brings questions of race in the

Problems: Open Double Consciousness and Mulatinidad in Edwidge Danticat's *The Farming of Bones*," *The C. L. R. James Journal: A Review of Caribbean Ideas* 10, no. 1 (Winter 2004): 123–53; and Nelson Maldonado-Torres, "Thinking from the Limits of Being: Levinas, Fanon, Dussel and the Cry of Ethical Revolt" (Providence, RI: Brown University Dissertation in Philosophy of Religion, 2002), *Against War: Views from the Underside of Modernity* (Durham, NC: Duke University Press, 2008), and as an editor, *New Caribbean Philosophy*, in *Caribbean Studies* 33, no. 2 (2005): vii–248; see also, among Maldonado-Torres's many articles, "The Cry of the Self as a Call from the Other: The Paradoxical Loving Subjectivity of Frantz Fanon," *Listening: A Journal of Religion and Culture* 36, no. 1 (2001): 46–60 and "Walking to the Fourth World of the Caribbean," *Nepantla: Views from South* 4, no. 3 (2003): 561–565. As well, there are the historical sources of Afro-Latin Caribbean philosophical thought that are still to be studied primarily because of the absence of translation into English and the near neglect of their contributions because of the tendency to avoid the Afro-dimension of Latin American life. Two cases in point are the work of the Brazilian social theorist Alberto Guerreiro Ramos (1915–1982), whose work is a correlate to W. E. B. Du Bois's sociological work on black folk, and Abdias do Nascimento, the father of Brazilian Negritude. See e.g. Alberto Guerreiro Ramos's *A Reducão Sociológica* (Rio de Janeiro: Editoria UFRJ, 1996) and Abdias do Nascimento's *O genocído do negro brasileiro* (Rio de Janeiro: Editoria Paz e Terra, 1978) and *A luta aro-brasileira no senado* (Brasilia: Senado Federal, 1991).

[49] See Nelson Maldonado-Torres, "Toward a Critique of Continental Reason: Africana Studies and the Decolonization of Imperial Cartographies," in Gordon and Gordon, *Not Only the Master's Tools*, pp. 51–84.

[50] This is the subject of Nelson Maldonado-Torres, *Against War*.

[51] See also Maldonado-Torres's article, "The Cry of the Self as a Call from the Other."

Latin-Caribbean context to the fore with connections to the rest of Latin America, especially Panama.[52]

Paget Henry's reflections on phenomenology have also been joined by groups of North American scholars in dialogue with Afro-Caribbean philosophy. The late Iris Marion Young (1949–2006) co-organized a conference with Jacob Levy in 2004, which brought the Caribbean into conversation with other regions on questions of postcoloniality.[53] Other scholars include the philosopher and therapist Marilyn Nissim-Sabat, who had already begun exploring the postcolonial phenomenological dimensions of Afro-Caribbean philosophy on developmental questions of maturation in contemporary thought.[54] Kenneth Knies has also taken on the question of the constitution of the self in phenomenology, and he raises the question of their disciplinary underpinning in what he calls, as we saw in the previous chapter, "post-European science."[55] I have characterized this development in the field as "shifting the geography of reason."[56] In effect, this research asks what happens when reason no longer runs out the door when the black walks in the room. The argument here takes several turns. First, it addresses the metatheoretical question of theory itself. Critics of Afro-Caribbean philosophy take the position that building new theory is an imperial project and that properly postcolonial thought, as Afro-Caribbean thought should be, should focus on criticism, on tearing down the master's house, so to speak. The response to this approach argues that being locked in negative critique collapses into reactionary thought and politics. The aim should not be about what to tear down but what to build up.

---

[52] See especially part IV of Alcoff's *Visible Identities: Race, Gender, and the Self* (New York: Oxford University Press, 2005).

[53] The conference was held on the 23 and 24 April 2004 under the title *Colonialism and Its Legacies*. Henry's paper was entitled, "The Creolization of Caribbean Philosophy: A Peculiar Colonial Legacy." For a commentary on that conference, see Neil Roberts, "Colonialism and Its Legacies: New Directions in Contemporary Political Theory," *Philosophia Africana* 7, no. 2 (2004): 89–97.

[54] See Nissim-Sabat's forthcoming book, *For Love of Humanity*. See also, Marilyn Nissim-Sabat, "Psychiatry, Psychoanalysis, and Race," *Philosophy, Psychiatry, and Psychology* 8, no. 1 (2001): 45–59.

[55] Kenneth Knies, "The Idea of Post-European Science: An Essay on Phenomenology and Africana Studies," in Gordon and Gordon, *Not Only the Master's Tools*, pp. 85–106; "Politics and Phenomenology: Beyond the Philosopher's Politics Toward a Political Eidetic," *Radical Philosophy Review* 4, nos. 1–2 (2001).

[56] See Lewis R. Gordon, "From the President of the Caribbean Philosophical Association," *Caribbean Studies* 33, no. 2 (2005): xv–xxii.

The role of theory is to use all of its resources – from its many genealogical trends (creolization) – to build livable homes.[57] This means, second, understanding what disciplinary formations could offer such a domicile. The error in most disciplinary formations is that they treat themselves as "closed," "absolute," or "deontological." The result is disciplinary decadence, which involves the closing off of epistemological possibilities of disciplinary work.[58] This form of decadence is particularly acute at the level of method, where a methodology does not surface since such questions are closed. In effect, the discipline and its method become "complete." Life returns to disciplinary practices, however, through being willing to transcend the disciplines, which, as we have seen, is a teleological suspension of disciplinarity. What this means is that the thinker concludes that there are issues so important to pursue that method and disciplinary commitment must fall by the wayside if they inhibit exploration of those issues. In the case of philosophy, its disciplinary suspension – that is, the decision to go beyond philosophy – enables the cultivation of new philosophy. Afro-Caribbean philosophy, from this point of view, is the construction of new philosophy through Afro-Caribbean philosophers' willingness to go beyond philosophy, paradoxically, for the sake of philosophy.

At the institutional level, what has resulted since 2000 is that there are now philosophy departments at the universities in the Anglo-Caribbean and the Dutch-Caribbean, and there are now institutes and centers for Caribbean thought. Richard Clarke and his colleagues at the University of the West Indies at Cave Hill held a conference on philosophy and Caribbean cultural studies in 2001, which stimulated discussions on philosophy on that island in the form of continued, annual symposia, and the University of the West Indies at Mona, Jamaica, held a series of large, public seminars honoring such people of letters as Sylvia Wynter (2002), George Lamming (2003), and Stuart Hall (2004), through which from the onset discussions

---

[57] For recent discussions and debates on creolization, see the first volume and issue of *Shibboleth: Journal of Comparative Theory* (2006), especially the first two articles: O. Nigel Bolland, "Reconsidering Creolisation and Creole Societies," pp. 1–14, and E. P. Brandon, "Creolisation, Syncreticism and Multiculturalism," pp. 15–19. See also Alexis Nouss, "Mestizaje, créolité, globalization," and Mickaella Perina, "Identity Negotiated: Créolité versus Negritude?" both of which appear in *The C. L. R. James Journal* (spring 2008).

[58] See Lewis R. Gordon, *Disciplinary Decadence: Living Thought in Trying Times*, especially the introduction and ch. 1.

led to the founding of the Caribbean Philosophical Association in 2003. With the motto of "shifting the geography of reason," the Caribbean Philosophical Association meets annually at alternative linguistic countries and provinces – that is, Anglophone (Barbados, 2004; Jamaica, 2007), Hispanophone (Puerto Rico, 2005), Francophone (Montreal, Quebec, 2006; Guadeloupe, 2008) – and has produced a volume, through the editorship of Clevis Headley and Marina Banchetti-Robino, addressing problems in the philosophy of science, language, religion, gender, and aesthetics in the Caribbean context. There are now also students pursuing graduate degrees in the Caribbean with a focus on Afro-Caribbean philosophy. Within those ranks, there is much interest in the thought of Caribbean women writers, and there is growing dialogue between Afro-Caribbean feminists and US feminist philosophers for the emerging area of Afro-Caribbean feminist philosophy. Developments include work on historical figures, such as T. Denean Sharpley-Whiting's study of the role of the Nardal sisters and Suzanne Césaire in the development of *Négritude* and Kristin Waters's work on the Jamaican Mary Seacole (1805–1881) as well as the emerging scholarship on such women as Jamaica Kincaid and Edgwin Danticat, and there is feminist constructivist work by such philosophers as Jeanette (Jan) Boxill on contemporary problems ranging from social justice to philosophies of sport.[59]

To conclude, then, Afro-Caribbean philosophy has placed the question of the Afro-Caribbean self as a primary concern of the identity dimension of its philosophical anthropology and explorations of how such conceptions of the self relate to historical questions of social change as its teleology. Afro-Caribbean philosophy is also concerned with a variety of questions in other areas of philosophy, such as the relationship of European philosophical categories to the creolized ones of the Caribbean, as well as the historical task of constructing Caribbean intellectual history. It is not, however, a philosophy that is obsessed with similitude or the pressures to be philosophy as understood in the northern hemisphere. In seeking its own path, Afro-Caribbean philosophy exemplifies the paradox of becoming more philosophical through the effort of going beyond philosophy itself.

---

[59] See T. Denean Sharpley-Whiting's *Negritude Women*, and the others have been presentations at the Caribbean Philosophical Association meetings, most of which will come to print through its series *Shifting the Geography of Reason*.

6   African philosophy

It could easily be argued that we have been discussing African philosophy throughout, if by that is meant the work of or pertaining to Africans both on the continent and in the diaspora. Although that is partially true, the fact remains that Africa itself as a point of departure raises unique questions in Africana philosophy, especially that, as we have seen at the beginning of this book, of modernity. There are several implications of modernity in the African context. One of them is the question of African modernism. Although we have discussed modernism at the outset, we will, in this chapter, explore it further. An implication of modernism is that the human being, whether as fixed or unstable, increasingly becomes the subject of study in reflections on reality. Another is that admission of the human being as the condition by which a human world is created leads to the question of how such a being or beings create such worlds. And finally there are the consequences of such actions on the kinds of world people live in. We could formulate these as problems of humanism, invention, and politics. African philosophy, as understood through the lens of Africana philosophy, offers creative insights into these problems.

The reader may, however, wonder why we will not be devoting much attention to ancient African philosophy. The answer is that the focus of this book is Africana philosophy, which requires us to focus on Africana African philosophy. That philosophy arose, as I have argued in the introduction, from the late medieval into the modern world.[1]

---

[1] For ancient studies, see Théophile Obenga, *African Philosophy: The Pharaonic Period: 2780–330 BC* (Popenguine, Senegal: Ankh, 2004) and "Egypt: Ancient History of African Philosophy," in *A Companion to African Philosophy*, ed. with introduction by Kwasi Wiredu (Malden, MA: Blackwell, 2004), pp. 32–49; D. A. Masolo, "African Philosophers in the Greco-Roman Era," in *A Companion to African Philosophy*, pp. 50–65; Maulana Karenga, *Maat: The Moral ideal in Ancient Egypt – a Study in Classical African Ethics* (Los Angeles, CA: University of Sankore

African humanism

I know of no African philosopher who has not argued that African philosophy is humanistic. A common misconception of African humanism is, however, that it is a set of values brought into instead of emerging from communities on the African continent. Such an error is a function of interpretations of humanism that locate its emergence in the European Renaissance and subsequent modern world.[2] If we define humanism as a value system that places priority on the welfare, worth, and dignity of human beings, its presence in precolonial African religious and philosophical thought can easily be found.[3] In religious thought such as that among the Akan in what is today Ghana, for example, human beings do not seek redemption in an afterlife because, for them, punishment or redemption exists only on earth. Consequently, there is a tendency to place great weight on human action and human subjects. The focus on earthly actions without an expectation of their effects on an afterlife is a key feature of many African religions, and African humanism reflects this fact. Death, in other words, is a return to the Creator (or Creators) and taking one's place among the ancestors instead of in an afterlife time of reckoning.

Despite the presence of many indigenous ethnic groups in Africa, there is much similarity in the cosmologies that ground their religious practices, especially those of people south of the Sahara. A major reason for this commonality is that many of them are descended from a set of communities along the ancient lakes and plains of the Sahara-Sahelian region of northern Africa that subsequently dried up and became a desert. We could call this the earliest foundational sources of those peoples. The second phase is connected to the history of ancient Egypt, particularly

Press, 2006); and Charles Finch, III, *Echoes of the Old Darkland: Themes from the African Eden* (Decatur, GA: Khenti, 1991).

[2] See e.g. Ernst Cassirer, *The Individual and the Cosmos in Renaissance Philosophy*, trans. with introduction by Mario Domand (Mineola, NY: Dover, 2000). Even postmodern discussions of humanism treat it as almost exclusively a European affair. For some discussion of this tendency and how it may be transformed in terms of "post" humanism, see David Fryer, *Thinking Queerly: Post-Humanist Essays on Ethics and Identity* (Boulder, CO: Paradigm Publishers, 2008).

[3] See e.g. Obenga, *African Philosophy*; Karenga, *Maat*; and Wiredu, *A Companion to African Philosophy* (through discussions of various authors in *The Companion*).

the Archaic or Thinite period (3100 BCE–2700 BCE), and the Old (2650–2134 BCE) and Middle (2040–1640 BCE) Kingdoms. As invasions, conquest, and colonization became a feature of the New Kingdom's plight (1570–1070 BCE) and subsequent Egyptian history – as witnessed by the Hyksos (1786 BCE–1539 BCE), Kushites (750 BCE–671 BCE), Assyrians (671 BCE–661 BCE), Persians (525 BCE–405 BCE, and then again 342 BCE–332 BCE), Greeks (332 BCE–30 BCE), Romans (30 BCE–638 CE), Muslim Arabs with subsequent Persian and other kinds of Muslims (638 CE–1517), Turkish Muslims/Ottomans (1517–1805), the French (1798–1800), and the British (1882–1952) – the peoples of those older kingdoms were pushed away from the northeastern regions of Africa and eventually became known as the variety of sub-Saharan groups of today. Scholars, particularly linguistic anthropologists, have shown the connections, however, between the languages of some of these peoples today and those of the ancient Egyptian past.[4] The cosmologies of these groups tend to have a concomitant ontology, or conception of being, and a system of values in which greater reality and value are afforded to things of the past. Thus, the Creator (sometimes Creators), being first, has the greatest ontological weight, and whoever is brought into being closer in time to the moment of the origin of the world is afforded greater weight. This view gives one's ancestors greater ontological weight and value than their descendants. Also, one's past actions are of greater ontological weight than one's present actions. One's future actions are of no ontological weight since they have not yet occurred.

Indigenous African systems affirm that human beings negotiate their affairs with the understanding that they cannot change the past (although it constantly reaches out to the present through ancestors). They must take responsibility for their future through realizing that it can only come into being through their actions. Kwame Gyekye has argued that this form of humanism does not require the rejection of religion but may exist alongside it. As he observed in his classic study of Akan humanism in Ghana:

---

[4] See e.g. Charles Finch, "From the Nile to the Niger," in *A Companion to African-American Studies*, ed. with introduction by Lewis R. Gordon and Jane Anna Gordon (Malden, MA: Blackwell, 2006), pp. 453–75. See also *The African Frontier: The Reproduction of Traditional African Societies*, ed. Igor Kopytoff (Bloomington, IN: Indiana University Press, 1987) and *The Archaeology of Africa: Food, Meals and Towns*, ed. Thustan Shaw, Paul Sinclair, Bassey Andah, and Alex Okpoko (London: Routledge, 1993).

> In Akan religious thought the Supreme Being is not He who must be feared and could cast one into eternal hellfire. (The Supreme Being is believed to punish evildoers only in this world.) Again, in spite of Akan belief in immortality, their conception of the hereafter does not include hopes of a happier, more blessed life beyond the grave. Western humanism sees religion as impeding the concentration of human energies on building the good society. In Akan thought this tension between supernaturalism and humanism does not appear; for the Akan, religion is not seen as hindering the pursuit of one's interests in this world . . . Akan humanism is the consequence not only of a belief in the existence of a Supreme Being and other supernatural entities, but, more importantly I think, of a desire to utilize the munificence and powers of such entities for the promotion of human welfare and happiness.[5]

Beyond the indigenous models of humanism there has arisen what may be called modern African humanism, which emerged from African responses to conquest, colonization, and the various slave trades along the African coasts. These forms usually involve engagements with Christian and secular liberal and republican (domination-free) values, or with ideas that emerged as a result of engagement with various Muslim empires in the Middle Ages, whose impact continues to be felt. We should bear in mind that much of eastern Africa is also populated by Semitic peoples, and that their Coptic and Abyssinian (or Ethiopian) Judaism and Christianity have left legacies that are as old as, if not older than, their European counterparts.

Many modern African humanists, as did their counterparts in the diaspora, address the problem raised in the end of the ancient into the early medieval African Christian philosophy in the thought of St. Augustine of Hippo (today, Algeria): the problem of theodicy, which, as we have seen in our various discussions of the subject in this book, involves accounting for the presence of evil in a universe ruled by an omnipotent, omniscient, and benevolent god or God. Before recounting this problem, some thoughts on St. Augustine's African location should strengthen the critique of not-out-of-Africa theses, which is a subtext of this book in general and chapter in particular. St. Aurelius Augustine was the son of a Roman father (Patricius) and a Berber mother (Monica). By now the reader should notice that "Berber"

---

[5] Kwame Gyekye, *An Essay on African Philosophical Thought: The Akan Conceptual Scheme*, rev. edn (Philadelphia, PA: Temple University Press, 1995 [first edn, 1987]), pp. 144–5.

people are usually evoked in the north African context as a way of referring to Africa without outright saying black Africa. The term often refers to almost any indigenous, nomadic group of Africans who happen to be in north Africa. The Berbers of today do not necessarily look like the Berbers of nearly two millennia ago, and as our discussion in our introduction showed, it is an error to look at the people of any region as morphologically and culturally static and homogeneous when the region has been undergoing conquest and colonization for thousands of years. In the case of north Africa the populations have been affected by waves of European and West Asian conquest and colonization in antiquity by Phoenicians, Greeks, and Romans, a Visigoth and then Islamic Arabic onslaught in the Middle Ages, and then, in modern times since the defeat of the Moors in Iberia Peninsula in 1492, the Spanish, French, and Italians. St. Augustine is exclusively Roman Christian only through a logic that denies mixture, where he supposedly cannot be Roman and Berber, a product of two sides of the Mediterranean. Nearly all of the philosophers we have examined are products of more than one civilization and more than one kind of people. The focus of this book has been the Africana side, but the organizing premise is more one of emphasis than exclusion. Being Africana does not exclude being something else.

To recapitulate the theodicean problem, St. Augustine argued that human beings are responsible for evil because evil actions are a necessary possibility of freedom. He also argued that human beings have limited knowledge of God's ultimate will or God's justice – the literal meaning of theodicy, *theo* (god) and *dikê* (justice). The modern African faces the same problem, as we saw in our discussion of theodicy and double consciousness in chapter 3, when he or she looks at such evils as the slave trade and colonialism. Recall that Wilhelm Amo and Ottobah Cugoano wrote treatises calling for the abolition of the slave trade. These authors argued that human beings are responsible for their actions, and that Europeans faced the negative moral consequences of the slave trade. Although couched in a Christian context, their work included reflections on the humanity of African peoples that have become a feature of modern African humanistic thought – namely, its concern with philosophical anthropology.

There has been an African Muslim discourse on humanism, as we saw in our first chapter. There has also been, and continues to be, a Jewish discussion, but it has been unfortunately eclipsed by a tendency to place Jews out of Africa. For instance, Moshe ben Maimon (Moses Maimonides,

1135–1204), the greatest Jewish thinker of the Middle Ages, was born in Cordoba, studied primarily with Muslim scholars, and from about 1165 spent the rest of his life in Al-Fustat (original Arabic capital now known as "Old Cairo"), Egypt. That he, along with other important Jewish thinkers, took refuge in a Muslim center reveals much about the Islamic world at the time and how Jews configured in the subsequent Inquisition succeeding the expulsion of the Moors from Iberia. Maimonides's concerns were primarily with the interpretation of Jewish law. His work, written in Arabic, often brought the Islamic and Muslim world together, as in the important role he played in the reception of the work of Ibn Rushd.[6] Recall that Ibn Rushd, most known by his Latin name Averroës, was a north African philosopher whose work came to prominence in Cordoba. He was a pioneer in formulating the set of issues that continue to dominate African Muslim thought, although his influence includes commentaries on Aristotle that affected European scholasticism and the struggles to transform it. Rushd argued for the secularization of political life and the dominance of reason.[7] For this position he was widely rejected in the Muslim world save for a small set of followers. The debate over these ideas, however, continued in the question of the place or role of modernity in the Muslim world. Among the many scholars who took up these issues was the Egyptian born Imam Muhammad Abdou (1849–1905), who argued for freeing thought from conventionalism and presenting a political theory of citizens' rights instead of blind obedience to the religious state.[8] Zaki Naguib Mahmoud (1905–1993) defended the dominance of reason through defending logical positivism in science and through that a form of secular naturalism as the basis of

---

[6] See Fred Dallmayr, *Dialogue among Civilizations* (New York: Palgrave Macmillan, 2002), p. 141. See also the selections on Maimonides in *Medieval Political Philosophy*, ed. Ralph Lerner and Muhsin Mahdi (Ithaca, NY: Cornell University Press, 1963), pp. 188–236.

[7] See Averroës, *The Book of the Decisive Treatise and Epistle Dedicatory*, trans. with introduction and notes by Charles E. Butterworth (Provo, UT: Brigham Young University Press, 2001). Commentaries are many, but see e.g. Majid Fakhry, *Averroes (Ibn Rushd): His Life, Works and Influence* (Oxford: Oneworld, 2001); Liz Sonneborn, *Averroes (Ibn Rushd): Muslim Scholar, Philosopher, and Physician of Twelfth-century al-Andalus* (New York: Rosen Central, 2006); Mourad Wahba, "Philosophy in North Africa," in Wiredu, *A Companion to African Philosophy*, pp. 161–2; and Dallmayr, *Dialogue among Civilizations*, pp. 121–46.

[8] The main source here on Muhammad Abdou, Zaki Naguib Mahmoud, and Abdel-Rahman Badawi is Mourad Wahba's insightful chapter, "Philosophy in North Africa," in Wiredu, *A Companion to African Philosophy*, pp. 161–71.

his humanism. Abdel-Rahman Badawi (1917–2002), also Egyptian born, presented his atheistic existential philosophy as a more radical humanism for the Muslim world by comparing it with Sufism. In both, he argued, the human subject is prioritized. More recently, the question of subjectivity and the impact of physical and historical limits has been brought to a new dimension in the writings of the Algerian novelist and historian Assia Djebar, who examines, in her historical work, the emergence of women revolutionaries under extraordinarily repressive circumstances and, in her novels, how reclamation of their voices and bodies exemplify liberation for women.[9]

In the twentieth century a form of secular humanism emerged in Africa primarily through the efforts of the Senegalese intellectuals Cheikh Anta Diop (1923–1986) and Léopold Sédar Senghor (1906–2001). Diop advocated a strong historicist humanism that focused on the achievements of ancient Africans as the first *Homo sapiens*, arguing that they laid the groundwork for the cultural life of the species. Although secular, the familiar theme of ancestral value is echoed in his work. Senghor is best known as a co-founder, with the Martinican poet Aimé Césaire, of the *Négritude* movement, which focused on the creative potential of an affirmed black standpoint.[10]

Whereas Diop represented what Paget Henry would call the historicist tradition of African secular humanism, Senghor is the father of the poeticizing tradition. He defended the humanity of black Africans primarily through literature, although his thought also included reflections on music. Senghor argued that African value systems were more properly humanistic than European ones because African models affirmed that the passionate or emotional side of a person carries the same value and legitimacy as the

---

[9] See e.g. Assia Djebar, *A Sister to Scheherazade* (London: Quartet, 1988); *So Vast the Prison*, trans. Betsy Wing (New York: Seven Stories Press, 1999); and "Writing in the Language of the Other," in *Word: On Being a [Woman] Writer*, ed. Jocelyn Burrell, foreword by Suheir Hammad (New York: Feminist Press, 2004), pp. 112–19. See also Nada Elia, *Trances, Dances and Vociferations: Agency and Resistance in Africana Women's Narratives* (New York: Garland, 2001), ch. 2.

[10] See e.g. Cheikh Anta Diop, *Civilization or Barbarism: An Authentic Anthropology*, trans. Yaa-Lengi Meema Ngemi, ed. Harold J. Salemson and Marjolijn de Jager (New York: Lawrence Hill Books, 1991); Aimé Césaire, *Notebook of a Return to My Native Land: Cahier d'un retour au pays natal / Aimé Césaire*, trans. Mireille Rosello with Annie Pritchard, introduction by Mireille Rosello (Newcastle upon Tyne: de Bloodaxe Books, 1995); Léopold Senghor, *Liberté: I* (Paris: Editions Seuil, 1964).

rational, analytic side. In Ghana the secular humanist tradition also took hold through the thought of Kwame Nkrumah (1909–1972), who in 1946 offered what he called consciencism, or critical material consciousness. For Nkrumah African humanism was a call for explicitly political, communalistic responses to social problems.[11]

The most famous formulation of secular humanism to emerge on the African continent came, however, by way of the thought of Frantz Fanon, the Martinican expatriate in Algeria who, as we have seen throughout this book, has had an impact across the entire spectrum of Africana philosophy. Fanon diagnosed a sick modern world premised upon human actions, where the tasks faced by contemporary Africans must be to build up their material infrastructure (based on national consciousness) and thereby transform negative cultural symbols into positive ones in the hope of setting afoot a new humanity.[12] The secular humanist tradition continued along historicist and poeticizing lines, and with political allegiances of the Marxist (and, occasionally, liberal) variety through such writers and political leaders as the Guinean Amílcar Cabral (1921–1973) and Tanzanian Julius Nyerere (1922–1999) until the emergence of leaders in the struggle against apartheid in South Africa took center stage.[13]

The most influential formulations of secular humanism to emerge in South Africa focused on the question of consciousness. The first was Solomon Tshekisho Plaatje (1876–1932), whose political writings include the novel

---

[11] Kwame Nkrumah, *Consciencism: Philosophy and Ideology for Decolonization and Development with Particular Reference to the African Revolution* (New York: Monthly Review Press, 1965).

[12] Frantz Fanon, *The Wretched of the Earth*, trans. Constance Farrington (New York: Grove Press, 1963). It took some time for Fanon's other writings to develop an impact in Africa. Many of the themes of his first book, *Black Skin, White Masks*, trans. Charles Lamm Markmann (New York: Grove Press, 1967), are influential in recent African postcolonial political thought, especially through the Lacanian-influenced work of Homi Bhabha, *The Location of Culture* (Routledge Classics) (New York: Routledge, 2004), which has had a great impact on postcolonial studies, especially Achille Mbembe's collection of essays *On the Postcolony* (Berkeley, CA: University of California Press, 2001).

[13] See Nkrumah, *Consciencism*; Amílcar Cabral, *Revolution in Guinea: Selected Texts*, trans. and ed. Richard Handyside (New York: Monthly Review Press, 1970); Julius K. Nyerere, *Ujamaa: Essays on Socialism* (London: Oxford University Press, 1973), *Freedom and Socialism = Uhuru Na Ujamaa: A Selection from Writings and Speeches, 1965–1967* (Dar es Salaam: Oxford University Press, 1976), *Freedom and Development: Uhuru Na Maendeleo: A Selection from Writings and Speeches 1968–1973* (London: Oxford University Press, 1974).

Mhudi (1930), in addition to his Boer War diary.[14] Plaatje defended the humanity of indigenous African peoples through a form of Black Nationalism that respected the multilingual and cultural diversity of Africans. The impact of Plaatje's political work, which included co-founding the South African Native National Congress in 1912, which in 1926 became the African National Congress, and his commitment to a diverse understanding of nationhood, influenced Steven Bantu Biko (1946–1977), who developed a theory of black consciousness that drew upon the political dimension of racial oppression. "Black," for Biko, designated a political identity that was a consequence of oppression that could be faced by an East Indian, an East Asian, or a colored (in South Africa, a person of mixed race whose parents are indigenous and Afrikaaner) as well as an indigenous African. Afrikaaners are descendants of white Dutch settlers in southern Africa. Many were farmers known as "Boers."[15] More recently, Biko's thought has been expanded by Rozena Maart, a South African from the colored community of District Six. Maart was among the 60,000 people forcibly moved from that area when it was declared for "whites only" in 1965, and she has chronicled it in her fiction, essays, and poetry.[16] Her philosophical work draws upon Fanonian explorations of consciousness, Freudian and Lacanian psychoanalysis, and Derridian semiotics of traces and absence from which Maart argues that Biko's advancement of Black Consciousness also brings to the fore the dynamics of repression exemplified by white normativity. The effect is a political-epistemological critique of whiteness as the signification of neutrality.[17] Noël C. Manganyi, advisor to the vice-chancellor and principal of

---

[14] Solomon Tshekisho Plaatje, *Mafeking Diary: A Black Man's View of a White Man's War*, ed. John Comaroff, with Brian Willan and Andrew Reed (Cambridge: Meridor Books, 1990).

[15] For a historical anthropological study of South Africa, see John and Jean Comaroff, *Of Revelation and Revolution*. Vol. I: *Christianity, Colonialism, and Consciousness in South Africa* (Chicago, IL: University of Chicago Press, 1991) and vol. II: *The Dialectics of Modernity on a South African Frontier* (Chicago, IL: University of Chicago Press, 1997). And for Biko, see Steve Bantu Biko, *I Write What I Like: Selected Writings*, ed. with a personal memoir by Aeired Stubbs, preface by Desmond Tutu, introduction by Malusi and Thoko Mpumlwana, new foreword by Lewis R. Gordon (Chicago, IL: University of Chicago Press, 2002) and the discussions of Biko in Mabogo Samuel More, "Biko: Africana Existentialist Philosopher," *Alternation* II, no. 1 (2004). See also *Biko Lives: Conversations and Contestations*, ed. Amanda Alexander, Nigel Gibson, and Andile Mngxitama (New York: Palgrave, 2008).

[16] See e.g. Rozena Maart, *Rosa's District Six* (Toronto: Tsar Publishers, 2004).

[17] See Rozena Maart, *The Politics of Consciousness, the Consciousness of Politics: When Black Consciousness Meets White Consciousness*. Vol. I: *The Interrogation of Writing* (Guelph, Canada:

the University of Pretoria, is also an exemplar of South African humanistic thought. Manganyi is a psychologist whose writings during the apartheid years were of an existential phenomenological variety, with many similarities to the work of Fanon and Jean-Paul Sartre.[18] There have, however, also been highly political Christian humanist responses in the South African context that should be considered, the most noted representative of which is the Nobel Peace Prize laureate Bishop Desmond Tutu, whose leadership in forming South Africa's Peace and Reconciliation Commission exemplifies what might be called the Christian liberal tradition.

The last quarter of the twentieth century has also been marked by the rise of African academic intellectuals as chief spokespersons for secular African humanism. Many of these writers present their case from the disciplinary perspectives of philosophy, political theory, and political economy (especially as critics of development studies), and many of them, save, for example, Kwame Gyekye (Ghana), Noel Manganyi (South Africa), Mabogo P. More (South Africa), Benita Parry (South Africa), Achille Mbembe (Cameroon, but teaching in South Africa), Ernest Wamba dia Wamba (Democratic Republic of the Congo) and Samir Amin (Egyptian in Senegal), are expatriates living in North America and Europe. They include, among others, V. Y. Mudimbe (Congo/Zaire), Ato Sekyi-Otu (Ghana), Ali Mazrui (Kenya), Kwasi Wiredu (Ghana), K. Anthony Appiah (born in Britain and grew up visiting Ghana), Nkiru Nzegwu (Nigeria), Oyèrónké Oyěwùmí (Nigeria), D. A. Masolo (Kenya), Tsenay Serequeberhan (Eritrea), Clarence Sholé Johnson (Sierra Leone), Teodros Kiros (Ethiopia), Souleyman Bachir Diagne (Senegal), Elias Bongmba (Cameroon), Hlonipha Mokoena (South Africa), Luc Ngowet (Gabon), and Samuel Imbo (Kenya). To this academic group can be added East Indian and white (though ambiguously so for those who are born Jews) Africans such as Mahmood Mamdani (Uganda), Pal Ahlulawia (Kenya), Ashwin Desai (formerly in the academy), Ebrahim Moosa, Leswin Laubscher,

---

Awomandla Publishers, 2006) and *The Politics of Consciousness, the Consciousness of Politics: When Black Consciousness Meets White Consciousness.* Vol. II: *The Research Settings, the Interrogation of Speech and Imagination* (Guelph, Canada: Awomandla Publishers, 2006). Maart is, to my knowledge, the only South African woman of color to have received a doctorate in philosophy, which she earned at the University of Birmingham through the famed Centre for Cultural Studies in 1996.

[18] See e.g. Noël Chabani Manganyi, *Being-Black-in-the-World* (Johannesburg: Ravan Press, 1973) and *Alienation and the Body in Racist Society: A Study of the Society that Invented Soweto* (New York: NOK Publishers, 1977), and for discussion, see More, "Sartre and the Problem of Racism," pp. 223–35.

Jean Comaroff, John Comaroff, Sander Gilman, David Theo Goldberg, Neil Lazarus, Jonathan Judaken, and Richard Pithouse (all from South Africa), and Hélène Cixous (Algeria). Among those who have become ancestors, African expatriates such as Algerians Albert Camus and Jacques Derrida, although associated more with Europe, were nevertheless affected by the African colonial context in their intellectual formation. A similar analysis could be made of the Tunisian Albert Memmi, who is from an older generation and exemplifies a lineage similar to St. Augustine's in terms of a Berber mother and an Italian father. The list could go on. This stage of African secular humanism is marked by such themes as postmodern skeptical humanism, liberal cosmopolitanism, New Left Marxism, and feminism. Because of this, none of these intellectuals should be read in exclusively academic terms, although their achievements in academe are extraordinary.

The poeticist–humanist tradition has continued through many novelists and dramatists, all of whom have played significant roles in the transformation of the contemporary literary canon, such as Wole Soyinka (Nigeria), Chinua Achebe (Nigeria), Ngugi wa Thiong'o (Kenya), Ama Ata Aidoo (Ghana), Ayi Kwei Armah (Ghana), Assai Djebar (Algeria), and white authors, the best known of whom are the South African Nobel laureates Nadine Gordimer and John Coetzee. There is also the emergence of a form of musical poeticist humanism that has been part of the rise of "world music," whose artists come from all parts of Africa and nearly all its traditions. They serve as critical commentators on Africa's contemporary condition. Perhaps the most famous of such artists was the Nigerian Fela Anikulapo-Kuti (1938–1997). It is the question of black Africans that has afforded the most challenges, as we have seen throughout this study, for philosophical problems in the African context. How those Africans struggled with this problematic in the world of ideas has been primarily through exploring the impact it has had on the constitution of the African self. A major thematic of such reflection has been that of invention or of how that self came into being.

The theme of invention in recent African philosophy

The word "invention" is derived from the Latin infinitive *invenire*, which means to devise, discover, or find. Although Europe and Africa were not strangers to each other in premodern times, the history that unfolded since 1492 was one of increased estrangement that paradoxically haunted even efforts of knowing. Thus, the relationship between invention and activities in this age of discovery was not accidental, as is clearly revealed by their etymological convergence; both to discover and to invent means to reveal the hidden, to find what stood in the dark.

African peoples, as we have seen over the course of the pages in this book, in the midst of all the creation and expansion of Europe, began to discover that they had two identities imposed from without – namely, the continental identity of being African and the racial identity of being black. They also discovered, as a consequence of their racial identity, a temporally displaced identity of signifying *primitives*.[19] And they began to discover that beyond the dignity afforded by their understood indigenous identities, which in the emergence of scientific anthropology became known as "tribes" – Asante, Fanti, Yorùbá, Ibo, Masai, Twa, etc. – they were regarded in European and Asian regions as less than human. For people whose humanity has long been denied, the value of philosophical anthropology, as we have seen, became their *philosophia prima*.

Differentiating the European self from the African one raises the question of the degree of difference between peoples on the two continents. The racial subtext of this question becomes, "How different are whites in Europe from blacks in Africa?" European and African thinkers have not been unanimous in their response to this question. Thomas Paine argued that the differences were superficial enough not to warrant the practice of slavery, whereas David Hume and Immanuel Kant argued that they were substantial enough not to take seriously the status of blacks as human beings.[20] G. W. F. Hegel, in the introduction to his *Philosophy of History*, presented the most influential support for radical, substantial difference by virtue of his

[19] See e.g. Nkiru Uwechia Nzegwu, "Colonial Racism: Sweeping Out Africa with Mother Europe's Broom." Following Nzegwu, I here say "black" and "primitive" since the former was not always the operating factor of race, especially in West Africa, where whites were considered inferior at the level of the body but superior with regard to technological mastery; the consequence of this was the notion of African technological and cultural primitiveness (pp. 134–5). For a discussion of the construction of the primitive beyond the West African context see also V. Y. Mudimbe, *The Invention of Africa: Gnosis, Philosophy, and the Order of Knowledge* (Indianapolis, IN: Indiana University Press, 1988), pp. 72–5.

[20] See Thomas Paine, "African Slavery in America," in *The Thomas Paine Reader*, ed. Michael Foot and Isaac Kramnick (New York: Penguin Classics, 1987), pp. 52–6. Relevant selections from Hume's and Kant's writings are reprinted in *Race and the Enlightenment: A Reader*, ed. Emmanuel Chukwudi Eze (Oxford: Blackwell, 1997), chs. 3–4.

claim that history did not even pay a courtesy visit to the black peoples of Africa. Even the virtue of religiosity should not be ascribed to Africans, in Hegel's view, for genuine religion requires a movement of spirit (*Geist*) and the emergence of consciousness, whereas Africans, as he saw them, were capable only of sorcery and primitive beliefs in magic.[21] The impact of the Hegelian view becomes acute when the question of philosophy is raised in the African context, for the movement of history for Hegel is also the unfolding realization of reason; thus, to search for the practice of reason as manifested in philosophy in the place that exemplified the antipode of reason was a contradiction of terms. Philosophy was for a long time since rejected by Europeans as existing in Africa not on the basis of empirical evidence but on the conviction that it could not exist there by virtue of Africa's indigenous people.[22]

We have already discussed some of these issues in the introduction, the first, and the second chapters of this book. Recall that a result of the Hegelian thesis was much academic ignoring of medieval African thought and the complex intellectual history of various African nations well into the mid-twentieth century. Much of the continued failure to examine Africa in this light is premised upon the ongoing misrepresentation of Africa as a continent without indigenous forms of writing. Even in the age of deconstruction from the late 1970s through to the end of the twentieth century,

[21] See e.g. G. W. F. Hegel, "Introduction," *The Philosophy of History*, with prefaces by Charles Hegel and the translator, J. Sibree, and a new introduction by C. J. Friedrich (New York: Dover Publications, 1956), and Mudimbe, *The Invention of Africa*, as well as D. A. Masolo's *African Philosophy in Search of Identity* (Bloomington, IN: Indiana University Press, 1994).

[22] The response to the important role of ancient Egypt is well known: make it, in its origins, Asiatic in spite of all the evidence that demonstrates otherwise. The debate continues. See Martin Bernal, *Black Athena Writes Back: Martin Bernal Responds to His Critics*, ed. David Chioni Moore (Durham, NC: Duke University Press, 2001) and for a detailed critique of the civilization-not-out-of-Africa thesis, see Finch, *Echoes of the Old Darkland* and "From the Nile to the Niger: the Evolution of African Spiritual Concepts," in Gordon and Gordon, *A Companion to African-American Studies*, pp. 453–75. For an excellent, recent criticism of the not-out-of-Africa thesis, especially with regard to technology such as the production of steel, see John Ayotunde (Tunde) Isola Bewaji, *Beauty and Culture: Perspectives in Black Aesthetics* (Ibadan, Nigeria: Spectrum Books, 2003), chs. 1 and 2, especially pp. 37–40, 78–97, and "Philosophy in History and History of Philosophy as Academic Politics," International Readings on Theory, History, and Philosophy of Culture (UNESCO Moscow) 18: *Differentiation and Integration of Worldviews: Philosophy & Religious Experience* (2001), especially pp. 224–5.

where every aspect of reality, including culture itself, was treated as a form of written text, this misrepresentation presents Africa as a form of limit unless the divide between inscription and metaphors of inscription is completely blurred. Complicating the matter, as well, are the many roles of deconstruction articulated by Jacques Derrida, at least in his classic essay "Plato's Pharmacy," where the multitude of simultaneous economies of psychoanalysis, Marxism, and semiotics interplay as an anxiety over the father, authority, and speech. This appears both Eurocentric and culturally relative in relation to our question of African thought since it requires a variety of values premised upon family structures and sexual anxieties that are alien to many traditional African societies where the economy of even polygamy has strong matrilineal injunctions.[23] Nevertheless, it is safe to say that although philosophy does not rely on writing for its performance and existence, its place in intellectual history (of any kind) has been much facilitated by the existence of written texts. Our discussion has made the question of whether there was written African philosophical thought pretty much moot. And no doubt more will come to light as the African dimension of past thinkers is better understood and as new works re-emerge from the depths of obscurity and, literally, from beneath the ground. The current research on late medieval and early modern philosophy in Ethiopia and the excavation and preservation of writings from medieval Mali are such instances, and the effort to write down the origination narratives of many oral traditions worldwide is a function of the declining numbers of individuals with both the time and devotion to maintain such vast reservoirs of their cultures in their individual memory.[24]

[23] See Jacques Derrida, *Dissemination*, trans. Barbara Johnson (Chicago, IL: University of Chicago Press, 1983). On this matter of matrilineality, see e.g. Nkiru Uwechia Nzegwu's "Questions of Identity and Inheritance: A Critical Review of Anthony Appiah, *In My Father's House*," *Hypatia* 11, no. 1 (1996): 175–201, and *Family Matters: Feminist Concepts in African Philosophy of Culture* (Albany, NY: State University of New York Press, 2004). For influential, and controversial, metaphilosophical work on the question of writing in African philosophy, see Paulin Hountondji, *African Philosophy: Myth and Reality*, trans. Henri Evans with the collaboration of Jonathan Rée and introduction by Abiola Irele (Bloomington, IN: Indiana University Press, 1983) and P. O. Bodunrin, "The Question of African Philosophy," in *African Philosophy: An Introduction*, ed. Richard A. Wright (Lanham, MD: University Press of America, 1984), pp. 1–23, and for discussion of both, see Masolo, *African Philosophy*, pp. 195–204 and 241–3.

[24] See e.g. Teodros Kiros, "Zara Yacob and Traditional Ethiopian Philosophy," in Wiredu, *A Companion to African Philosophy*, pp. 183–90, and his book *Zara Yacob: Rationality of*

The "westernized African" returns, then, as academics raised by their local (African) traditions but trained in other (non-African) ones.[25] I write "traditions" because I know of no African scholar who has been raised in a single tradition. There is much creolization of various indigenous groups in Africa either literally through mixed ethnic relationships or through a cultural intermixture in which there is often great knowledge (including linguistic mastery) of at least two cultures. But more, it is a rather absurd demand, as Kwame Gyekye points out, to expect African authenticity to rest on Africans having no contact with Europeans and any other outside community.[26] It is not a standard used against the authenticity of Europeans, and at the heart of it is the old primitivist notion of child-like people untouched by civilization, where civilization is defined as white and European or Asian. The African academic philosopher thus usually faces three major tasks. The first is translation, where the task is to articulate the tenets of traditional African cultures in Western academic terms. This is a project geared not only at the non-African academic philosopher, but also at fellow African intellectuals, for the language of the academy becomes one of the many languages they face mastering in their life's journey. The second task is to formulate theories, interpretations, and criticisms of their own. The third is to articulate and offer viable responses to the political situation that plagues much of contemporary Africa. These aims could be explored in the language of the Western academy, but they need not be so. The rest of this chapter is an exploration of some of the recent efforts to tackle these problems from African theorists, some of

the *Human Heart* (Trenton, NJ: Red Sea Press, 205). See also Claude Sumner, "The Light and the Shadow: Zera Yacob and Walda Heywat: Two Ethiopian Philosophers of the Seventeenth Century," in Wiredu, *A Companion to African Philosophy*, pp. 172–82 and Timbuktu Manuscripts Project for the Preservation and Promotion of African Literary Heritage: www.sum.uio.no/research/mali/timbuktu/project/index.html and the UNESCO site: http://portal.unesco.org/ci/en/ev.php-URL_ID=14224&URL_DO=DO_TOPIC& URL_SECTION=201.html.

[25] For more on the westernized African see Tsenay Serequeberhan, *Our Heritage: The Past in the Present of African-American and African Existence* (Lanham, MD: Rowman & Littlefield, 2000), pp. 3–6. The reader might wonder why I used the term "non-African" instead of, say, "Western" or "European." This observation includes the small cadre of African intellectuals who were trained in northeast Asia during the Cold War, and those who have historically found their way to those countries, especially Japan, for other reasons.

[26] Kwame Gyekye, *Tradition and Modernity: Philosophical Reflections on the African Experience* (New York: Oxford University, 1997).

whom are not philosophers but whose work has had much philosophical influence.

African critiques of invention

A controversial text that exemplifies the first two tasks of translation and developing new theory is John S. Mbiti's *African Religions and Philosophy*.[27] Echoing some of the ethnophilosophical work of Father Placide Temples, Mbiti offers in that work a systematic account of the structures of Bantu-speaking societies through an analysis of their conception of time.[28] The importance of such a focus depends on a basic philosophical insight: there are no values without temporality. Eternal creatures, for instance, neither come into time nor go out of it, which presents serious metaphysical problems not only as to whether they can "act," but also whether their behaviors could translate into meaningful ones. Creatures who gain immortality face a similar dictate, only they have the addition of having been born. Yet it is no accident that many civilizations portray such mythic creatures as monsters. Not being able to die takes meaning from their lives and makes behaviors that for the rest of us – mortal and hence finite – are monstrous insignificant to them. Values are thus linked to the fact that we are born, we live for a time with knowledge of an accumulated past and awareness that we will eventually die, and even if we do not worry much about our own death, the eventual death of our loved ones is sufficient to stimulate much concern.[29] One could go further and present a transcendental phenomenological version of this argument thus: there is no consciousness

---

[27] John Mbiti, *African Philosophy and Religions*, rev. edn (Oxford: Heineman, 1990).

[28] Placide Tempels, *La Philosophie bantoue* (Paris: Présence Africaine, 1949). Originally published in Elizabethville, Congo, by Lovania in 1945, and is available in English as *Bantu Philosophy*, trans. Rev. Colin King (Paris: Présence Africaine, 1959). This is a controversial book, primarily because of its many essentialist claims. For discussion and criticism, see e.g. Masolo, *African Philosophy in Search of Identity*, pp. 42–67.

[29] The similarity here with existential treatments of value as a function of our consciousness of our own finitude is not accidental. Although the theological underpinnings of Mbiti's arguments are Christian, it can easily be shown that the common ground through which his theology meets his traditional African upbringing is an existential one. For an outline of this type of argument, see Paget Henry, "African and Afro-Caribbean Existential Philosophies," in *Existence in Black: An Anthology of Black Existential Philosophy*, ed. Lewis R. Gordon (New York: Routledge, 1997), pp. 11–36.

without intentionality, where consciousness is consciousness of something, but "something" cannot be apprehended without maintenance of it if only for a nanosecond. Such notions as sustaining a thought or a concept require temporality, which makes time a necessary condition of consciousness.[30] Since there is no point in talking about the values of a community without members of that community being conscious or at least aware of themselves as having values, then the argument for temporality advances through to the question of community. Mbiti's concerns require such a philosophical maneuver.

Mbiti's argument, which has been much criticized by other African philosophers, is that the metaphysics and cosmology of Bantu-speaking peoples are premised on the view that all being, all actuality, flows from God, which means that nothing ever "is" until the forces that constitute God's ongoing unfolding of reality are enacted.[31] What that means is that there is no future until the future occurs, which means that for it to be, it must become the present and then the past. In Mbiti's words,

> The future is virtually absent because events which lie in it have not taken place, they have not been realized and cannot, therefore, constitute time. If, however, future events are certain to occur, or if they fall within the inevitable rhythm of nature, they at best constitute only *potential time* not *actual time*. What is taking place now no doubt unfolds the future, but once an event has taken place, it is no longer in the future but in the present and what is past. It moves "backward" rather than "forward"; and people set their minds not on future things, but chiefly in what has taken place.[32]

Mbiti's argument can easily be misread to entail that Bantu-speaking people have no conception of time. What the argument does reveal is a theory of temporal realism. What this means is that the unfolding of events is all that constitutes reality. But more, if the source of such an unfolding

---

[30] The origin of this argument is, by the way, in Kant's classic response to Hume's attack on necessity. For Kant's argument, see *The Critique of Pure Reason*, trans. Norman Kemp Smith (New York: St. Martin's Press, 1965) and for David Hume's see *A Treatise of Human Nature* (London: Penguin Classics, 1969).

[31] For criticisms of Mbiti's conception of time see especially Gyekye, *An Essay on African Philosophical Thought*, pp. 169–77. See also discussions of Mbiti by Barry Hallen, *A Short History of African Philosophy* (Bloomington, IN: Indiana University Press, 2002) and Masolo, *African Philosophy in Search of Identity*.

[32] Mbiti, *African Religions and Philosophy*, p. 17.

constitutes the most dense exemplification of reality – namely, God – then each subsequent event is of less ontological potency than its predecessor. In effect, there is a metaphysical "fall" or "drying up" from the real to the eventual unreal. The significance of this schema becomes apparent in a striking dimension of many African axiologies: the importance of ancestors. The question of ancestors is perhaps the most dominating feature of African ethics, and it is analyzed in nearly every work on African philosophy. That ancestors precede us affords them a greater place both in the ontology and its accompanying order of values. Our parents, for example, are not simply more experienced than we are; they are more valuable than us, and so are we in relation to our children. This does not mean that we cannot value our children through loving them, and it can easily be argued that our children's appreciation of us should be a function of the enormous value of the love we offer them.

For our purposes, the importance of Mbiti's argument is that he has tapped into a concept that is a unique development in contemporary (and perhaps all) African philosophy and consequently the study of African culture. Although there are many metaphilosophical analyses of philosophy in the African context, many of which offer their advancement and criticisms of such developments as ethnophilosophy, sage philosophy, "professional" philosophy, and praxis philosophy, a striking feature of African philosophy that is often not discussed is the near obsession of African philosophers with ancient and even mythic times.[33] These philosophers, even the analytical ones among them, take on the past with the zeal of the proverbial drowning man attempting to make it to dry land. In accounting for this, we could consider the very practical goal of reconstructing what have been disavowed by antiblack and Eurocentric scholars. But this does not explain the peculiarity of the sense of normative urgency African (and African diasporic) philosophers bring to their historical work. Many of us know that racists resist the significance of proof that contradicts their racist attitudes; they collapse such evidence into the realm of "exceptions" to the point of there being no amount of sufficient evidence that could persuade them.

---

[33] For excellent recent summaries of these conceptions of African philosophy – sage philosophy, ethnophilosophy, "professional" philosophy, and praxis philosophy – see Hallen's *A Short History of African Philosophy* (Indianapolis: Indiana University Press, 2002) and Masolo's *African Philosophy in Search of Identity*.

This is so because, for those who hold onto them with claims of appealing to "reason" and philosophy, the collapse of their position means the end of the world.[34] The situation is similar for the historian. The past does not function for many African scholars of philosophy as it does for, say, most European intellectual historians. For such historians, the project is the articulation of their narrative about "what" happened or "what" was argued. But for many African philosophers and intellectual historians, the narrative is about the ancestors and their deeds and thoughts and their suffering. If part of their suffering was their "disappearance," which may be in effect similar to the wrong of an improper burial, then the act of getting the past right is also a corrective act of justice through the resources of truth. From this point of view the African philosopher and intellectual historian have ethical obligations that transcend scientific expectations of method and procedure. This poses a challenge that transcends aspirations enmeshed in the dialectics of professional recognition.[35] That philosopher works in a world in which ancestors are more real, in the sense of being closer to the source of all reality, than the present and future groups of human beings. The African philosopher thus faces the twofold and symbiotically related themes of identity and liberation, and even the debates on interpellation that we have seen manifest themselves in African-American and Afro-Caribbean philosophy take on a different dimension here, for naming is not a privilege of the individual subject. In many African communities the process by which one is named and literally exists comes from an understanding of a past of greater ontological and normative force. The idea that one names oneself would be patently absurd from this perspective. Many African philosophers take the position that there need not be a tension between identity and liberation, then, because both must appeal to the past as a ground of the present on which the future must be built. What we find at the heart of this view is a peculiar conception of agency that transcends stoic resignation.

The problem of invention in African philosophy is made explicit in V. Y. Mudimbe's *The Invention of Africa: Gnosis, Philosophy, and the Order of Knowledge*,

---

[34] On this matter of tenacious racism and its relationship to orders of rationality, see Lewis R. Gordon, *Bad Faith and Antiblack Racism* (Amherst, NY: Humanity/Prometheus Books, 1999), part II, and *Fanon and the Crisis of European Man: An Essay on Philosophy and the Human Sciences* (New York: Routledge, 1995), chs. 2 and 3.

[35] My focus here is history as it relates to a scholar whose value-system is governed by ancestral obligation.

a text that has influenced nearly every major work in African philosophy since the late 1980s. Africa, Mudimbe argues, is not only a continent but a mode of discourse that exemplifies what he calls a form of *gnosis* or way of knowing:

> Specifically, *gnosis* [from the Greek *gnosko*, which means "to know"] means seeking to know, inquiry, methods of knowing, investigation, and even acquaintance with someone. Often the word is used in a more specialized sense, that of higher and esoteric knowledge, and thus it refers to a structured, common, and conventional knowledge, but one strictly under the control of specific procedures for its use as well as transmission. *Gnosis* is, consequently, different from *doxa* or opinion, and, on the other hand, cannot be confused with *episteme*, understood as both science and general intellectual configuration.[36]

Gnosis is not as constrained a concept as the early Michel Foucault's notion of *episteme*, which is linked to the ancient Greek use of the term to refer to the kinds of knowledge involved in knowing how things work, of, that is, knowing the order and function of things. It is instead sufficiently broad in its reach to be a way of knowing that constitutes and maintains new forms of life. It is in this sense that Africa is "invented." It is invented by the systems of knowledge constituted by the process of conquest and colonization, which always erupted with discovery, on the one hand, and it is also constituted by the processes of resistance borne out of those events the consequence of which is an effect of both on each other. In both instances, the gnostic practices could function at subterranean levels. Colonial practices, for example, haunt modern gnostic practices that make no claim of colonial intent even to the point of being, in some cases, explicitly anti-imperial. The struggle for liberation, for instance, is difficult precisely because of its location within such gnostic practices, the result of which is the proliferation of more endemic identities and values, which in this case means more "Africanisms." We see here a return of the poststructural side of the identity debate, which questions identity itself and the notion of nondiscursive underlying subjects. Mudimbe concludes that "Even in the most explicitly 'Afrocentric' descriptions, models of analysis explicitly or implicitly, knowingly or unknowingly, refer to the same order."[37]

---

[36] Mudimbe, *The Invention of Africa*, p. ix.   [37] *Ibid.*, p. x.

Mudimbe's argument could easily be criticized as an exemplification of the practices it rejects because of its obvious genealogical poststructural form. The similarities here between Foucault's archaeological and genealogical writings could be such that one could see the influence of his notion of power/knowledge on Mudimbe's gnosis/colonialism argument, and Mudimbe uses the term "archaeology" to describe his approach to the study of African gnosis.[38] Yet we may ask why an African thinker's affinity with a European thinker requires a causal relationship in which the latter has an effect on the former. Could not the African philosopher be offering arguments that develop from poststructural commitments that he shares with the European poststructuralist? Mudimbe is, after all, also a novelist and literary scholar, in other words, a textualist. As with the Afro-Caribbean tradition, this means that his inclinations are more toward the poeticist approach to these issues, which locates him, as well, with philosopher novelists such as Charles Johnson and Sylvia Wynter. His, along with their, relationship to Foucault could be more associational, of similar mind set, than causal. For in the end what is absent in Foucault's analysis but present in Mudimbe's is (1) the historical significance of outside imposition and (2) the ontological weight of the past as manifested in African gnosis. Invention for Mudimbe is, in other words, more weighted down in reality by the ancestors than the more epiphenomenal notions that tend to accompany European poststructural readings of historical events.[39] What is more, for Europeans, or at least modern and postmodern Europeans, the present stands in a peculiar relationship with the past – one without commitment and against authority. Each generation presumes itself to be the judge of the past simply by living in the present. But in the African context, as we have seen, this is reversed. The past, having legitimation and ontological priority over the present, is more than the foundation of the present; it is also the judge of the present. While most Europeans and Euro-Americans often see themselves, at best, as "owing" the future, most Africans stand in a constant debt to a living past.

Kwame Gyekye picks up on this aspect of Mudimbe's work in *An Essay on African Philosophical Thought* when he criticizes K. Anthony Appiah's appropriation of Mudimbe's term. Appiah, the cosmopolitanist, is interested in an Africa that is freed of ancestral constraints. He is thus very critical of African

---

[38] *Ibid.*   [39] See e.g. *ibid.*, p. xv.

diasporic thought that appeals to a connection with common African ancestors and the use of that commonality as the basis of a pan-African identity. Appiah thus used the term invention to argue for a theory of maximum difference between African ethnic groups in his very popular and influential book *In My Father's House: African in the Philosophy of Culture* and subsequently in his work on cosmopolitanism.[40] The notion of a common black people of Africa is, in his view, not only fictitious, but also racist. Appiah places the blame for this ideology on New World pan-Africanists, especially Alexander Crummell and W. E. B. Du Bois. One wonders why Africans and African diasporic activists and scholars who met in London in 1900 to strategize the liberation of Africa receive such criticism in a text that ignores such matters as King Leopold II's Congo and the Berlin Conference of 1884–5. What is more, as Kwame Gyekye has shown in his critical discussion of the conception of invention that Appiah is offering, the claim of maximum difference and disunity of African peoples is empirically false, and even Appiah contradicts himself on this assertion in various instances. Drawing primarily on the work of Igor Kopytoff and Philip Curtin and his colleagues Gyekye points out that many African communities south of the Sahara are descendants of cultures that once inhabited the northern fertile regions many thousands of years ago.[41] These and many other scholars who have actually conducted comparative studies of African ethnic groups marvel at the commonalities they discover.[42] He concludes: "It would be methodologically aberrant, unscientific, and intellectually facile to just shrug off the conclusions of these elaborate empirical investigations of the cultures of African peoples."[43] With regard to Appiah's contradictions, he posits:

---

[40] Criticisms of this book abound. For criticism of its logicism, see Paget Henry, "African Philosophy in the Mirror of Logicism: A Review/Essay," *The C. L. R. James Journal* 4, no. 1 (1993): 70–80; for criticisms of its race theory, see Gordon, *Bad Faith and Antiblack Racism*, part II; and for criticisms of its attack on a black-based pan-Africanism, see Lewis R. Gordon, *Her Majesty's Other Children: Sketches of Racism in a Neocolonial Age* (Lanham, MD: Rowman & Littlefield, 1997), ch. 6. Appiah's work on cosmopolitanism is brought together in *Cosmopolitanism: Ethics in a World of Strangers* (New York: W. W. Norton, 2006).

[41] See Igor Kopytoff, *The African Frontier: The Reproduction of Traditional African Societies*, reprint edn (Indianapolis, IN: Indiana University Press, 1989); Philip Curtin, Steven Feierman, Leonard Thompson, and Jan Vansina, *African History: From Earliest Times to Independence*, 2nd edn (New York: Longman, 1995).

[42] Cf. e.g. Shaw et al., *The Archaeology of Africa*; Finch, *Echoes of the Old Dark Land*; and Graham Connah, *African Civilizations: An Archaeological Perspective*, 2nd edn (Cambridge: Cambridge University Press, 2001).

[43] Gyekye, *An Essay on African Philosophy*, p. xxvii.

Also, can Appiah say, "Most Africans, now, whether converted to Islam or Christianity or not, still *share* the beliefs of their ancestors in an ontology of visible beings," and at the same time absolutely deny "a metaphysical unity to African conceptions" or "*an* African worldview?"[44]

Finally, Gyekye rejects Appiah's argument that any cultural borrowing of a group is evidence of traditions that are not theirs. Gyekye's response:

> It can hardly be doubted, I think, that cultural borrowing is an outstanding *historical* phenomenon in the development of all human cultures . . . Given this historically justifiable assumption, I find it difficult to endorse Appiah's skepticisms regarding the possibility of identifying some precolonial system of ideas or values of a particular African people as (part of) *their* tradition . . .[45]

He concludes by advancing his own view of what he calls a "weak sense of the idea of unified cultural life," which

> does not imply or suggest a monolithic cultural life for a people who live in what may be described as a shared cultural environment. Rather, it allows for the expression of individual or group sentiments, preferences, tastes, and different ways of responding to local or particular experiences. Social stratification, occupational differences, and differences in individual talents, endowments, desires, and aesthetic perceptions insistently constrain the homogenization of particular forms of cultural life even in the same cultural milieu. To say this, however, is of course not to deny that people belonging to the same cultural environment would generally share certain cultural values – a proposition that logically derives from the notions of culture and community.[46]

Gyekye here addresses a theme that has recurred throughout the course of our treatment of Africana philosophy in North America and the Caribbean – namely, the impact of Western impositions. His argument, that there is a creative, dynamic process of cultural formation internal to African communities the consequence of which is both commonality and the unfolding of creative possibilities of individual expression, matches much lived reality. Africa is not, in other words, simply invented but continues to be invented and reinvented, both inside and outside the terms of African peoples. Such a conclusion enables Gyekye to argue that African philosophy is a critique

---

[44] *Ibid.*, p. xxvii. The references are to, consecutively, pp. 134 and 81 of *In My Father's House*.
[45] *Ibid.*, p. xxviii.   [46] *Ibid.*, p. xxxii.

of and systematic inquiry into the general principles that constitute the fundamental thought and values of African peoples.[47]

Mudimbe's and Gyekye's formulations of invention are not, however, the final story of the concept in African philosophy. Oyèrónké Oyěwùmí, a Nigerian-born Yorùbá social theorist, has advanced a provocative conception of invention in which she argues for a more radical use of the term. Her main target is the anti-essentialism and constructivism in Western feminist thought.[48] If gender is constructed as the proponents of such thought claim it is, then why, echoing Judith Butler, should it follow that gender (1) be constructed the same way everywhere and (2) have been constructed at all everywhere?[49] Could there not have been some societies in which gender has never been constructed, has, that is, never appeared? Oyěwùmí offers an analysis of Yorùbá society in which gender, she claims, is not basic. Other factors of social life, such as trading and age hierarchy, are. The difficulty in seeing how Yorùbá society was historically invented by the Yorùbá and how subsequent invasion of different social practices constitute a recent engendered discourse is a function of what she describes as a Western obsession with the body and visual perception.[50] In societies that do not center such perception, the identities that emerge from social relations premised upon other senses – such as hearing, smelling, and touching – may be radically different and in some cases, as with gender, not present at all. Gender and sexual difference are, after all, ways of differentiating types of human bodies; without focus on the body, the necessity of such terminology is eliminated and perhaps more fluid instead of fixed subjects and social relations prevail.

It is not only Western feminist poststructuralists who receive the brunt of criticism from Oyěwùmí. She writes on the concept of invention in the thought of Mudimbe as follows:

> As a prologue to his acclaimed book *The Invention of Africa*, Mudimbe disseminates what he calls the "good news" – that the African now has "the freedom of thinking of himself or herself as the starting point of an

---

[47] *Ibid.*, p. 4.
[48] Oyèrónké Oyěwùmí, *The Invention of Women: Making an African Sense of Western Gender Discourses* (Minneapolis, MN: University of Minnesota Press, 1997).
[49] See our discussion of Judith Butler on interpellation in ch. 4 (above), and, of course, her classic work, *Gender Trouble: Feminism and the Subversion of Identity* (New York: Routledge, 1990).
[50] *Ibid.*, pp. 1–17.

absolute discourse." His claim is surprising given that the content of his book does not derive epistemologically from Africa and is heavily dependent on European thought. This is hardly the multicultural heritage that Appiah wants us to believe obtains in African studies. It is clearly a Western heritage and explains why Ogún does not stand a chance against Zeus and why Africa remains merely an idea in the minds of many African scholars. Of course, in reality Africa continues to unfold in the march of history. The original human history at that![51]

Oyěwùmí here affirms an observation from Frantz Fanon: "The Black has no ontological resistance in the eyes of the White."[52] Yet *The Invention of Women* is not without blind spots. For example, there is no discussion of ancestral obligation or even ancestors even though the social role of seniority receives much treatment. It is perhaps this absence that occludes, in her analysis, the kind of reading I have offered of Mudimbe's and Gyekye's notions of invention. Oyěwùmí's is a radical constructivism, which demands a rigorous articulation of construction. Her argument about impositions suggests that something is lost by European influences on our readings of the history of Yorùbáland. For her, history, too, is invented (and I shall presume that so too are notions of ancestors but by African peoples themselves), which leads to a distorted discourse of the past. What she favors, in this regard, is the notion of "invented traditions." She writes:

> I deploy it to acknowledge the implication of the present in the past, rather than making a "presentist" claim that the past is solely fabricated to reflect present interests . . . The notion of invented traditions does not necessarily imply dishonesty; the process is usually much more unconscious. In fact, it is a testament to the immediate nature of evidence and the positionality of any particular recorder of the past . . . What is permissible is culture-bound. The idea expressed in the notion of permissibility is that the extent to which the past is malleable for present purposes is limited. Although many things can change, some things must remain the same.[53]

We find here much affinity between Oyěwùmí and Gyekye because both want to draw upon what was invented by African people outside of the discourses that were a function of Western imposition, although Gyekye is

---

[51] *Ibid.*, p. 27. The Mudimbe quote is from p. 200 of *The Invention of Africa.*
[52] Fanon, *Black Skin, White Masks*, p. 110 (my translation).
[53] Oyěwùmí, *The Invention of Women*, p. 81.

not as radical as she is on the elimination of such influence. This conclusion is clearly exemplified when Oyĕwùmí writes,

> Since the colonial period, Yorùbá history has been reconstituted through a process of inventing gendered traditions. Men and women have been invented as social categories, and history is presented as being dominated by male actors. Female actors are virtually absent, and where they are recognized, they are reduced to exceptions.[54]

Notice that this argument does not entail the rejection of a feminist response to the historical present of Africa, which Oyĕwùmí here suggests is perhaps even required given the occlusion of "female actors."[55] Oyĕwùmí is concerned with the power of language and the social realities maintained by the use of those linked to one order of knowledge over others. *The Invention of Women* thus demands a more radical interpretation of invention because its author regards the consequences of failing to make this interpretation to be detrimental to the people who have been invented as invisible or abnormal beings. The consequence of Western inventions, in other words, is not only Western normativity, but also its accompanying baggage of white and male normativity as manifested in the production of gender.

Yet not all contemporary African philosophers with an affinity for post-structuralism see radical invention as the best alternative. A danger, as the Wimbum philosopher Elias Kifon Bongmba from the Cameroons sees it, is that of moral and epistemological relativism. He criticizes notions of radical constructivism and radical difference on ethical grounds by drawing upon the thought of Emmanuel Levinas. Bongmba agrees with the inventionists that European colonization of Africa led to a structure of white scholars as also theorists who reflect upon Africans as offering only their experience. Transforming this relationship requires Africans taking responsibility for theoretical reflection as well, which entails exploring ontological, epistemological, and political questions. As we have seen in our earlier discussions,

---

[54] *Ibid.*, p. 82.

[55] For contemporary African feminist philosophical work, see Safro Kwame, "Feminism and African Philosophy," in *Readings in African Philosophy: An Akan Collection*, ed. Safro Kwame (Lanham, MD: University Press of America, 1995), pp. 25–38. And for more discussion in regard to Oyĕwùmí, see Doug Ficek, "Distinction without Difference: Oyèrónké Oyĕwùmí and the Invention of Women," *Philosophy and Social Criticism* 32, no. 4 (2006): 543–9.

Western intellectuals have long considered themselves the custodians of bringing the light of reason to the understanding of African experience. The result has been a terrible situation in, for example, African studies, which is in much of its appearance a white-dominated field with scholars who would like to keep it as such. Consider, for example, the white scholar Philip Curtin's editorial opinion, "Ghettoizing African Studies," in which he protested against preferential treatment for African candidates for employment in the field with the usual set of anti-affirmative action complaints about such things as an absence of merit and lowering standards.[56] Thomas Spear, in an editorial response entitled "Ghettoizing African History?" questioned the hysteria of his white male colleague when all the demographics indicated that the field continued to be mostly white, and especially as white male dominated as it was and, unfortunately, continues to be.[57] One of the fallouts from those exchanges was the loss of some of the most eminent black scholars who were briefly members of the African Studies Association. The counterfactual consideration is, of course, what Curtin would have said about European studies becoming a discipline in which it would be illegitimate to seek out European scholars if the demographics revealed that it was dominated by people of color, if, that is, Europeans were a tiny minority in the field. Would Curtin protest that seeking European scholars for European studies programs would make it a "ghettoized" field?

The reality is that it has been difficult for black scholars to play roles beyond those of ethnographic informants or sources of experience on the continent of Africa. In philosophy, the situation has been similarly phobogenic. The inclusion of black philosophers has often raised the problem of the particularity of Western philosophy in spite of its avowed universality.[58] Even Emmanuel Levinas, upon whose work much of Bongmba's ethics is based, suffered from such centrism in his well-known effort to forge a

---

[56] Phillip Curtin, "Ghettoizing African Studies," *Chronicle of Higher Education* (March 1995). For recent discussion, see Michael West, "Summary Report of 'Ghettoizing African Studies?' The Question of Representation in the Study of Africa – a Roundtable held at the 38th Annual Meeting of the African Studies Association, November 4, 1995," *ACAS Bulletin*, no. 46 (1995). URL: http://acas.prairienet.org/bulletin/bull46toc.html.

[57] See Thomas Spear, "Ghettoizing African History?" *ACAS Bulletin*, no. 46 (April 4, 1995). URL: http://www.hartford-hwp.com/archives/45/311.html.

[58] For discussion, see Gordon, *Her Majesty's Other Children*, ch. 2.

Graeco-Semitic torch for humanity's night.[59] Bongmba thus admits that the task faced by him and other African scholars is to think through ideas in fields saturated by many practitioners who neither expect nor want people like him to think at all.

Bongmba begins *African Witchcraft and Otherness* by demonstrating the problem with simply applying the term "witchcraft" wholesale to a range of activities by African peoples from judgments on natural gifts to efforts to bring about supernatural occurrences. We find here an instance of the classic problem of cultural translation and indeterminacy. Although there is a rich language to deal with such phenomena beyond the terms of "witchcraft" in the European world, its application to African activities has been reductive, and indigenous African communities, in their effort to translate their activities to European ones, simply continue to use the misguided European terms. Thus, those scholars use the word "witchcraft" where in fact witchcraft as understood in the West is absent. In English, for instance, there are terms such as "genius," "gifted," "wizard," "sorcerer," "magician," "witch," and "warlock." Bongmba shows that at least among the Wimbum, the Cameroonian ethnic group of which he is a member, such terms as *bfiu*, *brii*, and *tfu* should not be lumped together under the term "witchcraft" because only the last comes close to Western analogues. Could one imagine Wolfgang Amadeus Mozart (1756–1791), Immanuel Kant, Albert Einstein (1879–1955), or Sigmund Freud (1856–1939) being referred to as "warlocks" instead of geniuses or gifted? But in effect, that is what is going on in some scholarly treatments of these communities. At this point of his analysis, Bongmba is in stream with Oyěwùmí and the other inventionists.

Bongmba then makes a maneuver that further challenges establishment approaches to the study of Africa and African religions. He offers a critique of how activities associated with such phenomena as *tfu* are manifested in contemporary Africa. To understand why he makes this move let us consider the two extremes in Western approaches to the study of African communities. On the one hand, there is the old-style civilized versus primitive thesis.

---

[59] See Elias Kifon Bongmba, *African Witchcraft and Otherness: A Philosophical and Theological Critique of Intersubjective Relations* (Albany, NY: State University of New York Press, 2001). For discussion of Levinas's exploration of Jewish and Greek thought, with a provocative examination of a Levinasian reversal of both, see Oona Ajzenstat, "Levinas versus Levinas: Hebrew, Greek, and Linguistic Justice," *Philosophy and Rhetoric* 38, no. 2 (2005): 145–58.

There, the criticism is that indigenous Africans are primitive, backward peoples who need to move forward through the adoption of Western civilization, which usually takes the form of Christianity. It is this conviction that motivated Christian missionaries, such as Placide Tempels from without and Mbiti from within, to look into the interstices of what they considered to be the African mind and search for an ethnophilosophy through which they could cultivate the Afro-Christian on a path, simply, to the Christian.[60] In response, ethnographers attempted to correct such efforts by simply aiming for description without judgment. Bongmba objects to both approaches on the grounds that they lead not only to cultural relativism but also ethical relativism, the consequence of which is the destruction of intersubjective relations. It is, in effect, a failure to meet another human community as a human community. "I question the anxiety scholars have about any attempt to criticize local African practices," Bongmba confesses. "If scholars feel awkward about critical discourse on Africa, then contemporary African scholarship has touched Africa with a 'fatal kindness,' to borrow a metaphor from Friedrich Schleiermacher."[61] It is on these bases that Bongmba parts company with most works on the study of witchcraft and advances a critical philosophy of witchcraft. This approach raises the problematics of the human sciences and offers an interdisciplinary methodology anchored in the critical resources of lived experience. By "critical philosophy" is here also meant an ethico-phenomenological investigation, which here means both taking seriously what members of a community say and speaking truthfully with that community; it is a call for genuine dialogue. Bongmba takes this dialogical point of departure to expand his analysis by adding the resources of Levinasian studies and ethics. There, he offers a reading and application that is more socially rich than the formulations offered by Levinas. Although he builds much on the Levinasian claim of the "face-to-face" dimensions of ethical encounter, where the Other exemplifies an ethical cry, it strikes me that the social resources to which he appeals in his discussion of the Wimbum are richer than the one-to-one formalism of Levinas. Bongmba's critical conclusion on *tfu*, the closest activity to witchcraft in the Western sense, is that

---

[60] Scholarly treatment of this effort abounds, but see especially Josiah Young, *A Pan-African Theology: Providence and the Legacies of the Ancestors* (Trenton, NJ: Africa World Press, 1992). The most famous instance of this practice was, by the way, Father Placide Temples's *Bantu Philosophy*.

[61] Bongmba, *African Witchcraft and Otherness*, p. xix.

Wimbum theology should adopt a theory of desire without consuming the Other through acts of totalization. The absence of such consumption leaves room for positive critical dialogue between Western and traditional African communities on questions of ethical life.

The question of ethical life raises questions of what is to be done in the African context. Frantz Fanon, it is well known, argued in *The Wretched of the Earth* that discussion of ethics before political resolutions leads to reassertions of what he called "the Graeco-Latin pedestal." He would no doubt be very critical of Bongmba's ethical turn, but some readers of Fanon have argued for a consolidation of the Fanonian and Levinasian engagements with ethics.[62] Drawing upon philosophical hermeneutics, Tsenay Serequeberhan has argued in *The Hermeneutics of African Philosophy* that the kind of emancipatory politics needed to precede ethics is one that is governed by the spirit of interpretation and criticism. A problem with hermeneutical approaches, however, is the kind of suspension they have on questions of truth. What happens to the "ancestors" when even they stand as indeterminate functions of open textual interpretation?

The question of ethical and cultural relativism has also been taken up by the Asanti philosopher Kwasi Wiredu in *Cultural Universals and Particulars*, where he also examines problems of human rights in the African context.[63] Drawing upon resources from pragmatism, linguistic analysis, and biological science, Wiredu argues against relativism by using *reductio ad absurdum* arguments. His critique is couched in a conviction of the unyielding force of reality. The problem with radical invention and its consequent relativism is that they function like ancient logical paradoxes advanced by Zeno of Elia (488 BCE–possibly 430 BCE), who argued against the reality of time, distance, and motion through demonstrating an infinitesimal series of points to cross before even the first movement of each. One simply need take a walk.[64] Although bad translations do surface, the fact of the matter is that different communities of people do manage to communicate with each other, and

---

[62] See e.g. Nelson Maldonado-Torres's "The Cry of the Self as a Call from the Other: The Paradoxical Loving Subjectivity of Frantz Fanon," *Listening: A Journal of Religion and Culture* 36, no. 1 (2001): 46–60.

[63] The discussion that follows focuses on pp. 21–41 of Kwasi Wiredu, *Cultural Universals and Particulars: An African Perspective* (Bloomington, IN: Indiana University Press, 1996).

[64] See *Early Greek Philosophy*, rev. edn, trans. and ed. Jonathan Barnes (London: Penguin Classics, 2002).

since they are able to do so, there must be cultural universals. That there are no instances of radical incommunicability – for even where a term cannot be translated from the language of one culture into that of another, the logical response has always been simply the adaptation of that new term to the stock of words in the other culture – the ability to communicate must be an inherent potential of human beings. Ironically, Wiredu is also providing a response to the poststructuralists who question the idea of an underlying subject on which is tagged the variety of social meanings, roles, or identities. For Wiredu the fact of intersubjective communication means that human beings must take biology more seriously as a foundation or transcendental condition of such an aspect of human behavior. His argument further suggests that the critics of an underlying human subject are taking what should be a natural consequence of contingent realities – that different communities will have their own histories and develop different ways of life (culture) and styles of languages – to entail untranslatable human differences. Human communities are founded on communication, however, which means that there are underlying norms of thought that come into play not only within communities, but also between communities; the failure to develop them would not be an indication of the limits of language and meaning but instead a sign of some kind of malfunction in that particular group of human beings or individuals. Observe:

> Consider the implications of this last result [that the whole species must have some norms of thought in common]. It cannot be history, culture, or ideology that accounts for this commonality, for these are the causes of the diversity rather than the unity of the species. And, in any case, they all presuppose that very same commonality. Why? Because the norms of thought that make it possible for us to think and make history and everything else are the same conditions that make social interaction with others (of whatever identities) possible. It is, I suggest, nothing other than our common basic biology that underlies the particular mental affinity of all the members of the human race with which we are concerned.[65]

The poststructural commitments of some inventionists have unfortunately led to antipathy on their part toward offering the biological as a category of analysis. This is explicit in the thought of Oyěwùmí, but it is also

---

[65] Wiredu, *Cultural Universals*, p. 34.

there, as we have seen, in the thought of Judith Butler, where the biological is a socially or discursively conditioned category.[66] In the words of
Oyěwùmí:

> That many categories of difference are socially constructed in the West may
> well suggest the mutability of categories, but it is also an invitation to
> endless constructions of biology – in that there is no limit to what can be
> explained by the body-appeal. Thus biology is hardly mutable; it is much
> more a combination of the Hydra and the Phoenix of Greek mythology.
> Biology is forever mutating, not mutable. Ultimately, the most important
> point is not that gender is socially constructed but the extent to which
> biology itself is socially constructed and therefore inseparable from the
> social.[67]

Biology is, under this view, simply part of an epistemic ordering of life. But
is this so?

There is a fallacy that involves confusing the conditions of meaning with
that which is meant by a particular term or sentence. That meaning must
be social is clearly a consequence of its being part of language and communication, and, as Wittgenstein has shown, in principle understandable
and dependent on a set of rules and norms that are not "private."[68] But
being of the social does not entail referring to the social. Signification can
be such that it points, as most semioticians have observed, beyond itself.[69]
The fallacy is, in effect, much like taking a pointing finger to be the thing
it is pointing at. Of course the biological is a function of social reality and
its concomitant episteme. But it does not follow that biological phenomena
are social objects, and I do not see how the reduction of such things to such
objects could work without ontologizing or, worse, solipsizing sociology and
thereby collapsing into sociologism.

Yet Wiredu's argument about our common underlying biology can easily
be shown to be compatible with an inventionist position. His claim is that
we are creatures in whose biological makeup is the propensity to invent

---

[66] Recall, e.g., Judith Butler, *Bodies that Matter: On the Discursive Limits of Sex* (New York:
Routledge, 1993).

[67] Oyěwùmí, *Invention of Women*, p. 9.

[68] See Ludwig Wittgenstein, *Philosophical Investigations*, trans. G. E. M. Anscombe (Oxford,
UK: Blackwell Publishers, 1997), section 243.

[69] See Wiredu, *Cultural Universals*, pp. 15–16, and for a general discussion of semiotics, see
John Deely, *Basics of Semiotics* (South Bend, IN: St. Augustine Press, 2004).

or discover activities that generate the social world. Within that world is a multitude of meanings that mark cultural variety across communities of the same species, which, in this case, is our own. Wiredu thus brings the human science question back into the discussion of studies of Africa, and he does so by advancing a philosophical anthropology premised upon communicable human variation. Like Gyekye he does not wish to ignore empirical evidence, and since he is not using natural science as the final arbiter but only a factor in the course of the argument, his position is not reductive nor positivist.

Many of Wiredu's conclusions have been similarly advanced in the phenomenological tradition, proponents of which would immediately see similarities not only between Wiredu's position and Alfred Schutz's *Phenomenology of the Social World*, but also with the arguments I have expanded in my discussion of human science and notions of problem people in *Existentia Africana* and those developed much earlier in South Africa by Noël Chabani Manganyi in such books as *Being-Black-in-the-World* and *Alienation and the Body in Racist Society*.[70] In the expansion of the question of invention in African philosophy to that of African diasporic philosophy, the strongest recent developments are, no doubt, Paget Henry's *Caliban's Reason: Introducing Afro-Caribbean Philosophy* and the work of Nkiru Nzegwu.[71]

Recall from our discussion of Afro-Caribbean philosophy that Henry begins his text with a discussion of the important contributions of traditional African thought (the ancestors) to the formation of Afro-Caribbean communities, which he regards as creolizations of Africa, Asia, and Native America, and then he advances a conception of philosophy in which the consequence of critical, systematic reflections on reality is the formation of a community's self-consciousness – the spirit of its culture – in a tension of what he calls historicist and poeticist prescriptions. These

---

[70] Noël Chabani Manganyi in such books as *Being-Black-in-the-World* (Johannesburg: Ravan, 1973) and *Alienation and the Body in Racist Society: A study of the Society that Invented Soweto* (New York: NOK, 1977).

[71] Nzegwu's work consists of an impressive array of articles and books in philosophy, art history, and feminist politics, as well as work as a poet and visual artist, and her leadership as president of the International Society for African Philosophy and Studies. See Nzegwu, *Family Matters: Feminist Concepts in African Philosophy of Culture* (Albany, NY: State University of New York Press, 2000) and for her work on art, her anthologies *Contemporary Textures: Multidimensionality in Nigerian Art* (Binghamton, NY: ISSA, 1999) and *Issues in Contemporary African Art* (Binghamton, NY: ISSA, 1998).

two prescriptions/approaches are the return of the liberation and identity themes, for the historicist wants to change the world and the poeticist argues for understanding the self that is to be changed, especially through resources of imagination for the semiosis of things cultural. That both can be reconciled is evidenced by such thinkers as Léopold Senghor, Aimé Césaire, C. L. R. James, and Frantz Fanon, each of whom appealed to liberating thought through poetic resources. It seems that the living great Afro-Caribbean thinkers are mostly of the poeticist bent, as witnessed by Sylvia Wynter, Wilson Harris, Eduoard Glissant, Kamau Braithwaite, Derek Walcott, Jamaica Kincaid, Maryse Condé, and George Lamming's contemporary appeal. Among the Africans, the same could be said with regard to Ngugi wa Thiong'o, Chinua Achebe, Ama Atta Aidoo, and Wole Soyinka. There is irony here, for the historicists are mostly dead, and the few who are alive and have not taken heed of recent developments seem "outdated."[72]

Nzegwu charts the complexity of West African history and art and demonstrates the fallacy of simply applying West African cultures, intact, to the New World African diasporic condition, which, like Henry, she regards as creolized communities with unique historical and political developments. She adds, however, in agreement with Oyěwùmí, that a unique influence is the impact of European ontological categories that include the primacy of the body as the location of identity. The geopolitical-epidemiological consideration to bear in mind in tropical west Africa, however, is the impact of malaria on the scale of white settlements, which made it difficult to maintain a body-racial politics in that region. Not only was white presence small in number, but white bodies appeared frail, pale, and weak in West African tropical environments. What needed to be invented, in her view, was the notion of the cultural and technological inferiority of the local West African populations – namely, the notion of primitives.[73] The result is the hegemony of European culture as "modern," which has an effect not only on the value of West African cultures, but also on their study. Her conclusion on what her analysis offers warrants a lengthy quotation:

[72] For a recent treatment of great black historicists, all of whom are unfortunately dead, see B. Anthony Bogues, *Black Heretics, Black Prophets: Radical Political Intellectuals* (New York: Routledge, 2003).

[73] This is so with the myth of Tarzan, "Lord of the Apes," notwithstanding. That myth is an expression of the desire for whites to be gods over nature.

The epistemological consequences of taking seriously the radically different histories of Africa and the United States are having far-reaching effects. For one, the experiences of colonial racism and the politics of area studies in the United States are increasingly forcing African scholars to interrogate the motives of scholars who purport to be responsive to the best interests of Africa and Africans, yet who end up creating an alienated discourse *of* Africa rather than *about* Africa. This interrogation is primarily a response to the invidious de-Africanization that results from the works of both the old-time Africanists and the New Africanists, whose knowledge of Africa tends to be breathtakingly superficial. The consensus of opinion is that this de-Africanization process is a colonial strategy that has effectively been used for decades to gain control of the production of knowledge about Africa. In de-Africanization, the conceptual categories of the different African nations are obscured, then the political, economic, social, and philosophical issues are conducted on the basis of Western categories and interests. If Africa were really placed at the center of such analyses, as it rightly should, it is debatable that old-time and new Africanists would begin with the currently used set of research issues and assumptions.[74]

Yet, as at least our examination of the field attests, Africana philosophy or African diaspora philosophy seems to have been able to negotiate its place between the historicist–poeticist divide and the unyielding misrepresentations by mainstream or Eurocentric approaches to human studies.[75] One could argue that this is because of how squarely it has placed at the forefront not only the question of how Africana peoples should be studied, but also the constitutive question of the grounding of such peoples in the first place – namely, their humanity. The impact of this turn cannot be underestimated since it is raising a question that crosses disciplinary divides as hoped by the philosophical anthropological critique with which we began our discussion. This is certainly the case in the historical-phenomenological and poststructural-psychoanalytical reflections of Achille Mbembe's *On the Postcolony*.[76] Writes Mbembe: "[T]he African

---

[74] Nzegwu, "Colonial Racism," p. 135.

[75] Evidence for this claim of Africana philosophy thriving consists of the several book series housed by influential publishers, the several societies worldwide, and the many journals and newsletters devoted to its study. A good source on such developments is the award-winning *Journal of Africana Philosophy*, now *Philosophia Africana*, formerly edited by the late Emmanuel Eze (1963–2007) housed at De Paul University.

[76] Achille Mbembe, *On the Postcolony* (Berkeley, CA: University of California Press, 2001).

subject is like any other human being: he or she engages in *meaningful acts.*[77] In the anthropology of Africa, the impact of at least philosophical language, particularly in the foundational rationalizations of ethnographies of peoples on the continent, has clearly been advanced through fusions of Marx and Foucault by leading scholars in the field such as Jean Comaroff and John Comaroff.[78] The philosophical challenge of contemporary African philosophy is whether they and other social scientists – those in history, political science, and sociology – and scholars in the humanities who study Africa will draw upon the insights and intellectual resources of contemporary African philosophical thought. For it is the case that the natives have transcended the status of informants and now offer an opportunity to co-invent a new relationship beyond African studies as white hegemony the achievement of which would be, at least in part, a genuinely new world. To explorations of such questions we now turn.

Recent African political thought

An immediate distinction between recent African political thought and its correlates in Europe and North America is that the situation of Africa demands an engagement with the legacy of modern colonialism and racism. Although one could make a case for the same in North America, as most Africana philosophers have, the fact remains that much of North America is also European, and in that regard the philosophical problematics become genealogically hybrid with a history of examining problems ranging from the institution of republicanism to the kinds of justice possible in an avowed democratic state on the one hand and the challenges posed by the use of laws and justice for the sake of racial and other kinds of oppression on the other hand. The reminder of the indigenous populations of North America and those of Europe makes the cultural addition to this mixture all the more complicated.

Most of the issues laid out in recent African political thought were formulated by Frantz Fanon in *The Wretched of the Earth* nearly fifty years

---

[77] *Ibid.*, p. 6.

[78] See especially their introduction to the second volume of their influential work *Of Revelation and Revolution*, where, too, the question of invention is explored through the missionaries' efforts to Christianize the indigenous population.

ago. Recall that Fanon began that text with the provocative observation of decolonization as a violent process that rendered ridiculous the "Graeco-Latin pedestal" of Western values. For if those values were instruments of colonization, how could they legitimate themselves as anything other than its salvation? What happens in a world of suspended values both old and new in a situation of imposed scarcity and poverty in the face of enormous wealth? Is it not the case that in a world without values all is permitted? And what more holds the possibility of violence than such a world, a world of poverty, wealth, and claims to the absence of limits?

The colonial condition is one of competing rights. The indigenous peoples see lands around them that have been stolen or acquired through trickery and the implements of unjust wars. The settlers see themselves as simply going through legal transactions that give them the right to the land they own. The stage is thus set for a conflict of "rights" – both with legal claims from different systems and shared moral claims against theft and unjust acquisition – that is no less than tragic. Fanon then takes us into the world faced at the moment of decolonization. His argument – that the absence of an infrastructure at the moment of decolonization, both at the level of land and idea, leads to a neocolonial situation through the affirmation of metropoles under the auspices of Third World elites, the response to which necessitates revolutionary mobilization that requires the peasantry and the lumpen-proletariat – stimulated outcries of "heretical Marxism."[79] Having built his thought on the importance of seizing one's freedom and taking responsibility for one's values, Fanon is careful to raise the question of how a transition could be made from necolonialism to a genuine *post*colonialism. He returns to criticizing *Négritude*, for instance, on the ground that it is not only a negative moment in a historical dialectic but also a form of reductionism akin to nationalism, racism, and all self-interests-laden models of group organizations instead of those premised upon the common good. Here Fanon is making concrete the old problem of participatory politics, where policy can be premised upon a collective of interests or the interest of the collective. As Jean-Jacques Rousseau famously formulated it in

[79] See, especially, Jack Woddis's *New Theories of Revolution: A Commentary on the Views of Frantz Fanon, Régis Debray, and Herbert Marcuse* (New York: International Publishers, 1972). And on this question of "hereticism" in black radical thought, see B. Anthony Bogues's *Black Heretics, Black Prophets: Radical Political Intellectuals* (New York: Routledge, 2003).

The Social Contract – between the will in general and the general will.[80] Fanon provided case studies of nationalisms that collapsed into ethnic conflicts and offered, in their stead, the option of national consciousness, where the task, as he formulated it, was to build the nation. In the course of his critique of neocolonial values, Fanon advanced both a geopolitical and a class critique. The geopolitical critique challenged the necessity of the capital city as the site of political residence and the organization of social life. The modern African city, for example, faces the reality of the complex political demands of rural Africa. The urban elite that emerges in this structure is one, he argues, that lacks material capital but relies on political capital as mediators with colonial metropolises. The result is a neglected infrastructure, mismanaged national loans, and the emergence of what, as we have seen in our earlier discussions of Fanon's thought, can be called a "lumpenbourgeoisie," an elite that, he concludes, serves no purpose.[81]

Fanon then returns to the colonial and decolonizing moments to illustrate a chilling point. The colonial condition forces the colonized, he argues, to question their humanity. This interrogation occasions alienation of the spirit in the face of loss of land and thwarted, indigenous teleological processes such as their own forms of self-critique. The decolonization process unleashes an array of violent forces that bring to the surface the many double standards of the colonial system and contingency in a world that once seemed to be absolute and necessary. At the heart of this "hell" is the classic direction of consumed hatred. As Virgil showed Dante's protagonist two foes, one of whom is so consumed by hatred that he gnaws on the head of his enemy while frozen from the neck down, Fanon presented the horrific implications of being consumed by hatred. There are some attachments, values, of which we must let go, and in so doing, we will find our way outside, where we could emerge, in the words of Dante, "to see – once

---

[80] For an elaboration of this concept and its connection to Fanon, see Jane Anna Gordon, "Of Legitimation and General Will: Creolizing Rousseau through Fanon," *The C. L. R. James Journal* (2008).

[81] Fanon, *The Wretched of the Earth*, pp. 175–6. This critique places Fanon in the company of E. Franklin Frazier and Amílcar Cabral, where both argue that the cultivation of racial and ethnic alliances create a mediating class with no material capital. See Frazier's *Black Bourgeoisie* and Cabral's *Unity and Struggle: Speeches and Writings*, with an introduction by Basil Risbridger Davidson (New York: Monthly Review Press, 1979). See also Olúfémi Taíwó, "Cabral," in *A Companion to the Philosophers*, ed. Robert L. Arrington (Malden, MA: Blackwell Publishers, 1999), pp. 5–12.

more – the stars."[82] This is what Fanon ultimately means when he implores us all, echoing the final verses of the *Internationale*, to "make a new start, develop new thoughts, and set afoot a new man."[83]

In contemporary Africa these considerations come to the fore in discussions of the postcolonial state, which is further contextualized by the global reach of neoliberalism and a growing neoconservatism in the countries that once ruled over most of the continent. The general goals of neoliberalism are to expand the hegemony of the market economy or capitalism, dwindle away the role of the state in human affairs as much as possible, especially the economy, and to facilitate the growth of Anglo-civil libertarian democracy.[84] Neoconservatism is similar, but it prioritizes order over civil liberties and is also willing, for the sake of such order, to cultivate a relationship with conservative, even radically right-wing, religious groups. In the West this often means Christians and Jews. In the Middle East, such expansion has meant a near eradication of moderate and especially progressive Muslim opposition, with the result that mostly conservative or right-wing forms of Islam dominate many countries in the region.[85] This is the context in which the African postcolonial state is located today.

It has been a longstanding view in studies of colonialism in Africa that it follows a different logic in different regions. Issues around Islam dominate the north, and an insufficient European cultural stronghold applies to the central regions, save for the coasts, where slavery has had an enormous impact. Then there is South Africa, which, because of a permanent white settler population, and its concomitant bourgeoisie, follows more the logic of North American and Australian colonization and postcolonization, except that indigenous Africans continue to be the majority population. This standard interpretation has been challenged by Mahmood Mamdani, the Ugandan-born East Indian political economist and political theorist, who argues that the logic of colonization that governed South Africa is the

---

[82] Dante Alighieri, *The Divine Comedy of Dante Alighieri. Vol. I: Inferno* (Toronto, Canada: Bantam Books, 1982), XXXIII, line 139.

[83] Fanon, *The Wretched of the Earth*, p. 316.

[84] Studies abound, but see Zygmunt Bauman, *Globalism: The Human Consequences* (New York: Columbia University Press, 2000) and David Harvey, *A Brief History of Neoliberalism* (Oxford: Oxford University Press, 2005).

[85] See e.g. Danny Postel, *Reading Legitimation Crisis in Tehran: Iran and the Future of Liberalism* (Chicago, IL: Prickly Paradigm Press, 2006).

same one that was deployed across the continent.[86] That being so, the logic of the postcolonial state can be studied through examining the neoliberal state that stands in the wake of apartheid.

Mamdani begins with a distinction between direct and indirect colonial rule, which was formulated by Lord Frederick John Dealtry Lugard (1858–1945).[87] According to Lugard indigenous Africans are more like children. They should be governed or ruled, and the failure to understand that leads to the misguided notion of having political relations with them. Such relations, designed for mature people known as "citizens," would require equality between colonizers and colonized, between, since we are referring to a highly racialized situation, whites and the varieties of color all the way down to blacks. Offensive though this argument may be, we should bear in mind, as Laurence Thomas showed in his discussion of Kant's racism, that within a framework in which the "factual" bases on which this kind of argument rests are true, it is not only a valid consequence but a highly reasonable one.[88] The more equality indigenous Africans are "given," the more disastrous the results. But like children, they crave for this equality. Thus, fighting them against it only increases their determination to achieve it. A better tactic, similar to reverse psychology, which is pretty effective with children, is to make them think they are in control by delegating levels of ruling. The historical result was the setting up of systems of chiefs who maintained supposedly native rule while organizing citizenship between white settlers. This practice, implemented in the Nigerian situation among others, is well documented by Nkiru Nzegwu, who points out that some of the people who became known as "chiefs" were actually servants in precolonial times, and that along with this newly developed leadership were also new sets of relational concepts that facilitated a disruption of the societies and more effective exploitation of local resources by foreign agents.[89] Lord

---

[86] Mahmood Mamdani, *Citizen and Subject: Contemporary Africa and the Legacy of Late Colonialism* (Princeton, NJ: Princeton University Press, 1996).

[87] See F. D. Lugard, *The Dual Mandate in British Tropical Africa* (Edinburgh: W. Blackwood and Sons, 1922).

[88] See Laurence Thomas, "Moral Equality and Natural Inferiority," *Social Theory and Practice* 31, no. 3 (2005). For recent discussion of the distinction between governing and politics, see Lewis R. Gordon, *Disciplinary Decadence: Living Thought in Trying Times* (Boulder, CO: Paradigm Publishers, 2006), ch. 1, and for a classic discussion of rule, see Ortega y Gasset, *Revolt of the Masses* (New York: W. W. Norton, 1960).

[89] Nzegwu, *Family Matters*. For discussion of the socio-linguistic dimensions of this incursion, see Oyěwùmí, *The Invention of Women*.

Lugard argued that the situation was too far gone in South Africa, where indigenous people had already begun a fight for their "rights," but it could be avoided in the rest of Africa.

Mamdani adds to this discussion the distinction between state and civil society that organizes political reflections on modern democratic societies. States have citizens, who collectively rule either by parliamentary representation or some other form of representative means, for whom there is equality before the law. Civil society enables these relations to emerge as the sets of customs, mores, or ways of life that are conducive to social order. Mamdani points out that modern racism, with its creation of the primitive, leads to the thesis that blacks cannot properly have a "civil" society because they are by definition not civilized. Thus, the notion that black rule can translate into self-rule is already fallacious in such a system, and it also does not work with coherent notions of state and citizenship. Returning to the South African situation, which had already gone "too far," there was the problem of the fight against apartheid. A goal of that struggle was to effect full citizenship for all South Africans. To that end, a new constitution was drafted and national elections were held in 1994, and the African National Congress Party, once outlawed, achieved a majority of the seats in the new parliamentary government, and its then leader, Nelson Mandela, became the first indigenous person to become the head of state of that country. What followed, however, was the implementation of neoliberal policies in South Africa, which have resulted, argues Mamdani, in new forms of indirect rule.

Under neoliberalism, there is supposedly a reduction of state intervention into civil society but much realignment of inequalities within the state apparatus. Thus, as equality increases in the image of the state, inequalities could increase within the now supposedly free civil society. Since the society was affected by racism, the aim of social justice, of eliminating the inequalities created by racism and colonial exploitation, required affirmative action. It required recognizing that racism was an attack that was not on individuals but on groups. Thus, a form of response such as affirmative action was needed since it recognized discrimination against groups. The problem was that, just as in the logic in which the concept of civil society collapsed into that of civilization, that of "individual" worked for whites in ways that it especially did not for blacks. (Asians and coloreds continued to play more ambiguous and mediating roles.) That the new state clearly had a strong black presence in a country whose majority was black made it clear that the question of at least white supremacy was taken on by the state. But because this new state abandoned affirmative action at the level of civil society, because it abandoned responding to issues of social and economic inequalities along racial lines, it in effect became the harbinger of a new, more rigorous form of apartheid, one in which the distances between whites and other groups, especially blacks, continue at the level of civil society but without the charge of being a function of a white supremacist state.

Mamdani's critique in effect reveals the neocolonial structure of the post-colonial state but without the classic neocolonial model of the logic of outside forces manipulating inside leadership. We see here processes of hegemonic practices of political legitimation that lead, paradoxically, to very undemocratic forms of purported democracies. This question of the meaning of postcolonialism today and the nature of the postcolonial state has been taken up and defended in a concerted effort by the Kenyan-born East Indian scholar Pal Ahluwalia, who argues for the independence of postcolonial studies by offering a critique of those who locate it as a subcategory of postmodernism and poststructuralism.[90] In many ways, such conclusions, he contends, result from confusing the field with the biographies and methodological preferences of some of its practitioners. It is true that there are postcolonial scholars who use poststructuralism to decenter Western epistemic practices, and it is also true that the convergence of modernity with the kinds of colonization they examine often leads to a critique of the former; but whereas postmodernism is primarily concerned with its relation to things modern, postcolonialism transcends such concerns. For the postcolonialist many problems could be raised against the postmodernist rejection of subjectivity and of the forms of humanism that may ground the humanistic dimensions of postcolonial thought. Can, in other words, the postcolonialists, whose struggle involves the assertion (recognition for some) of their humanity, afford to reject the value of articulating what Sylvia Wynter has called "the human after the age of man?"[91] Taking on a variety

---

[90] Pal Ahluwalia, *Politics and Post-Colonial Theory* (London: Routledge, 2001).

[91] See Sylvia Wynter, "On How We Mistook the Map for the Territory, and Re-Imprisoned Ourselves in Our Unbearable Wrongness of Being, of *Désêtre*: Black Studies Toward the Human Project," in Lewis R. Gordon and Jane Anna Gordon (eds.), *Not Only the Master's Tools: African-American Studies in Theory and Practice* (Boulder, CO: Paradigm Publishers 2006), pp. 107–72. For discussion, see also *After Man, Towards the Human: Critical Essays on Sylvia Wynter*, ed. Anthony Bogues (Kingston, Jamaica: Ian Randle, 2006).

of critics of postcolonialism, Ahluwalia argues that many of them appeal to unsustainable reductionism to support their case. For instance, the claim of the field being primarily work done by English departments fails to account for work produced by scholars in the social sciences, of which Ahluwalia's is a case in point. His main response relies on the meaning of "post" in postcolonial studies. It is not entirely clear what Ahluwalia means in his use of the prefix. It transcends, he argues, the temporal and spatial notions of "after" and "beyond," and he suggests that the question must be examined by going beyond geopolitical specificity to the controlling forces of the imagination, to the social dynamics that constitute new forms of activities that produce, and reproduce, freedom-inhibiting practices.[92] One thing is certain: the historical context for the prefix is its relation to the institutions built in the period of high colonialism and whose transcendence marks the ongoing effort of subaltern peoples in the present age, a point on which his and Mamdani's thought converge.

Ahluwalia's conception of postcoloniality has, however, led to his issuing a critique of Mahmood Mamdani's analysis of African postcolonial states. Recall that civil society, Mamdani argues, became another way of saying "civilization," and that concept was restricted to whites, which meant that the notion of "black civil society" became an oxymoron. Rejected as civil, the organization of black indigenous social life became one of authoritarian rule. Mamdani also pointed out that this bifurcation led to a situation in which the deracialization of the state did not necessarily mean a similar alignment of civil society. The paradox of deracialization is that it required the recognition of racial categories for its success (affirmative action). A deracialized state that was formerly reserved only for whites meant, quite simply, that other racial groups could be active participants in state institutions. For the state to implement such a policy in "civil society" meant, however, affirmative action, and the resistance to affirmative action in many efforts at deracializing civil institutions entailed policies of recognizing other factors. The result was that deracialization was not occurring in the communities in a system that left management of non-state institutions in the hands of "traditional" or "custom" authorities. Such authorities were state supported without the correlative demand of being aligned with state deracialization. The result, then, was a deracialized state in the face of a heavily racist civil

---

[92] See e.g. Ahluwalia's introduction, *Politics and Post-Colonial Theory*.

society. The best example of this, Mamdani argued, is contemporary South Africa, which got rid of apartheid and achieved a deracialized state (as the African National Congress-run Parliament and heads of state exemplify) but a civil society that continues to look pretty much like, and at times is even worse than, its apartheid predecessor.[93]

Ahluwalia offers empirical evidence against Mamdani's thesis:

> Why have African countries managed to remain intact, preserving borders demarcated by the colonial powers? All these questions suggest that, if Mamdani is correct in asserting that a system of decentralised despotism was imposed upon rural peoples who had successfully fought colonial rule, then we should have witnessed a severe crisis of legitimacy that would have made rule in the post-independence period unsustainable.[94]

His main criticism, further, is that the logic of Mamdani's approach is an appeal to "binaries": "Mamdani has argued for new forms of analysis . . . and, while his work goes a long way to providing such an answer, it ultimately fails to do so. This is because Mamdani has reverted to another set of binaries, citizen and subject, which cannot be sustained under careful analysis."[95] Drawing upon a bevy of recent thought on citizenship and subject ranging from that of Etienne Balibar to Chantal Mouffe, Michel Foucault, and Ruth Lister, Ahluwalia argues that the structure of citizen and subject fails to account for the complex, symbiotic structure of citizen/subject or citizen-subject through which each is productive of the other. He concludes that Mamdani only attributes agency to colonized peoples during the process of decolonization but not at the moment of independence.[96]

Ahluwalia's criticisms of Mamdani have some ironic features. The attack on binary analysis, for instance, is a main feature of postmodern and poststructural analyses, two governing narratives from which, he argued at the

---

[93] On this matter, see some of the writings of contemporary South Africa's dissident intellectuals such as Ashwin Desai, *South Africa: Still Revolting* (Johannesburg: Impact Africa Publishing, 2000); *The Poors of Chatsworth: Race, Class and Social Movements in Post-Apartheid South Africa* (Durban: Madiba Publishers, 2000); *We Are the Poors: Community Struggles in Post-Apartheid South Africa* (New York: Monthly Review Press, 2002); *Challenging Hegemony: Social Movements and the Quest for a New Humanism in Post-Apartheid South Africa*, ed. Nigel C. Gibson (Trenton, NJ: Africa World Press, 2005); and *Asinamali: University Struggles in Post-Apartheid South Africa*, ed. Richard Pithouse (Trenton, NJ: Africa World Press, 2006).

[94] Ahluwalia, *Politics and Post-Colonial Theory*, p. 104.   [95] *Ibid.*, p. 105.   [96] *Ibid.*, p. 112.

outset, postcolonial theory is supposed to be independent. The rejection of binary as binary does not address the question of whether the instance of binary analysis in question accurately addresses reality or the aspect of reality under discussion. In other words, is it not a-contextual to argue that binary analysis is never appropriate? Racism, for instance, aims at producing Manichaean structures on people whose purported origins are different from that of the dominating group, and although the lived reality of social life, even in colonialism, may not be binary, there is the reality of the constant imposition of binary relations on the colonized and racialized subject. It stands to reason, then, that an analysis that reveals the binary dimension of colonial and racial logic would not be fallacious but accurate. In similar kind, if a neocolonial environment is governed by the same stratifying logic, then it also stands to reason that the "neocolonial postcolonial state" is better understood as the working out of a new binary structure. If this is correct then Mamdani's point is not that there is no agency manifested by the ruled in the postcolony but that the structure of indirect rule is aimed at chipping away the social efficacy of such agents. It simply is not the case, for instance, that black citizen-subjects have the same opportunities within African independence as white citizen-subjects, even though they may exert enough cultural influence to create creolized behavior among whites, and this is because of the global economy of white life over black and other non-whites. Ahluwalia is correct that the governed Africans are not passive. But Mamdani concedes that. What is complicated is that the avenues for exercising agency could become the least effective ones as the new set of state and civil institutions foster their diminution. Ahluwalia's response is to broaden the context of discussion, which he does in his treatment of globalism, where he concludes that it is necessary to "examine the global system and discern the patterns through which hegemony is maintained," and he insists that "[p]ost-colonial theory offers a way to break down the tyranny of the structures of power which continue to entrap post-colonial subjects."[97]

Beyond his critique of Mamdani, Ahluwalia clearly regards postcolonial studies as the exploration of subaltern subjects as human agents. In his empirical studies, for example, they are shown to be actively engaged in practices of "resistance," by which he means that they are not passive recipients

---

[97] *Ibid.*, pp. 130–1.

of governmental dictates.[98] I should like to add here that it is his focus on what Frantz Fanon calls "actional subjects" that distinguishes Ahluwalia's thought from (ironically orthodox) poststructuralism. The resources, and even the foci of much of his theoretical work, are poststructuralists such as Jacques Derrida and Michel Foucault, although he is equally indebted to Edward Said (1935–2003) and Frantz Fanon. He is right to assert that although he uses their thought as, in effect, tools, his interest in the actional subject separates his thought from problems of undecidability (Derrida) and genealogical impositions of power constitutive of subjectivity (Foucault) since, for Ahluwalia, there is always room in which action, in a word, matters.

We arrive, then, at a situation in African political thought where in all instances liberalism, at least in its neoliberal form, receives much criticism on the one hand, and where there is a conflict between scholarship organized along critical modernist lines (usually neo-Marxist) and the kinds of postmodern poststructuralist approaches that are heavily influential in the humanities and growing in the social sciences, on the other hand. Kwame Gyekye, whose work has informed much of our re-examination of traditional African thought, has offered a way forward on the question of liberalism.[99] The dominating social and political philosophy of the postcolonial African state is, he contends, communitarianism. In Anglo-political philosophy, communitarianism stands in opposition to individualized liberalism.[100] The influence of Marxism on African thought, especially by way of such legendary pan-African intellectuals and political leaders as Kwame Nkrumah (1909–1972) in Ghana and Julius Kambarage Nyerere (1922–1999) in Tanzania, led to an indigenous African form of Marxist thought premised upon communal values which they referred to as "communalism" instead of communism. Communalism invariably meant socialism.[101] Although Nkrumah was ousted by the United States' Central Intelligence Agency (CIA)

---

[98] See e.g. *Post-Colonialism and The Politics of Kenya* (Hauppauge, NY: Nova Science Publishers, 1996).

[99] See Gyekye, *Tradition and Modernity*.

[100] Discussions abound, but see especially the works of e.g. John Rawls, Charles Taylor, Alasdair McIntyre, Bruce Ackerman, Robert Nozick, Ronald Dworkin, Martha Nussbaum, K. Anthony Appiah – in other words, contemporary theorists of the Anglo-liberal political tradition.

[101] For representative works of these legendary figures in African politics, see Kwame Nkrumah, *Africa Must Unite* (New York: F. A. Praeger, 1963); *Consciencism*; *Neo-colonialism:*

and died in exile in Bucharest, Romania, in 1972 while seeking medical treatment, Nyerere led Tanzania through to his retirement with a record of great honor for such decisions as Tanzania's role in ousting the brutal dictator Idi Amin (mid-1920s–2003) from Uganda and the many efforts Nyerere organized in the promotion of human rights and education. Unusual for a politician with so much power, he was willing to admit when he failed as well as when he succeeded. What is not often admitted after the end of this period of African leadership is the even worse scale of failure on the part of those who accepted the task of transforming those state-managed economies into free market ones.

Although less the case in Tanzania, the path of development premised upon communalism took authoritarian forms in many African postcolonial states because of demands for unanimity, which logically meant an appeal to the absence of dissent. The result was the occlusion of oppositional discursive practices. Without opposition, there can be no politics, only rule. Thus, Gyekye argues, a problem of African political philosophy becomes the absence of a genuinely political dimension. What is left is only thought on governing or rulership. To create a space for the political, Gyekye argues for moderate communitarianism, where the preference for the common good is acknowledged with an understanding of the importance of spaces for dissent, or minority rights, as an essential element of that good. In effect, Gyekye is arguing for a debate among Africans on the possibility of a form of African liberal communitarianism.

Mamdani's concern for politics in Africa instead of indirect rule is supported by Gyekye's diagnosis of the contemporary African situation.[102] Gyekye argues, however, in stream with Ahlulawia, that there can be more dissent and critical opposition within indigenous thought that could be constitutive of such a politics and that philosophical thought – whose history is full of examples of politically engaged intellectuals, such as John Locke (1632–1704), whose thought provided the framework for the kinds of economic and social thought that informed the bourgeois revolution in Anglo-Europe – has an important role to play in its development. In fact,

The Last Stage of Imperialism (New York: International Publishers, 1966); and Nyerere, Freedom and Socialism; Freedom and Development; Ujamaa: Essays on Socialism (London: Oxford University Press, 1977) and Crusade for Liberation (Dar es Salaam: Oxford University Press, 1979).

[102] Gyekye, Tradition and Modernity.

the relationship is symbiotic: philosophy argues for such discursively free spaces or a free public realm, and such an environment facilitates philosophical reflection. An added reason for the need for such spaces, Gyekye argues, is the problem of corruption, which has become a mundane feature of the postcolonial African state. The dominance of rule over politics leads to a situation of unaccountability since the weight of public opinion, which requires a public sphere in which condemnation of certain deeds could be voiced, is rendered ineffective by, in effect, stifling it. The result is the absence of external assessment: the statesman, working on a notion of unanimity, asserts an isomorphic relationship between his will and the will of the people. As one, they literally lose an "outside," and since accountability requires being accountable to something or someone other than oneself, the road to unaccountability follows. Without accountability legitimation collapses into sheer will and force. Thus, legitimation of such rulers becomes mostly a legal matter. But for normative legitimacy, which plays a central role in politics, the voice and will of the people must matter, and they can only develop where paradoxically there are safeguards for minority expressions, for speech, and for other facets of liberal democracy. Gyekye is here presenting, out of the African context, the very argument posed by Ortega y Gasset in the European struggle against fascism and hyperdemocracy in *Revolt of the Masses*. But Gyekye's moderate communitarianism argument suggests a greater faith in participatory democracy than Gasset's preference for British-style liberal, parliamentary democracy.[103]

It seems, however, that Mamdani's and Gyekye's encomia have fallen on proverbial deaf ears. For what has emerged as the most influential recent development in African political thought is reminiscent of the form of philosophical idealism that preceded Marxism in Germany in the nineteenth century. This could be attributed to the undisputed domination of neoliberalism in post-apartheid South Africa. Whereas it stands as an external imposition on the rest of Africa, the post-apartheid South African government seems to have taken the neoliberal bull by the proverbial horns, and the effect of this policy is reflected in the kind of thought that dominates its most influential universities – namely, the thought that, in effect, holds

---

[103] See Ortega y Gasset, *The Revolt of the Masses*, reissued edn, trans. anonymous and authorized (New York: W. W. Norton, 1994), ch. 13, "The Greatest Danger, the State," and ch. 14, "Who Rules the World?" pp. 115–86.

no governments accountable and prefers, instead, formulations that conflate cultural life as politics without an articulation of what differentiates a political field of activity from other kinds.[104] As with African-American philosophy, what this turn has meant is a near hegemonic rise of postmodern cultural criticism as representative of nonconservative thought. I say "nonconservative" because "left-wing" would not be an appropriate ascription to postmodern cultural critics because of its obvious binary structural relation to "right wing," unless, of course, a genuinely neutral third were possible, which postmodern and even liberal scholarship rejects, and, in the main, postmodern and liberal intellectuals would not describe themselves as conservative. As Raymond Guess observes:

> Another line to which some recent liberals seem committed has been the claim that liberalism is "neutral" in the struggle of ideologies, and that it has no specific positive values of its own or substantive conceptions of a "good life" it seeks to realize. That this claim is itself false and ideological seems to me too self-evident to require detailed discussion.[105]

For a conservative African voice, we must turn to, among others, the Nigerian-born philosopher Polycarp Ikuenobe.

In *Philosophical Perspectives on Communalism and Morality in African Traditions*, Ikuenobe enters this debate on rule and politics in Africana political thought.[106] He correctly places philosophers such as Kwasi Wiredu and K. Anthony Appiah in Kwame Gyekye's camp of advocating liberalism as a viable response to African problems. This lumping of them together does not mean that their views are exactly the same. For instance, Appiah's opposition to communalism leads to a form of cosmopolitanism.[107] Wiredu is, however, a more complex story since his arguments are also rooted in pragmatism and its concomitant naturalism, through the work of John Dewey, which is a far cry from the kind of individualism endorsed by Appiah.[108] Ikuenobe defends communalism through arguing for the formation of moral personhood as

---

[104] See e.g. Gibson, *Challenging Hegemony*, and for discussion of the political role of intellectuals in these unfolding events, see Pithouse, *Asinamali*.

[105] Raymond Guess, *Outside Ethics* (Princeton, NJ: Princeton University Press, 2005), p. 128.

[106] See Polycarp A. Ikuenobe, *Philosophical Perspectives on Communalism and Morality in African Traditions* (Lanham, MD: Lexington Books, 2006).

[107] See K. Anthony Appiah, *Cosmopolitanism: Ethics in a World of Strangers* (New York: W. W. Norton, 2006).

[108] See Wiredu, *Cultural Universals*.

a function of communal values. Since he is offering a defense of African communalism, he must also respond to the criticism that such a value often collapses into unanimism and authoritarianism in the African context. His response is that authoritarianism is not in itself a bad thing. To bring home his point, he appeals to "rational authoritarianism," where criteria of evidence and other forms of assessment are demanded from the community to adjudicate between conflicting beliefs. An error of liberal conceptions of the person is, for example, their presumption that the individual can be the source of assessing such things. Ikuenobe's response is to point out the ineluctability of individual fallibility and prejudice. It is not that the community cannot be wrong. It is that its constant criterion of publicity reduces the likelihood of the advancement of false beliefs. The main point is that rational authoritarianism depends on what he calls "evidentialism," of being subject to criteria beyond the self. From this argument, Ikuenobe is able to defend, as well, a form of "moderate indoctrinarianism."[109] His argument is that for evidence to do its bidding, indoctrination will always encounter its own limits. It is where indoctrination collapses into "brainwashing," he cautions, that it is bad.[110] Finally, he argues that liberalism is more applicable to western Europe, where such values are already held as dominant (though not always historically so), than it would be in places where the value system might be quite different. Given his demand for the role of evidence in human social life, Ikuenobe concludes, like Gyekye, with a preference for moderate communalism, but unlike Gyekye, he insists that this is already a feature of traditional African cultures.

At this point, let us consider some questions in need of a response or adjustment in Ikuenobe's thought. The first relates to the focus on "moral philosophy" in the African context. Alasdair MacIntyre, following Nietzsche, has shown that much confusion characterizes contemporary axiology through a failure to distinguish morals from ethics.[111] The focus of the former is on rules, whereas that of the latter is on character or the good life. It is no accident that Ikuenobe, although focusing primarily on Africa, finds

---

[109] Ikuenobe, *Philosophical Perspectives*, pp. 8, 225–9.   [110] *Ibid.*

[111] See Friedrich Nietzsche, *On the Genealogy of Morals*, trans. Walter Kaufmann and R. J. Hollingdale, ed. with commentary Walter Kaufmann (New York: Vintage, 1967); and Alasdair MacIntyre, *After Virtue: A Study in Moral Theory*, 2nd edn (Notre Dame, IN: Notre Dame University Press, 1984). See also Jerry Miller, "Ethics without Morality" (Santa Cruz: University of California Doctoral Dissertation, History of Consciousness, 2001).

himself referring to Plato and Aristotle in his defense of communitarianism. This is because his argument lends itself to worlds in which there is a guiding teleology or purpose. In such worlds there is an ethos, where virtue may count more, and since, as both the Greek and the Egyptian/Kamitan ancients argued, such character requires cultivation; the importance of habit and controlled experiences for the child raised by the proverbial village comes to the fore.[112] Yet Ikuenobe's text works within the framework of modern moral philosophical thought as though there were not a fissure between that world and the ancient one via the medieval. This is all the more odd since there is a demonstrated rupture in the modern world between European and African value systems to begin with. Gyekye, for instance, situates his discussion of Akan values in the context of their cosmology, which is a teleological system premised upon values emanating from the beginning in decaying reach to the present. A major feature of liberal moral philosophy is its rejection of teleological reasoning. Even where consequences are taken into account, as with utilitarianism, they are not located within an overarching teleology. What Gyekye suggests should be taken into account is that which brings value to African traditional communities in their own terms, from this point of view – literally a metaphysics of values from the past onward. Ancestors become valuable, as we saw in our discussion of invention, because they are older and thus closer linked to the center from which values emanate. The human community becomes the focus in a form of humanism, but it is one that is not premised upon a moral rule in itself but on the community, which is considered part of a larger whole that includes the never entirely dead (ancestors). In other words, there is an understanding of subjects through whom human-made rules can be broken. Since everyone will one day become an ancestor, the focus is on agency, character, and earthly existence. Because of this emphasis on human subjectivity, it means that there is always something an individual can do to make amends for his or her action. There is thus, for example, not a constant anxiety about an afterlife. Thus, in many African communities, an individual can really be brought back into a community after having paid the proper respects for violating a law or moral rule. There is no metaphysical addition of deferred judgment. Although this is not a uniform perspective across the continent,

---

[112] The classic Greek statement is Aristotle's *Nicomachean Ethics*, which receives discussion in MacIntyre, *After Virtue*, and for the classic Egyptian/Kamitian formulations through the concept of *Ma'at*, see Karenga, *Maat*, pp. 50 and 254–7.

it is a highly influential one in the central western region, which is the focus of Ikuenobe's prescriptions.

An additional criticism is as follows. Although Ikuenobe is critical of liberalism, the approach of focusing on moral rules, epistemic criteria, and moral education in political thought is quintessentially not only analytical but also a prime example of liberal political theory. A criticism that could be added of liberal political theory is that it focuses on normative rules over and against political practice to the point of there being an absence of genuine politics in liberal political theory. John Rawls, for example, developed rules that hardly exemplified an understanding of politics but, instead, were more fitting for administration and distribution.[113] It is as if the political theorist were simply a social engineer. The argument avowed by Ikuenobe seems more suitable for governing than politics proper. This is one reason why his concern with moral education becomes crucial; it is a theory about what is necessary at the pre-political levels for the political to have a suitable civil society from which to emerge.

Yet it is difficult to see how Ikuenobe's counsel makes much sense in a world where, as Fanon and Cabral have shown, there is the absence of a genuine bourgeoisie and their economic correlate – material capital – from which their nation can be built. How would moral education intervene beyond the question of the corruption of such people in the face of the wider social problems that affect them? As we have seen, much of recent African political thought is informed by the problems raised in the writings of Fanon. He has, in effect, situated the political and methodological fields of research as the dialectics of freedom in tandem with changing traditions and the decolonization of knowledge. The first calls for democratization and the latter demands a phenomenological self-reflective critique. These themes have been taken up again from Francophone Africa through the thought of the Cameroonian social and political theorist Achille Mbembe.

As with many of the other thinkers in this book, I will not be able to explore all the themes of Mbembe's thought because of limited space. Our focus, then, will be on how he retells the Fanonian-affected ones of sociogenesis, human agency, time, corruption, and the epistemic conditions of

---

[113] See John Rawls's classic work, *A Theory of Justice* (Cambridge, MA: Harvard University Press, 1971) and for a critique along the lines I am offering here, see Bonnie Honig, *Political Theory and the Displacement of Politics* (Ithaca, NY: Cornell University Press, 1993), pp. 126–61.

human genesis. In his most influential book, *On the Postcolony*, Mbembe walks along theoretical roads paved by Fanon, but this path is taken with the effect of not following its lessons. Whereas, for example, Fanon, as we saw, in his exploration of Lacanian thought in Africa, revealed its relativism, its dependence on the European context, Mbembe simply applies Lacanian psychoanalysis to the African situation without a response to Fanon's sociogenic critique. Such an application in effect presumes the universality of Lacanian psychoanalysis.[114] The result of such a presumption is a reassertion of the universal legitimacy of modern Western human sciences, even in the face of their avowed critical interrogation.[115] There are, as well, the added elements of the text offering a more Heideggerian-inspired phenomenology, where the approach is to focus on beings over metaphysical efforts to read them in terms of a particular being. This emphasis offers a response to the Fanonian critique of application through the possibility of positioning Mbembe's thought as premised upon Fanon's consideration instead of ignoring it. In other words, Fanon's critique, in effect, takes Western human sciences to task for reducing black beings to Black Being or, worse, to a form of being that will always fail to be incorporated as a human being. To analyze that phenomenon, one may wish, as Mbembe does, to offer a reading of the misreadings, of the misread beings. Critics of this approach could argue, however, that some form of connecting the assertion is needed to make dominating forces accountable for phenomena such as oppression, which moves across beings, and that a failure to do so is inherently conservative, perhaps even right-wing, with genealogical resources in such a strand that grew out of the thought of Hegel. Right-wing Hegelianism, for instance, builds on the market from *Philosophy of Right* and world history in *Lectures on the Philosophy of History* and follows a path to Heideggerian *Volk*ism, which found a home in postmodern textualism. The consequence of this is an academic line that is today well known as postmodern forms of French poststructuralism and as, in its most explicit right-wing formulation, at least through Heideggerianism and its legacies through Leo Strauss, conservative and neoconservative political thought.[116] Left-wing Hegelianism, which worked its way through Marx and on through to Du Bois, Sartre,

---

[114] See e.g. *On the Postcolony*, ch. 5, especially p. 175, and ch. 6.   [115] *Ibid.*, introduction.

[116] For these genealogies, see Tom Rockmore, *On Heidegger's Nazism and Philosophy*, rev. edn (Berkeley, CA: University of California Press, 1997); Anne Norton, *Leo Strauss and the Politics of Empire* (New Haven: Yale University Press, 2004); and Nelson Maldonado-Torres,

and Fanon, focuses on a human-oriented social world in which freedom is constituted beyond questions of epistemic or textual limits; but it departs from the Hegelian teleology of progress by placing strong emphasis on the contingency of human situations, a notion crucial for the formation of discursive opposition or political life.[117] These two lines reveal, in effect, the continued dialectic of rule and politics.

Mbembe's Lacanian psychoanalytical readings are situated in the Heideggerian-affected textualist approach which leads to a phenomenology of African experience in which, paradoxically, the African does not seem to appear. Given the Heideggerian consideration of beings versus Being, one could argue that it is a good thing that the African is invisible. Africans, however, are another story. Consider Mbembe's use of the terms "us" and "them." Africans appear in this sense, but they do so in the third-person pronoun, whereas only European perspectives in the text stand in the first person, which raises a serious question of what the author is in this displaced "we," given his biography. Observe:

> It is assumed that, although the African possess a self-referring structure
> that makes him or her close to "being human," he or she belongs, up to a
> point, to a world we cannot penetrate. At bottom, he/she is familiar to us.
> We can give an account of him/her in the same way we can understand the
> psychic life of the *beast*. We can even, through a process of domestication
> and training, bring the African to where he or she can enjoy a fully human
> life. In this perspective, Africa is essentially, for us, an object of
> experimentation.[118]

Added to this poignant passage is the power of the rhetorical force of the text. It is without question that Mbembe is perhaps one of the greatest living prose-writers in contemporary African thought. To find his equal, one needs to step outside of scholarship into the world of what Paget Henry calls the poeticist imagination, or the world of the novelists and the poets.[119] This

"Toward a Critique of Continental Reason: Africana Studies and the Decolonization of Imperial Cartographies in the Americas," in Gordon and Gordon, *Not Only the Master's Tools*, especially pp. 52–9. Cf. also Danny Postel, *Reading Legitimation Crisis in Tehran: Iran and the Future of Liberalism* (Chicago, IL: Prickly Paradigm Press, 2006), pp. 111–15.

[117] For discussion of the left-wing Hegelian genealogy, see Robert Nisbet, *The Social Philosophers: Community and Conflict in Western Thought* (New York, Crowell, 1973) and Nigel Gibson, *Fanon: The Postcolonial Imagination* (Cambridge: Polity Press, 2003).

[118] Mbembe, *On the Postcolony*, p. 2.

[119] See our discussion of Henry in the previous chapter and his formulations in *Caliban's Reason*.

makes his work especially appealing in literary and cultural studies circles. But part of the aim of political thought is to offer some content along with style. Where style alone stands as a contribution, the effect is a form of implosive disciplinary decadence.

Mbembe, like Fanon, does not make his methodological moves explicit but instead goes through them in the course of his descriptions of contemporary African life. Thus, although he raises questions of experience, it is not clear whether they are advanced through acts of suspension, as one finds in Husserlian forms of phenomenology, or a dialectical unfolding of epistemic clarity and ontological scope, as one finds in Hegelian phenomenology. What does emerge, in stream with most philosophical phenomenology, is a reflection of and on the lived and metacritical impact of time. In one sense, time emerges as an unsettled feature of the African subject or subjects of study:

> Time – "it was always there," "since time immemorial," "we came to meet it" – is supposedly stationary: thus the importance of repetition and cycles, and the alleged central place of witch-craft and divination procedures. The idea of progress is said to disintegrate in such societies; should change occur – rare indeed – it would, as of necessity, follow a disordered trajectory and fortuitous path ending only in undifferentiated chaos.[120]

The theme of time returns in his discussion of temporality, where different dimensions of African societies from traditional to colonial to post-colonial state rulers occupy different temporal spaces in a paradoxical simultaneity.[121]

> More philosophically, it may be supposed that the present *as experience of a time* is precisely that moment when different forms of absence become mixed together: absence of those presences that are no longer so and that one remembers (the past), and absence of those others that are yet to come and are anticipated (the future).[122]

For such an analysis to make sense, a form of subjunctive articulation of temporality is needed, where one deals with what was, is, would and could be as indexical points on each other in both conflicting and intersecting subjectivities. In stream with Gyekye he points out that "in these societies the 'person' is seen as predominant over the 'individual,' [which is]

---

[120] Mbembe, *On the Postcolony*, p. 4.   [121] *Ibid.*, pp. 15–17.   [122] *Ibid.*, p. 16.

considered (it is added) 'a strictly Western creation,'" and reminiscent of Fanon's introduction in *Black Skin, White Masks*:

> More than any other region, Africa thus stands out as the supreme receptacle of the West's obsession with, and circular discourse about, the facts of "absence," "lack," and "non-being," of identity and difference, of negativeness – in short, of nothingness . . . In fact, here is a principle of language and classificatory systems in which *to differ* from something or somebody is not simply *not to be like* (in the sense of being non-identical or being-other); it is also *not to be at all* (non-being). More, it is *being nothing* (nothingness).[123]

We see here not only the reassertion of what Fanon called "the zone of nonbeing," but also themes from *The Wretched of the Earth*, where Fanon revealed, in similar, phenomenologically rich descriptions, the Manichaean colonial world.

Mbembe is not, however, describing the colonial world but instead what purports to be the "postcolonial" one. This world, or effort, marked by claims of African independence, is guided by teleologies of social evolution and "ideologies of development and modernization."[124] Although Mbembe does not make it explicit, these mantras reveal the rallying cry of "civil society" discussions in academic treatments of Africa, which, as we might recall, Mamdani astutely points out collapses into "civilizing" discourses in the dualistic dialectics of white and black, civilized and uncivilized. Mbembe's interest stops at the descriptive level, however, which means that the teleologies are observed but ultimately not necessarily theorized.

Many themes are taken up in the course of Mbembe's explorations, such as the kinds of rationalizations that enable legitimacy in the postcolonial state in the face of constant, imposed scarcity (the first chapter, "Of Commandments"), the privatization of violence and power (the second chapter, "On Private Indirect Government"), or the structural psychoanalytical semiotics of death (the sixth chapter, "God's Phallus"). I should here like, however, to consider his meaning of the term "postcolony." Mbembe writes:

> The notion "postcolony" identifies specifically a given historical trajectory – that of societies recently emerging from the experience of colonization and the violence which the colonial relationship involves. To be sure, the

---

[123] *Ibid.*, p. 4.   [124] *Ibid.*

postcolony is chaotically pluralistic; it has nonetheless an internal coherence. It is a specific system of signs, a particular way of fabricating simulacra or re-forming stereotypes. It is not, however, just an economy of signs in which power is mirrored and *imagined* self-reflectively. The postcolony is characterized by a distinctive style of political improvisation, by a tendency to excess and lack of proportion, as well as by distinctive ways identities are multiplied, transformed, and put into circulation. But the postcolony is also made up of a series of corporate institutions and a political machinery that, once in place, constitute a distinctive regime of violence. In this sense, the postcolony is a particularly revealing, and rather dramatic, stage on which are played out the wider problems of subjections and its corollary, discipline.[125]

Reading this passage from the third chapter, "The Aesthetics of Vulgarity," it is difficult to discern the extent to which the postcolony is not, in the end, the *neo*colony. One reason why this is difficult to fathom is the absence of analyses that go beyond the mere fact of such phenomena. Thus, it seems, these ongoing social dynamics exist independent of a wider, international geopolitical economy of power. By in effect ontologically suspending the roles of North America, Europe, and even Asia, the *post* in postcolony becomes an unquestioned prefix in the domain of cultural interpretation. What this means is that a genuine independence is conceded in the equation, even though possibly not intended, and the onus of responsibility becomes evidently local. Even though Mbembe concedes that he does not mean to use the prefix "post" in terms of referring to succession over time, of "before" and "after" colonialism, the absence of a wider context leaves little room for other interpretations.[126] Yet an interpretation could be made that is not offered by Mbembe's analysis, including his notion of temporality. The "post" in postcolony could signify the absence of legitimacy afforded colonialism itself. Thus, as opposed to the days of old or high colonialism when leaders could gain public approval, political legitimacy, by openly announcing the acquisition of colonies for the sake of securing national wealth, contemporary colonization dares not speak its name. Colonies continue to be acquired on the condition that colonizers are no longer called colonizers and colonies are no longer called colonies. Such a logic could only work in a world in which word was divorced from reality in

---

[125] *Ibid.*, pp. 102–3.   [126] Cf. *Ibid.*, pp. 15–16.

an idealism of language itself, and as such, reality is or becomes what it is called. Lord Lugard's prescience is validated here. Recall that he argued for not making in Africa the kinds of "mistakes" that occurred in Asia. There, colonialism created a hybrid structure whose legacy includes a local ruling class linked to material sources of wealth. In Africa the aim was to get the resources more efficiently through blocking the cultivation of an indigenous, manufacturing or industrial elite. This was achieved through fanning the flames of custom and traditional conflicts and creating a conception of cultural authenticity that monopolized a very manipulative site of power. Mbembe astutely characterized this concentration as the privatization of power and its concomitant violence. We will return to this concept shortly. For now, what is significant is that the *post* has become the absence of colonial legitimacy in the face of colonial aspiration. The lived experience of continued colonial practices becomes, then, the realization of the "effects" of their misnamed continuation.

The question that follows, then, is what would happen to this analysis if the context were broadened, the language shifted from third-person Africans to a first-person African, and the general anonymity of actors afforded by third-person analysis shifted to the disclosing effects of proper names. In *The Dialectics of Transformation in Africa*, philosopher and theologian Elias K. Bongmba, also from Cameroon, does just that, and the result is a critique of the kinds of argument that collapse into exclusive disjunctions of one possibility versus another.[127] That is to say, in agreement with Mbembe, that it is an affront to African people to treat their leadership as not also responsible for the contemporary situation of Africa because of the colonialism that preceded their rule. But ascribing such responsibility does not entail absolving the rest of the world of the role the imperial powers played, and continue to play, in the contemporary predicament of Africa either. Bongmba argues, in agreement with Mbembe, that the afflictions that currently besiege African societies are a function of the privatization of power and the failure of African leadership. But, unlike Mbembe, he builds his case through a detailed analysis of the contemporary situation with a scale of specificity rarely seen in recent political thought. Rulers, especially the most abusive ones, are not anonymous in this text, and the process by which

---

[127] Elias K. Bongmba, *The Dialectics of Transformation in Africa* (New York: Palgrave Macmillan, 2006).

they go about achieving power is demystified through Bongmba's copious use of examples of historical evidence. The result is, in effect, an updating of Fanon's *The Wretched of the Earth*, especially the second chapter, "The Pitfalls [Misadventures] of National Consciousness."

A crucial feature of Bongmba's text is its absence of disciplinary limits. Although not made explicit in most social and political thought, a division between secular and theological sources has often taken the form of ignoring the impact of the sacred and the profane on the constitution of social and political life. It has also had the unfortunate consequence of ignoring the important contributions of religious thinkers in the theorizing of freedom, as Cedric Robinson revealed.[128] Bongmba, however, brings these forces to the forefront of the analysis and spells out, systematically, their relationship to secular, philosophical anthropological assumptions, dynamics of social transformation, and the reflections on method, disciplines, and reason deployed in their advancement. The result is a work in social and political theory whose scope cannot receive justice in this introduction.

The Dialectics of Transformation in Africa offers a sustained analysis of power. One could argue that the postmodern moment and the rise of postmodernist readings of social reality have led to a mystification of power through, by way of Foucault, asserting its ubiquity. What is the point in talking about how anyone achieves power if everyone already manifests it? Bongmba, on the other hand, points out that even if power were in some way manifested by all, the relations of power could be such that they could be consolidated into individuals in ways that would render meaningless the forms in which they remained in others. Recall that Mbembe identified this phenomenon as the "privatization of power," which he portrays as a haphazard unfolding of the privatization process. Bongmba, however, sees it as a pattern of predictable, instrumental dynamics – in short, a methodology. He defines it as "an exclusionary political praxis that has reserved political power and the spoils of power to a few self-anointed rulers."[129] We see here, in spite of that difference, a convergence of concerns of rulership in the thought of Gyekye,

---

[128] I am of course referring to *An Anthropology of Marxism* (Aldershot, UK: Ashgate, 2001), discussion of which appears in ch. 4 above.

[129] Bongmba, *Dialectics*, p. 10. Cf. Mbembe, *On the Postcolony*, ch. 2, "On Private Indirect Government," especially pp. 77–89.

Mamdani, and Mbembe. Privatization here does not refer to a space, as in the private space versus public one. It refers, literally, to asserted ownership of a society's political and civil institutions; in short, to the ownership of a country in practice if not avowedly so in law. I say "if not avowedly so" since the laws themselves are dictated by such rulers and can be appealed to in the processes of mystification.

Privatization of power in the African context is achieved by (1) appealing to a form of precolonial African authenticity of a single ruler or small set of rulers led by a supreme ruler; (2) bureaucratic centralization; (3) eliminating political opposition; (4) monopolizing the press; and (5) using occult forces.[130] In response Bongmba points out that the first technique appeals to a notion of Africans that is not historic, and that in fact, there was a broad distribution of power among the leadership in precolonial African states with checks and balances on power and expectations of changes of leadership over the course of time.[131] The process from (1) leads the leadership into a process the outcome of which is divination, with its expectations of omniscience and omnipotence. The effort to become omniscient, which requires central bureaucratic centralization, controlling the press, and the manipulation of occult forces, leads to the desperate effort to extend control to metaphysical levels. Omnipotence requires full control over opposing forces, which, in effect, means their elimination, which in Africa often means single-party rule. Part of the privatization of power is deification of the leader and, by implication, the leadership. Thus, again, the use of occultism is not surprising since the leader's "reach" becomes more than physical but supernatural. This is not uniquely African, as Bongmba points out by appealing to Nancy Reagan's consultations with astrologers during

---

[130] Bongmba, *Dialectics*, pp. 11–17. Although Bongmba is referring to the contemporary African political situation, he notes throughout the book that he is not treating these processes as uniquely African and that part of the problem of analyzing them is the tendency on the part of some scholars to treat Africa as somehow outside of the human community. Thus, although he does not mention this, one could see continuities between his analysis of the privatization of power and Elias Canetti's study of abusive acquisition of power over several millennia in *Crowds and Power*, trans. Carol Stewart (New York: Farrar, Straus, and Giroux, 1984).

[131] Bongmba provides copious cases to support his claims, the most familiar of which to some readers was the precolonial Yorùbá council of elders in Nigeria who were entrusted with "appointing, installing, supervising, and deposing chiefs," *Dialectics*, p. 11; see also pp. 177–9.

Ronald Reagan's presidency, but the difference, he reminds us, is that the US president is not expected to stay in office beyond two elected terms.[132] What is missing from most African nations, in other words, is a peaceful transition of leadership on a regular basis because of an absence of checks and balances on the scope of the leadership's power, which, in the end, becomes the reality of rulership over politics.

The realization of rulership over politics leads Bongmba to explore Mamdani's analysis of the postcolonial African state as a two-tier system of citizenship and indirect rule. He regards Mamdani's analysis as accurate with an important shortcoming. Mamdani

> does not discuss the role of religion and theology in the invention of the subject, especially in South Africa, where theological beliefs created apartheid. In particular, he has ignored the theological and anthropological literature[,] especially the work of Jean and John Comaroff and other scholars of South African history, who discuss the missionization, colonization, and proletarianization of South African society in remarkable detail.[133]

Here, Bongmba is bringing up the methodological flaw of working through a form of radical secularism in the human sciences that leads to ignoring the role of religious phenomena in human life. But, more significant, Bongmba decides to take on the existential political legacy of the failure to transcend the two-tier structure and its consequences in most (if not all) African countries: "Since political reforms have failed to overcome this legacy, Mamdani has concluded that Africa faced a new situation, Afro-pessimism."[134] The task at hand is to offer non-pessimistic responses to the African situation. In effect, Bongmba's work could be characterized as African existential political thought in that it addresses social and political nihilism head on, as does Cornel West in the US context, but with a more detailed set of arguments against critics of a constructive politics in Africa.[135] His argument is existential also in the sense that he places necessity as an *ex post facto* dimension of the social world, which means that the human being is in a contingent relationship with the future. What this means, then, is that failure cannot be a predisposition. Bongmba's ultimate

---

[132] *Ibid.*, p. 14.   [133] *Ibid.*, pp. 42–3.   [134] *Ibid.*, p. 42.

[135] I am referring to Cornel West's important essay "Nihilism in the Black Community," which is included in *Race Matters* (Boston, MA: Beacon Press, 1994).

response is that a genuinely public sharing of power facilitated by an environment of accountability for the leadership, which also requires meeting criteria of good governing, must be cultivated in Africa through rallying all of the resources necessary for their achievement. These resources include the development of a form of African civil society that could lead, in concert with Gyekye, to African forms of liberal distribution of power protected by social institutions that impose limits on the leadership. This leads him to offer a critique of Mamdani's argument that the task at hand is to develop democratic subjects who could in turn fight for their rights. "I do not think that this distinction between individual bearers of rights and the 'democratic subject' weakens the case for liberal democracy," writes Bongmba.

> I am also not convinced that one ought to separate a democratic "content" such as rights from the "democratic subject" as Mamdani does. The "democratic subject" ought to struggle for democracy, but I contend that democratic "contents" such as rights must inspire and propel the struggle. The needs of each political community ought to determine the democratic content, and all democratic subjects should have the right to choose the vision and context of their struggle. Mamdani's disquiet about the imposition of nineteenth-century liberal ideas on Africa ought to be taken seriously, but I still think that liberal democratic ideals could be reformulated in the African setting.[136]

Bongmba then offers an existential phenomenological theory of social reality premised upon intersubjective relations through which to articulate and develop a "political ethics."[137] Here Bongmba's argument is in stream with the thought of other Africana existential philosophers who argue that dehumanization, exploitation, racism, colonialism, and hate are functions of a breakdown of social relations; the leadership, in effect, become solipsists, people whose radical sense of self becomes so inflated, narcissistic, and overwhelming that they live as though there is no one else in the world or worse – as though they are the world.[138] Bongmba is taking seriously the fact that social institutions play a role in cultivating or blocking human

---

[136] *Ibid.*, p. 81.   [137] *Ibid.*, p. 139.

[138] See e.g. Lewis R. Gordon, *Bad Faith and Antiblack Racism* and *Existentia Africana*, ch. 4. See, as well, the essays in Robert Birt (ed.), *The Quest for Community and Identity: Critical Essays in Africana Social Philosophy* (Lanham, MD: Rowman & Littlefield, 2002), and, as well, discussions of various thinkers in this book, above.

relationships, and that leaders in structures without accountability are literally in worlds without others.

A question to consider here, among others, is the status of agents in Bongmba's (and Mbembe's) thought. As greedy, manipulating, and cunning as the leadership may be, there are many stages of their efforts that develop before the Hobbesian situation of, in effect, violence against the people takes place. In other words, it is not necessarily the case that public opinion plays no role in the process of the privatization of power. On this matter, the South African Lemba philosopher Rabson Wuriga offers an explanation for why and how this process of legitimation along the way to privatization of power is possible. Many scholars of the postcolonial moment often forget or ignore the realities of colonialism. But for the people who lived through colonialism and decolonization, the scale of humiliation meted out by colonizers and settlers was sufficiently traumatic to enable the individuals who fought against such forces to become men, and sometimes women, of the people. Put differently, a bond is established between the people and the anti-colonial leadership.[139] Wuriga calls this the "revolutionary bond." The logic of this bond is that one should be loyal to someone who fought on behalf of indigenous African peoples and against white supremacist settlers. It is not only an act of gratitude for formal decolonization but also a response to a historical fact: the modern European world has difficulty seeing the humanity of black people. Although the counter argument is that the indigenous African leaders have also not proven themselves to be trustworthy, the historical weight of European and Euro-American and Euro-Australian antiblack racist activities wins the day. A bad African leader may be disgracing his nation, but his acts are within a specified territory, not over the entire black diaspora. The history of antiblack racism among the European nations and their extensions that constitute the West reveals a war against the entire black world. Thus, the (often wise) reluctance to trust whites when it comes to the welfare of black people leads to putting stock in black leadership, however volatile their record might be, and the ensuing logic of like-with-like-kind follows the slippery slope into the kinds of intra-African racism that Fanon predicted in *The Wretched of the Earth*.

---

[139] Rabson Wuriga, "Revolutionary Bond and Opposition Politics in Post-Independent Africa: The Case of Zimbabwe," *Newsletter on Philosophy and the Black Experience* (forthcoming).

In all, in the path from Fanon to Bongmba, we see, then, the three themes of philosophical anthropology, social transformation and liberation, and reflection on reason come to the fore in a portrait of philosophy that engages the world in matters of the age-old consequence of life and death. The debates between African philosophers on social and political responses to these concerns reveal the global significance of African thought, for the problem of a two-tier structure of citizenship and rule and the privatization of power no doubt strike North American, European, and Australian readers with chilling familiarity as one thinks of the course of eroding civil liberties and enriching and bolstering oligarchical approaches over all other forms of rule that governments in first world countries have taken over the past decade. What the rest of the world stands to learn from Africa, if I may use an expression from John and Jean Comaroff, may very well be a renewed understanding of the vital character of thought in the age-old proverb of our not being able to live by bread alone.

Conclusion

It is impossible to cover every dimension of so vast an area of thought as Africana philosophy in one volume. It is my hope that the explorations and reflections in this book have offered the reader some insight into this important field of study. At its core is the paradox of reason, that reason must be able to evaluate itself, which means it must transcend itself.

That we cannot control all of the conditions through which and by which reason is manifested does not mean we should abandon it. Wilhelm Amo, Ottobah Cugoano, Anténor Firmin, W. E. B. Du Bois, Anna Julia Cooper, Frantz Fanon, and Steve Bantu Biko understood this. They knew that the misuse of rationality does not entail the elimination of activities that enable us to meet each other with dignity and respect. Thinking and language, resources of the mind made concrete in a social world rich in symbolic meaning, have brought much to our species in, from the standpoint of the cosmos, not even a blink in the unfolding of time. Africana philosophy is one of those resources, one born, as Leonard Harris characterized its African-American line, of struggle.

Africana philosophy exemplifies what it means to do philosophy in a hostile world. Its practitioners are aware that, like Caliban in Shakespeare's *Tempest*, what they do, and sometimes they themselves, appear to the Prospero-inspired world of Eurocentric philosophy more as the production of beasts than creatures of reason. Yet there is an ironic dimension of this misrepresentation. Recall our discussion of Plato's *Symposium*. Socrates' lover Alcibiades intrudes upon the party after the invited guests have completed their speeches on love. Learning of the topic under discussion, he decides to speak on his beloved, Socrates, whose countenance, he reminds us, is far from beautiful. He speaks of the ugly object of his affection as emanating a unique, intoxicating beauty, a way of thinking that brings one to higher levels of understanding through great toil and suffering. In speaking of his love of the philosopher, Alcibiades creates a doubled moment of revealing what it is to love the lover of wisdom and to become poisoned, which is what intoxication is, by such pursuits. The love of wisdom is revealed to come to us from an encounter with the superficially ugly; it is a function of our ability to see beyond what things at first appear to be. It is not a stretch, then, to argue, as black theologians such as Howard Thurman and James Cone have argued about the message of a God of the oppressed, or the Moor Ibn Rushd, who attempted to articulate a voice of reason along-side the demands of faith, that perhaps Africana philosophy too exemplifies the spirit of even its persecutors' greatest ancestor. The spirit of the gadfly continues, after all, in the contradictions it offers to the narcissistic consciousness of the modern world, and in so doing its practitioners remind all of us of the challenge of reason always to look further.

Guide to further reading

This is the first comprehensive treatment of Africana philosophy to be offered in a single volume. The information on each work I have discussed is available in the footnotes. Aside from this text, the Stanford Online Encyclopedia of Philosophy includes a section on Africana philosophy that the reader might find useful. For more on the areas of Africana philosophy discussed in this volume, the reader is also encouraged to consult the following texts, which I have selected because of the comprehensiveness of some and the movements stimulated by others.

For African philosophy

The Companion to African Philosophy, ed. Kwasi Wiredu, Malden, MA: Blackwell Publishers, 2004. This anthology is the best in the field. It is well conceived, with discussions that do not place North Africa out of Africa. Another strength of this volume is that it offers discussions of the philosophical arguments of African philosophers. A shortcoming of some texts is that they present the biographies of African philosophers over and against their thought.

In terms of detailed monographs on African philosophy, D. A. Masolo's *African Philosophy in Search of Identity* (1994) is comprehensive and erudite. For beginners, Barry Hallen's *A Short History of African Philosophy* (2002) is concise and useful. Both are published in Indianapolis by Indiana University Press.

The classic works in the field such as those written by Ibn Rushd, Wilhelm Amo, Cugoano, Fanon, Cabral, Biko, and others have been discussed and documented in the main text. There are certain recent monographs that have stimulated professional philosophical debates and with which advanced scholars and students of the field are expected to be familiar. To make this bibliography brief, I will only list a small set of texts here. They include, but are not limited to, the following.

Kwame Anthony Appiah, *In My Father's House: Africa in the Philosophy of Culture*, New York: Oxford, 1992. This work has stimulated debates on the role of race in the formation of pan-African thought. The author offers several novel conceptual tools that have affected much of the discussion in analytical philosophical treatments of race and racism, and the work has also stimulated a critical discussion on topics ranging from the study of gender and colonization to debates in African aesthetics.

John Ayotunde Isola Bewaji, *Beauty and Culture: Perspectives in Black Aesthetics*, Ibadan, Nigeria: Spectrum Books, 2003. Although not as known as the other texts because of the limits of distributing work published in Africa, this is an important volume that organizes questions of disciplinary formation and the relationship of African philosophy to more explicit philosophies of culture.

Kwame Gyekye, *An Essay on African Philosophical Thought: The Akan Conceptual Scheme*, rev. edn, Philadelphia: Temple University Press, 1995 (first edition 1987). This work is one of the living classics of the field. It offers an integration of critical analysis in dialogue with traditional African philosophical thought (sage philosophy) and presents, through a detailed discussion of Akan thought, a contemporary example of African philosophical work. The work offers novel discussions of topics ranging from ontology and theodicy to epistemology and ethics.

Kwame Gyekye, *Tradition and Modernity: Philosophical Reflections on the African Experience*, New York and Oxford: Oxford University Press, 1997. This is an important work in recent African political philosophy. It offers a theory of modern communitarianism and presents one of the few cases (along with Appiah) for a liberal political philosophy in Africa.

Mahmood Mamdani, *Citizen and Subject: Contemporary Africa and the Legacy of Late Colonialism*, Princeton, NJ: Princeton University Press, 1996. This work has inaugurated much debate on the understanding of colonization, liberalism, and the postcolonial state. It has stimulated a critical literature of both rejection and support of its discussion of the rule-governed indigenous communities versus a settlement citizenship as well as the author's analysis of how deracialized states could be used in the interest of heavily racialized and unequal civil societies.

Achille Mbembe, *On the Postcolony*, Berkeley, CA: University of California Press, 2001. There is almost an obverse relationship between proponents of Mamdani's text and those in support of Mbembe's. This work is considered a prime exemplar of postmodernist African thought, although there are concrete connections that have been developed from its themes, especially the privatization of violence and power.

John Mbiti, *African Religion and Philosophy*, 2nd enlarged and rev. edn, Oxford: Heinemann, 1990. Although this text originally came to print in the 1970s, it is included here because of the continued debate it has stimulated over the conception of time in African thought.

Valentin Y. Mudimbe, *The Invention of Africa: Gnosis, Philosophy, and the Order of Knowledge*, Bloomington, IN: Indiana University Press, 1988. This is the text that initiated the discussion of invention in African philosophy. It also, more than any other work, inaugurated contemporary African philosophy in the Anglophone academy.

Oyèrónké Oyewùmí, *The Invention of Women: Making an African Sense of Western Gender Discourses*, Minneapolis: University of Minnesota Press, 1997. Although Africana feminist philosophy was under discussion in journals and anthologies, this work offered a novel discussion of invention that radicalized not only the question of African history but also the scope and tensions of philosophical anthropologies that presuppose, even in the instances of constructivists analyses, a transcendental, gendered subject.

Nkiru Uwechia Nzegwu, *Family Matters: Feminist Concepts in African Philosophy of Culture*, Albany, NY: State University of New York Press, 2006. This text takes the constructivist thesis to the question of family formation and offers a critical anthropology that calls for an African feminist philosophy without a closed conception of a female subject.

Théophile Obenga, *Ancient Egypt and Black Africa*, Chicago, IL: Karnak House, 1992 and *African Philosophy: The Pharaonic Period: 2780–330 BC*, Popenguine, Senegal: ANKH, 2004. These two books are perhaps the most influential philosophical treatments of Diop's call for a close study of ancient Egyptian thought as African thought. It has stimulated a contemporary debate on the ancient philosophical world.

Tsenay Serequeberhan, *The Hermeneutics of African Philosophy: Horizon and Discourse*, New York: Routledge, 1994. This work is the main exemplar of African Euro-continental philosophy. It is inspired by the thought of Martin Heidegger and Hans Gorg-Gadamer on the one hand, and Frantz Fanon and Amílcar Cabral on the other.

Kwasi Wiredu, *Cultural Universals and Particulars: An African Perspective*, Bloomington, IN: Indiana University Press, 1996. There are many brilliant subtleties in this work. It offers clear, methodical discussions of the conditions of cross-cultural communication and critical discussions of Cartesianism as they emerge in Akan thought. It is a work that deserves study in its own right.

For African-American and Afro-British philosophy

A bona fide classic is *Philosophy Born of Struggle: Anthology of Afro-American Philosophy from 1917*, ed. Leonard Harris, Dubuque, IA: Kendall/Hunt, 1983. There are two versions of this text. The second edition is nearly entirely different from the first. This text pretty much created the academic study of the field. Both editions offer discussions either by or on nearly every central figure in African-American philosophy.

Another classic anthology is *African-American Perspectives and Philosophical Traditions*, ed. John Pittman, New York: Routledge, 1997. It was originally a special issue of the *Philosophical Forum* (1992). The main strength of this anthology is the excellence of the essays. They are philosophical in their own right, and many of them have been reprinted many times and have framed many of the debates ranging from discussions of race and xenophobia to modernism and metaphilosophy.

Reflections: An Anthology of African-American Philosophy, ed. James Montmarquet and William Hardy, offers a broad spectrum of influential essays in the field.

The Companion to African-American Philosophy, ed. Tommy Lott and John Pittman, Malden, MA: Blackwell Publishers, 2003, is perhaps the best recent anthology of essays by professional philosophers and innovators from related disciplines. The essays in this volume are not meant to be encyclopedic and stand as philosophical arguments in their own right.

African American Philosophers: 17 Conversations, ed. George Yancy, New York: Routledge, 1997, offers an insight into the lives and thought of recent African-American philosophers. Yancy is a philosopher himself, and this is reflected in the high quality of the questions he asked each interviewer. These interviews are much referenced and discussed in the field, and they offer much on its recent history.

Existence in Black: An Anthology of Black Existential Philosophy, ed. Lewis R. Gordon, New York: Routledge, 1997, offers philosophical essays by scholars in philosophy, religious thought, intellectual history, and political theory. Although black existentialism was known in its literary form, this text formerly inaugurated the field in professional philosophy. It is also a text used in existentialism courses, which makes it a bridge between Africana philosophy and other areas of philosophy.

A Companion to African-American Studies, ed. Lewis R. Gordon and Jane Anna Gordon, Malden, MA: Blackwell Publishers, 2006, and *Not Only the Master's Tools: African-American Studies in Theory and Practice*, ed. Lewis R. Gordon and Jane Anna Gordon, Boulder, CO: Paradigm Publishers, 2006, are two anthologies that are heavily influenced by philosophical thought. Together they offer important discussions not available in the other anthologies, such as more engagement with the Francophone and Hispanophone contributions to African-American philosophy, critical formulations of its location in African-American studies, and articulations of an African-American decolonial epistemology.

Influential recent monographs that have organized debates in the field include, *inter alia*, the following.

Linda Martín Alcoff, *Visible Identities: Race, Gender, and the Self*, New York: Oxford University Press, 2006. This work, which puts together important essays by the author from works that span little more than a decade, is one of the best discussions of the role of identity in recent philosophy, and it engages the thought of many African-American and Latin philosophers. It is the leading volume in Afro-Latino American philosophy.

K. Anthony Appiah and Amy Gutmann, *Color Conscious*, with Amy Gutmann, Princeton, NJ: Princeton University Press, 1996. Along with Appiah's *In My Father's House*, this work situates much of the analytical discussions of race and racism in contemporary African American philosophy.

Molefi Kete Asante, *The Afrocentric Idea*, rev. edn, Philadelphia: Temple University Press, 1998. There are many works by this author (65 books as of 2007), but this one is the most concise summary of Afrocentricity/Africology. This work has stimulated debates on the relationship of Afrocentricity to other areas of Africana thought. Most significant, it is one of the main texts against the applied approach to Africana philosophy. It is a defense of the field standing on its own terms. Its discussions include a formulation of African-American philosophy as African philosophy, a philosophy of history, a philosophy of communication and language, and a radical theory of agency. It has stimulated many debates, some of which have been outlined in the fourth chapter of this introduction.

Bernard Boxill, *Blacks and Social Justice*, rev. edn, Lanham, MD: Rowman & Littlefield, 1992. This is a pioneering work in analytical liberal political philosophy. Many of the debates in analytical political philosophy are built on it, and it serves as a bridge between Africana philosophy and other areas of philosophy, in this case, Anglo-analytical political theory.

Patricia Hill Collins, *Black Feminist Thought: Knowledge, Consciousness, and the Politics of Empowerment*, rev. 10th anniversary edn, New York: Routledge, 2000. This, too, is a pioneering work. A central feature is its focus on standpoint epistemology and postmodern feminist thought. It too is a text that bridges many gaps. It has been especially influential in bridging gaps between African-American philosophy and feminist philosophy and women's studies.

James H. Cone, *Black Theology and Black Power*, New York: Seabury Press, 1969, and *A Black Theology of Liberation*, Philadelphia: Lippincott, 1970. These are among the works that brought philosophy of liberation to the North American Academy and inaugurated Black Liberation Theology. They were central in invigorating Africana philosophy of religion and have stimulated debates in nearly every area of Africana philosophy.

Paul Gilroy, *The Black Atlantic: Modernity and Double Consciousness*, Cambridge, MA: Harvard University Press, 1993. This is an extraordinarily influential work across many fields. It has led to the formation of Black Atlantic studies programs and it has stimulated debates in African-American and Afro-British philosophy on the study of Hegel's master–slave dialectic from the standpoint of slaves. The author argues that the enslaving dimensions of modernity hold within them as well their transformation from the underside with more cosmopolitan possibilities. It is also a work that has brought the resources of North American philosophical categories to the British context.

David Theo Goldberg, *Racist Culture*, Oxford: Blackwell, 1993. This is also a very influential work in race theory. It stands as a historicist work that presents the case for the study of racisms, instead of only racism, and for the understanding of why culture and rationality cannot be separated.

Lewis R. Gordon, *Bad Faith and Antiblack Racism*, Amherst, NY: Humanity/Prometheus Books, 1999 (originally published in Atlantic Highlands, NJ, by Humanities International Press, 1995), and Lewis R. Gordon, *Fanon and the Crisis of European Man: An Essay on Philosophy and the Human Sciences*, New York: Routledge, 1995. These two books inaugurated the phenomenological and recent decolonial epistemic movements in Africana philosophy. They are also the books that initiated, along with *Existence in Black*, black existentialism in professional philosophy. As well, they have initiated discussions on philosophical anthropology and, through the theory of disciplinary decadence, the role of disciplinary formation and metaphilosophy.

Lewis R. Gordon, *Existentia Africana: Understanding Africana Existential Thought*, New York: Routledge, 2000. This text outlines and offers the author's response to the main problems in Africana existential philosophy through a discussion of several African-American philosophers and religious thinkers.

Joy James, *Transcending the Talented Tenth: Black Leaders and American Intellectuals*, Foreword by Lewis R. Gordon. New York: Routledge. This is a work in black political thought that argues for engagement with the black radical tradition in black feminist thought.

Bill E. Lawson and Howard McGary, *Between Slavery and Freedom: Philosophy and American Slavery*, Bloomington, IN: Indiana University Press, 1992. This work presents the case for analytical philosophical discussion of slavery and its impact in contemporary liberal political philosophy.

Charles W. Mills, *The Racial Contract*, Ithaca, NY: Cornell University Press, 1999. This work has brought debates on social contract theory to the fore in African-American and Afro-Caribbean political philosophy. It is also a text that has bridged some divides since it calls for dialogue with liberal political theory, especially on debates on the significance of ideal social contract theory.

Lucius T. Outlaw, Jr., *On Race and Philosophy*, New York: Routledge, 1996. This influential text offers the first philosophical formulation of Africana philosophy, engagements with deconstruction, and a theory of race that does not require its dismissal in African-American life.

Cedric Robinson, *An Anthropology of Marxism*, Aldershot: Ashgate, 2001. This is perhaps the most creative recent engagement with Marxist thought in Africana philosophy. The author's treatment works through the three themes of philosophical anthropology, social transformation, and metacritique of reason.

Cornel West, *Race Matters*, Boston: Beacon Press, 1993. This is perhaps the most popular recent work in African-American philosophy. It is accessible to lay people, and the author offers discussion of a range of issues in popular culture and American politics. Its most enduring discussion is the chapter on nihilism in black communities.

Cornel West, *Prophesy, Deliverance! An Afro-American Revolutionary Christianity: An Afro-American Revolutionary Christianity*, anniversary edn, Louisville, KY: Westminster John Knox Press, 2002 (first edn, 1982). This classic work inaugurates prophetic pragmatism. It has many novel discussions ranging from the role of deconstruction and genealogical methods in the study of racism to a theory of humanistic responses to racism.

Naomi Zack, *Race and Mixed Race*, Philadelphia, PA: Temple University Press, 1994. This book builds on many of the arguments in Appiah's work and argues for the fictionality of race. It takes the argument to the point of arguing against the moral validity of race on the grounds of its being false and for the notion of mixed-race people as "raceless." It has stimulated much criticism not only from opponents of mixed-race theory but among proponents as well.

In Afro-Caribbean philosophy

The first anthology explicitly devoted to Caribbean philosophy is *Shifting the Geography of Reason I: Gender, Science, and Religion*, ed. Marina Paola Banchetti-Robino and Clevis Ronald Headley, Kingston, Jamaica: University of West Indies Press, 2001. It is part of a series of anthologies organized through the Caribbean Philosophical Association.

New Caribbean Thought: a Reader, ed. Brian Meeks and Folke Lindahl, expands the discussion in terms of theorists from a variety of perspectives.

Influential recent monographs are the following.

B. Anthony Bogues, *Black Heretics, Black Prophets: Radical Political Intellectuals*, New York: Routledge, 2003. This book presents a theory of Caribbean prophetic thought in which Rastafari take center stage. The text brings Caribbean political thought in dialogue with North American and British Africana political thought.

Sibylle Fischer, *Modernity Disavowed: Haiti and Cultures of Slavery in the Age of Revolution*, Durham, NC: Duke University Press, 2004. This work has transformed the discussion of the Haitian Revolution in Caribbean thought. Nearly every important theme, including the discussion of Hegel's master–slave dialectic, receives a novel reading through the author's analysis of disavowal. As well, the text examines the philosophy of history through raising the question of its formation as an avowal of supposedly truthful narratives premised upon disavowal.

Edouard Glissant, *Caribbean Discourses*, trans. with introduction by J. Michael Dash, Charlottesville, VA: University of Virginia Press, 1989. This is the major text of the *creolité* movement and one of the best exemplars of Caribbean poeticism.

Paget Henry, *Caliban's Reason: Introducing Afro-Caribbean Philosophy*, New York: Routledge, 2000. This is the most influential recent text in Afro-Caribbean philosophy. It organizes the entire field from poeticism to historicism, analytical thought, traditional Afro-Caribbean thought, poststructural analysis, existentialism, phenomenology, Marxism, *creolité*, and offers discussion of nearly every central figure in the Anglophone and Francophone Caribbean. For a growing understanding of the Hispanophone and Lusophone Caribbean, the readers should examine the *Shifting the Geography of Reason* anthologies.

Walter Mignolo, *The Idea of Latin America*, Malden, MA: Blackwell, 2006. This work examines the French formation of Latin America as a founding act of erasing the African and indigenous American dimensions of the region. This work explores the task of developing decolonial epistemologies as a response among others. It also brings Hispanophone and Lusophone elements to the fore.

Journals

Although scholars in all areas of Africana philosophy publish in a variety of journals, there are some whose focus is African diasporic thought.

The American Philosophical Association Newsletter for Philosophy and the Black Experience is an important resource for short articles and announcement in the field.

Philosophia Africana (formerly *The Journal of Africana Philosophy*), formerly ed. by Emmanuel Eze (1963–2007), speaks for itself.

The C. L. R. James Journal: A Review of Ideas, edited by Paget Henry, publishes articles in Africana philosophy, although the majority of the articles focus on Caribbean thought.

Sapina: A Bulletin of the Society for African Philosophy in North America has writings by nearly every influential scholar in African philosophy in its archives.

Every journal in Africana studies such as, *inter alia*, *The Journal of Africana Studies*, *The Journal of Black Studies*, *The Western Journal of Black Studies, African Studies Review*, has published articles in Africana philosophy. The same applies to journals generally designated under philosophy, political science, religion, literature, and cultural studies.

Index

Abdou, Imam Muhammad, 190
Abolitionist movement (US), 49
Abraham, William, 36
Academy of St. Louis, 147
Accasa (Fanti king), Ambro, 40, 42
Achebe, Chinua, 195, 218
Ackerman, Bruce, 230
Addell, Sandra, 78
Adeleke, Tunde, 48
affirmative action, 112, 211, 225
Africa, 3, 22, 25, 34, 62, 78, 108, 132; cities
    in, 222; etymology of, 15, 17, 116; history
    of, 24; indigenous languages of, 17;
    modern European colonization of, 189;
    North, 4, 8, 15, 189; Phoenician, Greek,
    Roman, Visigoth, Arabic invasions and
    colonizations of northern regions, 189;
    political situation of, 199; Sahara-
    Sahelian region, 186; trade in and
    across, 18, 25
African(s), 10, 13, 14, 25, 28, 31, 41, 109;
    academic philosophers, 199; ancient, 15,
    16; authenticity standards on, 199, 207,
    242; becoming black, 78, 79; Christian
    salvation of, 38, 64; conceptions of time,
    187, 200–2; cosmopolitanism, 205, 233;
    creolizations of, 199, 217; differences
    and disunity of, 206; historians, 203;
    historicist–poeticist divide, 219;
    infantilization of, 224; political thought
    (see political theory/political thought);
    secular humanist academics, 194–5;
    value systems, 200–2, 208, 235;
    Westernized, 199, 207; writing, 198–9

Africana, versus black, 1
Africana philosophy, passim, but see
    especially, 248, 249; African, 7, 15, 35,
    109, 185, 208; African-American, 69, 91,
    109, 171, 172, 173; Canadian, 110, 120,
    203; Caribbean, 116, 157, 159, 167, 173,
    175, 183, 184, 203, 217; as a modern
    philosophy, 21, 37; particular, 31; a
    species of Africana thought, 1; exclusion
    of, 15; historical scope of, 15; Latin
    American, 181; metaphilosophy, 14;
    Native American, 105
African Community League (ACL), 163
African National Congress, 193, 225
Africanism, 204
Afrikaaner(s), 193
Afro-Arab(s), 22, 23, 125, 159
Afrocentricity, 106–10, 138; as an
    existential philosophy, 139
Afrocentrism, 91, 106–10, 204
Agbeyebiawo, Daniel, 73
agency, 108, 129, 139, 141, 167, 175, 229,
    247; in African cosmologies, 200, 203;
    female, 210; adverbial, 239
Ahluwalia, Pal, 194, 226, 227, 228, 229,
    230, 231; critique of Mamdani, 228
Ahmed, Sara, 153, 154, 155; on disciplines,
    153; Fanon, 154; queering
    phenomenology, 153; tables/tabling, 154
Aidoo, Ama Ata, 195
Ajumako, in Ghana, 39
Ajzenstat, Oona, 212
Akan, the, 132, 186, 187, 235; (see also
    Gyekye, Kwami; Wiredu, Kwasi)

Akron, Ohio, 102

Al-Andalus, 4

Alcibiades, 250

Alcoff, Linda Martín, 121, 141, 144, 145,
146, 147, 148, 149, 155, 180, 181, 182; on
Judith Butler, 146, 148, 150;
hermeneutics, 147; interpellation, 146,
148; phenomenology, 147, 148; race, 147,
148, 149; recognition, 146; theorizing
the self, 147; women, 147, 148

Algeria, 167; Algerian War, 167; Algerian
National Liberation Front, 167; Hippo
(ancient), 188

Ali, Ben, 125

Allen, Ernest, Jr., 77

Allen, Samuel W., 73

America(s), the, 8, 17, 42; conquest of, 28;
colonies of, 35; Americanism, 96;
post-continental critique of, 181

American Declaration of Independence, 56

American Negro Academy, 51, 54

Americans, Native, 15, 28, 70, 105, 157,
158, 217

Amerigo Vespucci (see Vespucci, Amerigo)

Amin, Samir, 194

Amo, Anton-Wilhelm, 35, 36, 37, 38, 39,
189, 249

African identity of critique of
Cartesianism, 38

Amsterdam, 35

ancestors, 187, 205, 209, 217, 235

Anderson, Elijah, 75, 78

Anderson, Victor, 97

Andrews, William L., 73

Anikulapo-Kuti, Fela, 195

anthropology, 13, 60, 162, 196;
philosophical, 13, 60, 80, 91, 93, 98, 115,
123, 132, 139, 142, 145, 168, 170, 171,
173, 243, 248

Anthropology Society (French), 57

Antigua, 172

anti-Semitism, 115

Appiah, Kwame Anthony, 52, 111, 112, 117,
194, 205, 206, 230, 233; opposition to
communalism, 233; (see also Gyekye,
Kwame)

Aptheker, Herbert, 30, 73

Arabic, 159

Arawaks, 157

Aristotle, 26, 29, 63, 85, 124, 130, 146, 190,
235

Armah, Ayi Kwei, 195

Asante (people), 196

Asante, Molefi Kete, 103, 106, 107, 108, 109,
110, 138; on Africology, 108, 109; agency
in history, 108, 138; classical African
civilization, 108; critique of
postmodernism, 108, 110; djed, 109;
existentialism of, 110; homelessness,
138; language, 108

Asia(ns), iii, 3, 15, 25, 62, 78, 116, 199, 225,
242; Western, 17, 27

Atlanta University, 74

Augustine, St. bishop of Hippo, 26, 43, 188,
189, 195

Austin, Allan D., 99

Australia, 78, 158, 223

Averroës [Ibn Rushd], 23, 24, 190, 249

Axim, Ghana, 35, 37

Aziz Al-Azmeh, Ibn Khaldūn, 24

Aztecs, 30

Babbit, Susan E., and Sue Campbell, 79

Bacon, Francis, 30

bad faith, 140, 141, 173

Badawi, Abdel-Rahman, 190, 191

Bahamas, the, 4

Baldwin, James, 95, 134, 135

Bales, Kevin, 18, 161

Balibar, Etienne, 228

Bambara, Toni Cade, 101

Bamikole, Lawrence, 180

Banchetti-Robino, Marina Paola, 184

Banneker, Benjamin, 31

Bantu linguistic group, 15

Barbados, 171, 184

Barnes, Jonathan, 214

Barrington, Massachusetts, 73

Bauman, Zygmunt, 223

beauty and ugliness, 135

Beauvoir, Simone de, 133, 152

Bell, Bernard W., and Emily Grosholz, 73

Berbers, 159, 189

Bergson, Henri, 148

Berkeley, Bishop George, 30

Berlin, Germany, 74, 92

Berlin Conference (1884–5), 206

Bernal, Martin, 1, 2, 6, 197

Bernasconi, Robert, 120

Bernasconi, Robert, and Anika Mann, 105

Bethesda, Maryland, 167

Bewaji, John Ayotunde Isola, 39, 180, 197

Bhabha, Homi, 81, 192

Bhan, Esme, 70, 71, 72

Biko, Steve Bantu, 120, 193, 249

biology, 148, 215, 216–17

Birt, Robert, 121, 122

Black Consciousness, 120, 193; (see also Biko, Steve; Maart, Rozena)

Black Women's Club Movement, 54

Blida-Joinville Hospital/Frantz Fanon Hospital, 167

Blues, the, 97

Blyden, George Wilmot, 56, 63, 64

Bodunrin, P. O., 198

Boers, 193

Bogues, B. Anthony, 6, 165, 172, 177, 180, 218, 221

Bolland, O. Nigel, 183

bondage, 14; (see also slavery)

Bongmba, Elias Kifon, 194, 210, 211, 212, 213, 242, 244, 246, 248; critique of Mamdani, 245; on privatization of power, 242, 243, 247; tfu, 212, 213

botany, 85

Boxill, Bernard, 33, 111, 112, 171, 176

Boxill, Jeanette (Jan), 184

Braithwaite, Kamau, 218

Brandon, E. P., 183

Braunschweig-Wofenbüttel (duke), Anton Ulrich von, 35

Broad, Jacqueline, 11

Brock, Lisa, and Otis Cunningham, 169

Brown, Scott, 107

Buddhists, 10

Buhle, Paul, 165

Burke, Edmund, 16

Burrell, Jocelyn, 191

Butler, Judith, 121, 146, 148, 150, 151, 208, 216; (see also Alcoff, Linda); on Fanon, 121

Cabral, Amílcar, 192, 222, 236

Caliban, 167, 174, 249

Cambridge University, 51

Cameroon, 212

Campbell, Alexander, 40

Camus, Albert, 84, 195

Canetti, Elias, 244

Canada, 116, 157, 159–60, 167, 171

Cannon, Katie Geneva, 102

capitalism, 107, 129–30, 223; state, 165; (see also slave trades; Marxism)

Capitein, Jacobus, 37, 38

Caribbean, 15, 56, 100, 169, 174; creolization, 177, 178, 179, 183; etymology of, 157; historicists, 173, 175, 176, 177, 217; Indo-, 178, 179; poeticists, 175, 176, 177, 217; political economy of, 178

Caribbean Philosophical Association, 181, 184

Caribs, the, 157; etymological basis of "cannibal," 157

Carolina (colony of), 34, 35

Casas, Bartolomé de Las, 28, 29, 158; on slavery, 28, 29, 130

Cassirer, Ernst, 84, 124, 186

Castro, Fidel, 169

Caute, David, 167

Caws, Peter, 11

center(s), 3, 4, 17; centeredness, 109; of the world, 21; de-, 226

Central Intelligence Agency (CIA), 230

Centre for Contemporary Cultural Studies (Birmingham, UK), 128, 176

Césaire, Aimé, 14, 89, 164, 166, 218; on Negritude, 166, 184

Césaire, Suzanne, 166, 184

Chandler, Nahum Dimitri, 76, 78

Charlemagne, The Emperor, 22

Charles I (king), 28

Charles, Asselin, 59

Chekhov, Anton, 95, 136

Cherki, Alice, 81, 84, 136, 167, 169
Chevannes, Barry, 164
China, 162; ancient, 6, 9, 30
Christendom, 4, 21, 158
Christianity, 4, 46, 47, 52, 53, 95, 130, 137, 213; Coptic, 188; Afro-Christian philosophy, 188; Episcopalian, 51, 188; Ethiopian, 188
Christians, 4, 213, 223; missionaries, 213; South African political Christian humanism, 194
citizenship, 116, 161, 162, 228; egalitarian demands of, 224
Civil Rights March (1963), 74
civil society, 42, 225, 226, 227, 240; black, 227; racist, 227
Cixous, Hélène, 195
Clarke, Richard, 183
class struggle, 129; (*see also* Marxism)
C.L.R. James Journal, The, 173
Coetzee, John, 195
Collins, Patricia Hill, 103, 104, 106, 107, 108
colonialism, *passim*, but especially, 85, 88, 99, 116, 141, 159, 168, 170, 173, 175, 204, 220, 221, 222–5, 226–30, 241, 242, 247; inspiring hatred, 222; neo-, 226, 229
colony, *passim*, but see especially, 16; neo-, 241; post-, 229, 240, 241, 242
Colored(s), South African, 193, 225
Coltrane, John, 96
Columbia University, 70
Columbus, Christopher (Cristóbal Colón), 4, 16, 21, 28, 30, 116
Comaroff, John L., and Jean Comaroff, 193, 194, 220, 245, 248
committee on the Status of Blacks in Philosophy (American Philosophical Association), 137, 171
communication/communicability, 125, 153, 216; incommunicability, 125, 215
Communist Party USA, 74
Comte, August, 60
Conaway, Carol B., 47
Condé, Maryse, 218

Cone, James H., 96, 102, 137, 250
Confucius, 9
Congo, 206
Connah, Graham, 18
Conquistadors, 28
consciencism, 192
Conyers, James L., Jr., 74
Cooper, Anna Julia, 54, 55, 59, 69, 70, 71, 90, 100, 104, 112, 249; as black feminist, 71, 72, 100; theory of value, 71, 72
Cooper, George, 70, 90
Copernicus, Nicolaus, 30
Cordoba, 190
Cornell, Drucilla, 121
Corsica, 26
Cortez, Hernando, 28
Cosway, Richard, and Mary Cosway, 40
Cotkin, George, 98
Covey, Edward, 50
Cox, Oliver C., 172
Creole, 108
Crisis magazine, 74
critical reflection, 8
Crummell, Alexander, 51, 52, 53, 64, 206; as institution builder, 53, 137; conservatism of, 52; critique of Marxism, 51; founding the American Negro Academy, 53, 54; on black women, 52, 54; on "Leaders of Revenue," 54; philosophy of civilization, 52, 53, 73
Cruse, Harold, 106
Cuban Revolution, 169
Cugoano, Quobna Ottobah, 11, 40, 41, 42, 46, 189; adopted the name John Stewart, 40; critique of dominating political theory, 42; critique of Hume, 42; on language, 44, 45; on slavery, 41; theodicy, 42, 43, 44, 45
Cullen, Christopher, 8
cultural studies, 101, 173, 220
culture, *passim*, but see especially, 93, 110, 218; creolized, 133, 199; translation and indeterminacy of, 212
Curtin, Philip, 211
Curtin, Philip, Steven Feierman, Leonard Thompson, and Jan Vansina, 206, 211

Daigne, Soueyman Bachir, 194

Dallmayr, Fred, 21, 190

Dante Alighieri, 109, 222

Danticat, Edgwin, 184

Dark Ages, 23

Darwin, Charles, 53, 63

Dash, J. Michael, 59

Davis, Angela Y., 101, 105

Davis, Gregson, 164, 165

Davis, Robert, 5, 30

death, 50, 144, 186, 200;
   -bound-subjectivity, 116, 139–40;
   semiotics of, 240

decadence, 53, 141, 165, 183; disciplinary,
   183; teleological suspension of, 183; (see
   also Gordon, Lewis; Kierkegaard, Søren;
   Nietzsche, Friedrich)

decolonization, passim, but see especially,
   220–2, 247

Deconstruction, 197; (see also Derrida,
   Jacques)

Delany, Martin Robinson, 47, 48, 51, 55,
   64

Deloria, Vine, 99

DeMarco, Joseph P., 73

democracy, 131, 220; black self-rule, 225;
   development of, 246; hyper-, 232;
   libertarian, 223; parliamentary, 232;
   subjects, 240

Derrida, Jacques, 9, 81, 94, 112, 120, 125,
   195, 198, 230; deconstruction, 120, 123,
   129, 198; on différance, 125

Desai, Ashwin, 194, 228

Descartes, René, 10, 11, 21, 22, 24, 30, 43;
   dualism of, 38; on existential
   predication, 39; on mathematics, 44

Deuteronomy, Book of, 44

Dewey, John, 10, 93, 94, 95, 97, 233; (see
   also West, Cornel)

Diop, Cheikh Anta, 18, 26, 62, 108, 191

disappointment, 113

discipline(s), 153; (see also decadence;
   Foucault, Michel; Gordon, Lewis;
   Ahmed, Sara)

discovery, 204; age of, 196; etymology of,
   196

District Six, Cape Town, South Africa, 193

Djebar, Assia, 191, 195

Djed, 109

double consciousness; epistemological
   dimension of, 79; phenomenological
   aspect of, 79; potentiated, 177; (see also
   Du Bois, W. E. B.; Henry, Paget)

Dougla, 179

Douglass, Frederick, 49, 55, 58, 112, 122,
   136, 139

Dred Scott v. Sanford, 35

Du Bois, W. E. B., 37, 50, 55, 59, 69, 73, 74,
   81, 82, 90, 104, 112, 128, 163, 181, 206,
   238, 249; on double consciousness, 77,
   78, 79; history, 79, 80, 129, 136, 143, 177;
   problem people, 75, 76, 87, 114, 119, 126,
   141; secularized theodicy, 75, 76, 119; US
   Reconstruction, 80, 113; white
   normativity, 79; pragmatists' reading of,
   associated with pragmatism, 91

Dumas, Léon Gontian, 166

Dunbar, Paul Laurence, 55

Dussel, Enrique, 1, 2, 3, 17, 21, 22, 26, 88,
   181

Dutch East India Company, 36

Dworkin, Ronald, 230

Earl of Shaftesbury, 33

Ebonics, 108

Edwards, Jonathan, 98

Egypt (ancient), 2; Arab colonization of,
   187; Assyrian colonization of, 187;
   British colonization of, 187; etymology
   of, 2, 17, 108, 109; French colonization
   of, 187; Greek colonization of, 186;
   history of, 186; Hyksos invasion of, 187;
   Kushite colonization of, 187; Persian
   colonization of, 187; Roman
   colonization of, 187; Turkish/Ottoman
   colonization of, 187; (see also Km.t)

Egyptians (ancient), 6, 17, 26, 30, 107;
   Asianizing of, 62; cosmological views of,
   187

Eichhorn's Repertorium, 27

Einstein, Albert, 212

Elia, Nada, 191

Elisabeth von der Pfalz (of Bohemia or
    Princess Palatine), 11
Ellington, Duke, 96
Ellison, Ralph, v, 95, 126, 134
Emerson, Ralph Waldo, 98
Engels, Friedrich, 129, 130, 131, 170
England, 35, 41, 49, 128; abolitionist
    community in, 41; outlaw of slavery in,
    40
Enlightenment, 24, 30
epistemology, 10, 22, 79; colonial, 85, 143,
    167, 204–5, 236; relativism in, 210;
    standpoint, 103, 104, 106, 108, 183; as a
    politics, 125, 193
essence, 22, 124
essentialism, 103, 123, 127, 148; anti-, 123,
    127, 153, 208
ethics, 82, 87, 88, 98, 104, 105, 181, 211; as
    opposed to morals, 234, 236;
    Graeco-Latin pedestal, 214, 221; liberal,
    107, 115, 167, 188, 195;
    phenomenological, 213; responsibility
    for, 221; political, 246
Ethiopia(ns), 26, 27, 78, 198
etymology, 2
Euben, Roxanne, 21
Eurocentrism, 32, 62, 106, 110, 149, 166,
    174, 202, 219, 249
Europe, 5, 15, 18, 22, 23, 25, 36, 48, 63, 155;
    bourgeois revolution in, 231; expansion
    of, 24; treatment of blacks in, 37
Europeans, 5, 15, 25, 56, 99, 109, 162;
    civilization of, 52, 199; perspective, 238
evidence, 37, 142
existentialism and philosophy of existence,
    50, 53, 84, 98, 105, 106, 132–4, 169, 172,
    191; American, 98, 245, 246; (see also
    phenomenology; philosophy, existential)
Exodus, Book of, 43, 44
explanation, problem of, 75
exploration (modern), 3, 24, 29, 158, 159
Eze, Emmanuel, 219, 259

Fakhry, Majid, 190
Fanon, Frantz, 32, 39, 40, 42, 47, 48, 50,
    69, 80, 104, 110, 126, 128, 136, 140, 142,

149, 158, 166, 167, 168, 169, 170, 172,
    174, 176, 192, 209, 214, 218, 220, 221,
    222, 223, 230, 237, 239; as teleological
    suspension of philosophy, 82; existential
    phenomenologist, 84; on Aimé Césaire,
    166; epistemic colonization, 85, 141, 167,
    236; embodied schema, 152, 154;
    failure(s), 81, 85, 86, 119; human
    sciences, 87; language, 168; liberty and
    freedom, 83, 86, 157; narcissism, 86;
    nationalism and national consciousness,
    89, 192, 243; Negritude, 109, 157;
    neocolonialism, 90; nonbeing, 240;
    normality, 88; normative political
    theory, 88; phobogenesis, 134;
    postcolonialism, 90; postcolonial
    bourgeoisie, 90, 97, 221, 236;
    primitivism, 167; psychoanalysis, 85, 87,
    168; racism and colonialism, 41, 48, 85,
    88, 116, 167, 168; reason and rationality,
    81, 116, 167; recognition, 86, 87, 119,
    136, 140, 167, 168, 249; Self–Other
    dialectic, 87, 88, 168; sociogenesis, 84,
    85, 87, 118, 140, 143, 168, 237; the
    individual, 86; violence, 88, 161, 220;
    will in general and general will, 89, 222;
    (see also Rousseau, Jean-Jacques);
    phenomenological reduction of,
    85; postcolonial philosophy of, 85,
    89
Fanti (people), 196
Farrington, Benjamin, 63
Fascism, 120, 138, 232
Fasi, M. El, 78
Faulconer, James E., and Mark A. Wrathall,
    120
Feagin, Joe R., 33
Feder, Ellen K., 152
Fehrenbacher, Don E., 35
feminist thought, 71, 72, 100–2, 103–4,
    126, 184, 191; on embodiment and the
    body, 208; poststructural, 148, 207–10;
    womanist, 103
Ferdinand V, king of Castile, 4, 28,
    158
Ficek, Doug, 210

Finch, Charles S., III, 16, 18, 25, 27, 28, 78, 186, 187, 197; on Semitic classification, 28

Firmin, Anténor, 56, 57, 58, 59, 60, 61, 89, 162, 249; critique of Europeanizing and Asianizing Egypt, 62; Kant and Hegel, 60; of naturalistic reductionism, 60; polygenesis, 50; of racial difference, 60, 61; on the "primitive" as a modern construction, 162; regeneration, 62; social life, 62; underdevelopment, 62; republicanism of, 59, 63

Fischer, Sibylle, 57, 163

Fleur-Lobban, Carolyn, 58, 59

Foner, Philip S., 47

Foster, Guy Mark, 135

Foucault, Michel, 61, 81, 112, 129, 152, 162, 220, 228, 230; archaeological poststructuralism of, 129, 205; episteme, 119, 131, 173, 204; genealogical poststructuralism of, 123, 205

France, 36, 56, 167, 169

Frank, Philipp, 31

Frankfurt school critical theory, 120, 171

Franklin, Benjamin, 31

Franklin, Todd, and Renee Scott, 121

Frazier, E. Franklin, 97, 222

freedom, *passim*, but see especially, 14, 50, 51, 75, 133; assault on, 25, 27, 80, 114, 133, 135, 139, 172; as distinguished from liberty, 83, 86; seizing, 221

French Resistance, 167

French Revolution, 56

Freud, Sigmund, 120, 151, 212

Fryer, David, 153, 154, 186

Gadamer, Hans Georg, 124

Galileo (Galilei), 30

Garcia, Jorge, 181

Garrison, William Lloyd, 49

Garvey, Marcus, 163, 164

Gasset, José Ortega y, 224, 232

Gates, Henry Louis, Jr., 121

Gates, Sylvester James, 11, 12

Gendzier, Irene, 81, 167

genocide, 115

George III (king), 41

Germans, 6, 160

Geuss, Raymond, 233

Ghana, 74, 192, 230

Gibson, Nigel, 81, 228, 233, 238

Gilman, Sander, 194

Gilroy, Paul, 50, 78, 120, 151, 176, 177

Gines, Kathryn, 105, 106, 121, 133, 134, 152; existential defense of race, 152

Giroux, Henry, and Stanley Aronowitz, 248

Glaude, Eddie, Jr., 97

Glissant, Edouard, 176, 218

Gobineau, Count Arthur de, 58

God, 11, 43, 44, 76, 82, 137, 188, 189; Akan conception of, 188; Bantu-speaking people's conception of, 200–2; of the oppressed, 250

Goldberg, David Theo, 111, 118, 121, 194

good, the, 43

Goodin, Patrick, 180

Gooding-Williams, Robert, 121, 171

Gordimer, Nadine, 195

Gordon, Jane Anna, 14, 76, 77, 89, 149, 222

Gordon, Lewis R., 1, 11, 14, 18, 32, 50, 62, 69, 74, 76, 77, 81, 82, 95, 97, 99, 117, 120, 124, 125, 140, 142, 143, 144, 151, 173, 174, 182, 183, 187, 203, 206, 211, 224, 246; existential phenomenology of, 140, 141; postcolonial phenomenology, 141, 142; on bad faith, 140, 141; decolonized methodology, 141, 142, 182; double consciousness, 143; disciplinary decadence, 141, 182, 183; problem people, 142; epistemic closure, 143, 183; evidence, 142; incompleteness, 142; irreplaceability, 143; liberation, 141; options, 143; shifting the geography of reason, 182; social reality, 141, 143; teleological suspension of philosophy, 82, 153, 183; Cornel West, 95

Gottlieb, Karla, 57

Gracia, Jorge, 181

Gramsci, Antonio, 10, 128, 129

Granada, 4

Granny Nanny, 57

Grant, Jacquelyn, 72, 102

Greece (ancient), 2, 3, 6, 16, 23

Green, Thomas Hill, 94

Greenberg, Joseph, 27

Grenada, 40

Grimke, Archibald H., 56

Grimshaw, Anna, 165, 188

Grosfoguel, Ramón, Nelson
 Maldonado-Torres, and José Saldívar,
 78

guilt/blame/responsibility (*Schuld*), 160–1,
 162; (*see also* Jaspers, Karl)

Gutmann, Amy, 111

Guyana, 179

Guy-Sheftall, Beverly, and Johnetta B. Cole,
 55

Gyekye, Kwame, 10, 76, 107, 132, 133, 188,
 194, 199, 206, 207, 208, 209, 217, 230,
 231, 235, 239; critique of K. Anthony
 Appiah, 205, 206; on African
 authenticity, 199; communitarianism,
 230, 231, 232, 234, 235; humanism, 188;
 invention, 205, 206, 207, 208, 209;
 liberalism, 230, 231, 233, 246

Haiti (Hayti), 16, 50, 57, 58, 59, 60, 62, 160;
 US occupation and destablization of, 57,
 60, 163

Haitian Revolution, 56, 57, 71, 89, 160, 161,
 162, 165

Hall, Stuart, 128, 183

Hallen, Barry, 201, 202

Ham, 44, 144

Hanke, Lewis, 29, 99

Hare, Nathan, 75

Harlem Renaissance, 92

Harries, Karsten, 137, 138

Harris, Joseph E., 16, 25

Harris, Leonard, 92, 93, 95, 96, 119, 171,
 249

Harris, Leonard, Scott L. Pratt, and Anne
 Waters, 98

Harris, Wilson, 172, 176, 218

Hart, William D., 106

Harvard University, 48, 73, 92

Harvey, David, 223

Haymes, Stephen, 151

Hayward, George Washington, and Hannah
 Stanley, 69

Headley, Clevis Ronald, 152, 180, 184

Hebrews, 44

Hector, Leonard Tim, 175

Hegel, Georg W. F., 6, 10, 60, 80, 89, 93, 94,
 121, 122, 142, 165, 168, 176, 197, 237; on
 Africa and blacks, 196, 197;
 phenomenology of, 239

hegemony, 129, 218, 223, 226

Heidegger, Martin, 2, 7, 120, 136, 237

Henry, Paget, 41, 107, 108, 119, 121, 128,
 132, 156, 165, 166, 172, 173, 174, 175, 176,
 177, 179, 182, 200, 206, 217, 218; critique
 of logicism, 176; poststructuralism, 127,
 176; on double consciousness, 174, 177;
 ("potentiated"); historicism, 173, 175,
 176, 177, 191, 218; C.L.R. James, 165, 166,
 173, 175; phenomenology, 176, 177, 182;
 poeticism, 168, 175, 177, 218, 238;
 predestination, 175; transcendentalism,
 177, 178, 179

Herbermann, Charles, Edward A. Pace,
 Thomas J. Shahan, and John J. Wynne,
 27

Hick, John, 43, 76

Higgenson, Thomas Wentworth, and James
 M. Mcpherson, 29

Hindus, 9, 178, 179

Hinks, Peter P., 46

Hispaniola, 160

history, *passim*, but see especially, 61, 62,
 130, 171; intellectual, 44, 175, 203, 219;
 universal/world, 165, 196, 237; (*see also*
 philosophy of history)

Hobbes, Thomas, 21, 42, 112, 247

Holmes, Oliver Wendell, Sr., 48

homelessness, 138, 139

Honnig, Bonnie, 236

Hook, Sidney, 93

hooks, bell/Gloria Watkins, 101

Hountondji, Paulin, 198

Hourani, Albert, 22, 25

Howard University, 51, 92

Hume, David, 11, 30, 37, 43, 115, 126, 201;
 on Africa and blacks, 42, 196;
 naturalistic fallacy, 43

Humanism, 123, 137, 185; African, 186–95,
 226, 235; historicist, 191; Muslim, 190,
 191; poeticist-humanists, 195; post-, 153

Husserl, Edmund, 121, 124, 136, 142, 152, 154, 239

Iberia, 3, 26, 158, 189
Ibo (people), 196
identity, 144–6, 149, 150, 204; political, 193
Ikuenobe, Polycarp A., 231, 233, 234; defense of authoritarianism, 233; indoctrination, 234; moral education, 234, 235, 236
Imbo, Samuel, 194
India, 21, 162, 178
Indians (East), 16, 193
Indo-European, 18
Indus Valley, 5
interpellation, 146, 148, 203
intersubjectivity, 14
invention, 169, 196, 200, 210–13, 214–20; etymology of, 195; of gender, 208, 209, 210
invisibility and visibility, 134, 144, 149
irreplaceability and replaceability, 143
Isaac, Walter, 99
Isabella I, queen of Castile, 4, 28, 158
Islam, 4, 23, 158, 190, 223; Sufism, 191
Italy, 4

Jackson, Fatimah, 31
Jacobs, Harriet, 139
Jamaica, 57, 164, 170, 171, 184
James, C.L.R., 17, 30, 57, 89, 165; on Marxism of, 128, 164, 165, 170
James, Joy, 103, 104, 105
James, William, 73, 91, 94
James Gonzalez de Allen, Gertrude, 180, 181
JanMohamed, Abdul R., 115, 116, 136, 139, 140
Jaspers, Karl, 7, 12, 81, 84, 121, 160; on citizens, 161, 162; blame, guilt, and responsibility (*Schuld*), 160, 161; *right*, 161
jazz/ African-American classical music, 95, 113
Jefferson, Thomas, 31, 56
Jesus of Nazareth, 23

Jews, 4, 158, 189–90, 223; in Medieval Muslim world, 190
Jim Crow (system of), 80, 114
Johnson, Charles, 136, 137, 138, 139, 205
Johnson, Clarence Sholé, 194
Johnson, Claudia Durst, 30
Johnson, James Weldon, 56, 133
Jones, William R., 136, 137, 171
Judaism, 44; Coptic and Ethiopian, 188; Jewish law/*Halacha*, 190
Judaken, Jonathan, 195
Judy, Ronald A.T., 99, 120, 121, 125
justice, 43, 76, 112, 113–14, 115, 117, 119, 220; (*see also* Boxill, Bernard; Rawls, John; Roberts, Rodney)

Kala pani, 178, 179
kitsch, 138, 139
Km.t/ Kamit/Kemet, 2, 7, 15, 17, 109
Kamugisha, Aaron, 18, 180
Kant, Immanuel, 12, 13, 31, 60, 89, 115, 201, 212; on dark people, 37, 116, 145, 196; *noumena*, 150; transcendental argumentation of, 109
Karenga, Maulana [Ron], 106, 107, 108, 185, 235
Keller, Frances Richardson, 70
Kesteloot, Lilyan, 166
Kierkegaard, Søren, 12, 82, 95, 136
Kincaid, Jamaica, 172, 184, 218
Kirkland, Frank M., 21, 69, 121
Kirkland, Frank, and D.P. Chattopadhyaya, 49, 121, 122
Kiros, Teodros, 24, 194, 198
Knies, Danziger, 14, 155, 182
knowledge, *passim*, but see especially, 61
Kopytoff, Igor, 187, 206
Kpobi, David Nii Anum, 38
Ku Klux Klan, 114
Kush, iii
Kwame, Safro, 36, 210
Kwanza, 106

labor, 52, 72
Lacan, Jacques, 87, 120, 168, 237, 238
Laclau, Ernesto, 121

Lamming, George, 172, 183, 218
language, 11, 44, 45, 167, 215; "private," 216
Latin America, 169; (*see also* Americas)
Laubscher, Lewsin, 194
laws (categorical generalizations), 124
Lawson, Bill E., 111, 112, 113
Lazarus, Neil, 194
Le, C.N., 30
Leibniz, Gottfried, 30
Lemert, Charles, 55, 70, 71, 72, 90
Leopold II, King Louis Philippe Marie Victor, 206
Lerner, Ralphi, and Muhsin Mahdi, 190
Levinas, Emmanuel, 120, 181, 210, 211, 213
Leviticus, Book of, 44
Levy, Jacoby, 182
Lewis, David Levering, 73, 74
Lewis, Rupert, 163
Lewis, Shireen K., 176
Liberia, 49, 51, 64; Alexander High School, 64; College, 64
Lincoln, Abraham, 49
Lincoln University (Missouri), 70
Lister, Ruth, 228
Locke, Alain, 56, 91, 92, 93, 94, 96; on cultural pluralism, 92, 96
Locke, John, 30, 33, 34, 42, 112, 231; on slavery, 33, 34, 35
Lofts, Sebastian, S.G., 124
Lott, Tommy Lee, 33, 96, 110, 111, 112
Louis XVI (king), 36
Love, Monifa, 135
Lowe, Lisa, 180
Lubiano, Wahneema, 99, 125
Luft, Sebastian, 124
Lugard, Lord F.D., 224, 242
Lynch, Hollis, 64

M Street High School/Laurence Dunbar School, 70
Maart, Rozena, 120, 193
Ma'at, 107
Machiavelli, Niccolò, 4, 21
MacIntyre, Alasdair, 47, 124, 230, 234
Madison, Gary B., 120

Mahmoud, Zaki Naguib, 190
Maimonides, Moses (Moshe ben Maimon), 189, 190
Maldonado-Torres, Nelson, 96, 169, 180, 181, 214, 237
Mali, 198
Mallory, J.P., and Victor H. Mair, 25
Mamdani, Mahmood, 194, 223, 224, 225, 226, 228, 229, 231, 232, 240, 245, 246; on neoliberalism, 225; state and civil society, 225
Manganyi, Noël Chabani, 194, 217
Mankiewicz, Richard, 8
Mann, Anika Maaza, 105, 152
Maroons, the, 57
Martin, Tony, 163
Martinez, Jacqueline M., 153
Martinez, Roy, 120, 136
Martinique, 164, 166, 168
Marx, Karl, 51, 121, 129, 130, 131, 170, 220, 237
Marxism, 72, 89, 95, 101, 128, 166, 170; (–Leninism), 198, 230, 232; heretical, 221
Masai (people), 196
Masolo, D.A., 180, 185, 194, 197, 198, 200, 201, 202
Maters, Robert D., and Christopher Kelly, 83
mathematics, 8, 30, 44, 85
Mazama, Ama, 108
Mazrui, Ali, 194
Mbembe, Achille, 192, 194, 219, 220, 236, 237, 238, 239, 242, 243, 247; defining the postcolony, 240, 241; methodology of, 239; on absence, 240; privatization of violence and power, 240, 242, 243; time, 239; phenomenology of, 237; use of "we" and "us," 238
Mbiti, John, 133, 200, 201, 202, 213
McGary, Howard, 111, 112, 171
McKenzie, Renee Eugenia, 104, 105, 106, 121; dialectical logic of both-and, 105
McLendon, John H., III, 166
McWhorter, John, 100
Mead, George Herbert, 147
Mediterranean, 21

Meeks, Brian, 169
Mehta, Brinda, 178, 179, 180
melancholia, 151
Memmi, Albert, 195
Menand, Louis, 48
Mendieta, Eduardo, 3, 21
Merleau-Ponty, Maurice, 84, 136, 149, 150, 151
method, problem of, 75, 110, 119, 136, 141, 162, 183, 213, 239, 243
Meyers, Walter Dean, 30
Mićunović, Natlja, 180
Middle Ages, 130, 188
Middle East, the, 4, 26, 99, 159, 223
Mignolo, Walter, 3, 21, 22, 157, 169
Milian Arias, Claudia, 180, 181
Miller, Jerry, 145
Mills, Charles, 26, 111, 114, 116, 119, 171
mind–body dualism, 38; Cartesian, 38
modernity, 17, 21, 24, 25, 32, 64, 108, 130, 138, 176, 185
Mohammed, the Prophet, 22
Mokoena, Hlonipha, 194
Môle of St. Nicolas (Haiti), 58
Molina, Luis de, 130
Montreal, 184
Moore, David Chioni, 2, 197
Moors, the, 4, 23, 26, 28, 158, 189
Moosa, Ebrahim, 194
More, (Samuel) Mabogo P., 193, 194
Morley, David, Kuan-Hsing Chen, Stuart Hall, 128
Morris, George Sylveser, 94
Morrison, Roy D., II, 137
Morrison, Toni, 135, 140, 146
Moses (Moshe), 40
Moses, Wilson, 54
Mosley, Albert, 118
Mouffe, Chantal, 228
Mozart, Wolfgang Amadeus, 212
Mudimbe, Valentin Y., 1, 14, 79, 194, 196, 203, 204, 205, 208, 209; on *gnosis*, 204, 205; invention, 204; poststructuralism of, 205; relation to Foucault, 205
Munford, Clarence J., 108
Murdoch, Iris, 10

Muslim(s), 4, 64, 178, 190; empires, 25, 26, 188; existentialism, 191; political thought, 190–1
mystery/mysteriousness, 125

Naguib, Mahmoud, 190
narcissism, 86
Nardal, Jane, and Paulette Nardal, 184
Nascimento, Abdias do, 181
Natanson, Maurice, 62
National Association for the Advancement of Colored People, 74
National Association of Colored Women (NACW), 54
Nationalism, 89, 106, 120, 163, 164, 192, 193, 243
nature, 11, 22, 44, 45, 85; natural phenomena, 41; reductionism, 60; teleological naturalism, 85; Rastafari naturalism, 170
Neanderthals, 15, 63
Necho II, Pharoah, 17
Negritude, 109, 138, 157, 166, 184, 191; critique of, 221
Newton, Isaac, 30
Ngowet, Luc, 194
Niagra Movement, the, 74
Nicholls, Tracey, 150
Nietzsche, Friedrich, 52, 53, 72, 145, 234
Nigeria, 64, 224
Nihilism, 136, 144, 245
Niño, Pedro Alonso, 29
Nisbet, Robert, 238
Nishitani, Kejii, 12, 84, 182
Nissim-Sabat, Marilyn, 152
Nkrumah, Kwame, 106, 192, 230
Noah, 43
Nobel Prize, 194
Norment, Nathaniel, Jr., 74
Nouss, Alexs, 180, 183
Nozick, Robert, 116, 117, 230
Nussbaum, Martha, 103, 230
Nyerere, Julius K., 192, 230, 231
Nzegwu, Nkiru Uwechia, 79, 179, 194, 196, 198, 217, 218, 219, 224

Obenga, Théophile, 1, 2, 185, 186
Oberlin College, 70
O'Chieng Odhiambo, Frederick, 180
Oliver, Kelly, 84
Olyan, Saul, 103
Osiris, 109
Other, the, 87; production of, 228
Outlaw, Lucius T., Jr., 1, 110, 120, 136, 137, 171
orientation, 3
Owens, J., 164
Oxford Library of French Classics, 58
Oxford University, 92; Hertford College, 92
Oyěwùmí, Oyèrónké, 194, 207, 208, 209, 210, 212, 218; on Mudimbe, 208; female actors, 210; biology, 215

Padua, Marsilius de, 130
Paine, Thomas, 196
Pan-African Congress (first), 59, 71, 74, 206
Pan-Africanism, 165
Papua ne Guinea, 78
Parry, Benita, 194
Patterson, Orlando, 172
Paul III (pope), 28
Peace and Reconciliation Commission (South Africa), 194
Peirce, Charles Sanders, 94, 98
Perina, Mickaela, 180, 183
Perry, Ralph Barton, 92
phenomenology, 79, 85, 110, 124, 128, 136, 171, 172, 176, 177, 239; existential, 84, 91, 105, 131, 136, 140–5, 151–5, 173, 194, 217, 238, 246; bracketing/parenthesizing, 142; historical, 219; intentionality of consciousness in, 201; postcolonial, 142, 143, 182; queer, 153–5
Philadelphia, Pennsylvania, 75, 92
philosopher, 9, 10, 12, 211
philosophy, *passim*, but see especially, 8, 9, 12, 39, 249–50; ancient Greek, 7, 15; Anglo-analytical, 82, 110–17, 118–19, 171, 176, 202; anti-colonial, 82; black feminist or womanist, 104, 105; Chinese, 7, 15; Continental (European), 112, 120–7, 171; East Indian, 15; pre-Socratic,

7; ethno-, 213; Europeanization of, 7; etymology of, 1, 3; existential, 14, 50; (*see also* Existential Phenomenology; Gordon, Lewis); intoxicating, 9; North American, 21, 111; (*see also* African-American philosophy); Medieval, 130; methodology of, 39; of civilization, 52, 108; economics, 53; education, 152; German idealism, 232; heremeneutical, 214; history, 14, 80, 165, 202; moral, 234–5; science, 184; social science, 62; political, 21, 89, 230; postcolonial, 81, 89; "professional"/academic, 39, 171, 202; questions of, 8, 10; (*see also* Africana philosophy); Sage, 180, 202; teleological suspension of, 14, 82
Phoenicians, 6
Piper, Adrian Piper, 111, 115
Pippin, Robert B., 21
Pirenne, Henri, 22, 23
Pithouse, Richard, 195, 228
Pittman, John, 96, 110
Plaatje, Solomon Tshekisho, 192, 193
Plato (Aristocles), 9, 10, 23, 26, 130, 235, 249; condemnation of Sophists, 54
poetry, 12
Police des Noirs, 36
political economy, 130, 131, 171, 172, 175, 221; globalism, 229; (*see also* Marxism; Socialist Thought)
political theory/political thought, 88, 89, 117, 160, 179, 190; African, 220–1, 230, 231, 232, 239; communalism, 230, 234; communitarianism, 230, 232; conservative, 223, 233, 237; liberal, 230, 232–3, 236, 246; neoconservative, 223; neoliberal, 223, 230, 232; social and, 243; (*see also* justice; Marxism)
politics, 88, 97, 118, 125, 145, 185, 231; black feminist, 6, 104; geo-, 222; legitimation crisis of, 226, 228, 241, 247; requiring opposition, 231; role for philosophical thought, 231; versus rule/governing, 224, 225, 231, 236, 245
Polynesian Islands, 158
Portugal, 5, 159

postcolonialism, 90, 181, 226–7;
    postcoloniality, 182; postcolonial studies,
    226, 227; postcolonial theory, 229
Postel, Danny, 223, 238
postmodernism, 32, 103, 107, 108, 110, 122,
    126, 226, 230, 237; Afro-, 91, 105, 122,
    125; cultural criticism, 233
poststructuralism, 32, 62, 91, 123, 129, 148,
    151, 172, 204, 215, 226, 228, 230, 237;
    European, 205
Pottier, Eugène, 90
Poussaint, Alvin, 75
Power, 240, 242, 243; liberal distribution
    of, 246; privatization of, 243, 244, 247,
    248; public sharing of, 246
pragmatism, 91, 93–9, 128, 171–2; (see also
    Dewey, John; James, William;
    philosophy; West, Cornel)
Prah, K. K. Prah, 38
Pratt, Scott L., 98
pre-Socratics, the, 2
primitivism, 17, 24, 162, 167, 213, 218,
    225
problem people, 76, 77, 80, 87, 141
property, 13, 33
Prospero, 167, 174, 249
psychoanalysis, 85, 87, 120, 152, 168, 198
Puerto Rico, 171, 184

Queens College (Liberia), 51
Qu'ran/Koran, 22, 158

Rabaka, Reiland Rabaka, 80
race, passim, but see especially, 14, 57, 58,
    61, 145; Aryan, 58, 98, 111, 123, 129, 148,
    154, 206; de-racialization, 227; black,
    passim; Caucasian, 61; mixed, 61, 117–18,
    147, 152; polygenetic view of, 61;
    proliferation of, 149
racism, passim, but see especially, 14, 58,
    72, 88, 110, 116, 117, 118, 160, 173, 175,
    225, 229; in African Studies, 211–12;
    intra-African, 247; role of evidence and
    proof in, 202; reality of, 140
Ramos, Alberto Guerreiro, 181
Rampersad, Arnold, 73

Rashidi, Runoko, and Ivan Van Sertima,
    25, 78
Rastafari, 164, 170
rationalism, 24; authoritarian, 234;
    evidentialism, 234
rationality, passim, but see especially, 11,
    115, 116, 133; colonial, 141
Rawls, John, 112, 114, 115, 116, 117, 230,
    236
Reagan, Nancy, 244
Reagan, Ronald, 245
reality, 18, 143, 144, 151, 201, 214
reason, 11, 12, 14, 23, 24, 26, 40, 93, 116,
    167, 197, 203, 250; geography of, 182;
    metacritique of, 92; paradox of, 249
recognition, 86, 87, 119–40, 167–8, 177,
    249; (see also Hegel, Georg; Fanon, Frantz)
Reconquesta (Reconquest), 4, 158
Reed, Adolph, Jr., 73
Reinhardt, Catherine A., 36, 37
relativism, 210, 237; cultural, 212, 214;
    moral, 210
religion(s), 12; African, 186, 187, 197,
    212
religious thought, 186
Renaissance, Italian, 3, 186
reparations, 112, 113, 161
republicanism, 59
Rhodes Scholarship, 92
Richards, Catherine A., 48
Richardson, Marilyn, 47
Ricoeur, Paul, 124
right(s), 42, 161, 221, 225; and democratic
    subjects, 246; minority, 231; of women,
    50
Roberts, Neil, 180, 222
Roberts, Rodney, 105, 106, 111, 113, 114,
    119
Robins, Gay, and Charles Shute, 8
Robinson, Cedric, 3, 5, 22, 128, 129, 131,
    145, 170, 243; on Greek antiquity, 129;
    Marxism, 129, 131, 170; medieval and
    early modern Christianity, 130
Rockmore, Tom, 237
Rodney, Walter, 25, 62, 63, 169, 170
Rogonzinski, Jan, 157

Rolle, Daphne M., 46
Romans (ancient), 6, 15, 16
Rorty, Richard, 94, 129
Rossi, Corinna, 8
Rouman, Jacques, 90
Rousseau, Jean-Jacques, 31, 34, 35, 83, 89, 112; on liberty and freedom, 82, 83; on slavery, 34, 35; the will in general and the general will, 83, 221
Royce, Josiah, 92, 93
Rushd, Ibn (see Averroës)
Russell, Bertrand, 7

Said, Edward W., 81, 230
Saint Luke's Episcopal Church (Washington, DC), 51
Salih, Sarah, 121
Samir, Y., and F. Samir,, 78
Sanders, Mark, 103
San Sebastian (Dutch fort of), 37
Sartre, Jean-Paul, 84, 120, 121, 125, 133, 150, 151, 171, 238
Schleiermacher, Friedrich, 213
Schlesinger, Arthur, 145
Schlözer, August Ludwig von, 26
scholasticism, 22, 190
Scholz, Sally, and Shannon Mussett, 152
Schomburg, Arthur, 56
Schopenhauer, Arthur, 10
Schrag, Calvin O., 82
Schutz, Alfred, 62, 121, 136, 217
Schwartz, Gary, 135
Schweitzer, Albert, 52
science, 11, 12, 22, 30, 53, 85, 217; positivist, 60, 61, 190; post-European, 14, 75, 155, 182; connection to "sex," 147
Scotland, 49
Scott, David, 166, 176, 177
Scriven, Darryl, 46
Searls-Giroux, Susan, 80
Seacole, Mary, 184
secularization, 45; secularism, 53, 76, 188, 190, 191
Sekyi-Otu, Ato, 81, 194
Selassie, Haile/Ras Tafari Makonnen, 164

self, the, 15, 32, 78, 115, 143, 151; self–other dialectic, 87, 144, 147, 168, 203; African, 175; Caribbean, 176, 195; liberal conceptions of, 234; poststructural critique of, 177, 178, 179
Semite(s), 26, 27; Afro-, viii, 188; etymology of, 26
Senghor, Léopold, 191, 218
Sepúlveda, Juan Ginés de, 29, 130
Serequeberhan, Tsenay, 107, 194, 199, 214
Sertima, Ivan Van, 23
Shakespeare, William, 157, 174, 249
Sharpley-Whiting, T. Denean, 120, 126, 166, 184
Shaw, Thurston, and Paul Sinclair, 187, 206
Shelby, Tommie, 98
Sicily, 26
Sierra Leone, 64
slavery, 13, 22, 33, 41, 43, 45, 46, 50, 99, 115, 175, 223; the enslaved, 13, 28, 33, 34, 35, 41, 55, 86, 114, 161; responsibility for, 160–1
slave revolts, vii, 57; (see also Haitian Revoltion)
slave trade(s), 25, 63, 116; Atlantic, 18, 28, 29, 178; Middle Passage, 29
Smith, Adam, 30
Smitherman, Ginvea, 109
Snowden, Frank M., Jr., 16, 25
Snowden, Isaac H., and Daniel Laing, Jr., 48
social contract theory, 116; (see also Locke, John; Mills, Charles; Rawls, John; Rousseau, Jean-Jacques)
Socialism, 130
socialist thought, 130
social world, the, 15, 89, 116, 143, 148; social reality, 141, 216–17, 246
sociogenesis, 85, 119; (see also Fanon, Frantz)
sociology, 216
Socrates, 9, 26, 249
soldiers, 34
Sonneborn, Liz, 24, 190
Sorbonne, 71
Soto, Domingo de, 130

South Africa, 79, 192, 223–5; struggle for full citizenship, 225, 245; Apartheid, *passim*, but see especially, 226, 228; post-Apartheid neoliberalism in, 232
South African Native National Congress, 193
South America, 100
South Carolina, 49
Soviet Union, the (USSR), 165
Soyinka, Wole, 195, 218
Spain, 5, 159
Spear, Thomas, 211
Spencer, Herbert, 53
Spencer, Rainier, 111, 117, 118, 119
Spinoza, Benedicto (Baruch), 148
Spivak, Gayatri, 81
state, the, 225; accountability of, 232; deracialized, 227; neocolonial, 229; neoliberal, 224, 225; postcolonial, 223, 226, 230, 240; corruption in, 232
Sterling, Dorothy, 48
Stewart, James W., 46
Stewart, Maria W., 46, 47, 51, 101, 102
Strauss, Leo, 237
St. Augustine Normal School and Collegiate Institute for Free Blacks, 70
St. Thomas, Virgin Islands, 59, 64
Stubblefield, Anna, 98
Suárez, Francisco, 130
sugar, 56
Suffragette movement, 50
Swetz, Frank, and T. I. Kao, 8
symmetry, 126–7; a-, 126

Taínos, 157, 160
Taíwó, Olúfémí, 222
Tanzania, 231
Taraporevala and Mira Nair, 12
Taylor, Charles, 230
Taylor, Paul C., 97, 111
Temples, Placide, 200, 213
Terrell, Mary Church, 54, 100
Thales of Miletos, 7
theodicy, 43, 44, 76, 137, 188, 189–90

theology, 12, 102, 103; of Apartheid, 245; of slavery, 43, 137
Thomas, Laurence Mordekhai, 111, 115, 116, 224
Thurman, Howard, 96, 137, 250
Timbuktu, 24
Todorov, Tzvetan, 29
trade routes (Arabic and East Indian), 158
transcendentalism, 13, 177, 178, 179, 215
trauma, 152
Trinidad, 165, 179
Trotskyism, 165
Truth, Sojourner/Isabella Baumfree, 55, 100, 102
Tunstall, Dwayne, 92
Ture, Kwame, 106
Tuskegee Institute, 70
Tuskegee Machine, 70
Tutu, Bishop Desmond, 194
Twa (people), 196

undecidability, 127, 230
underclass, 113
underdevelopment, 62
United States of America (USA), 49, 51, 56, 71; Civil War, 49, 114, 117; history, 79; "Negro problem" of, 77; (*see also* America)
Universal Negro Improvement Association (UNIA), 163
University of Berlin, 74
University of Halle, 37, 38
University of Leiden, 38
University of Pennsylvania, 74
University of Pretoria, 193
University of the West Indies: at Cave Hill, Barbados, 180, 183; Mona, Jamaica, 180, 183
US Supreme Court, 35

Vandals, the, 4
vanquishment, 162
Vespucci, Amerigo, 17
Vest, Jennifer Lisa, 105
Vickery, Paul S., 30

violence, 89, 161, 247; decolonial, 221;
    privatization of, 240
Visigoths, the, 4
Vitoria, Francisco de, 130

Wahba, Mourad, 24
Walcott, Derek, 218
Waldseemüller, Martin, 17
Walker, Alice, 101, 102
Walker, Clarence E., 106
Walker, Corey D.B., 80, 99
Walker, David, 46, 69, 100
Wamba, Ernest Wamba dia, 194
Ward, Julie T., and Tommy Lee Lott, 112,
    120
Warrior, Robert Allen, 99
Washington, Booker T., 55, 70, 163
Waters, Anne, 98
Waters, Kristin, 47, 184
wa Thiong'o, Ngugi, 195, 218
Weber, Max, 124, 145
Weiss, Gail, 152
Wells-Barnett, Ida B., 54, 100
West, Cornel, 47, 91, 94, 95, 96, 100, 136,
    144, 171, 245; on Christianity, 94, 95, 96;
    John Dewey, 94, 99, 129; Marxism, 94,
    95, 96, 99, 128, 129; nihilism, 95, 113,
    245; philosophical writing, 94, 122;
    existentialism of, 95, 135; prophetic
    pragmatism of, 93, 94, 95, 96, 100,
    176
Whaba, Maourad, 23
Wheatley, Phillis, 133
Wheelock, Stefan Wheelock, 47
White, Renée T., 120
Whitehead, Alfred North, 148
Wilberforce University, 74
Willett, Cynthia, 121, 122

Wimbum (people), the, 212, 213;
    conceptions of witchcraft and the
    occult, 212
Williams, Eric, 25, 56
Wilmore, Gayraud S., 137
Wiredu, Kwasi, 22, 36, 38, 39, 180, 185,
    190, 194, 214, 215, 216, 217, 233
Wittgenstein, Ludwig, 125, 216
Woddis, Jack, 170, 221
Women's Era, The, 54
Women's Rights Convention (1854), 102
Woodson, Carter G., 55
working class, the, 52
world music, 195
World War II, 160, 167
Wright, Richard, 50, 133, 134, 139, 140
Wub-E-Ke-Niew, 99
Wuriga, Rabson, 246, 247
Wynter, Sylvia, iv, 100, 172, 175, 183, 205,
    218, 226

Xenia, Ohio, 49
xenophobia, 115

Yacob, Zara, 24
Yancy, George, 95, 172
Yorùbá (people), 107, 196
Yoruba Land, 49
Young, Iris Marion, 182
Young, Josiah Ulysses, III, 52, 96, 213

Zack, Naomi, 111, 117, 118, 145,
    171
Zahar, Renate Zahar, 81
Zeno of Elia, 214
Žižek, Slavoj, 121
Zuberi, Tubufu, 78
Zulus, the, 107